# The Ballad-Singer in Georgian and Victorian London

For three centuries, ballad-singers thrived at the heart of life in London. One of history's great paradoxes, they were routinely disparaged and persecuted, living on the margins, yet playing a central part in the social, cultural, and political life of the nation. This history spans the Georgian heyday and Victorian decline of those who sang in the city streets in order to sell printed songs. Focusing on the people who plied this musical trade, Oskar Cox Jensen interrogates their craft and their repertoire, the challenges they faced and the great changes in which they were caught up. From orphans to veterans, prostitutes to preachers, ballad-singers sang of love and loss, the soil and the sea, mediating the events of the day to an audience of hundreds of thousands. Complemented by sixty-two recorded songs, this study demonstrates how ballad-singers are figures of central importance in the cultural, social, and political processes of continuity, contestation, and change across the nineteenth-century world.

Oskar Cox Jensen is a Senior Research Associate at the University of East Anglia. He is the author of *Napoleon and British Song, 1797–1822* (2015), co-editor of *Charles Dibdin and Late Georgian Culture* (2018) and a special forum of *Journal of British Studies*: 'Music and Politics in Britain' (2021), and author of numerous book chapters and articles in journals including *Studies in Romanticism*.

T0384523

# The Ballad-Singer in Georgian and Victorian London

Oskar Cox Jensen

CAMBRIDGE
UNIVERSITY PRESS

Shaftesbury Road, Cambridge CB2 8EA, United Kingdom

One Liberty Plaza, 20th Floor, New York, NY 10006, USA

477 Williamstown Road, Port Melbourne, VIC 3207, Australia

314–321, 3rd Floor, Plot 3, Splendor Forum, Jasola District Centre, New Delhi – 110025, India

103 Penang Road, #05–06/07, Visioncrest Commercial, Singapore 238467

Cambridge University Press is part of Cambridge University Press & Assessment, a department of the University of Cambridge.

We share the University's mission to contribute to society through the pursuit of education, learning and research at the highest international levels of excellence.

www.cambridge.org
Information on this title: www.cambridge.org/9781108821087

DOI: 10.1017/9781108908108

First published 2021
First paperback edition 2023

*A catalogue record for this publication is available from the British Library*

ISBN   978-1-108-83056-0   Hardback
ISBN   978-1-108-82108-7   Paperback

Cambridge University Press & Assessment has no responsibility for the persistence or accuracy of URLs for external or third-party internet websites referred to in this publication and does not guarantee that any content on such websites is, or will remain, accurate or appropriate.

# Contents

# Figures

# Tables

# Musical Examples

# Recordings

Songs are numbered in the order in which they are first encountered in the text.

1 'Sprig of Shillelah' (Popularised by John Henry Johnstone, *c*.1800)
2 'The Black Joke' (Of Irish origin, 1720s)
3 'The Ladies' Fall' (English, 1619 or earlier)
4 'Tyburn Tree' (John Gay, 1728, to the tune of 'Greensleeves')
5 'Polly Will You Marry Me?' (Sung by Billy Waters, 1810s)
6 'The Primrose Girl' (John Moulds, 1790)
7 'Oh! Cruel' (First performed in Liverpool, 1810)
8 'Winter's Evening' (*c*.1770s, a variant of 'The Maid of Bedlam')
9 'Little Bess the Ballad Singer' (Samuel Arnold, 1794)
10 'The Ballad Singer' (George Linley, 1854)
11 'The Ballad-Singer's Petition' (Stephen Storace and Prince Hoare, 1790)
12 'Beggars and Ballad Singers' (*c*.1800)
13 'The Dustman's Brother' (After 1835, to the tune of 'The Literary Dustman')
14 'Billy Nutts, the Poet' (*c*.1840)
15 'For My True Love is Gone to Sea' (Thomas Arne, 1765)
16 'Lines on the Death of Eliza Fenning' (1815, tune chosen: 'Ned that Died at Sea')
17 'Gallant Cambridge Jumping Over Prince Albert' (1856, to the tune of 'Rory O'Moore')
18 'Fortune My Foe' (Of Irish origin, sixteenth century)
19 'Good People, I Pray, to these Lines now Attend' (Robert Wright, 1779, tune chosen: 'King John and the Abbot of Canterbury')
20 'Blooming Beauty of Surrey and her Father's Servant Man' (1865, to the tune of 'Lucy Neal')
21 'Lord Viscount Maidstone's Address' (1852, to the tune of 'Bow Wow Wow')
22 'Sit Down Neighbours All. Bow Wow Wow' (Charles Morris, *c*.1783)
23 'London Cries' (1800, to the tune of 'The Heaving of the Lead')

24 'The Arethusa' (William Shield and Prince Hoare, 1796, to the tune of 'The Princess Royal')
25 'Listen to the Voice of Love' (James Hook, 1795)
26 'The Death of Nelson' (John Braham, 1812)
27 'The British Grenadiers' (Of English origin, early seventeenth century)
28 'The Bay of Biscay' (John Davy and Andrew Cherry, 1806)
29 'The Storm' (George Alexander Stevens, c.1770, to the tune of 'The Sailor's Complaint')
30 'Tom Bowling' (Charles Dibdin, 1790)
31 'The British Seaman's Praise' (Or 'The Hardy Tar', William Boyce, 1770s)
32 'The Wooden Walls of Old England' (James Hook and Henry Green, 1773)
33 'The Sea' (Sigismund von Neukomm and Barry Cornwall, 1830s)
34 'A Life on the Ocean Wave' (Henry Russell and Epes Sargent, 1838)
35 'Lord Bateman' (Probably of English origin, early seventeenth century)
36 'The Outlandish Knight' (Of Scottish origin, eighteenth century or earlier)
37 'Sir Patrick Spens' (Of Scottish origin)
38 'Exile of Erin' (Thomas Campbell, c.1805).
39 'Gee Ho Dobbin' (Arranged by Thomas Arne, 1762)
40 'The Shufflers' (1801, to the tune of 'Gee Ho Dobbin')
41 'The Ivy Green' (Henry Russell and Charles Dickens, c.1840)
42 'The Cabbage Green' (1840s, to the tune of 'The Ivy Green')
43 'Alice Gray' (Virtue Millard, c.1828)
44 'Isle of Beauty' (Charles Shapland Whitmore and Thomas Haynes Bayly, c.1830)
45 'The Bold Pedlar and Robin Hood' (Of English origin, seventeenth century)
46 'Old Dog Tray' (Stephen Collins Foster, 1853)
47 'Black-Ey'd Susan' (Richard Leveridge and John Gay, c.1720)
48 'Cherry Ripe' (Charles Edward Horn and Robert Herrick, 1825)
49 'Just Before the Battle, Mother' (George Frederick Root, 1866)
50 'Early One Morning' (Of English origin, eighteenth century)
51 'Sally in Our Alley' (Henry Carey, 1710s)
52 'The Wolf' (William Shield and John O'Keeffe, 1798)
53 'The Beautiful Maid' (John Braham, 1802)
54 'Buy a Broom' (Arranged by Alexander Lee and D. A. O'Meara, c.1824, to the tune of 'O du lieber Augustin')

# Acknowledgements

I've been promising people this book for a while. For enough years, in fact, that practically everyone I've so much as mentioned it to has gone on to say or show me something brilliant that has gone into its making. Enough, indeed, that I'm sure I've forgotten as many debts as I've recorded. But this book has sprung from conversations, and some of the best of them have been with Christian Algar, David Atkinson, Georgina Bartlett, Giles Bergel, Siv Gøril Brandtzæg, Michael Burden, Gilli Bush-Bailey, Catherine Charlwood, Ross Cole, Sarah Collins, Isabel Corfe, Adriana Craciun, James Davey, James Davies, Patricia Fumerton, Vic Gammon, Andrew Gustar, Judith Hawley, Sarah Hibberd, David Hitchcock, David Hopkin, Matthew Ingleby, Louis James, Julia Johnson, Berta Joncus, Colin Jones, Peter Jones, Daniel Karlin, Georgina Locke, Ellen Lockhart, Brian Maidment, Christopher Marsh, Jo McDonagh, Angela McShane, Graeme Milne, Tony Montague, Brian Murray, Felicity Nussbaum, Sheila O'Connell, Eamonn O'Keeffe, Clare Pettitt, Carmel Raz, Brianna Robertson-Kirkland, Massimo Rospocher, Steve Roud, Jeroen Salman, Rosa Salzberg, Matthew Sangster, Derek Scott, Mary Shannon, Keith Shipton, Sally Shuttleworth, Simon Smith, Laura Smyth, Natalie Steed, Matildie Thom Wium, Wiebke Thormählen, Laura Tunbridge, Susan Valladares, Abigail Williams, Roderick Williams, and David Worrall. Thank you all for your insights, energy, and expertise – which I knew I could count on – and your sustained interest, which has come as a pleasant surprise.

Some people of course have had no real choice but to help – yet have done so with a warmth, courtesy, and generosity that was quite unnecessary. These include, most recently, the excellent Atifa Jiwa and Ruth Boyes at Cambridge University Press; Rashmi Motiwale and Allan Alphonse at Integra; my two beleaguered readers, who have made this book much better in the face of my errors, mulishness, and verbosity; Emily Dourish at Cambridge University Library; and – for many years now – the combined staff of the Rare Books and Music Reading Room at the British Library (it's taken a lot of them). Liz Friend-Smith, my editor at Cambridge, *did* have a choice, of course – and I am eternally grateful that she made it!

Of all the institutions whose resources I have plundered, whose names you will encounter at length in captions, footnotes, and references, two merit particular thanks. The Yale Center for British Art has a most enlightened attitude when it comes to giving people use of their images for free. And without the Bodleian Library's Broadside Ballads Online, I would probably never have written this book at all. I thank them both; and if you haven't already used their archives yourself, you really should do so! Lucia Rinolfi of British Museum Images was also especially helpful. Two other institutions even went so far as to employ me while I wrote this book: thank you to all the staff and students of the Music Department, King's College London, and the School of History, Queen Mary University of London.

So many people I've mentioned already have been not just colleagues and collaborators but friends. While it would be invidious to single out (et cetera), I'm still going to do so. Jacky Bratton has been an inspiration to many besides me; she has also been unswervingly kind, wise, and encouraging of this project. Joanna Hofer-Robinson has been and hopefully will always be a peerless partner-in-crime, in our work on both London and the theatre. Kirsteen McCue is the dynamic champion that this period's songs and their scholars both deserve. Mark Philp, once the best supervisor a person could have, continues to be the best of mentors, minds, and sounding boards, while simultaneously running a dozen more important projects. Susan Rutherford has guided my thinking on voice, music, and gender, and is generally a force for good in the world. And my wife and collaborator Emma Whipday is responsible for anything intelligent that is said about neighbourhoods and communities in Chapter 2. Emma's voice is one of those you will hear singing the songs referred to throughout this book, along with my sister and collaborator, Freyja Cox Jensen, who has once again lent her voice to an awful lot of songs that are too hard for me to sing. On which note (hah), thanks too to our Mama and Papa, who are, in the final analysis, the ones to blame for all our endeavours.

For an ordinary monograph, that would do. However, the reason this is already so lengthy is because of the incredible gravitational pull exerted by 'Music in London, 1800–1851', which has drawn so many brilliant scholars into its orbit. 'Music in London' is a project that ran at King's College London from 2013 to 2018, and it was funded by the European Research Council (ERC). This monograph forms one of its formal outputs. At the time of writing, it does not appear that the ERC will be able to fund many further such projects in the United Kingdom. I am proud to acknowledge that this book and, such as it is, my career were made possible by this ERC project.

At a personal level, this means more debts I can never repay. Angela Waplington, the project's administrator, is singularly competent, and it was both a joy and an honour to work with her. 'Music in London' meant I could research and write this book surrounded by peers and friends whose brilliance as both scholars and human beings is surely one of those freak historical events that normally results in a revolution. I cannot imagine this book, my life, or indeed civilisation being possible without the contributions made by Kathy Fry, James Grande, Katherine Hambridge, Jonathan Hicks, Erin Johnson-Williams, David Kennerley, Tessa Kilgarriff, Ian Newman, Gavin Williams, and Flora Willson.

One person has, of course, been saved for last and best: Roger Parker, the Principal Investigator of 'Music in London'. I owe him so much, both personally and professionally, that were I to begin to thank him properly he would at once tell me to shut up and not bang on about it. Nor am I alone. Perhaps the most telling, suitably indirect tribute that I can pay him and his vision for the project is that there are so many other scholars in the same indebted boat. Their loyalty and gratitude, like mine, are testament to Roger's indefatigable support and towering example. But then, he has always known how to pick 'em.

# Note on the Text

I have attempted, where possible, to supply a recording of every song discussed. If a recording is available, this is clearly indicated in the text by an underlining of the song title at its first mention. A list of all recordings may be found in this book's front matter. The recordings themselves are available to download at www.cambridge.org/ballads.

Unless specified, place of publication in all references is assumed to be London.

# Abbreviations

| | |
|---|---|
| BL Mus. | British Library Music Collections |
| Bod. | Broadside Ballads Online Collection, Bodleian Library, Oxford |
| *ODNB* | *Oxford Dictionary of National Biography* |
| *OED* | *Oxford English Dictionary* |
| POB | Proceedings of the Old Bailey |

# Introduction

[A]ny thing written in voice & especially to an Old English tune . . . made a more fixed Impression on the Minds of the Younger and Lower Class of People, than any written in Prose, which was often forgotten as soon as Read.

> – 'A friend to Church and State' to John Reeves' Association for the Preservation of Liberty and Property against Republicans and Levellers, 12 December 1792.[1]

If you happen to be a scholar of 1790s Britain, or of British ballads, then you are probably familiar with the quotation in the epigraph. Of the many excellent academics who have turned to the letter in recent years, most explain that they came across it in Roy Palmer's *The Sound of History: Songs and Social Comment*, published a generation ago in 1988.[2] Simon Bainbridge, Vic Gammon, and Ian Newman go on to include the anonymous correspondent's suggestion of 'putting them [i.e. copies of the song] . . . by twenties into the hands of Ballad Singers who might sing them for the sake of selling them'. So begins this book: in 1792, dawn of the ballad-singer's final heyday.

I reproduce this quotation for two reasons. The first is bibliographic: academics across the humanities are perhaps more interested in ballads,

---

[1] British Library Add. MSS 16922, fol. 43.
[2] Roy Palmer, *The Sound of History: Songs and Social Comment* (Oxford, 1988), 16–17. See, for example, Simon Bainbridge, 'Politics and Poetry', in Pamela Clemit (ed.), *The Cambridge Companion to British Literature of the French Revolution in the 1790s* (Cambridge, 2011), 190–205, 195; Vic Gammon, 'The Grand Conversation: Napoleon and British Popular Balladry', *RSA Journal* 137 (1989): 665–74, 667; Vic Gatrell, *The Hanging Tree: Execution and the English People, 1770–1868* (Oxford, 1994), 141; Ffion Mair Jones, *Welsh Ballads of the French Revolution: 1793–1815* (Cardiff, 2012), 1; Christopher Marsh, *Music and Society in Early Modern England* (Cambridge, 2010), 284; Ian Newman, 'Moderation in the Lyrical Ballads: Wordsworth and the Ballad Debates of the 1790s', *Studies in Romanticism* 55 (2016): 185–210. Mark Philp quotes a similar letter by a female correspondent of Reeves in 'Politics and Memory: Nelson and Trafalgar in Popular Song', in Mark Philp, *Reforming Ideas in Britain* (Cambridge, 2014), 232–59, 233–4.

and song in general, than ever. There is a growing demand for literature that is concerned, not with the content, but with the context of ballads, and that thinks extensively about how they worked. I hope this book will be helpful on that score. Secondly, as a first step in doing that thinking, the letter is worth one more look. Its writer does not use the terms 'ballad' and 'broadside', but rather 'voice' – suggesting something more, I think, than simply verse in contrast to prose – which she or he couples with 'tune'. It is the sonic, vocalised, lyrical, and explicitly musical object that makes the 'fixed Impression'. Furthermore, the correspondent goes on to hope that ballad-singers 'might sing them for the sake of selling them'. Songs did not operate in a vacuum, or in accordance with the dictates of their writers. They were sung by independent agents known as ballad-singers: people with their own agendas and their own living to make, who were already in the business of performing and selling songs *of all kinds*, not just moral or political pieces. These are the people – women, men, children – that I would like to think about: people plying a trade in the London street that centred on musical performance as a mechanism for selling printed songs, exactly as they had done since the start of the reign of Elizabeth I, and as they would continue to do well into the reign of Victoria, where both their story and this book end.

In this book, I seek to write the history of the ballad-singer: a central agent in numerous cultural, social, and political processes of continuity, contestation, and change across Western Europe between the later sixteenth and the late nineteenth centuries. The English term 'ballad-singer' appears to have been an invention of the 1590s,[3] and in the Victorian period it began to lose coherence among a raft of alternatives, all of which denoted something slightly different: chaunter, patterer, long-song seller, street vocalist, busker. For the three centuries in between, however, its usage remained remarkably consistent, referring to a low-status and low-income individual of questionable legality, whose primary occupation was the dissemination of printed songs, generally by direct sale for small change, in public places, primarily the street, and who sang these songs as part of the process. In the period under discussion in these pages, ballad-singers' songs' musical notation was almost never printed, the words being set instead as verse (often accompanied by image), leaving the onus upon the seller to supply – and sometimes even to choose – the tune.

'Ballad-singer' was an intrinsically loaded term, and while it would be interpreted differently by individuals of various class and interest groups,

---

[3] Angela McShane, 'Political street songs and singers in seventeenth-century England', *Renaissance Studies* 33 (2019): 94–118, 95 and 102.

those interpretations all rested on an engagement with the same central idea: that of a highly audible subaltern voice, playing a prominent and influential role in public discourse and public culture. This basic identity was often reduced to a stock type by the legislators, artists, playwrights, etymologists, and many other persons whose representations of ballad-singers figure so largely in the historical record, and to an extent this speaks to a historical truth. Anyone who took up ballad singing placed themselves within an immediately recognisable category, one that by 1792 had at least two centuries of associated meaning behind it. That category – shabby, scurrilous, loud – is worth holding on to. But it is equally true that, right from their beginnings across Renaissance Europe – England, Italy, and the Netherlands in particular – the profession was almost paradoxically defined by its heterogeneity, fluidity, and liminality. A recent special issue of *Renaissance Studies* has focused on this 'elusive' character, its editors remarking: 'Even more than the category itself, however, it was each individual street singer that could be (and typically was) extremely many-sided.'[4] Articles within that collection stress the 'remarkable social mix' and 'constant mobility' of such performers – not only spatially and culturally but also socially, in providing 'a focal point where the culture of the piazza and that of the *palazzo* collided'.[5] While this heterogeneity presents a historiographical challenge that I have occasionally failed to meet – there are many generalisations in what follows – it is also of vital importance in understanding the world in which ballad-singers worked. It is by appreciating singers as relatively autonomous individuals, rather than as uniform and unthinking mouthpieces for the songs they sold, that we come to grips with how culture and society operated through their mediation: not by a clear, structured separation of high and low cultures, or within a strict set of categories for politics and entertainment, but by means of a mainstream that was, above all, *mixed.*

London in the late eighteenth and nineteenth centuries was no exception to this rule. As one 1837 survey put it: 'John Bull ... has "stomach for 'em all" ... rich or poor, naked or clad, old or young, masculine or feminine, so as they have but something to sell, say, or sing, and present themselves in the streets of the metropolis, he is sure to stop and make a purchase.'[6] Thus, to draw solely on examples encountered in these

---

[4] Luca Degl'Innocenti and Massimo Rospocher, 'Introduction', in their edited collection, *Street Singers in Renaissance Europe*, special issue of *Renaissance Studies* 33, no. 1 (2019): 5–16, 7 and 12.

[5] McShane, 'Political Street Song', 118; Luca Degl'Innocenti and Massimo Rospocher, 'Urban Voices: The Hybrid Figure of the Street Figure in Renaissance Italy', in Degl'Innocenti and Rospocher, *Street Singers*, 17–41, 19.

[6] 'Jack Rag' (ed.), *Streetology of London; or, the Metropolitan Papers of the Itinerant Club* (1837), 82.

pages, a London ballad-singer could be a boy of twelve, a girl of nineteen, a mother of three, a blind ancient. Hailing from Wapping, Wexford, the West Indies, and residing in Seven Dials, Whitechapel, Southwark – in garret or gutter, boarding- or bawdy-house. They might be an orphan, a spouse, a discharged veteran; lately of the Opera House, a jeweller's, a merchant bank; of the army, scullery, or rookery; concurrently a beggar, tailor, thief, writer, pensioner, weaver, prostitute, preacher. By the name of David Love, an earnest old Scot; Ann Lee, a desperate young felon; Joseph Johnson, a disabled West Indian sailor. In short, a drunken, teetotal, rapist, evangelist, knowing, prudish, communist, liberal, xenophobic, cosmopolitan, patriotic, cynical, timid, upstart, deferential, oratorical, boorish wit. Their singing might be excellent, abysmal, idiosyncratic, or simply adequate, and their patter just as variable. Nor were the songs they sold any less disparate: of love or loss; the soil or the sea; conflicts of class, nation, gender; comedy or tragedy; sex or salvation. Composed any time from three centuries ago to earlier that morning, their lyrics written by Shakespeare, Dickens, or the penniless balladmonger John Morgan, by the anonymous bard of antiquity or the equally unknown Grub Street hack. Their tunes taken from opera house, theatre, pleasure garden, church, country dance, from anywhere across the Atlantic archipelago, America, Europe … and this product printed on a two-song broadside or single slip, or – as time went on – on a long sheet or in a songster, the paper uniformly poor and the words invariably smudged, cramped, pirated, the whole thing sold for small change, for the halfpennies that clinked in the pocket of all but the very poorest Londoner. A product that was at once literature and music, yet that was consistently denied the legitimacy of either by those whose words or images were printed by more respectable publishers.

### What Song Has to Offer (I)

Given this rather overwhelming variability, it is doubly important to remember the unifying factor: these people sold and sang printed songs in the street.[7] It is because of that function that they are of such

---

[7] I must concede that songs were not always – or not only – sung, but also viewed, read, or read aloud. Abigail Williams has noted the vast number of ballads that were incorporated into commonplace books, while of the many scholars to claim that ballads were often pasted onto 'the walls of cottages and little alehouses', only David Atkinson has traced this assertion to a source – the memoirs of Thomas Holcroft – in defence of his ongoing (and highly productive) argument that we should also consider songs as texts, separable from their sung iterations. Crucially, however, Atkinson sees this focus as complementary, not antithetical, to a consideration of their aural transmission. See Abigail Williams, *The Social Life of Books: Reading Together in the Eighteenth-Century Home* (Yale, 2017);

historical importance: as mediators – gatekeepers, in twenty-first-century parlance – of a dominant cultural product. Until the later nineteenth century, song was perhaps the only universal form of expression, accessible to all irrespective of age, class, or sex, excluding only, in its aural form, the deaf (and even here, it is worth noting that Harriet Martineau, the most notable and eloquent sufferer of deafness in Britain in the period, both wrote and enjoyed songs). The years under discussion were the last, in Western Europe at any rate, in which song, not 'music', was the dominant and indeed only universal category of musical expression and thinking; this was still a time when instrumental music was a minority interest, only consumed by the masses when subordinated to the function of dance, and song still reigned supreme in both theory and practice.[8] Song was cheaper, more comprehensible, and more portable than either the newspaper or the caricature; unlike the sermon it could cross (as well as reinforce) sectarian divides; the spaces of its enjoyment were exceptionally varied, bridging the public and private, the sociable and the solitary. As a hybrid form, song could appear by proxy within other types of music and literature – the dance, the march, the journal, novel, or chapbook – and even withstand the separation of its constituent elements, so that quotation of a lyric might bring to mind a melody, or the performance of a few bars summon forth the words. Song was used in everything from manual labour to court ceremony, worship to revelry, and there can have been few persons in the metropolis that did not hear song on a daily basis.

As such, there are precious few forms of historical enquiry to which song is not germane – not merely as incidental colour, but as a practice of some influence. Song mediated everything from gender and class relations to national identity, via race, empire, innovation and technology, sex, humour, faith, superstition, medicine, commerce, and education – there really was a song for everything. Rather wonderfully, given the inherent ephemerality of the medium, we still have access to many of these songs in their printed form: among many excellent digitised archives, the Bodleian alone has 'nearly 30,000 songs' available online, while the British Library has recently partnered with the English Broadside Ballad Archive (based at the University of California Santa Barbara) to digitise its own collection

David Atkinson, *The Anglo-Scottish Ballad and its Imaginary Contexts* (Cambridge, 2014); and Thomas Holcroft, *Memoirs of the Late Thomas Holcroft*, 3 vols. (1816), vol. 1, 135–6.
[8] Gary Tomlinson has long since suggested the term 'cantology' as a replacement for musicology, as the default mode of engagement with musical experience before the nineteenth-century rise of instrumental music: see especially his 'Vico's Songs: Detours at the Origins of (Ethno)Musicology' in Gary Tomlinson, *Music and Historical Critique: Selected Essays* (Aldershot, 2007), 197–230.

in sound and colour.[9] There is the opportunity here for a whole field of rigorous historical enquiry, and it is one that many scholars have begun to embrace.

## The Question of Contrafacta

Until very recently, the 'big idea' in ballad scholarship, among both the early modernists and the scholars of this period who have taken songs seriously as musical objects, has been that of contrafacta. Borrowed from medievalist scholarship of the mid-twentieth century, a contrafactum is defined in Grove as 'the substitution of one text for another without substantial change to the music ... most commonly applied to the practice of composing new poems to older melodies'.[10] Put simply, it means a song with new words but an old tune, a standard compositional practice for ballads, and one seized upon by scholars because of the associative potential for audiences if the substitution was recognised. Historians in particular have been drawn to the generation of political meaning by such juxtapositions – as, for example, a radical rewrite of a loyalist anthem.[11] At its best, thinking about contrafacta in this way allows us to use melody as a way of accessing nothing less than a secret history of meaning.

Even for a non-specialist, the semantic connection between melody and lyric is easy to grasp. Without thinking about it, try singing the Hebrew word usually written in English as either 'Hallelujah' or 'Alleluia'. If you are a scholar raised in a Western Anglophone tradition, the chances are that you will opt for one of three four-note melodies given in Example 0.1 and indelibly associated with, respectively: a much-covered pop song from the 1980s; the Hallelujah Chorus from Handel's *Messiah*; and a hymn learnt and sung in many English schools. In each case, the meanings and memories generated by the same word are both powerful and distinct – and easily grasped without recourse to the musical notation.

Example 0.1  Three settings of the word 'Hallelujah'

[9] ballads.bodleian.ox.ac.uk/about. The British Library project is being led by Christian Algar.

[10] www.oxfordmusiconline.com/grovemusic/view/10.1093/gmo/9781561592630.001.0001/ omo-9781561592630-e-0000006361

[11] Kate Bowan and Paul A. Pickering, *Sounds of Liberty: Music, Radicalism and Reform in the Anglophone World, 1790–1914* (Manchester, 2017), makes exceptionally good and frequent use of contrafacta throughout, and as defined ibid., 17.

As may be apparent even from this simple example, however, the significance of each melody is likely to vary depending on both the singer and the listener: on whether, for instance, you think of Leonard Cohen, John Cale, Jeff Buckley, Rufus Wainwright, k.d. lang, Alexandra Burke, or Susan Boyle performing the first song; on your religious creed or lack thereof; on whether you went to a Church of England school, or are familiar with the descending peal of church bells evoked by the third musical phrase. A melody alone does not contain semantic meaning. Rather, meaning is generated in the relationship between (performed) song and listener, and whether that listener identifies with it as an individual or as part of a collective. As Anindita Ghosh has written of street song in nineteenth-century Kolkata, listeners were constantly 'filtering the performances in the light of their own experiences and knowledge'.[12] To take another famous modern parallel: the Rodgers and Hammerstein composition 'You'll Never Walk Alone' from the 1945 musical *Carousel* often moves me to tears when sung at Liverpool football matches – but less because of the immediate context (I support Arsenal) than because I have sung it at the funeral of a close friend's father – and even then, I am loth to put my response down to association alone. Other factors are in play.

Thinking about songs as contrafacta remains extremely productive, even when we concede that the recognition of a melody by a listener and the range of meanings this might generate were contingent. Politically, the fact that only part of an audience might 'get' the association being made is in itself of interest – in our period, for example, there was a thriving culture of electoral contrafacta that circulated among exclusive, enfranchised, partisan communities, and in this context the sharing of a musical reference understood only by 'insiders' might reinforce both bonds and barriers. But I think that, as historians, we can overestimate the importance of melodic association. In our own twenty-first-century musical soundscape, contrafacta are rare artefacts confined largely to the realm of comic parody. In a world where, by contrast, contrafactum was the default mode of composition, we can attribute immoderate significance to a choice of tune: when the same melody provided a setting for dozens of songs, the associative power of the original must often (though by no means always) have been relatively weak, and susceptible to overwriting. The comic Irish song 'Sprig of Shillelah', originally the bawdy 'Black Joke', and 'God Save the King/ Queen', originally a Jacobite drinking song, are two prominent examples of ostensibly fixed but in fact overwritten associations.

---

[12] Anindita Ghosh, 'Singing in a New World: Street Songs and Urban Experience in Colonial Calcutta', *History Workshop Journal* 76 (2013): 111–36, 113.

While I do not wish to dismiss the undoubted importance of contra-facta, it is good to see discussion broadening into other areas. The risk of emphasising contrafacta – and I speak as a guilty party – is this: by assigning meaning to a *tune* based on that tune's earliest or most famous lyrical accompaniment, and then mapping that lyrical association on to a subsequent lyric, we effectively remove the musical component altogether: the tune becomes a shorthand, a signifier for old words, for an old title. At its worst this could become a way for us as scholars, despite our best intentions, to avoid talking about performance and music altogether, returning to a discussion centred entirely on written texts.[13] There is much more that thinking about songs as musical performances can bring to the historical conversation.

## What Song Has to Offer (II)

As I will elaborate later in this book, and as hinted at by the anonymous correspondent with whom I began, song was 'universally acknowledged' in this period to exert a 'magic power' over listeners – a belief that was not without justification.[14] The musicalised performance of text was a mode of discourse of such rhetorical potency that it preoccupied philosophers and politicians throughout the period, just as it had done for centuries.[15] Jean-Jacques Rousseau, in privileging song as 'the highest musical genre' due to what he perceived as the naturally affective power of melody in the manipulation of the passions,[16] was echoing the fifteenth-century Florentine philosopher Marsilio Ficino's belief that song 'imitates and enacts everything so forcefully that it immediately provokes both the singer and the hearers to imitate and enact the same

---

[13] In my own *Napoleon and British Song, 1797–1822* (Basingstoke, 2015), I sometimes make this lapse, for example, on 124–5 and 158. While I would not wish to cite others' examples, this is a tendency I have observed repeatedly in conversation at workshops and conferences, and it occasionally creeps in to the writing of historians and literary scholars. Current musicologists, by contrast, sometimes seem excessively sceptical of contrafacta, as part of a wider resistance to the erroneous idea of objective musical meaning and the work-concept; to the new musicology, melody is infinitely more protean than the folklorist or political historian would have it.

[14] 'National Odes', *The Satirist, or, Monthly Meteor* 2 (May 1808): 239–45, 239. Ian McCalman conflates various parts of this anonymous essay to summarise, not unfairly, 'that people like Hannah More were alarmed because the song possessed a special, deeply rooted "magic power" in English popular culture', in his *Radical Underworld: Prophets, Revolutionaries and Pornographers in London, 1795–1840* (Cambridge, 1988), 118.

[15] See Chapter 2.

[16] Carolyn Abbate, *Unsung Voices: Opera and Musical Narrative in the Nineteenth Century* (Princeton, 1991), 15; Tomlinson, 'Vico's Songs', 215. Tomlinson also observes that 'In secular and sacred arenas alike, song exerted a force worrisome on account of its evident strength' – ibid., 201.

things'.[17] In early modern England, song was held to delight, to ravish, and above all to compel its suggestible listeners.[18] This belief in song's practical agency also found expression in 1830s London, as one anonymous writer declared that 'of all songs I love a ballad – the delightful mixture of sense with melody, which, passing through the ear to the heart, not only conveys pleasure of the most thrilling kind, but leaves us in that mood best suited to the exercise of individual friendship, or good-will to our fellow men'.[19] Across five centuries and three European cultures, the idea endured that song exerted a powerful and above all a socialised force in performance, because of its unique combination of words and musical tones. Nor has this historical perspective been discredited since. In an influential study of post-war popular music, John Street has written of song's 'ability to draw people together and to find a common resonance in their private feelings', while the cognitive psychologist Bruce McConachie concludes that audiences *simulate* the emotions they encounter 'through sounds as well as sights', adapting the philosopher Robert Gordon's observation that 'you can catch an emotion, just as you can catch a cold'.[20] Song, in short, can be contagious, and like any contagion, it catches best in crowds:[21] it 'animates imagined communities, aggregating its listeners into virtual collectivities or publics'.[22]

At first, it is difficult to reconcile these grand claims with the rhetoric of ephemerality and vulgarity that dominates representations of ballad-singers and their repertoires. Yet it is in the sphere of the mundane, everyday street song that such arguments have most weight, for they apply irrespective of the level of musicianship in play. As Carolyn Abbate writes, a song 'takes things that might in themselves seem unremarkable ... and, by decking them out with acoustic aura and

[17] Cited in a modern translation in Gary Tomlinson, *Metaphysical Song: An Essay on Opera* (Princeton, 1999), 12.
[18] Simon Smith, *Musical Response in the Early Modern Playhouse, 1603–1625* (Cambridge, 2017), 26–68.
[19] W. R., 'Ballad Singers', *Leigh Hunt's London Journal* 27 (1 October 1834): 211.
[20] John Street, *Rebel Rock: The Politics of Popular Music* (Oxford, 1986), 223. Bruce McConachie, *Engaging Audiences: A Cognitive Approach to Spectating in the Theatre* (Basingstoke, 2008), 66–8.
[21] Recent research into physiological synchrony among theatre audiences also notes a tendency for audience members' heartbeats to synchronise during an affecting performance. See www.ucl.ac.uk/pals/news/2017/nov/audience-members-hearts-beat-together-theatre.
[22] Georgina Born, 'For a Relational Musicology: Music and Interdisciplinarity, Beyond the Practice Turn', *Journal of the Royal Musical Association* 135 (2010): 205–43, 232. For further influential formulations of the same idea, see especially Jonathan Culler (paraphrasing Robert von Hallberg) in Jonathan Culler, *Theory of the Lyric* (Harvard, 2015), 351; and Abbate, *Unsung Voices*, 12.

sonic gift wrap ... [makes] them less banal than they are by themselves. The ordinary becomes a revelation.'[23] It is hard to appreciate this when *looking* at a broadside, its paper torn, its rhymes clumsy. But in perform-ance, the addition of melody to even the most hackneyed words supplies the lyricism, injects the eloquence, and transcends the inadequacies of the verse. This is the essence of the 'magic power' of song: that it is a form of heightened speech, the achievement of rhetoric by other means. When a street urchin sang a common ditty, that singer assumed a higher rhet-orical status, engaging in a mode of cultural articulation that, for the duration of the song, could elevate the singer and beguile the listener. Thus it was that, in the words of another anonymous scribbler, 'Even the ragged beggar listened once as if entranced ... and forgot his misery a moment.'[24]

Best of all – and I cannot put this forcefully enough – the study of song has much to contribute to more traditional fields of history. As my second chapter makes clear, the phenomenon I have just described and the practical consequences it produced disturbed the sleep of magistrates and moralists, peers and politicians. Song made the disenfranchised articulate and the insensible susceptible: what was being sung in the streets was of national concern. Songs are not historically illustrative so much as they are historically *active*; they 'have their own temporality, and are themselves a constitutive force in history'.[25] Beyond the incendiary or insidious potential of their political or moral rhetoric, the performance of songs, especially by ballad-singers, affected other important historical processes: the racialisation of the urban poor; the (trans)formation of both local and national communities; experiences of migration and belonging; the operation of class relations in general and charity in par-ticular; controversies of urban improvement; the lower-class appropri-ation of self-consciously elitist cultural capital; the economy of makeshift and the balance of power within petty capitalism – in short, many of the issues that defined the nineteenth-century city.

This is why I have chosen to focus solely on the ballad-singer in London: while the scale is manageable, it avoids excessive parochialism, as things not only happened first in London, they happened *more*. As the capital of what became, during the period, the world's leading imperial power, London was in dialogue with its hinterland, the British regions,

[23] Carolyn Abbate, 'Music—Drastic or Gnostic?', *Critical Inquiry* 30 (2004): 505–36, 517–18.
[24] Q.Q., 'Old and New Ballads', *Monthly Magazine* Series 3, vol. 9 (March 1843): 185–92, 190.
[25] Georgina Born, paraphrasing the anthropologist Christopher Pinney, in Born, 'For a Relational Musicology', 239.

Europe, and the world. This meant that the contrast between the relative importance of the ballad-singer as citizen (vanishingly small) and as purveyor and performer of songs (absolutely central to society) was at its starkest in the metropolis.

## Scholarship

It helps that the study of nineteenth-century London is so interdisciplinary in its scholarship: the field requires and is enriched by dialogue between historians (economic, urban, social, theatre, art ...), literary critics, cultural geographers, archaeologists, and others. The study of London's ballad-singers and their songs sits within a longstanding and productive debate among historians in particular, prompted above all by Peter Burke's work in the late 1970s, about what is generally termed 'popular culture'.[26] In this book, I seek to make two key contributions to that discourse. The first is historiographical. Although I am well aware of the 'notoriously problematic' limitations of adopting a binary model for the discussion of culture – top-down and bottom-up, elite and popular – it is a vocabulary I have largely been forced to use in order to reflect the language of ballad-singers' contemporaries.[27] In this instance, those simply *were* the terms of discussion, however reductive, and to the historian, the culture of the ballad-singer will always remain 'defined by its relationship to the dominant culture', given that it is the latter that largely provides our sources.[28] Yet as this book progresses, I seek to move beyond that opposition, revealing a culture that – for all the 'othering'[29] it was subjected to by certain commentators – was in effect a far broader and more fluid mainstream: one in which the singers and their performances might be ghettoised as low or popular, but in which the songs they sung were the common repertoire of all types of audience, whether defined by class, education, age, ethnicity, or gender. This fundamental distinction between a binary discourse used to classify performers and performances

---

[26] Peter Burke, *Popular Culture in Early Modern Europe* (3rd edn, Abingdon, 2009, 1st edn, New York, 1978).

[27] Michael J. Braddick and John Walter, 'Introduction. Grids of Power: Order, Hierarchy and Subordination in Early Modern Society', in their edited collection *Negotiating Power in Early Modern Society: Order, Hierarchy and Subordination in Britain and Ireland* (Cambridge, 2001), 1–42, 3. See also the discussion in Andrew Hadfield, Matthew Dimmock, and Abigail Shinn, 'Thinking About Popular Culture in Early Modern England', in their edited collection *The Ashgate Research Companion to Popular Culture in Early Modern England* (Farnham, 2014), 1–9, esp. 5.

[28] Editor's preface to Tiffany Potter (ed.), *Women, Popular Culture, and the Eighteenth Century* (Toronto, 2012), xiii.

[29] John Storey, *Cultural Theory and Popular Culture: An Introduction* (5th edn, Harlow, 2009), 1.

on the one hand, and a universal mainstream repertoire of cultural material on the other, is at the centre of my narrative. By the conclusion, it will illuminate both why ballad-singers were so important, and why – in a nuancing of a narrative first advanced in 1984 by John Golby and A. William Purdue – they were ultimately displaced by a mainstream audience whose appetites could no longer be sated by what these singers had to offer.[30]

My second contribution is a disciplinary one. It has been the hope of the major research project 'Music in London, 1800–1851', from which this present volume stems, that musicology also has its part to play, in the study of both London and of that thing often called popular culture. I myself am a historian by training, but I am attempting to practise the sort of interdisciplinarity championed by the musicologist Georgina Born: that which 'springs from a self-conscious dialogue with, criticism of, or opposition to, the intellectual, aesthetic, ethical or political limits of established disciplines'.[31] That is, I am trying to get beyond the shibboleths of our separate disciplines, which are themselves historical constructs, and use the best bits of various fields to come to a fuller understanding of the past. This need not mean abandoning our disciplinary identities: it is more about an openness to what colleagues with different training find most interesting. I do not see how a phenomenon such as song – a composite form of verse, music, and (sometimes) image, theatrically performed in physical space and historical time – can be studied any other way.

My hope is that this happy, productive vision of (inter)collegiality sums up a field that has moved beyond Martin Hewitt's 2007 diagnosis that 'one of the problems with history as a discipline is not that it says "I see music history, I must take it over", but that it says "I see music history, and I'm glad that someone else is doing that because it doesn't interest me."'[32] The history of musicalised performance, far from having little to interest the trained historian, desperately requires the rigour and expertise

---

[30] John M. Golby and A. William Purdue, *The Civilisation of the Crowd: Popular Culture in England 1750–1900* (Revised edn, Stroud, 1999).

[31] Born, 'For a Relational Musicology', 211. This approach is, I hope, rather more inviting than the limited exchange proposed in one of the few works devoted to the topic – that: 'Musicologists can help to guide historians through the particular concerns about music as a text because of their intimate knowledge of it. They can tell historians about how musical styles have changed and why those changes in style are historically important. Musicologists can learn from historians about a deep engagement with historical context and the ways in which particular musical texts and practices can help to illustrate broader historical issues.' Jeffrey H. Jackson and Stanley C. Pelkey (eds.), *Music and History: Bridging the Disciplines* (Mississippi, 2005), xiii.

[32] In Martin Hewitt and Rachel Cowgill (eds.), *Victorian Soundscapes Revisited* (Leeds, 2007), 33.

that historians are accustomed to applying to sources: the considerations of context, mentality, and materiality, and of the conditions of (sonic) production. In thinking about the reception of a *sung* text, we are not trespassing upon hostile territory, but simply placing greater stress on contextual elements common to the reception of *any* text.[33] A book, for example, is read in historical time and space, interpreted differently by different readers, and indeed interpreted differently by the *same* reader depending on context – if read aloud or in silence, in a library, club, over breakfast, in bed, in a carriage, in company, in good light or poor, in a single sitting or sporadically, on an empty or full stomach, and so on.[34] Any historical source, whether image, words, music, landscape, is subject to its temporal and physical conditions of reception. We are happy to think of issues of seriality when considering the reading of newspapers, or of how the hanging of paintings in galleries (how high? adjacent to what?) affected the gazes of viewers.[35] We are accustomed to thinking about how pedestrians 'read' the city itself as they walked.[36] All of this is part of thinking historically, and the same applies to song. To think about song culture, we need only behave as diligent historians. Knowledge of musical notation, for instance, is by no means required. It is enough to look at a set of lyrics and see them as such – as words that *could* be sung, existing beyond as well as on the page – and the great imaginative leap is made. If anything, the study of song is an exemplary exercise in reminding us, not of its difference, but of its similarity to other media as text consumed in time and space, by human bodies.[37]

In thinking about this repertoire in particular – the songs performed by ballad-singers, and enjoyed in common by most of the population – the lack of a specialist musicological background can even be beneficial. Born contrasts the traditional musicological perspective (sometimes shared by

---

[33] Matthew Champion and Miranda Stanyon make a similar argument about representation: 'The representation of sound in both notation and words confronts in complicated ways the problems of representation faced by any academic discipline.' Matthew S. Champion and Miranda Stanyon, 'Musicalising History', *Transactions of the Royal Historical Society* 29 (2019): 79–104, 80.

[34] Since writing this, I have had the great pleasure of seeing these contexts properly explored in Williams' *Social Life of Books*, which should be essential reading for any scholar interested in texts and their reception. As Williams puts it, sometimes 'What is read is less important than how' – ibid., 2.

[35] Respectively, I have been most influenced by the work of and discussions with Clare Pettitt and Pamela M. Fletcher on these two modes of reception.

[36] Of the many treatments of this subject, those not in thrall to Walter Benjamin's enigmatic *flâneur* acknowledge instead the influence of Michel de Certeau, *The Practice of Everyday Life*, trans. Steven Rendall (Berkeley and Los Angeles, 1984), 91–110, esp. 97–9.

[37] In this belief I differ slightly from my colleague David Kennerley, whose introduction to a forthcoming co-edited forum on 'Music and Politics' is essential reading for this topic. See *Journal of British Studies* 60, no. 3 (2021).

scholars of art and literature) 'that research on music must be founded on aesthetic advocacy of the music to be studied' with anthropology's commitment to 'confront the full spectrum of human behaviour', rooted in what she describes as 'a value agnosticism'.[38] Historians, I think, tend to belong to the latter camp: we study things, not because we think they are *good* (whatever that means), but because they are historically significant. We need not be worried that, formally speaking, most of these songs are aesthetically 'thin'[39] and artistically generic, and when the nineteenth-century collector Francis James Child sticks his nose up at the 'veritable dunghills' of broadside ballads, our own noses twitch with interest rather than revulsion.[40] What we *can* do, of course, is consider what led Child to make that judgement, and, going further, take seriously the aesthetic judgements of those contemporaries who wrote about song – for it is in their appreciation or denigration of both songs and singers that we learn most as historians about the values of past societies, not in the unmediated texts of the songs themselves. The question becomes, not 'is this a good song?', but 'who did this song repel and attract, and why?' Our mission, as Born concludes, 'is not to supersede but to reconceptualise questions of value'.[41]

Happily, I am far from the first to make this case. While many of the most eminent social historians of this period have been content to use songs as silent, illustrative sources, expressive of working-class sentiment, others have been more discerning.[42] Since the 1960s, a number of articles, monographs, and collections across various disciplines, rarely bearing any relation to each other, have contributed significantly to the study of vernacular singing as a historical phenomenon.[43] In recent years,

[38] Born, 'For a Relational Musicology', 217.
[39] Jeanette Bicknell and John Andrew Fisher, adapting the terminology of Stephen Davies in their *Song, Songs, and Singing* (Chichester, 2013), 4.
[40] See esp. Roy Palmer, '"Veritable Dunghills": Professor Child and the Broadside', *Folk Music Journal* 7, no. 2 (1996): 155–66.
[41] Born, 'For a Relational Musicology', 218.
[42] To cite just two towering examples, consider the use of ballads in E. P. Thompson's *The Making of the English Working Class* (Revised edn, 1991) and Patrick Joyce's *Visions of the People: Industrial England and the Question of Class, 1848–1914* (Cambridge, 1991).
[43] As such, many of these works overlap significantly in their thinking. A representative complementary corpus might include, among others, ordered chronologically: Bertrand H. Bronson, *The Ballad as Song* (Berkeley and Los Angeles, 1969); Eleanor R. Long, 'Ballad Singers, Ballad Makers, and Ballad Etiology', *Western Folklore* 32 (1973): 225–36; Mark W. Booth, *The Experience of Songs* (New Haven, 1981); Breandán Ó Madagáin, 'Functions of Irish Song in the Nineteenth Century', *Béaloideas* 53 (1985): 130–216; Jacky Bratton (ed.), *Music Hall: Performance and Style* (Milton Keynes, 1986); Mike Pickering and Tony Green (eds.), *Everyday Culture: Popular Song and the Vernacular Milieu* (Milton Keynes, 1987); Colin Neilands, 'Irish Broadside Ballads: Performers and Performances', *Folk Music Journal* 6 (1991): 209–22; Laura Mason, *Singing the French Revolution: Popular Culture and Politics, 1787–1799*

numerous landmark history journals have all devoted space to the thematic treatment of song and sound.[44] Perhaps the most fruitful and genuinely interdisciplinary conversations have taken place among early modernists rather than scholars of the eighteenth and nineteenth centuries.[45] Lacking an equivalent focus within the academy, scholarship on these latter centuries has fallen into three main categories. The first stems from a far longer tradition of antiquarian and folkloric research, and its energies are accordingly devoted principally to *collecting*; where once this meant almost exclusively collecting songs, it has led of late to extremely useful gathering of information about printers and singers.[46] This sort of work has been stimulated by the mass digitisation of primary

(Ithaca, NY, 1996); Phil Eva, 'Home Sweet Home? The "Culture of Exile" in Mid-Victorian Popular Song', *Popular Music* 16 (1997): 131–50; Peter Bailey, *Popular Culture and Performance in the Victorian City* (Cambridge, 1998); Jessica S. Sack, 'Street Music and Musicians: The Physical and Aural Nature of Performance' (Oxford University MPhil thesis, 1998); Michael Bywater, 'Performing Spaces: Street Music and Public Territory', *Twentieth-Century Music* 3 (2007): 97–120; Éva Guillorel, David Hopkin, and William G. Pooley (eds.), *Rhythms of Revolt: European Traditions and Memories of Social Conflict in Oral Culture* (Abingdon, 2018). The wider literature is hugely variable: see the bibliography for what is, I hope, the most comprehensive list of works on the subject yet compiled.

[44] For example, Daniel Bender, Duane J. Corpis, and Daniel J. Walkowitz, 'Sound Politics: Critically Listening to the Past', *Radical History Review* 121 (2015): 1–7; Champion and Stanyon, 'Musicalising History'; and a 2021 special forum of *Journal of British Studies* edited by David Kennerley and myself.

[45] A series of excellent monographs from literary scholars and historians has been complemented by something of a glut of innovative collections, three of the latter appearing in 2016 alone, while more recent monographs from a new generation of scholars hail from increasingly diverse perspectives. See especially: Bruce R. Smith, *The Acoustic World of Early Modern England* (Chicago, 1999); Adam Fox, *Oral and Literate Culture in England, 1500–1700* (Oxford, 2000); Arnold Hunt, *The Art of Hearing: English Preachers and Their Audiences, 1590–1640* (Cambridge, 2010); Marsh, *Music and Society*; Mark Hailwood, *Alehouses and Good Fellowship in Early Modern England* (Woodbridge, 2014); Jeroen Salman, *Pedlars and the Popular Press: Itinerant Distribution Networks in England and the Netherlands, 1600–1850* (Leiden, 2014); Luca Degl'Innocenti, Massimo Rospocher, and Rosa M. Salzberg (eds.), *The Cantastorie in Renaissance Italy: Street Singers Between Oral and Literature Cultures*, special issue of *Italian Studies* 71, no. 2 (2016); Patricia Fumerton (ed.), *Living English Broadside Ballads, 1550–1750: Song, Art, Dance, Culture*, special issue of *Huntington Library Quarterly* 79, no. 2 (2016); Dieuwke van der Poel, Louis Peter Grijp, and Anrooij van Wim (eds.), *Identity, Intertextuality, and Performance in Early Modern Song Culture* (Leiden, 2016); David Hitchcock, *Vagrancy in English Society and Culture, 1650–1750* (2016); Simon Smith, *Musical Response*; Degl'Innocenti and Rospocher, *Street Singers*; Angela McShane, *The Political World of the Broadside Ballad in Seventeenth-Century England* (forthcoming).

[46] In the United Kingdom, much of this work has been tied to the commendably active English Folk Dance and Song Society, based at Cecil Sharp House. The most recent such volume has some claim to constitute a textbook of sorts for the field: David Atkinson and Steve Roud (eds.), *Street Literature of the Long Nineteenth Century: Producers, Sellers, Consumers* (Newcastle, 2017). In relation to the present subject, see especially its introduction, and chapters by Isabel Corfe and Vic Gammon. Musicologists have also begun to specialise in this area, however, resulting most recently in Paul Watt, Derek B. Scott,

sources, allowing full-text searches of all manner of print, particularly periodical and trial literature, resulting in the collation of a mass of otherwise disparate and disconnected material relating to ballad singing. The second category has been concerned with what might be done in future, resulting in works of great conjectural vigour.[47] Most sorely lacking, to date, are works of the third type: studies of these centuries that use song culture as a means of historical analysis, in order to advance our understanding of the period.[48] The field of literary scholarship has again led the way, embracing both song and ballad, and producing landmark publications including a special issue of *Studies in Romanticism* that historians will find particularly valuable.[49] Perhaps the most notable example within the discipline itself is Katie Barclay's body of work, and it is especially encouraging that Barclay is primarily a historian of the emotions, whose facility in the study of song has produced work of great value to that field as well as to ours – just as some of the best work on ballad-singers of the period, by the social historian Tim Hitchcock, is concerned with the profession as 'a type of begging' rather than as a mode of musical performance.[50]

## Structure

I hope that this book will count as work of this last kind, appealing to a broad and interdisciplinary readership, of use both to those interested in the songs for their own sake, and those primarily concerned with the society such songs helped to shape. Above all I am interested in the singers: their lives, their artistry, how they were viewed, and how they

---

and Patrick Spedding (eds.), *Cheap Print and Popular Song in the Nineteenth Century: A Cultural History of the Songster* (Cambridge, 2017).

[47] Two notable calls-to-arms concern song, labour, and class formation: these are Kate Bowan and Paul A. Pickering, '"Songs for the Millions": Chartist Music and Popular Aural Tradition', *Labour History Review* 74 (2009): 44–63; and Marek Korczynski, Michael Pickering, and Emma Robertson, *Rhythms of Labour: Music at Work in Britain* (Cambridge, 2013). Bowan and Pickering's subsequent book *Sounds of Liberty* vastly exceeds their initial exhortation, and is undoubtedly the richest extant treatment of the wider subject.

[48] But see the previous footnote on *Sounds of Liberty*, and, in a comparative context, Ghosh, 'Singing in a New World'.

[49] Meredith L. McGill, 'What Is a Ballad? Reading for Genre, Format, and Medium', *Nineteenth-Century Literature* 71 (2016): 156–75; Ian Newman (ed.), *Song and the City*, special issue of *Studies in Romanticism* 58, no. 4 (2019).

[50] For the former, see especially 'Composing the Self: Gender, Subjectivity and Scottish Balladry', *Cultural and Social History* 7 (2010): 337–53; 'Singing, Performance, and Lower-Class Masculinity in the Dublin Magistrates' Court, 1820–1850', *Journal of Social History* 47 (2014): 746–68; and 'Sounds of Sedition: Music and Emotion in Ireland, 1780–1845', *Cultural History* 3 (2014): 54–80. For the latter, see primarily his *Down and Out in Eighteenth-Century London* (2004). The phrase quoted is on 67.

behaved. I have come to see them as practitioners of an inherently early modern occupation in a modernising metropolis – as both agents and victims of the historical process. Undone by time, they have since been overshadowed by their own wares, with the scholarship on ballads dwarfing that on ballad-singers, and in structuring this book I have tried to avoid replicating that disservice. Of four substantial, thematic chapters dealing with aspects of ballad singing, only the fourth has many songs in it, allowing the singers to remain the focus of discussion. Each of these chapters is, however, succeeded by an interlude built around an individual song that serves to expand or elaborate upon the theme of the preceding chapter, and move discussion on towards the next chapter, so that the whole book ends up echoing one of those patter ballads that alternates between recitations in prose and short sung refrains.[51] It may help to think of these interludes as stepping stones or pivots, as well as case studies: while each develops its theme from the chapter it follows, they also serve as standalone discussions that move the book forward.

My first chapter, 'Representations: Seeing the Singer', addresses perhaps the greatest problem to the historian of song culture, that of its sources, and in so doing serves also as a comprehensive introduction to the ballad-singer and her place in metropolitan life. It is constructed chiefly as an analysis of images of singers, supported by comparison with other media of representation, from plays to novels. I have tried to tackle head on the fact that in the historical record we see the singer almost entirely from above – and almost never hear them. Several key themes emerge: the extent to which ballad-singers were both silenced (or ventriloquised) and stripped of their crowds, thereby diminishing their potential to disturb viewers; the process of Othering whereby singers became synecdochal for an underclass within London, helping to create a domestic narrative of internal colonialism; and above all, the complex articulation of immorality in imagery. This lay less in a focus upon the female body than in the associations of the open mouth – a vulgar, sexualised trope that located vice, not in the singer's person, but in their song. This chapter is also something of an exercise in source methodology, and I hope it will deter both reader and author from treating too many sources as simply illustrative over the course of the book.

'Oh! Cruel', the first interlude, extends this source analysis to songs about or purportedly by singers, centring on the song 'Oh! Cruel' itself. The performance of this and other songs prompted especial anxieties

---

[51] For an example of this type, see the early-Victorian 'Jimmy Jumps the Rhymer'. Bod. Firth c.21(7) is a notably well-preserved edition.

around issues of charity and class relations. I contend that, though many of these songs share the stock characteristics and prejudices of the representations considered in Chapter 1, their crucial difference is that, because they were actually performed by ballad-singers, they afforded the singer a degree of agency and self-expression denied them in other media. It is this sort of autonomous performance that I see as central to the role of the ballad-singer in society.

Chapter 2 is 'Progress: Ancient Custom in the Modern City'. Here I pursue sociopolitical questions prompted by ballad singing, in an analysis shaped by an understanding of historical time and process whereby the chief tension lay between an early modern conception of order, public space, and neighbourhood, as embodied by the singer, and a self-consciously modern urban programme of improvement and capital, advanced by journalists and the judiciary. I situate debates over ballad singing at the centre of this historical process, the better to understand both issues. I analyse the threats singers were said to represent, in moral and legal writing; the political power accorded to the song by authorities (centring on the endlessly repeated maxim of the early Enlightenment thinker Andrew Fletcher); contemporary medical views on the inflammatory power of music; the vexed question of public space; and the steps taken both to repress and to coerce ballad-singers. I focus on the few documented occasions when a ballad-singer had a demonstrable impact on the actions of a community, from Kennington, to Camden, to Whitechapel market, and I come to see the singer, not as analogous to rough music as such, but as a paradoxical, anachronistic voice of authority within those communities. At a time when both moral and political reform was hotly contested, the singer emerges as a potent point of tension between articulate, self-regulating, traditional local communities, and the modernising forces of capitalism and civic authority.

Interlude II, 'Lord Viscount Maidstone's Address', pursues themes of localised community formation and articulation (mentioned in Chapter 2) through close analysis of a single election ballad of 1852, set to a popular political tune of the late eighteenth century, 'Bow, wow, wow'. I situate the song within the political and spatial context of the Westminster election, and demonstrate its suitability as a satirical form based on both the tune's associations and its innate melopoetic properties. In contrasting the Liberal Party's continued use of such songs with the Tory preference for more modern campaign media, I apply the chronological contentions of Chapter 2 to this mid-century case study, demonstrating the continued effectiveness, within a spatially contained neighbourhood, of this early modern form of political expression.

My third chapter – 'Performance: The Singer in Action' – is an extensive consideration of the practice of singing in the streets. Its focus homes in repeatedly upon the act of performance itself: from citywide topography and issues of calendar and clock time; to performance in specific sites; to voice, body, and audience engagement; to the singer's relationship with the physical ballad sheet in performance. I explore how balladeers overcame numerous challenges – geographic, sonic, social – by means of specific strategies, from the pitch of their voices, to the use of props, to borrowing the psychological weaponry of beggars. The chapter is therefore also in conversation with histories of charity and disability, as well as aspects of human geography. I am especially interested in the creation and maintaining of crowds, the appropriation of public space, the manipulation of codes of moral obligation, and above all in the musical and theatrical aspects of singing: it is central to my argument that we take ballad-singers seriously as being, on some level, artists. This is most evident in my discussion of voice, which – though it borrows heavily from musicology – is unrepentantly historical and leads us inevitably back to issues of class consciousness.

In the third interlude, 'The Storm', I examine the performance of a single song by one singer, the disabled black sailor Joseph Johnson. Taking an approach somewhat indebted to Timothy Brook's *Vermeer's Hat*, I pursue the elements bound up in Johnson's performance right across the globe, from the Antipodes to Jamaica, from Versailles to the West End stage, placing this East End performance within an imperial narrative of cultural appropriation, assimilation, and identity formation. Johnson emerges as in many ways the epitome of the ballad-singer: a marginal figure disadvantaged by both race and injury, whose self-fashioning (based on Jamaican Jonkonnu practice) was designed to reposition himself at the heart of both metropolitan and national notions of patriotism.

Fourth and finally I come to 'Repertoire: Navigating the Mainstream'. This chapter explores singers' repertoires, from whence these were derived, and their networks of dissemination, and centres on my formulation of a cultural 'mainstream' of songs. I begin by placing the notoriously mixed repertoires available to us within a theoretical framework of the miscellaneous as a form of cultural consumption, before moving beyond specific lists of songs to a consideration of historical process. I examine the remarkable ways in which singers appropriated tunes from other cultural spaces, and the varying methods by which a lyric might be sourced. I look at the question of circulation both within and without London, and the movement of songs between different physical and social sites, demonstrating in particular the overwhelming musical importance of the theatre to mainstream song culture. I construct an image of this 'mainstream' as a working model for understanding how songs were produced, performed, and consumed in an age before sound recording: a model that necessarily takes issue with Peter Burke's influential theory of the separation of elite and popular cultures by 1800. This is enlarged upon in three case studies of 'Black-Ey'd Susan', 'The Wolf', and 'Cherry Ripe', which together move my argument to a chronological contention: that the success of the mainstream was predicated on the portability of songs that, because they were written primarily as melodies, could easily be mediated by solo ballad-singers. As the century progressed and harmonic forms of songwriting, based on chord progressions, came to prominence, this cultural model was no longer tenable, and newly literate workers with a slightly improved disposable income began to consume songs in both physical and performative forms that bypassed the ballad-singer – a development that leads into the book's final stages.

The fourth interlude, 'Old Dog Tray', discusses one of the ballad-singer's last great mainstream hits, the sentimental American song 'Old Dog Tray'. I regard this song as something of a paradox: both an ideal solo ballad and an indication of the ballad-singer's failings, considering the song's harmonic possibilities as realised by performances on keyboard, barrel-organ, or by vocal ensembles – possibilities not available for songs written and sung in the early part of the century. This discussion leads naturally into the book's Conclusion. Developing the thesis elaborated in the latter part of Chapter 4, I contend that the demise of the ballad-singer was primarily due to a shift in mainstream taste and musical potential, as the masses developed both the appetite for, and access to, a wide range of more sophisticated music. By 1864, when this book ends, the ballad-singer was almost entirely absent from the debate around the Street Music Act championed by Michael Thomas Bass MP, indicating the irrelevance of the ballad-singer to the contemporary street scene. This argument, predicated upon technological change, literacy, economics, and class consciousness, is essentially optimistic, running counter to the rhetoric of decline and nostalgia found in nineteenth-century elite writing on the subject. I contend that the primarily musical transformation by which melodic *song* became subordinated within a new and totalising conception of *music* was itself symptomatic of the great historical forces of reform, education, improvement, and enfranchisement that were at work in Victorian London.

Several of the songs discussed in the interludes and Chapter 4 are accompanied by replications of their scores from contemporary editions of sheet music. However, these songs and many others throughout the book have also been recorded as solo vocals, and may be heard and downloaded at www.cambridge.org/ballads. These recordings should be taken as indicative of the songs' original notated melodies only, rather than as approximating to any historical performance by ballad-singers, which may of course have been different in tune, words, and above all in delivery. In addition to reading or listening to these examples, it is my hope that you will try to sing some of them yourself, and thereby reflect upon the choices made and the challenges faced by the London ballad-singer.

# 1   Representations
## Seeing the Singer

> 'Our manners will not suit your gentleness,' replied Jessy at last; 'our ways are low, our occupation very mean, and it requires a boldness and assurance which your modest nature could never assume. I am a ballad singer, [I] sing in the streets by night; could you – could you do that?'[1]

Like good Victorian children, London's ballad-singers are seen and not heard. For no one now living has ever heard such a singer, the last of whom vanished before the first age of field recording. In the epigraph, 'Jessy' warns us that they were bold and immodest, an affront to polite sensibility – yet she does so from the confines of a sentimental novel. Her cautions, directed at the pure yet fallen heroine Joscelina, speak of a shocking gulf between cocksure singers and genteel society – yet she is being ventriloquised by and for the delectation of genteel persons, in the form of the author Isabella Kelly and her readership. Across the seventy years of this study, in all forms of media, we are told time and again that ballad-singers are noisy, rude, eloquent, intrusive – yet who tells us? Not ballad-singers or their immediate paying audiences, but novelists, artists, poets, and playwrights. The one voice we do not hear is the singer's, though we see them everywhere. We must make do with representations.

Reflecting that 'History writing cannot make present – represent – what once was, in the past', Carolyn Steedman encourages us 'to conceptualise language and texts in the past *as things* that afforded social actors both use of them and cognition about them: as things that made people behave, think, and believe in certain ways, out of their quiddity'.[2] Nowhere is the ephemerality of that-which-once-was so intangible as in the realm of performance, which is what this book is after all about: the singing of songs. 'Without a copy, live performance . . . disappears into memory, into the realm of invisibility and

---

[1] Isabella Kelly, *Joscelina: or, the Rewards of Benevolence. A Novel*, 2 vols. (2nd edn, 1798), vol. 1, 193.

[2] Carolyn Steedman, 'Cries Unheard, Sights Unseen: Writing the Eighteenth-Century Metropolis', *Representations* 118 (2012): 28–71, 28–9.

the unconscious where it eludes regulation and control.'[3] As Peggy Phelan observes, however, 'The pressures brought to bear on performance to suc-cumb to the laws of the reproductive economy are enormous.'[4] And this is what we are left with: the texts – or *things* – that constitute the reproductive economy of our period. In the case of ballad singing, those things left to represent the historical performer (besides the printed songs themselves) are novels like *Joscelina*, plays, anecdotes, histories, and images, most of which are caricatures. In this chapter, building upon recent and comparable projects concerned explicitly with the representation of street figures, I will consider these representational objects, and what they reveal about singers, the metro-politan society within and beneath which they operated, and the ways in which these objects actively mediated the relationship between the two.[5]

Laura Mason observes of eighteenth-century Paris that street singers 'were recognisable as a coherent group only through the contradictory images found in idealised literary representations and largely hostile police reports' – so that the very first thing these representations did was to impose a false collectivity upon ballad-singers, presenting both con-temporary consumers and historians with a 'type', rather than with dis-crete individuals.[6] While it is important to remember that this generalising view of the singer is not a historical fact but a historical process (and one that undoubtedly influenced the opinion of numerous contemporaries), it is equally important to make the same point about the representations themselves. We must consider the specificity of the media employed to represent singers, bearing in mind the conventions, restraints, and possibilities of form. I have chosen to focus on eighty images (see Tables 1.1 and 1.2). However, these images do not form anything like a coherent corpus: while 'London Cries' constituted a minor, recognisable genre throughout the seventeenth to nineteenth centuries, the ballad-singer as a subject did not, and the representations of singers I have found are a motley bunch, ranging from the sole focus of a portrait to a literally marginal detail, in works ranging from the political to the pastoral. The word 'image' itself, meanwhile, encompasses every-

---

[3] Peggy Phelan, *Unmarked: The Politics of Performance* (1993), 148.     [4] Ibid., 146.

[5] These are Brian Maidment, *Dusty Bob: A Cultural History of Dustmen, 1780–1870* (Manchester, 2007); Salman, *Pedlars and the Popular Press*, chapter 1 'Reputation and Representation', 11–96; and Chriscinda Henry, 'From Beggar to Virtuoso: The Street Singer in the Netherlandish Visual Tradition, 1500–1600', in Degl'Innocenti and Rospocher, *Street Singers*, 136–58. For a more sustained treatment of the wider theme of representing the itinerant poor, see Hitchcock, *Vagrancy in English Society and Culture*.

[6] Mason, *Singing the French Revolution*, 16.

thing from oil paintings to book illustrations.[7] The only thing uniting these images is that they are the only ones I have found from London in this period that depict ballad-singers. I will supplement their analysis with reference to other representational media: poetry, prose, masquerades, and that most intermedial of forms, the play.

The material available – though not a complete record of what was once extant – admits of clear patterns and generic tropes that reveal much about gender, class, and power, especially when we think about representations of the human mouth. The neutralising of singers by capturing them in print or paint played into a wider bid by elements of London society to tame its noisy, feral streets. There is a historical irony to be unpicked here. It was the ballad-singer who, by their trade, apparently gave voice to the demonisation of the French and to the racial exoticising of the British Empire's colonial subjects, in the form of xenophobic ballads. Yet if anyone was consistently represented as 'other' in this imperial era, it was the ballad-singer. In spite of all of which my argument begins not in India or Jamaica, nor even London's Seven Dials, but in a still less likely part of the empire: Nottingham.

### David Love's Likeness

In or after 1814, the minor provincial portraitist Thomas Barber, a pupil of Sir Thomas Lawrence, executed a large half-body portrait in oils of an old man in a hat (Figure 1.1). Barber specialised in Whig politicians, from Charles James Fox to Thomas 1st Baron Denman, and in members of aspirational families: though he exhibited at the Royal Academy, his manner of living in Derby enabled him to offer cut-price yet cutting-edge services to the newly monied of the Midlands.[8] Even so, it is unlikely that the old man in the hat commissioned his portrait from Barber in the usual manner: for his name was David Love, and he was a ballad-singer.

Love, a Scot by birth, settled at Nottingham in late 1812 after a peripatetic life, and remained there until his death, save for a brief, panicked escape to London in 1814 for fear of repatriation to his parish of origin. During this time, he and his (third) wife were in and out of the workhouse, lodging on Leenside – then something of a slum – when they could afford it. He was nonetheless a local celebrity, and Barber's portrait, if not a 'calling-card' kept by the painter to impress prospective patrons,

---

[7] The caution not to conflate different forms of image comes courtesy of Nancy Rose Marshall, *City of Gold and Mud: Painting Victorian London* (New Haven, 2012), 6.

[8] Richard Walker, *Regency Portraits*, 2 vols. (1985), vol. 1, 486.

Figure 1.1  Thomas Barber, 'David Love (1750–1827), Ballad-Writer',
*c.*1814.
Oil on canvas. By permission of Nottingham City Museums & Galleries:
NCM 1946–42

may have been a speculative arrangement with Love, sold to a local benefactor with a strong sense of civic patriotism. This would accord with Love's
other attempts to capitalise upon his small stock of fame: he published two
memoirs, the second, sold by subscription, running to three editions within
a year. This volume includes the only other known depiction of Love, from
1824 – and this one, reproduced as Figure 1.2, he certainly commissioned
himself.[9] Although it is of a wholly different artistic register to Barber's
portrait, the similarities are striking – in features, dress, pose, and accessor-
ies. In both, Love would have been instantly recognisable as a *typical* male
ballad-singer, by virtue of his top hat, shabby but sober clothing, and above
all by his stance, a ballad slip held in both hands at the level of his stomach,
ready to sing. Given the images' goal of capitalising upon Love's fame, this
gesture to his profession is unsurprising. The remarkable thing is that these

[9] David Love, *The Life, Adventures, and Experience of David Love* (3rd edn, Nottingham,
1823 [1824]).

Figure 1.2  Anon, 'David Love, Aged 74', 1824.
Etching. Love, *The Life, Adventures, and Experience*, front matter

appear to be the only extant depictions of ballad-singers in Britain that
originate at the instigation or with the evident consent of the singer.

We must take care not to privilege a representation simply because it
comes first-hand: Love was of course engaged in active self-fashioning. In
the British Library's copy of his *Life*, the etched portrait is hand-coloured,
adding vitality to the background street scene. Love figures himself in the
heart of his adopted city, its quotidian routines and neo-Palladian architecture forming a theatrical backdrop to his likeness as he goes about his
celebrated business. He highlights his integration within a place while
subordinating that place to his own agency. Readers are invited to 'look'
at Love 'in his present state'. They presumably did this regularly in the
street – yet in this book, as author, self-publisher, and portrait commissioner, Love controlled their perspective, focusing attention on his valor-
ised person. In this, he was unique among ballad-singers, yet he was just
one of several, all of whom we will encounter in subsequent chapters, who
engaged in the comparable practice of life-writing. Their accounts are
consciously constructed, so that, as David Vincent observes: 'We are

presented not with a collection of remembered facts, but rather with a pattern of recollected experiences.[10] Memory moreover 'tends to sift out the merely uninteresting rather than the unpalatable', leaving a selection of atypically colourful incidents.[11] These might be further distorted, not merely to furnish potential readers – who were, of course, customers – with a compelling narrative but to serve an ulterior purpose, often evangelical or socialist. A born-again Methodist might embellish depravity, thereby bringing the conversion moment into sharper relief; a socialist might exaggerate injustice or poverty to strengthen the cause for social reform. In turning to life-writing at second hand, it is similarly tempting to give greater weight to biographical sources that focus on a single, known individual. Yet the creation of such 'legends', whether in the etchings of John Thomas Smith or in the journalism of Douglas Jerrold, was a recognised bourgeois strategy of containment, rendering the alien known, the tawdry romantic, and the dangerous 'interesting'.[12] In moving beyond Love's likeness to consider the representations of others, we too must allow ourselves to be interested, not in prosaic accuracy, but in the subtler stuff of motive, effect, and social relation.

## The Problem with Singers

The clue is in the name. Ballad-singers sang ballads, and when, from the mid-nineteenth century, they shifted to simply calling out titles, the terminology shifted too: Henry Mayhew's *London Labour and the London Poor*, compiled in the early 1850s, is full of ballad-*sellers*, patterers, and pinners-up, explicitly distinguished from the disappearing 'singers' and 'chaunters'.[13] Ballad-singers sold lyric sheets for domestic consumption, unaccompanied by notation. Thus, it was vital to their trade that they communicated a song's melody to purchasers, who learnt by ear. Auditors would be more likely to buy a song if it were sung accurately and audibly. Yet – though there were dissenting voices, such as the Bavarian artist George Johann Scharf – the

[10] David Vincent, *Bread, Knowledge and Freedom: A Study of Nineteenth-Century Working Class Autobiography* (1981), 5. See also Jeroen Salman, 'Pedlars in the Netherlands from 1600 to 1850: Nuisance or Necessity?', in Roeland Harms et al. (eds.), *Not Dead Things: The Dissemination of Popular Print in England and Wales, Italy, and the Low Countries, 1500–1820* (Leiden, 2013), 53–74.
[11] John Burnett (ed.), *Useful Toil: Autobiographies of Working People from the 1820s to the 1920s* (Harmondsworth, 1984), 11, 12.
[12] Thomas Lord Busby, *Costume of the Lower Orders of London. Painted and Engraved from Nature* (1820), iii. See also Mason, *Singing the French Revolution*, 31, and this chapter on street portraiture.
[13] Henry Mayhew, *London Labour and the London Poor*, 4 vols. (1861), vol. 3, 213–20, 226, 273–7. Mayhew himself is discussed later.

prevalent bourgeois and genteel discourse on singers condemned them as hoarse and unmelodious: makers of noise, not music.[14]

It is this question of disputed identity, and the distinctiveness of the ballad-singer's wares, that differentiates an analysis of singers from other existing studies of marginal, subaltern street figures in visual culture, of which the most comprehensive is Sean Shesgreen's *Images of the Outcast* – a rich, absorbing, imperfect study that, along with works by Vic Gatrell, Colin Jones, Saree Makdisi, and Nancy Rose Marshall, has done much both to inform and to provoke this chapter.[15] Admittedly, ballad-singers often featured within the broader pictorial genre of London Cries. Yet the ballad was more subversive than the groceries, services, or artefacts ped-dled by other street-sellers, and its disseminators attracted a specialised discourse. As the ephemeral, mobile, unlegislated product of the lowest and murkiest gutters of Grub Street, the ballad's potential to corrupt listeners and readers was a vexed issue, forming much of the subject of Chapter 2. Jeroen Salman observes of the late eighteenth century that:

> The ballad singer, who had begun as just one of many stock figures in a series of London street cries and as an appealing subject for the genre scenes that proved attractive to new classes of art buyers, came to embody allusions to the irreverent and rapid spread of the latest news and gossip.[16]

It is clear that such stock perceptions obtained in society, attested by the frequency with which singers were used in simile and metaphor, usually to represent nuisance or vulgarity.[17] So powerful was this trope that, in one Old Bailey trial, a witness made the assumption that because a woman 'came to me, in a very ragged dress, and looked very hard at me, I took her to be something of a ballad singer'.[18] Crucially, it was her appearance and stare alone that misled him, so indelibly fixed was the association of the singer with that particular combination of rags and effrontery.

---

[14] One of Scharf's private pencil sketches of singers, from 1844 (Table 1.1, number 67), contains the annotation that 'This woman had a very good voice'. For a broader discus-sion of elite attitudes, see Cox Jensen, *Napoleon and British Song*, 27–30.

[15] Sean Shesgreen, *Images of the Outcast: The Urban Poor in the Cries of London* (Manchester, 2002); Vic Gatrell, *City of Laughter: Sex and Satire in Eighteenth-Century London* (2007); Colin Jones, *The Smile Revolution in Eighteenth Century Paris* (Oxford, 2014); Saree Makdisi, *Making England Western: Occidentalism, Race, and Imperial Culture* (Chicago, 2014); Marshall, *City of Gold*. See also footnote 5 for more closely related specialist studies.

[16] Salman, *Pedlars*, 56.

[17] For example, *Britannic Magazine* 1, no. 12 (1793): 376; *Will Whimsical's Miscellany* (Chichester, 1799), 57; Oliver Goldsmith, *The Vicar of Wakefield* (1800), 56; POB t18120701-11 (testimony of Joseph Withers); *Scourge* 5 (1813): 227; *Satirist* 14 (1814): 454; *Lady's Monthly Museum* 6 (1817): 154.

[18] POB t17840225-26.

Nowhere was this archetype more evident than in the images produced by London's caricaturists, who tended towards a reductive and unsympathetic portrayal that tallies with the 'conservative tenor' of the genre, and the satirists' general sense of themselves as moral arbiters.[19] As licensed scandal-mongers themselves, too much a part of the establishment to require regulation by the Stamp Act, there was something slightly disingenuous in their condescending, even controlling depictions of their gutter-level counterparts, characterised by Brian Maidment in relation to a close cousin of the ballad-singer, the dustman, as forming 'part of the narrative of threat and danger which they constructed for their middle-class customers, who were always willing to have their perceptions of appetites of the lower orders confirmed'.[20] Conversely, the images that Salman terms 'fancy pictures', in which singers were 'cleaned-up and presented as a non-threatening or even appealing entity', were – as I discuss in detail later – more controlling still, reducing these unruly subaltern elements to a pastoral ideal.[21]

It would be reductive to suggest that all visual depictions of ballad-singers were solely and explicitly motivated by a civic desire to 'catalogue [and] control'.[22] Yet the question of power lies behind all the images I have found, for there is power in the gaze of both the artist and the viewer. At a basic level, this is exemplified by the artist's ability to control singers' surroundings. In images that take the singer as their subject, rather than including one or more as appendages to a wider scene, only two versions of Thomas Rowlandson's 'The Ballad Singer' (Table 1.1, nos. *14, 15*) depict her at the centre of a crowd: a crowd that is unruly, unsavoury, and infiltrated by pickpockets. Even this exception to the rule has an explanation that reinforces the rest: Rowlandson was conducting a painterly argument, offering a self-consciously grubby travesty of the Royal Academician Francis Wheatley's more typically sanitised street scenes.[23] Even in the two Rowlandsons the knowing addition of a pickpocket, visible to the viewer if not to the victim on the canvas, may be read as a way of sanitising the threat of crime, simultaneously titillating and reassuring the viewer by granting an omniscience of surveillance denied them when actually walking those streets.[24] Meanwhile in the vast majority of images, whether

---

[19] Eirwen E. C. Nicholson, 'Consumers and Spectators: The Public of the Political Print in Eighteenth-Century England', *History* 81 (1996): 5–21, 14. For extensive biographical details of the leading printmakers that reinforce the sense of a prosperous, well-educated, conservative milieu, see Tim Clayton, *The English Print, 1688–1802* (New Haven, 1997), esp. 214 onwards.

[20] Maidment, *Dusty Bob*, 145–6.      [21] Salman, *Pedlars*, 64, 61–3.

[22] Marshall, *City of Gold*, 39.

[23] Sean Shesgreen, 'The Cries of London from the Renaissance to the Nineteenth Century: A Short History', in Harms, *Not Dead Things*, 139.

[24] See Marshall, *City of Gold*, 52, for further discussion of pickpockets in painting.

represented in abstract space or against a rural or urban background, singers are shorn of their attentive crowds, rendered either as isolated specimens subject to the viewer's gaze alone or allotted individual listeners, whose social status varies according to the artist's agenda. This act of selective extraction placed singers within a bourgeois comfort zone by treating them as curious 'characters'. As Makdisi writes: 'While this tactic may have raised the risk of blurring all-important social distinctions, it was much to be preferred over the depiction of the masses as a coarse and undifferentiated mass.'[25]

This perspective is perhaps the victory of the visual over the aural: of the power of the gaze to confer ownership, which in depictions of street life was given unreservedly to the viewer or purchaser, generally ensconced in a private room or select convivial space such as a coffee house. It is more than twenty years since Eirwen Nicholson deconstructed the myth that visual prints circulated among a broad market, her painstaking research making clear the restricted print runs (rarely above five hundred), high prices (rarely under a shilling in this period, and often much more), carefully demarcated spaces of display, and exclusivity of allusion and reference, that characterised even the cheapest of the images under discussion here.[26] Of the eighty images I have found only three might be classed as, in Sheila O'Connell's terms, 'popular prints', sold for no more than sixpence and with a broad circulation that extended to the artisan classes.[27] In the overwhelming majority of cases, and unlike their flesh-and-blood counterparts, these represented singers were viewed by a select minority of London society. Gatrell has made us familiar with these sorts of viewers, especially in the earlier part of the period: persons both able and motivated to buy the images in question; a mixed audience, relatively well educated, obsessed with their own city and its endless sources of conversation. These viewers looked at the images they bought – especially caricatures, but also most other kinds of prints, paintings, illustrations – in a mode more often sociable than solitary, relying on the images to generate discourse, and ready to be simultaneously titillated and censorious, cynical and credulous – though this mercurial facility perhaps

[25] Makdisi, *Making England Western*, 35.

[26] Nicholson, 'Consumers and Spectators', 9–11, 12, 16, and 17. See also her 'English Political Prints and Pictorial Argument *c*.1640–*c*.1832: A Study in Historiography and Methodology' (University of Edinburgh PhD thesis, 1994); Harry T. Dickinson, *Caricatures and the Constitution, 1760–1832* (Cambridge, 1986), esp. 14; and Clayton, *The English Print*, 227, for a discussion of the expense of production, and ibid., 232, on sale price.

[27] Sheila O'Connell, *The Popular Print in England, 1550–1850* (1999). The three exceptions are *24, 45,* and *63.* The first is a 'straight' portrait naming the singer, Thomas Fox, and recalls David Love's commissioned print. The second is a print of the 1814 Frost Fair featuring two tiny singers in an immense crowd scene, and the third is a (rather charming) joke at the hungry singer's expense, distracted from his love song by the sight of a pile of dumplings in a shop window.

diminished as the nineteenth century wore on. As an advertisement by William Holland, perhaps the most risqué publisher of prints, claimed, even the edgier sort of caricature often 'embellished Dressing-Rooms, alcoves, Billiard Rooms &c'.[28] Physically, these images could also be repurposed, particularly when cut up and pasted or bound in new configurations and contexts, and could generate multiple registers of response even in the same individual. As objects they also enjoined close attention, a type of informed, concentrated viewing tantamount to reading, especially prevalent in the mixed medium of caricature, embellished by text and crammed with allusion. For a ballad-singer to be fixed before such a gaze was to reinforce for the viewer the power relations implicit in the social and financial hierarchy, and offered a reassurance, an omniscience, that was often quite absent from the face-to-face, mouth-to-ear encounter risked daily on the street. This gaze could only triumph at the expense of the aural: besides effecting the disappearance of the troubling crowd, these images enforced a more eloquent absence. For these represented ballad-singers, famed for their 'loud discordant lungs', are effectively rendered dumb.[29]

### The Denial of Articulacy

The scholarly consensus is that, in reality, 'the ballad was coupled with the balladeer, a thing of rags and tatters'.[30] Yet though authorities could not take the ballad-singer out of the ballad, artists could do the opposite, by depicting inarticulate singers. This is not to say that images of singers read as *silent*. Perhaps the most famous historical source in sound studies is William Hogarth's 'The Enraged Musician' of 1741, described by Shesgreen as 'the noisiest picture in English art', and by Hogarth's contemporary, the novelist Henry Fielding, as 'enough to make a man deaf to look at'.[31] Hogarth's ballad-singer in the left foreground bawls, mouth agape (see Figure 1.3). Uniquely and rather ambiguously, the song in her hand, 'The Ladies' Fall' (for more on which, see later), is drawn so as to contain musical notation, perhaps to draw better attention to the association of the tune's title. Yet even with this explicit reference to music, the composition places her below – and in contrast to – the titular figure, who stands for literate, learned, aestheticised music. Even though the image is usually read as a xenophobic attack on the Italian violinist, or

---

[28] Clayton, *The English Print*, 216.     [29] George Saville Carey, *The Balnea* (1799), vii.
[30] Andrew C. Rouse, *The Remunerated Vernacular Singer* (Frankfurt am Main, 2005), 12. See also Georgina Born, 'Listening, Mediation, Event: Anthropological and Sociological Perspectives', *Journal of the Royal Musical Association* 135, no. 1 (2010): 88; and Hitchcock, *Down and Out*, 65.
[31] Shesgreen, *Images*, 113.

Figure 1.3  William Hogarth, 'The Enraged Musician', 1741.
Engraving. Yale Center for British Art, Paul Mellon Collection

castrato, it is he who is acknowledged as the musician, and the ballad-
singer who is placed among so many other discordant noises, part of
a cacophony, not a choir.

Satires such as Hogarth's were far noisier than illustrations or paintings of
a subject of the type characterised earlier as 'fancy pictures'. Images in which
ballad-singers are 'audible' are almost exclusively satirical in genre, and in
only a single instance are they depicted in a way suggestive of sympathy on
the part of the artist.[32] Nor do these represented singers impose their own
choice of song upon the defenceless ears of society. Rather, they are pressed
into service to make the satirist's point. If wordless, then they invariably

---

[32] Twenty-four in total (6, 9–11, 16, 27, 29–30, 32, 34, 36, 39–40, 42–43, 50, 56–58, 61–63,
66–67). The four exceptions to the satirical rule (14–15, 37–38) are all by Rowlandson
and are at least semi-comical or with satirical undertones. The only 'positive' image is the
private study by Scharf mentioned earlier (67).

stand as symbols of noise, chaos, vice: they are not allowed to make music, but only to bawl in dumb, because unvoiced, symbolism. Without depicted lyrics or a legible title on the sheet they hold, they are denied articulacy. The literary parallel here is Wordsworth's 'single and alone, / An English ballad-singer', whose wares 'dangle from dead walls' in a description read variously as a condemnation of metropolitan mass culture or a poignant symbol of precisely a 'lack of narrative, even the lack of narration'.[33] If by contrast singers are made articulate by means of a speech bubble or a legible ballad sheet, it is to furnish the scene with a comment put in their mouths by the artist. Thus in Isaac Cruikshank's caricature 'The freemen triumphant, or the mare foal'd of her folly' (16), he pillories the Mayor of Rochester, indicted on a charge of embezzlement, in part by depicting, at right, a ballad-singer singing 'Downfall of the Ma[yo]r and Mules' – symbolising public opprobrium – and holding a ballad entitled 'At Maidstone Assizes' by way of an explanatory footnote. Here the audible singer, far from constituting a threat to the viewer, represents righteous public opinion as envisaged by the satirist, showing how far the target of their words has fallen that they can be shamed by so low a figure: the singer becomes an eloquent, because bathetic, mouthpiece. The same is true of prose accounts. In Charles Johnstone's famous novel *Chrysal: or, the Adventures of a Guinea*; in tales by Harriet Martineau and Allan Cunningham; and in a piece by the young Charles Dickens, ballad-singers admonish corrupt priests, tyrannical enclo-sers, and callous pedestrians.[34] Though the authors all accord a degree of moral authority to the singer, in ventriloquising those singers they arrogate that authority to their own writings, just as in caricature it is not really a balladeer singing, but an artist annotating an image. In these cases, the singer comes off relatively well – but only because they have lost their most troubling characteristic, their individual agency.

The question of articulacy transcends semantic meaning, extending beyond the rendering of lyrics to the subtler question of whether these representations can be interpreted by more sympathetic viewers as *musical*, rather than mere makers of noise. It is debatable whether a depicted ballad-singer could ever actually be made to look as if she were *singing* before the twentieth-century innovation of decorating speech bubbles with symbolic

[33] William Wordsworth, *The Prelude* (New York, 1850), 178–9; Tim Fulford, 'Fallen Ladies and Cruel Mothers: Ballad Singers and Ballad Heroines in the Eighteenth Century', *The Eighteenth Century: Theory and Interpretation* 47, nos. 2–3 (2006): 309–30, 320; Makdisi, *Making England Western*, 65.
[34] Charles Johnstone, *Chrysal*, 3 vols. (*c.*1797), vol. 2, 7–12; Harriet Martineau, *Illustrations of Political Economy: No. III, Brooke and Brooke Farm, a Tale* (3rd edn, 1833), 22–8; Allan Cunningham, *London Magazine* 4, no. 22 (1821): 405–6; Charles Dickens, 'Scenes: The Streets – Night' (1836, repr. in Michael Slater (ed.), *Dickens' Journalism* (1996), 58–9).

musical notation. It is easy to write 'they sang'; far harder to draw it.[35] Without any instrument save their voice to indicate musicality, depicted ballad-singers are either silent, or appear to emit, not music, but merely sound. This is partly due to gestural convention. The stock pose of the represented singer was to stand flat-footed, hands clasped across the stomach, holding the physical ballad from which they read – a gesture singularly unindicative of *music*. While anecdotal evidence states that some singers accompanied their songs with dance and gesture, there is none of this in the extant images.[36] Instead the singer's pose, however conducive in practice to both reading and vocal projection, is figured as rhetorically passive rather than declamatory. There is nothing, no gestural grace, no enraptured expression, to elevate their depicted performance from utterance to musical art, so that, if viewers wished to see these figures as musical, they had to contradict the evidence within the image. The only variable was the mouth: open or closed.

An open mouth, unlike a manufactured instrument, has no inherently musical connotations. While at other times – for example, the Netherlands of the seventeenth century – the open mouth might conventionally indicate an unfettered jollity associated with artists and musicians, to the contemporary London market for these images it was far likelier to suggest imbecility and impoliteness.[37] As Richard Leppert has long since brought to our attention, 'The body is a sight and a sound': in an age before recording, music was an embodied practice represented visually and corporeally.[38] In Nicholas Cook's words, 'musicians represent music'. Context was key, framing the expectations that caused listeners to interpret sound as music or not: for 'nothing can be music if it is not heard as music'.[39] It seems reasonable, then, to posit that, for many artists and the majority of their genteel and bourgeois viewers, the possibility of reading these depictions as musical was occluded by the visual taint of the ballad-singer's stock rags, bare feet, inanimate posture – and above all their black hole of a mouth.[40]

---

[35] It is worth noting that perhaps the most famous balladeer in nineteenth-century literature, Dickens' Silas Wegg in *Our Mutual Friend*, never actually sings either. See Caroline M. Jackson-Houlston, *Ballads, Songs and Snatches: The Appropriation of Folk Song and Popular Culture in British Nineteenth-Century Realist Prose* (Aldershot, 1999), 113–17; and Goldie Morgentaler, 'Dickens and the Scattered Identity of Silas Wegg', *Dickens Quarterly* 22, no. 2 (2005): 92–100.

[36] For example, Anon., 'London Ballad Singers', *The Mirror of Literature* 6, no. 150 (July 1825): 42.

[37] On the cultural connotations of the open mouth, see Jones, *The Smile Revolution*, 10, 29–31. For the Dutch case, see James Welu and Pieter Biesboer (eds.), *Judith Leyster: A Dutch Master and Her World* (Yale, 1993), 162–3.

[38] Richard Leppert, *The Sight of Sound* (Berkeley and Los Angeles, 1993), xix–xx.

[39] Nicholas Cook, *Music, Imagination, and Culture* (Oxford, 2002), 4, 12.

[40] The archetypal image here is *62*, a Cruikshank illustration of Jack Cartar, mocking his pretensions to legitimate singing, the visual cues reinforced by a 'flash' or slang verse

How, then, might a more sentimental artist, wishing to provoke a sympathetic response in their viewer, depict a recognisably musical ballad-*singer*, without resorting to the opprobrious convention of the open mouth? The universal solution seems to have been to relocate the musical signifier from the image to its paratexts, relying on an accompanying title or lines of verse to indicate the singing, and to represent their subject with a mouth either fully closed or, at the very most, pursed a little, as if whistling – and therefore to continue to deny that subject an articulate voice. Generally these images are sentimentalised prints – etchings, mezzotints, or stipple – compromising between artistic sophistication (many were based on oil paintings that were increasingly composed with a print afterlife in mind)[41] and affordability for a middling market.[42] They were the visual counterparts of sentimental poetic effusions produced for a middling readership, such as Eaglesfield Smith's maudlin 'On seeing a surly watchman drive a little beggar-child from the streets, for singing ballads',[43] or Felicia Hemans' more highly aestheticised 'To a Wandering Female Singer' of 1829, which seeks to sympathise (though stopping short of empathy) with its wretched but mellifluous subject:

> By its fond and plaintive lingering,
> On each word of grief so long,
> Oh! thou hast loved and suffer'd much –
> I know it by thy song![44]

Substantial overlap may be observed with images of London Cries in the same period, responses to a tradition established in the seventeenth century by Marcellus Laroon. Mark Bills, discussing Wheatley's series of Cries (of which 'A New Love Song', Figure 1.4, is of a ballad-singer), emphasises such images' relatively high aesthetic status: 'Wheatley elicited praise from connoisseurs who saw his "fragrant pictures" as charming, and praised their idealisation "where there is no suggestion of crowd or noise, no woman or girl who is not comely"'. Bills concludes rather tellingly that: 'never a raucous note is heard'.[45]

From the works of Amigoni in the earlier eighteenth century to the photography of Lewis Carroll and Julia Margaret Cameron, this tasteful

purporting to be Cartar's own, in which he compares himself bathetically to John Braham, the foremost tenor of the age.
[41] Clayton, *The English Print*, 220.
[42] For more on the particular concerns of this emerging 'middling' market, see Maidment, *Dusty Bob*, 214.
[43] *European Magazine* 64 (1813): 147.
[44] Reproduced in Daniel Karlin, *The Figure of the Singer* (Oxford, 2013), 48.
[45] Mark Bills, 'The "Cries" of London by Paul Sandby and Thomas Rowlandson', *Print Quarterly* 20, no. 1 (2003): 41.

Figure 1.4 Anthony Cardon after Francis Wheatley, 'A New Love Song', 1796.
Stipple. Yale Center for British Art, Paul Mellon Collection

representation of distasteful subjects persisted throughout the period. Key elements included delicacy of technique – Landseer apparently tried to stigmatise stipple, a common technique in these images, as 'effeminate' – attention to detail of attire and deportment, and an appeal to a pastoral idyll, embodied by the humble, carefree singer brightening the dull city streets.[46] In this pictorial discourse, even a singer's rags, 'with their uneven edges and rough texture', could stand in for the rural picturesque.[47] As such, these images appealed to an aspirant urban market, keen to celebrate aspects of their native city's streets in an idealised and tasteful form, or even to indulge in a little Romantic licence, imagining themselves vicariously into pastoral poses of freedom and adventure, in a harmless fantasy of liberation that would evolve later in the century into a mania for 'tramping',

[46] Shesgreen, *Images*, 89, 132–3. See also Marshall, *City of Gold*, 146.
[47] Marshall, *City of Gold*, 161.

and had its exponents even in the Hanoverian period, in the likes of Thomas Bewick and Charles Cochrane.[48]

Shesgreen highlights primary exponents of the sentimental taste around 1800 in Joshua Reynolds and John Rising, both of whom also produced notable images of ballad-singers (*8; 19, 41*).[49] Dozens of similar depictions exist, all offering consumers an idealised alternative to the troubling reality of the streets. The singers are pretty or at worst hand-some, but above all, they are modest. Their eyes are usually downcast – though doe-eyed child singers are permitted to answer the viewer's gaze with a charmingly pitiable countenance – and they never inflict sound upon the viewer.[50] They may hold ballads. They may be depicted before an audience. Yet they do not *sing*, as their mouths are invariably closed. Nowhere is this more apparent than in the representation of children. Subject paintings prettified and stylised them in a manner inescapably suggestive of the noble savage; diamonds in the rough; antecedents of the Oliver Twist model of virtuous Victorian urchins (*4–5, 19, 21–22, 33, 41, 59–60*). These rosy-cheeked ragamuffins were designed to appease and affect a sentimental middling market, happy to indulge in feelings of becoming, even salutary pity, from the comfort of their drawing rooms. This limited form of pity was critiqued at the time by Edmund Burke, who contrasted it unfavourably with 'sublime sympathy'. Burke was especially censorious of occasions such as this, in which 'the beholder is pleased by the representation rather than the reality of suffering'.[51] At the very most, images of suffering nobly borne might feed into the agenda of charitable reformers, who would subscribe to precisely the sort of societies – such as the Mendicity Society – that were committed to the removal of all persons such as ballad-singers from the public streets.[52] Potentially, then, these images were every bit as controlling and demeaning as the hostile carica-tures in which words were put into (or taken out of) singers' mouths. By this reading, the ribbons and bows with which Rising decorates his

---

[48] As Maidment writes of images of dustmen, these could be 'shot through with a sense of potentially more liberating otherness represented by the freedom dustmen had to be diverted, to lounge and observe, and to work when they pleased' – Maidment, *Dusty Bob*, 217. On tramping, see especially the various works of Luke Seaber, and for the earlier examples, see Thomas Bewick, *A Memoir of Thomas Bewick* (Newcastle, 1862), and [Charles Cochrane], *Journal of a Tour made by … J. de V., the Spanish Minstrel of 1828–9, through Great Britain and Ireland, a character assumed by an English gentleman* (1847).

[49] Shesgreen, *Images*, 89.

[50] As Marshall notes, represented grown men never presume to hold the viewer's gaze: only subordinate, aestheticised figures are allowed such licence. See *City of Gold*, 161.

[51] As paraphrased by Jonathan Lamb in his *The Evolution of Sympathy in the Long Eighteenth Century* (2009), 42.

[52] Clayton, *The English Print*, 248–50.

Figure 1.5 John Jones after John Rising, 'The Young Ballad Singers',
*c*.1790–8.
Mezzotint. © The Trustees of the British Museum

'Young Ballad Singers' (Figure 1.5) are as constrictive as manacles.
Daniel Karlin's criticism of the Hemans poem mentioned earlier – that
she 'exploits her subject; the sympathy she offers in her title, and in the
poem's intimate form of address, turns inward' – applies equally to these
depictions.[53] Romanticised, pitied, sterilised: these are singers subjected
to a gaze that denies both their agency and their articulacy.

## Colonising the London Street

If a closed mouth was prerequisite for an idealised depiction of the singer,
then the reverse – the open maw – could suggest far more than mere noise.

---

[53] Karlin, *The Figure*, 49.

There were multiple forms of 'savagery' invoked by this form of representation.[54] In the twenty-first century, a street figure with an open mouth might prompt associations of want, of hunger: of the mouth to be fed.[55] To contemporaries, by whose conventions of charity and sympathy the deserving supplicant should never be so vulgar as to impose their neediness directly upon the benefactor, this was already distasteful enough, that open mouth transgressing the boundary between want and wantonness.[56] Consequently, no artist seeking to evoke a sympathetic reaction in the viewer would indicate pitiable distress in this manner – especially in the earlier part of the period, in the context of the French Revolution. As Britain endured several successive failed harvests, the gaping mouth desirous of bread took on a political charge, with hunger interpreted by alarmed loyalists as synonymous with the threat of violence, even of cannibalism of the body politic. This fear was most memorably captured in James Gillray's caricature 'Un Petit Souper a la Parisiènne'.[57] When it came to ballad-singers this fear was heightened, partly due to the content of their songs – discussed in more detail later in this chapter – and partly because of the fact that, of all London's low-life, they were the element that was, in reality, the most audibly articulate.

Charles Williams played upon this tension in his provocative caricature of 1805, 'The Enraged Politicians or Political Ballad Singers', reproduced as Figure 1.6. The five singers' powerful physiques, wild hair, and bestial expressions are a potent vision of an underclass that, even as it aimed to provoke laughter, might unsettle the viewer as much as it does the vexed members of government who fume at their balconies in a deliberate echo, reinforced by the print's title, of Hogarth's 'Enraged Musician' (Figure 1.3). We are reminded of Brenda Assael's question, posed in relation to the Street Music Act of 1864: 'who owned the streets?'[58] Williams seems to be suggesting it is the mob – a mob made articulate by the speech bubbles

[54] '"Savages" are precisely what a reasonably sophisticated middle-class Englishman (or woman) would expect to see when surveying the lower orders of his (or her) country in the years around 1800, and in fact quite further [sic] into the nineteenth century as well.' Makdisi, *Making England Western*, 20.

[55] My thanks to Georgina Locke for raising this point in discussion at a 2017 conference.

[56] See Chapter 3 for a wider discussion of the 'socioemotional economy' of charity – a term derived from Candace Clarke, *Misery and Company: Sympathy in Everyday Life* (Chicago, 1997), 14.

[57] Published in 1792: see, for example, British Museum no. 1851,0901.620. While ragged clothing was similarly provocative around 1800, by the Victorian period this became the default mode of summoning a sympathy that often bordered on the erotic, a phenomenon discussed extensively in, among other works, Marshall, *City of Gold*; and Seth Koven, *Slumming: Sexual and Social Politics in Victorian London* (Princeton, 2006).

[58] Brenda Assael, 'Music in the Air: Noise, Performers and the Contest over the Streets of the Mid-Nineteenth-Century Metropolis', in Tim Hitchcock and Heather Shore (eds.), *The Streets of London: From the Great Fire to the Great Stink* (2003), 191.

Figure 1.6 Charles Williams, 'The Enraged Politicians or Political Ballad Singers', 1805.
Etching (hand-coloured). © The Trustees of the British Museum

that quote lines of political song, demonstrating the singers' knowing engagement with the political nation, and made dangerous by their open, toothy mouths. The two singers on the right appear most threatening, their bulk and bulging arms contrasting with the extreme slightness of the belea-guered premier, William Pitt the Younger. The male singer's lines, taken from a ballad, 'Tyburn Tree', sung by Macheath in *The Beggar's Opera* and set to the tune of 'Greensleeves', are especially disquieting in this context:

> For if rich rogues like us were to swing
> 'T'would soon thin the land such a Number to string
> Upon Tyburn Tree!

Scarcely a decade after the Parisian Terror, and within living memory of the 1780 Gordon Riots, this was strong stuff on Williams' part, wherein the 'savage' in the street threatens to usurp the state's function of judicial and political violence.[59] While it may have amused opposition supporters among his viewers, it surely disquieted others. The provocation is only

[59] See Chapter 2 for a deeper exploration of the singer's relationship with capital punishment.

defused within the image by the jovial, chuckling faces of respectable yeomen and citizens in the background – they, the viewer's stand-in, are visibly at ease with the humour – and by Williams' metatextual allusions: a song from *The Beggar's Opera* was unlikely to be taken at face value, it was too bound up with a familiar and satirical theatrical tradition, while the eliding of the enraged Pitt (and, at left, Melville) with Hogarth's original Italian virtuoso deflected the joke away from the middling viewer: *politicians*, it is saying, *are not like us, they are foreigners*. It helps, of course, that the word 'politician' was largely used pejoratively at the time.[60]

Williams' ballad-singers in this image are exceptional, a rare case in which the established order teeters on the edge of the open-mouthed abyss. On the street, as the subsequent chapters make clear, this must have been reflected in the experiences of concerned auditors of a high social status, exposed daily to the sound and sight of the uncouth singer. Yet in most representations that troubling articulacy could be denied, and the open mouth degraded from an instrument of democratic music to a source of sound *devoid* of fury, signifying nothing and therefore perturbing no one. Drawing on Raymond Williams, Shesgreen has observed that many representations of street-dwellers manage to tame their subjects, almost paradoxically, by making them *less* civilised, figuring them as 'either a harmless domestic savage from rural England or a childlike native from the colonies'.[61] Two caricatures, published soon after 'The Enraged Politicians', also perform this sort of safe savage-making, distorting the physiognomy of open-mouthed singers to the point of undermining their humanity. Gillray's 'Triumphal Procession of Little-Paul-The Taylor upon his new-Goose' (*34*) is typical in its composition, placing the two female singers on the periphery. With half their bodies cut off by the page edge, they become quite literally marginal figures – a fit treatment for persons whose performances were inherently liminal.[62] In profile their faces, dominated by distended mouths, become non-human, instead mirroring the goose at the image's centre. Similarly, Samuel De Wilde's 'Triumphal procession of the hog in armour' depicts a porcine boy singer (*40*). De Wilde is referencing Gillray's earlier image here, as made explicit by the similar title, though his bestial singer is fully in the frame. In both cases, of all the people depicted in the crowds, only the ballad-singers echo the animal appearance of the image's titular subject, be it goose or hog.

---

[60] Mark Philp is currently conducting research into the changing connotations of this term in the decades after 1789.
[61] Shesgreen, *Images*, 174.
[62] For a full discussion of the negotiation of liminality and space in singers' performances, see Bywater, 'Performing Spaces', esp. 97–8, 103–8.

Figure 1.7 Johann H. Ramberg, 'The Humours of St. Giles's', 1788.
Etching. Library of Congress PC 3 – 1788

This tradition of the therianthropic singer was well established by the
1800s. In an anonymous caricature of 1783 (6), two ballad-singers are
given asses' heads: one of them brays her song aloud. The impact is lessened,
however, by the similar transformation of other figures in the scene. More
powerful, though incidental, is Ramberg's 'The Humours of St. Giles's'
(Figure 1.7). At left are two child singers. One, a tiny boy, scratches his
rump in a crouching posture, as it is simultaneously sniffed by a curious
dog. The effect is to suggest the boy's own status as a yapping cur, allowing
the dog to treat him as one of its own kind. The composition reinforces this:
a strong diagonal line sweeps downwards from the pipe-smoking publican at
the centre, via a prostitute, lecher, and a literally fallen woman whose foot
stretches out to the urchin singers and the dog. Ramberg constructs
a narrative of moral causation in this line for the attentive viewer to appreciate – from liquor to sex, to unwanted children, to a bestial state – but also
stages a clear hierarchy that effectively elides the child singer with the
animal.[63] Less subtle was Robert Seymour's 1833 lithograph, 'Ballad

---

[63] Curiously, the causal line runs not only downwards, but right to left, contrary to conventions of narrative painting (perhaps simply an oversight in the printing process, which of
course creates a mirror image).

Singers. Any thing for an honest living' (*61*), which depicts a ballad-singing couple (he fiddles, she sings) with five children – or rather, kittens, as all seven figures are anthropomorphised cats. They are simultaneously therianthropised ballad-singers, wherein lies the image's humour: far from being respectable musicians, ballad-singers caterwaul. The joke is a knowing wink from artist to viewer – *isn't it awful how badly these street-people sing?* – that flatters the viewer by letting them in on the joke, implicitly reinforcing their own sense of possessing good taste. This denial of musical status to singers is simply the bluntest realisation of a trope of at least fifty years' standing, figuring balladeers as amusingly unhuman.

Unhuman is not the same as *sub*human, and the artist's capacity to suggest the latter was in many ways the more insidious element in this mode of exoticising or Othering a would-be articulate underclass. In a second caricature that places words in a singer's open mouth in order to pillory a politician, Williams retreats from the foregrounded threat of 'The Enraged Politicians' to the subtler, perhaps unintentionally crueller representation of 'The Close of the Poll', in which a female singer who mocks a despondent Richard Brinsley Sheridan – who grumbles 'Curse those ballad singers what a noise they make' – is given the punning line 'The same is a New song entitled and called – Sherry done over' (Figure 1.8). This ballad-singer is of course a mere mouthpiece for Williams, joking at Sheridan's expense, and this subordination is made uncomfortably clear by her appearance: tilting her head back so that her eyes are lost in her hair, Williams reduces her face to two nostrils and an enormous open mouth, red and round, with the black dot of her gullet at its centre. The fact that she is hemmed in by a grinning, respectable, male audience, presumably of propertied electors, and whose features are more conventionally rendered, only underlines her subordinate status. She is reduced to an orifice, no more, denied the facial features that would signify intelligence. The contemporary viewer is denied the impression that this woman truly understands, let alone had penned, the words she vocalises. This vein of imagery invites a reading of the ballad-singer as subhuman: an unsavoury yet passive, necessary Other.[64]

In an age of global imperial expansion, the streets of London were frequently depicted and discussed as themselves an outpost of empire, home to a lesser species in need of patriarchal civilising: a species typified by the ballad-singer. Interestingly the physical deformities given to singers, centred on the mouth, did not map on to the contemporary

---

[64] The function of the Other, as both Makdisi and Marshall have observed in this instance, is by its inversion to be constitutive of what it is not: respectable bourgeois whiteness. Makdisi, *Making England Western*, 10; Marshall, *City of Gold*, 117–18.

Figure 1.8 Charles Williams, 'The Close of the Poll' (detail), 1807. Etching (hand-coloured). © The Trustees of the British Museum

visual tropes used to portray racial difference. One illustration of the black singer and fiddler Billy Waters (53) shares much with the central male singer in Figure 1.6: a rictus grin, prominent teeth, and staring eyes. Yet the casual racial stereotyping in John Thomas Smith's etching of the black ballad-singer Joseph Johnson (46) bears no resemblance to other views of singers. Smith gives Johnson exaggeratedly rounded features, with huge lips and eyes, but his mouth is closed in a smile, and Smith's image and accompanying text suggest warm though condescending sympathy.

Of the two men, Johnson is of greater interest as a ballad-singer: here was a man who knew a bit about representation.[65] Waters by contrast is something of a red herring. Thanks primarily to his inclusion in Pierce Egan's *Life in London*, he attracted a unique degree of attention, featuring in the

[65] See Interlude III, 'The Storm'.

aforementioned book[66] and stage adaptations thereof,[67] at least five prints,[68] and three articles,[69] becoming the subject of a poem,[70] a ballad,[71] a hugely fanciful biography,[72] three portraits,[73] and a series of ceramic figurines from Derby and Staffordshire derived from the painting by Thomas Lord Busby.[74] In many of these representations, race and exoticisation is a central feature. Yet although Waters is known to have sung (specifically, 'Polly will you marry me?', of which only one verse is extant), he was more a busker than a seller – a distinction insisted upon by contemporary writers[75] – and more a celebrity than either. These were representations, not of a generic ballad-singer, but of the dancing fiddler, the 'African prince', the 'King of the Beggars': in short, legend-making at its most blatant (as Mary Shannon has recently and expertly discussed), entirely removing Waters, as an exceptional curiosity, from the wider category of ballad-singers.[76] In returning to this broader group for signs of racialised images, we find one white singer drawn with a black infant on her back (*39*), yet once again the dehumanisation lies in the slackness of her distended mouth. We might conclude that the ballad-singer as a type was not associated with a racial Other, but rather treated in some representations as an under*class*, figuratively rather than literally comparable to an aboriginal population.

Shesgreen perceives the same phenomenon in the 'proto-anthropological' anecdotes of John Thomas Smith and the proto-ethnography of Mayhew.[77] He quotes Smith himself: '"Few persons", he assures us, "particularly those in elevated life, can witness or even

[66] Pierce Egan, *Life in London, or, the Day and Night Scenes of Jerry Hawthorn, Esq.* (1821).
[67] For example, William Thomas Moncrieff, *Tom and Jerry; or, Life in London: An Operatic Extravaganza, in Three Acts* (2nd edn, 1828).
[68] British Museum Images, nos. 1859,0316.148; 1859,0316.142; 1864,0611.408; 1935,0522.7.214; 1886,0513.1856–1860.
[69] Busby, *Costume*, 1; Douglas Jerrold, 'The Ballad Singer', in *Heads of the People: Being Portraits of the English*, 2 vols. (1840), vol. 2, 297; Charles Hindley, *The True History of Tom and Jerry* (1888), 102–8.
[70] William Reeves, 'Lines on Billy Waters' (1823), in Hindley, *Tom and Jerry*, 108.
[71] 'The Merry Will & Testament of Master Black Billy' (1823), in James Hepburn, *A Book of Scattered Leaves: Poetry of Poverty in Broadside Ballads of Nineteenth-Century England*, 2 vols. (Cranbury, 2000–1), vol. 2, 308–9.
[72] Also by Moncrieff; in Hindley, *Tom and Jerry*, 103–7.
[73] An oil painting attributed to David Wilkie, *c.*1815, Royal Museums Greenwich, no. ZBA2427; Busby's portrait (*53*); and an anonymous lithograph *c.*1830, British Museum Images, no. 2006,0929.46.
[74] For example, Victoria & Albert Museum, nos. C.38–2002 (Staffordshire, 1828–30) and C.317–1916 (Derby, 1862).
[75] 'Rag', *Streetology*, 83.
[76] Mary L. Shannon, 'The Multiple Lives of Billy Waters: Dangerous Theatricality and Networked Illustrations in Nineteenth-Century Popular Culture', *Nineteenth Century Theatre and Film* 46 (2019): 161–89.
[77] See Makdisi, *Making England Western*, 8, for Mayhew's own conception of this division.

entertain a true idea of the various modes by which the lowest classes gain a livelihood.'"[78] Mayhew, the archetypal re-presenter of nineteenth-century social investigation, has been interpreted similarly. His work was originally read, in journal form, by artisans as much as by the middling classes. Much like Francis Place his initial goal, informed by Chartist connections, was social reform.[79] Yet the resulting volumes are essentially 'a form of travel narrative'; a pseudo-scientific series of encounters, worked up into coherent narratives for an avid readership. Rather than aiming for realism, Mayhew 'adopted Platonist theories of representation: his ambition was to convey the *idea* of a character or a place ... to work the "ghost raising" to the level of an aesthetic experience.'[80] Put bluntly, this meant that he passed off his own literary reworkings as the authentic voice of the street, drawing on the techniques he had learnt from his early years in London's theatrical circles. Shannon has drawn attention to the inherent 'theatricality' of the first-person narratives Mayhew presents, and the speed and frequency with which they were, like Egan's *Life in London*, adapted for the stage in the 1850s.[81]

Mayhew's accounts are perhaps the single greatest challenge and temptation to scholars of the Victorian metropolis, holding out the prospect of unrivalled insight into the lives of street-dwellers. In this book I will return to Mayhew time and again, unable to resist the richness of his narratives. Yet I hope to reach for them with due circumspection. Admittedly, twenty-first-century ethnographers have sought to reclaim him as the detached, impartial founder of their discipline; others have praised the sober discretion with which he preserved his informants' anonymity.[82] Yet as Bernard Taithe observes and Steedman has demonstrated, 'Mayhew also wrote that his interviews and his descriptions were a mere *reflection* of the real.'[83] Tellingly, those recurrent themes of the control and containment of a potentially bestial mass are everywhere in evidence

---

[78] Shesgreen, *Images*, 165–6; 167.
[79] Sally Hayward, '"Those Who Cannot Work"', *Prose Studies: History, Theory, Criticism* 27, nos. 1–2 (2005): 53–71, 57; Bernard Taithe, *The Essential Mayhew: Representing and Communicating the Poor* (1996), 4, 17, 19; Anne Humpherys, *Travels into the Poor Man's Country: The Work of Henry Mayhew* (Athens, Georgia, 1977), 31–3. For Place, see Chapter 2.
[80] Taithe, *The Essential Mayhew*, 16.
[81] Mary L. Shannon, *Dickens, Reynolds, and Mayhew on Wellington Street* (Farnham, 2015), 155.
[82] Bryan S. Green, 'Learning from Henry Mayhew: The Role of the Impartial Spectator in Mayhew's London Labour and the London Poor', *Journal of Contemporary Ethnography* 31, no. 2 (2002): 99–134, 103–5, 125–6; Humpherys, *Travels*, 92.
[83] Taithe, *The Essential Mayhew*, 16; Carolyn Steedman, 'Mayhew: On Reading, About Writing', *Journal of Victorian Culture* 19 (2014): 550–61. Added emphasis.

in Mayhew's writings.[84] Derisive authorial asides undercut his informants, mitigating the disruptive potential of 'the tolerable and the intoler-
able performers'; of 'those who do not cry, but (if one may so far stretch
the English language) *sing* the contents of the "papers" they vend.'[85] His
unsubstantiated statistics, which give us 'above 250 who live by ballad-
singing alone', and his mania for categorisation – 'the long-song-sellers;
the wall-song-sellers (or "pinners-up," as they are technically termed);
the ballad sellers; the vendors of playbills' – purport, like the rash of 'flash'
street-language dictionaries that appeared earlier in the century, to docu-
ment the minutiae of street life.[86] Yet in truth they impose a spurious
sense of order; they are the wholly unsubstantiated metadata that frame
the individual accounts, the whole serving to render explicable, account-
able, and therefore containable, that which was alien and amorphous:
a social Other in the heart of the capital.

### Sex and the Singer

By claiming to reproduce the exact words of his anonymous interviewees – but in all likelihood amalgamating and editing various testimonies –
Mayhew was echoing the work of those caricaturists who had placed
words into the open mouths of depicted ballad-singers. It was ultimately
this open mouth, and what might otherwise come out of it, that appears to
have most exercised reformers, improvers, observers, and reactionaries –
to the point that, in imagery, it often appears to have been transformed (in
both men and women) from a speaking organ to a sexualised orifice. It
was not merely female singers' bodies that were represented sexually, but
their entire function. Deborah Epstein Nord has made a perfectly reasonable link between the 'implied sexual taint of the [Victorian] street singer'
and female prostitution – an unavoidable parallel when singers were
selling wares in the street by means of embodied performance.[87] But
the provocation of these performances concerned more than the female
body: it related directly to the act of ballad singing itself. Once again, the
explanation begins in Hogarth.

'The Enraged Musician' of 1741 (Figure 1.3) is a touchstone of sound
studies for a reason, offering academics unending scope for interpretation. Yet it also remained a touchstone for both artists and the viewing
public in our period – hence the reference in Williams' 'The Enraged

---

[84] Hayward, 'Those Who Cannot Work', 61; Humpherys, *Travels*, 73.
[85] Mayhew, *London Labour*, vol. 3, 158; vol. 1, 15, original emphasis.
[86] Ibid., vol. 3, 190; vol. 1, 3.
[87] Deborah Epstein Nord, *Walking the Victorian Streets: Women, Representation, and the City*
(New York, 1995), 74–5.

Politicians' (Figure 1.6) – referenced not only in histories of Hogarth, but in theatrical culture: most notably in the 1789 afterpiece 'The Enraged Musician' by George Colman and Samuel Arnold, staged at the Haymarket, and in a burletta of the same title performed at Astley's Amphitheatre the following year.[88] Periodic bouts of 'Hogarthomania' recurred in subsequent generations, prompting imitations as much as interest in the originals.[89] As such, Hogarth's image – the most iconic, but also typical, of the numerous female ballad-singers he depicted – remained highly influential in our period. Shesgreen's interpretation is that Hogarth 'contends that the commerce of ballad singers is sex', even while describing the depicted singer as a 'ballad hag'.[90] There is a contradiction here, caused by Shesgreen's use of the present tense. In fact Hogarth gives us, in his ballad-singer, a potted narrative – a series of clues that effectively reimagines his own 1731 series *The Harlot's Progress* in a single figure. The singer holds both her infant and, to clarify further, a sheet entitled 'The Ladies' Fall' (a famous seventeenth-century song).[91] Her breasts are bare, but presumably not in order to titillate the eighteenth-century male viewer: rather, they are an attempt to render squalid the fact that she has a baby to feed. The logical inference is that the commerce of this ballad-singer *was* sex but that *now* it is singing: the consequences of her fallen state have rendered that occupation untenable, necessitating this turn to balladry. While sex and sin are a crucial part of her history, she represents not their presence but their consequence, and may be interpreted as a cynical warning to the ostensibly pure milkmaid at the image's centre. As such, this singer-as-mother is just one of a great number of representations that feature, according to the dominant visual codes of the time that influenced the male gaze, a sex*less* female. Stout, saddled with inconvenient children, and dressed in a mass of shapeless rags and shawls, these were not images designed to provoke eroticised thoughts in contemporary male viewers.[92]

In fact, there are remarkably few overtly sexualised depictions of female singers. Daniel Maclise's 'The Ballad Singer' of 1846 (Figure 1.9) could be classed as such, given the singer's idealised physiognomy, the fact that she caresses the slip in her hands in a manner that draws attention to her fingers

---

[88] John Ireland, *Hogarth Illustrated*, 3 vols. (1793), vol. 1, xxxvii–viii. I have written a chapter on the former production, 'Of Sight and Sound: Realising *The Enraged Musician*', that will appear in a volume currently in preparation by James Grande and Carmel Raz; for the latter, see John Greene, *Theatre in Dublin, 1745–1820: A Calendar of Performances* (Lehigh, 2011), 2585, and a note in the *Annual Review* 6 (1807): 606.

[89] Clayton, *The English Print*, 232–3.     [90] Shesgreen, *Images*, 127.

[91] I hesitate to call it a ballad since the sheet appears, as I have discussed earlier, to include musical notation.

[92] See Chapter 3 for further discussion of female singers accompanied by infants.

Figure 1.9  James Stephenson after Daniel Maclise, 'The Ballad Singer',
1846.
Etching and engraving. © The Trustees of the British Museum

and bare forearms, and the allegorical detail that she carries a basket of ripe
fruit. Her infant, coupled with the title of the slip she holds ('Sailor's Wife'),
the pastoral background, and the light on her open face – expressive of purity
in the conventions of contemporary devotional imagery – might all serve to
counteract this impression. Then again, as Tim Clayton notes of the genre,
'Innocence and eroticism were an appealing combination.'[93] In an earlier,
more permissive context, George and Isaac Cruikshank are more frank in
a famous illustration to Egan's *Life in London* (55) featuring a ballad-singer at
its centre. They give their otherwise 'stock' female singer additional bawdy
attributes: a mug of beer, a knowing stare into the eyes of Corinthian Tom,
and bared breasts, without the excuse of a dependent infant. Beyond this
atypical illustration, I have found only two depictions, both (unsurprisingly)
by Rowlandson, that are arguably intended to be read as sexualised. 'The

[93] Clayton, *The English Print*, 253.

Figure 1.10 Thomas Rowlandson, 'The Ballad Singers', c.1789. Watercolour, graphite, pen. Yale Center for British Art, Paul Mellon Collection

Ballad Singer' (15) features a lecherous audience member ogling the singer – the male gaze as diegetic, if you will – while 'The Ballad Singers' (Figure 1.10) features two young women bent over a sheaf of slips, their posture and the colour tones focusing attention on their lips and skin. The hand of the one is draped in a charged but anatomically implausible attitude over the other's chest, recalling Rowlandson's sideline in pornography and resulting in an image that hovers between the picturesque and the bawdy subgenres of his repertoire. Other depictions of young, idealised singers resist a sexual interpretation, either by the sober dignity of their execution (such as Henry Robert Morland's 'The Ballad Singer', 1), or by depicting children rather than young women. This is as much to do with attire as age: since these infants are literally 'dolled' up in respectable costume, there is none of the exposed flesh and ragged vulnerability pinpointed by Marshall as key to the eroticisation of street children in nineteenth-century art.[94] These child

[94] Marshall, City of Gold, 163–4. See also Koven, Slumming; and Clayton, The English Print, 253.

ballad-singers are desexualised *because* rather than in spite of their conventional prettiness.

This general lack of eroticisation runs counter to Nord's gendered reading of ballad-singers' sexual connotations, especially as the vast majority of images are of female subjects by male artists. To attempt a loose and unscientific statistical summary of my data: in factual written accounts, men outnumber women nine to one when singers are named, and by nearly four to one when unnamed. In more 'literary' texts – primarily poetry, songs, and anecdotes in magazines and novels – the numbers are even. Yet in images, women outnumber men by more than two to one.[95] It seems implausible that, given the prevailing mentalities of both artists and viewers, this gender imbalance across different media has no connection to sex – and indeed, I would resist any such conclusion. The explanation lies, once again, in the open mouths.

As demonstrated earlier, it was a contradiction in terms to depict an attractive, open-mouthed singer. The sole attempt is Rowlandson's 'The Ballad Singer' (*15*), one of just three or four images that locate sex as present (rather than past) in the singer's body. Yet there was one crucial difference between the occupations of the prostitute and the ballad-singer. The former invited sex, renting her body to be exploited in a private place by the (often respectable) active male customer.[96] By contrast, the ballad-singer's function as a performer enabled her *or him* to impose sex and various other forms of immorality, in the form of bawdy song, upon the (often respectable) passive public, in public space. In envoicing lewd songs, the singer engaged in an act that was the precise inverse of the prostitute's, yet just as frequently demonised as detrimental to the moral health of society. In imagery, this act was embodied in the open mouth – envisaged, as it had been through the history of art, whether in Roman fresco or Lutheran anti-witch woodcut, as a sexual orifice.[97] In an age when caricaturists were obsessed with bodily functions, it is no surprise that it was primarily in Georgian satirical prints, rather than in 'fancy pictures', that ballad-singers' subversive sexuality was depicted, in

[95] The sample size for these approximations is in the hundreds. I will refrain from tabulating my data, so as not to impart a pseudo-scientific authority to what remains anecdotal information. There is also the obvious factor that women may have been more readily objectified and thus depicted, but taken less seriously by male writers, therefore receiving disproportionately little attention in biographical and anecdotal accounts of individual singers.

[96] I am aware that this is something of a simplification, and have no wish to deny the agency often involved in sex-work: however, the overall direction of the power relations surrounding the act cannot be denied.

[97] See also Jones, *The Smile Revolution*, 32.

a form that involved the orifice (in this case, the mouth) voiding noxious matter upon the public (in this case, by vocal ejaculation).[98]

These are unlikely analogues for an artistic form combining music and poetry, yet they reflect the opprobrium – and the denial of aesthetic validity – that was heaped upon street ballads in written sources. The implicitly gendered comparison to the vulva is further endorsed by the fact that, of twenty-five apparently hostile images featuring open-mouthed singers, only six include 'men'. One is 'The Enraged Politicians', depicting two men and three women. Another is George Cruikshank's 'Grievances of London' (*43*), in which the ghoulish singer is effectively androgynous. The third is 'Triumphal Procession of the Hog in Armour', where the singer is the porcine boy – a far from masculine figure. 'Jack Cartar' (*62*), another Cruikshank, uses the open mouth as travesty, ironising the singer's claim to musicality, and is something of an outlier here. 'The Rose Shall Cease To Blow' (*63*) turns the elderly male singer three-quarters away, so that the stretched opening of his mouth is effectively hidden. In 'Ballad singer's' (*58*), the open mouth belongs to Sir Robert Peel – but he is travestied as a female ballad-singer for satirical purposes. His open mouth thus becomes as much a signifier of gender as his apron, shawl, or bonnet, reinforcing the strong association between the open mouth and the represented female. In reality, men were as likely as women to sing and sell bawdy material. Yet by the artistic conventions of the day, it was simpler for artists to depict a sexual taint as female. In truth, it was not the singer's body that challenged decency, but their song.

## Simulating Singers: Page, Stage, and Masquerade

There is a degree of hypocrisy in caricaturists allowing themselves free rein in sexual and scatological references, while reinforcing the concerns of moral, legal, or political reformers that ballad-singers might exercise the same licence in their songs – a hypocrisy accounted for, I think, by a reductive but convincing consideration of social status. Singers, belonging to an underclass and exercising influence over the masses, could not be permitted the same freedom as their educated artistic betters: what was playful in the one sphere became dangerous in the other. (We need not accept the existence of those separate spheres to acknowledge their rhetorical role in contemporary discourse.) It follows, then, that in representations of singers operating purely within a middling and genteel milieu of entertainment and pleasure, rather than in relation to questions of reform, a similar degree of licence might be allowed – thereby replacing concern and disapproval with excitement and amusement. Especially in the pre-Victorian period, this

---

[98] See esp. ibid., 23–4; and Gatrell, *City of Laughter, passim.*

essentially ludic engagement with the idea of the ballad-singer was found in fiction, the theatre, and the masquerade. All three operated at a crucial representational remove from their subject, for whereas visual sources were concerned with *actual* ballad-singers, these forms were preoccupied with impersonation, and dealt almost exclusively in the theme of the respectable person disguised – always temporarily – as its disreputable counterpart. An examination of these forms highlights both similarities to and points of departure from the issues bound up in visual representations, enriching our understanding of the array of intermedial cultural engagements with the ballad-singer.

In the twenty years following the 1798 publication of Kelly's *Joscelina*, with which this chapter began, literary London experienced a glut of chaste, vulnerable maidens who, for one reason or another, found themselves in the perilous position of the female ballad-singer, in publications written primarily for and often by women. In this context, unlike in imagery, the obvious connection with prostitution came to the fore: it appears that to the polite sensibility the pose of ballad-singer was – while *affectively* synonymous with that of prostitute – the lowest state to which a young woman might be reduced that still allowed for the prospect of rescue and redemption; a fall that just remained within the thresholds of ultimate grace. If anything, this reinforces the earlier conclusion that the real challenge posed by ballad-singers was in their performances, not their persons: for no well-brought-up young lady fallen on hard times ever sings anything immoral or vulgar in these stories, instead falling back upon a more genteel repertoire, sung beautifully, and thereby demonstrating their continued virtue. The situation thus afforded an enticing metaphorical imaginary within which both sexes could safely entertain risqué musings, enjoying the vicarious thrill of sex and the street without transgressing the imaginative pale. To invoke Edmund Burke's categories of feeling once more, this was to cross the line from the passivity of pity to the thrill of embodied, empathetic sympathy.[99]

In one case – an 1807 tale from the *Lady's Monthly Museum* – the aim appears to have been philanthropic, wherein a male narrator assuming the worst of 'one of those common beggars' discovers her to be a virtuous widow deserving of charity, the story ending in an exhortation to its readers to conduct themselves in an open spirit of Christian charity.[100] In every other instance, however, this imagining of oneself into the plight of another seems to have been calculated to excite rather than to instruct, the stories' cheap thrills bordering on what we would now call acts of cultural appropriation.

[99] Lamb, *Evolution of Sympathy*, 42; and see Edmund Burke, *A Philosophical Enquiry into the Origin of Our Ideas of the Sublime and Beautiful* (1757).
[100] 'A Pedestrian', *Lady's Monthly Museum, or, Polite Repository of Amusement and Instruction* 2 (March 1807): 114–15.

In *Joscelina* itself, Kelly places her heroine's ballad-singing episode at the climax of her novel's first volume: it is the ultimate depth to which the titular innocent is forced to sink. In a single passage, she narrowly escapes the carriage of the dastardly Captain Harrison by taking 'refuge in a narrow dark passage', the language invoking moral as well as physical danger. It is shown at once to be no refuge when 'a croud [*sic*] of those poor nightly beings who invade the streets, violently rushed upon her exhausted frame'.[101] Overwhelmed to the brink of death, Joscelina is revived by the prostitute Jessy, who is too ashamed to confess her real occupation to the heroine. Instead Jessy claims to be what she had in fact been at an earlier stage of her own descent: one who must 'sing ballads at some tavern door' (191; 193).[102] There follows an intricate performance of impersonation: Jessy, the prostitute, and Joscelina, the innocent, both resolve to play the part of something in between: the ballad-singer. They take a sheaf of ballads to St James's coffee house, outside which they sing 'My name is Poor Mary, Primroses I sell'.[103] That is, these two impostor-singers ventriloquise a flower-seller, a subtly different class of street-vendor, generically female, again implicated with both the urban pastoral aesthetic and the taint of prostitution, these things simultaneously reified (as with the ballad) in her wares: the flower. Just to complicate matters further, the book's genteel readers would be most familiar with this song, not from street performances, but via its original incarnation as an on-stage hit for the famous singer Maria Bland. For the character of Joscelina, however, these knowing references are unavailable: instead, she is too much in sympathy with the part she plays, and is consumed by shame as she sings words that exactly represent her own situation.

[T]he fair unfortunate innocent, after convulsive repeated sighs, in a voice affecting, soft, plaintive, tremulous, began.
    'Friend – nor – parent – I've none, I am – look'd on – with – scorn – Ah – better – for – me – had – I – never – been – born.' –
    The last word sunk in indistinguishable sound: she could utter no more, her spirit failed, she shrieked, she gasped, shuddered, staggered, fell. (195–6)

---

[101] Kelly, *Joscelina*, vol. 1, 183–5. Further page references are given in brackets following the relevant quotation.

[102] Note that the sequence of her descent, by degrees, is the inverse of Hogarth's 1741 ballad-singer.

[103] This was a genuine street ballad, 'The Primrose Girl', dating from 1793, though Kelly has Joscelina begin with the second verse of the street editions to achieve the effect described following this footnote. See http://ballads.bodleian.ox.ac.uk/search/roud/V5 448 for editions. The song was presumably known to Kelly via its origin as a stage number, written by John Moulds and sung by Maria Theresa Bland in *The Sultan* (Drury Lane, 1792). See BL Mus G.360.(33).

Her voice, quiet as it is, is recognised by one of the establishment's patrons: her former friend, Errington, who calls for her to be given a room. "'A room!" repeated one of the waiters, somewhat scornfully; "a room! what for a ballad singer, a street walker?"' (198) 'Street walker' is clearly a euphemism for prostitute, and the waiter's conflation of the two occupations is echoed by Errington, who assumes by her 'occupation and companion' that Joscelina is ruined. Joscelina, so innocent that she still does not recognise Jessy for what she really is, is wholly indignant at Errington's exhortations that she must mend her ways, but her protestations convince nobody (200–3). Here the first volume ends. Readers will be unsurprised that the *second* volume ends with Joscelina and Errington triumphantly married – a generic expectation that formed part of the bargain for contemporaries, a necessary promise of catharsis, restoration, and forgiveness, that prevented the affectiveness of these passages from discomforting Kelly's readers overmuch, providing instead just the right level of playful peril. Today, we may roll our eyes at the predictability of *Joscelina*'s trials, but we must allow that, as sentimental fiction, it is perfectly judged.[104]

Subsequent works may be read as subtle variations upon this successful formula. In a short story of 1811, 'The Ballad Singer', published in the women's magazine *La Belle Assemblée*, a male narrator saves a mysterious hooded singer from the molestations of two gentlemen, who feel licensed to interfere with 'a person of her description'.[105] It transpires that the singer is in fact respectable, awaiting a substantial legacy from an aunt, and is only impersonating a ballad-singer in order to obtain the funds necessary to care for her ill nurse. She is sixteen, beautiful, and named Georgiana into the bargain, so inevitably the narrator ends the story in pressing his suit upon her. In the context of the magazine this offers an additional twist upon the sexual politics involved, offering the intended female reader two contrasting forms of predatory behaviour: both physical harassment (bad) and opportune gallantry (good). Maria Edgeworth's four-volume novel *The Ballad Singer* is more in Kelly's line, boasting the nobly born but abandoned orphan Angeline as its beautiful child heroine. By the fourth volume she has suffered a series of misfortunes that lead her to Mrs Horton's brothel, where she contemplates the only possible alternative to vice: ballad singing. 'But instantly the lily of her cheek gave place to a momentary suffusion of the

---

[104] Its success, particularly among women of fashion, is attested in Jenifer Buckley, *Gender, Pregnancy and Power in Eighteenth-Century Literature: The Maternal Imagination* (Basingstoke, 2017), 205. The fact that the critic for the *Monthly Review* panned the novel, lamenting that Kelly's 'imagination sometimes hurries her beyond the bounds of propriety' and referencing the ballad-singer incident, may have done more good than harm to its sale. 'Novels', *Monthly Review* 2, no. 24 (1797): 339–41.

[105] In 'Stories of Seven Days', *Belle Assemblée; or Court and Fashionable Magazine* (October 1811): 185–9.

deepest carnation, as with the natural feelings of a gentlewoman, she dismissed the degrading idea'.[106] Forced to reconsider, she 'ventured *alone*, at *night*', the italics stressing her exciting plight, 'into the public streets of this vast metropolis, to SING BALLADS!' (62) Angeline's voice is 'mellifluous' and strong, and she is invited inside to entertain diners at a public function (64). Sex is of course in the air, as 'the only female amongst so many men' (68) – but so is larceny.

'Oh! the light-fingered practices of those gentry are pretty well known,' said a spruce Baronet: 'and this said BALLAD SINGER, I presume, is of eminence in her profession. We had better keep a good eye on the plate; those sugar-dispensers and fruit-spoons are all portable.' (71)

Thus, just before her parentage is fortuitously discovered and her fortune restored, Angeline's simulation implicates her as a threat to property as well as propriety.

Most intriguing of all is a twenty-four-page chapbook, printed in Falkirk in 1818 but set in London, purporting to be *The Surprising History of a Ballad Singer*. Its story is conventional: an honest childhood and a happy end, with a nadir of ballad singing in the middle. The eleven-year-old heroine, Ermina, is taken in by two poor but honest singers; learns their trade; is later, aged fifteen, 'decoyed into the house of a vile procuress', but escapes, only to be 'kept' by a Baronet. Yet the detail differs: salvation comes, not with marriage, but in service as a nursery-maid to a good family, while her older ballad-singing friend takes charge of a glove shop. Far from plumbing the depths, her two companions are soberly dressed and rent a decent room; their back-stories rail graphically against male abuse, with an unsparing degree of detail carried through pregnancies, shocking death, and a wealth of description of the ballad-singing trade including details of repertoire and practice, how to source new material and where best to sing it, whose songs were most successful, and so on. It is, in fact, tempting to believe that this lurid moral adventure, published not for London society but for Scottish artisans, might actually be a legitimate – if melodramatised – piece of life-writing.[107]

Though etymologically precise, 'melodramatic' is ironically less appropriate when considering the theatre. Here the ballad-singer was more often a stock character in short afterpieces or interludes, usually burlettas or farces, than in the evolving genre of melodrama – though the very natural interpolation of diegetic ballads into the onstage action was a device

---

[106] Maria Edgeworth, *The Ballad Singer; or, Memoirs of the Bristol Family: A Most Interesting Novel in Four Volumes*, 4 vols. (1814), vol. 4, 60. Further page references are given in brackets following the relevant quotation.

[107] A belief that alters its generic status very little, but that may prove significant in justifying my drawing upon it in subsequent chapters!

common to most types of play, in part as the inescapable legacy of *The Beggar's Opera*, alluded to earlier. The role of *male* ballad-singer seems to have been the exclusive preserve of the low comedian, played for predictable laughs.[108] The portrayal of female ballad-singers, however, was very similar to their representation in prose fiction, not least in the tendency for these roles to involve an intermediary layer of impersonation. Such parts were more psychologically than visually provocative, and did not feature the revealing costumes associated with, for example, cross-dressed 'breeches' roles. Margaretta's ballad-singing costume in the 1790 afterpiece *No Song No Supper* is a 'cotton gown, stuff petticoat, white apron, red cloak, and straw hat' – all the trappings familiar from images, down to the iconic red shawl, beneath which her body was comprehensively hidden, and her virtue preserved.[109] The excitement lay instead in the simulation, taken quite literally a stage further than in prose fiction. The female ballad-singer in a play was invariably a guise assumed by a character revealed by the plot to be highborn or wealthy, and was in turn played by a celebrated actress – and this in an age when, partly due to the taint of prostitution that still dogged the profession, an actress' stage persona was inevitably conflated with her personal character.[110] It was therefore imperative for all concerned that the heroine remained technically virtuous – but as long as this was evidently the case, first to the censor and then to the audience, then the 'ballad-singer' could be implicated in all manner of disreputable scenarios by the rest of the cast. Thus in Moncrieff's 1839 *The Ballad Singer*, first staged at the New Strand Theatre,[111] the eponymous (and picturesquely rustic) Ruth is subjected to sauciness by Nykin (f. 253); lechery by Alured (257); physical harassment, violence, and later shameful imprisonment by Nobbs (257–8; 304); a murderous attack by Fitzatherley (272); punishment by other beggars (276); and remorseless pursuit (280–94); before a birthmark proves her to be Geraldine, the noble heiress of Montfalcon (325).[112] The degree of gendered and class-based frisson this generates is only made possible by

---

[108] In 1804, William Blanchard played an unnamed 'Ballad-Singer' in a stock pantomime: see 'Theatrical Journal', *European Magazine* 45 (1804): 58. In 1837, William Thomas Hammond, playing Sam Weller, impersonated an Irish ballad-singer in an adaptation of *The Pickwick Papers*: see William Thomas Moncrieff, *Sam Weller or, The Pickwickians: A Drama in Three Acts* (1837), 99.
[109] Prince Hoare, *No Song, No Supper; A Musical Entertainment, in Two Acts* (1830), ix.
[110] See David Kennerley, 'Debating Female Musical Professionalism and Artistry in the British Press, c.1820–1850', *Historical Journal* 58 (2015): 987–1008.
[111] Vic Gammon, 'Street Ballad Sellers in the Nineteenth Century', in Atkinson and Roud, *Street Literature of the Long Nineteenth Century*, 119–53, 140.
[112] *Plays from the Lord Chamberlain's Office. Vol. LXXXVIII. June–Aug 1839* (BL Add. MS. 42952) No. 10 '*The Ballad Singer.*'

her pose – in which even she believes – as a ballad-singer, a make-believe at once daringly down-to-earth and bucolically fantastic.

Increasingly, it becomes clear that – though literally visible and audible on the London street – the ballad-singer's simultaneous taming and exoticisation in representation was in part related to that wider vogue, most commonly if reductively associated with Marie Antoinette, for dressing up as an archetypal commoner, as a milkmaid or flower girl – with the ballad-singer perhaps representing the bolder end of the picturesque.[113] As a means of experiencing vicarious, transgressive sensations denied to women within the constraints of respectable society, the role had much to offer on both page and stage, but perhaps reached its apogee in a still more social form: the masquerade ball. Between 1801 and 1844 – though the phenomenon seems heavily concentrated in the years up to 1815 and again in the early 1820s, perhaps prompted by analogous incidents in Egan's smash hit *Life in London* – gossip columns recorded at least twenty-one separate instances of members of the *beau monde* attending society functions in the character of ballad-singers (see Table 1.3). The fact that the names of most of these masqueraders were reported gives the lie to the pretence at anonymity, of course, and it seems significant that only two cases seem to have involved unmarried women (*14, 17*), whose reputations were most at stake, and of whom one was accompanied by her sister, and the other by two girlfriends as matching street-criers. Most others were married, often titled, and as likely to be men as women, with two of the men cross-dressed as female singers for presumably low comic effect, and several others appearing in married couples. The role was ideal, appealing to the carnivalesque penchant for low travesty while providing the exhibitionist with an excuse to sing to the company, and it is far from remarkable that members of the late-Georgian elite donned the characteristic red shawls or shabby top hats. It does, however, return us from the individualism and personal experience of the impersonated ballad-singers of page and stage to the homogenising, stock identity peddled in caricature, once again reducing these articulate and problematic figures to a safe space of condescension.

The power relations and layers of irony that governed these sorts of imaginative impersonation never risked the impersonator either taking their subject too seriously, or collapsing the boundary between self and Other – indeed, the more the 'ballad-singer' was recognisable as a performable type, the greater the distance became between the two. On the only known occasion when a respectable woman appears to have been genuinely mistaken for a ballad-singer, any tension in the scenario was defused by its

---

[113] For an astute treatment of this complex phenomenon, see Meredith Martin, *Dairy Queens: The Politics of Pastoral Architecture from Catherine de' Medici to Marie-Antoinette* (Harvard, 2011). Improbably, we will return to Marie Antoinette in Interlude III.

incorporation into humorous, innocuous anecdote – though the story's subject, Sarah Banks, the renowned antiquarian and sister to Sir Joseph Banks, may have felt a degree of mortification.

After making repeated inquiries of the wall-venders of half-penny ballads for a particular one which she wanted, she was informed by the claret-faced woman, who strung up her stock by Middlesex Hospital-gates, that if she went to a printer in Long Lane, Smithfield, probably he might supply her ladyship with what her ladyship wanted. … He then gave Miss Banks what is called a book, consisting of many songs. Upon her expressing her surprise when the man returned her eightpence from her shilling, and [at] the great quantity of songs he had given her, when she only wanted one; 'What, then!' observed the man, 'are you not one of our chaunters? I beg your pardon.'[114]

Had Banks been a blushing debutante rather than a serious and supposedly 'eccentric' scholar, the misapprehension might not have been so easily laughed off – but it would almost certainly not have been reported either. One is left with the impression that this story circulated in part because the confusion with a disreputable street singer mitigated the threat to the patriarchal order posed by Banks' unorthodox activities. Perhaps the real message was meant to be that, in real life, only an individual already transgressing the social norms could ever find herself in such an iniquitous position.

### Conclusion: Singers on Ballads

It was precisely because the reality of the metropolitan street could prove so hazardous to negotiate that the singer was treated as a fixed type in so many media. In representing the noisy, corrupting ballad-singer, society – for these artists and writers, whatever their perspective, were all *of* society – subjected them to a controlling gaze. Thus safely contained, the singer could signify notional dangers in order to warn, instruct, or thrill viewers, without possessing the agency actually to trouble them.

Someone is missing from this story: not the real singer, but the representation of one sometimes carried in their hand. The songs sold as slips or broadsides were normally headed by an image, usually an antique (or pseudo-antique) woodcut, as illustrative – if often rather obliquely – of the song's subject. On very rare occasions, this image was itself of a ballad-singer. I have identified just seven unique instances, in the Bodleian Library's archive of nearly 30,000 songs, of the image of a ballad-singer being used to illustrate a song that dates from our period and originates, at

---

[114] John Thomas Smith, *A Book for a Rainy Day: or, Recollections of the Events of the Last Sixty-Six Years* (1845), 211–12.

least plausibly, from London. These images do not admit of the same level of close analysis as those earlier: aesthetically they are a case apart, as the difficulty of rendering detail in a minuscule, poorly reproduced wood-cut prevents us reading anything into mouths and facial expressions. Yet it remains remarkable how closely they conform to what we have already observed. There is the rustic singer in a rural idyll (Table 1.2, *ii*); the singer as detail within a crowd scene (*iii*, *v*); the wretched, beshawled woman accompanied by infant or family (*vi*, *vii*); and the idealised beauty, dressed in the clothes of an earlier age, the decorous adornment to the surprisingly innocent if knowing song, 'Don't let me Die a Maid'[115] (*iv*). Indeed, the theme of the urban pastoral accrues an extra layer of nostalgia in the ballad woodcut – a printing technique retained long after the invention of superseding technologies because of its sentimental appeal to the public, with older woodblocks becoming prized by printers as antiques: this was the ballad trade colluding, for financial gain, in its own sentimentalisation.[116]

On only one occasion (*i*) is the singer given unusual prominence in a ballad image, in this case an exceptionally large one: he is central to the composition, mounted on a street bollard (a hint at contemporary practice?) in the manner of a town-crier.[117] His intrinsic liminality is refigured from the margins to the middle: he divides paving from cobbles just as he divides the crowd; on one side the street-sellers and plebeians, on the other the long-legged 'quality' – a lady and her two foppish beaux – and as such he assumes a dominant symbolic role in the society depicted. This woodcut reminds me of David Love, with whom we began: of both his second, self-commissioned portrait, in which he positions himself with similar prominence at the centre of a decorous street scene; and of his actual mode of performance – mount-ing a stool and dividing his audience in two – as described in Chapter 3. But in the main, these tiny images – produced, it should be remembered, not by singers themselves, but by artists employed by printers who would match one of their images to the song before ever the singer saw it – confirm our broader findings: these were the docile, picturesque archetypes of the singer that purchasers wished to take home and, in some cases, paste on their walls.[118] Even here, on the ballad itself, we have only one single instance wherein the represented singer is permitted to imitate his flesh-and-blood seller, and become the noisy, noticeable centre of attention.

---

[115] Sadly, the tune is unknown.

[116] *The Life of Old Jemmy Catnach, Printer* (Penzance, 1965), 5–7.

[117] This image appears on Bod. Harding B 2(3) and (4), and Bod. Douce Ballads 4(18) and (19). It is also used in the Bod. header, at top right, at ballads.bodleian.ox.ac.uk.

[118] As mentioned in the Introduction, see Holcroft, *Memoirs*, vol. 1, 135–6, for a practically unique written confirmation of this practice.

Table 1.1 *London images (Female artists and publishers are italicised)*

| No. | Date (range) | Title | Artist | Publisher | Medium | Genre | Gender | Source |
|---|---|---|---|---|---|---|---|---|
| 1 | c.1764 | The Ballad Singer | H. R. Morland | N/A | Oil on canvas | Subject | Female | Yale Center for British Art B1981.25.456 |
| 2 | c.1775–1804 | The Ballad Singer | J. Eginton after H. Singleton | Unknown | Colour stipple (hand-coloured) | Subject | Female | BM 1884,0209.14 |
| 3 | 1777 | The Old Ballad Singer | J. R. Smith | Unknown | Mezzotint (hand-coloured) | Subject | Male | Yale Center for British Art B1970.3.760 |
| 4 | c.1780–1847 | A Young Ballad Singer | T. Barker | N/A | Oil on canvas | Subject | Male | Holburne Museum of Art, Bath: A108 |
| 5 | c.1781 | The Ballad Singers | C. W. White after *E. Creeve* | C. W. White, Stafford Row, Pimlico | Stipple, etching (hand-coloured) | Subject | Female (2) | BM 1917,1208.3079 |
| 6 | 1783 | The Westminster Electors Charing their Favo[u]rite Candidate | Anon | *E. Darchery,* 11 St James's St | Etching (hand-coloured) | Satire (politics) | Female (ass's head) | BM J,4.86 |
| 7 | 1785 | The Young Maid & Old Sailor | F. Bartolozzi after H. Walton | R. Wilkinson, 58 Cornhill | Stipple, etching (hand-coloured) | Subject | Male | BM 1868,0808.2890 |
| 8 | 1787 | Untitled | S. Okey after Sir J. Reynolds | Unknown | Mezzotint | Subject/portrait | Male | BM 1839,1012.55 |
| 9 | 1787 & 1796 | Preparing to Start | R. Earlom after R. Dighton | Bowles & Carver, 69 St Paul's Church Yard | Mezzotint, etching (hand-coloured) | Subject/satire | Female | BM 2010,7081.1665 |

Table 1.1 (cont.)

| No. | Date (range) | Title | Artist | Publisher | Medium | Genre | Gender | Source |
|---|---|---|---|---|---|---|---|---|
| 10 | 1788 | Charley's return from over the water | W. Dent | W. Moore, 308 Oxford St | Etching | Satire (politics) | Female | BM 1868,0808.5794 |
| 11 | 1788 | The Humours of St. Giles's | J. H. Ramberg | T. Harmar, 164 Piccadilly | Etching | Satire (society) | Female, Male | Library of Congress PC 3 – 1788 |
| 12 | 1788 | Norwich Market Place | T. Rowlandson | N/A | Oil on canvas | Landscape | Female | Wiki Commons |
| 13 | c.1789 | The Ballad Singers | T. Rowlandson | N/A | Watercolour, graphite, pen | Subject | Female (2) | Yale Center for British Art B1977.14.367 |
| 14 | c.1789 | The Ballad Singer | T. Rowlandson | N/A | Watercolour | Subject | Female | Wiki Gallery |
| 15 | 1789 | The Ballad Singer | T. Rowlandson | N/A | Watercolour | Subject | Female | National Library of Wales PZ52 |
| 16 | 1789 | The freemen triumphant, or the mare foal'd of her folly | I. Cruikshank | S. W. Fores, 3 Piccadilly | Etching (hand-coloured) | Satire (politics) | Female | BM 1868,0808.5884 |
| 17 | 1789 | The Tavern Door; Laetitia deserted by her Seducer is thrown on the Town | J. R. Smith after G. Morland | R. Ackermann, 101 Strand | Stipple | Series (moral) | Female | BM 1872,0511.226 |
| 18 | c.1790 | Untitled | J. Heath after R. Corbould | Unknown | Etching, engraving | Book illustration | Female | BM 1867,0309.1337 |
| 19 | c.1790–98 | The Young Ballad Singers | J. Jones after J. Rising | R. Cribb, 288 Holborn | Mezzotint | Subject | Female (2) | BM 2010,7081.2456 |

| # | Year | Title | Artist | Publisher | Technique | Genre | Gender | Collection |
|---|---|---|---|---|---|---|---|---|
| 20 | 1793 | He would be a soldier, or the history of John Bull[']s warlike expedition | I. Cruikshank | S. W. Fores, 3 Piccadilly | Etching | Series (satirical, moral) | Female | BM 1851,0901.653 |
| 21 | 1793 | Love Songs and Matches | J. Russell | N/A | Pastels | Subject | Male | Holburne Museum of Art, Bath: A366 |
| 22 | 1794 | The Country Ballad Singers | Anon | Laurie & Whittle, 53 Fleet St | Mezzotint | Subject | Female | Yale Center for British Art B1970.3.793 |
| 23 | 1794 | The Farmer Come to Town on a Foolish Errand | Anon | Laurie & Whittle, 53 Fleet St | Mezzotint (hand-coloured) | Satire (society) | Female | BM 1948,0214.426 |
| 24 | 1796 | The Celebrated Thos. Fox, Favorite [sic] of Comus | I. Jenner | I. Jenner, 26 Little Argyle St | Stipple | Portrait | Male | BM 1851,0308.267 |
| 25 | 1796 | A New Love Song | A. Cardon after F. Wheatley | Colnaghi & Co., 127 Pall Mall | Stipple | Series (subject) | Female | BM 1940,1109.90 |
| 26 | c.1798 | The Wandering Sailor | H. Singleton | N/A | Oil on paper | Subject | Male | Yale Center for British Art B1981.25.571 |
| 27 | 1799 | Last dying speech & Confession | T. Rowlandson | R. Ackermann, 101 Strand | Etching (hand-coloured) | Series (satirical) | Female | Cries of London, no.3 |
| 28 | 1799 | Untitled | T. Rowlandson | E. Jones | Etching | Songbook cover | Female | Madden Collection 1:3 |
| 29 | c.1800 | Picture of London | G. Cruikshank | Unknown | Etching (hand-coloured) | Satire (society) | Female | BM 1871,0429.725 |
| 30 | 1800 | Rapture | T. Rowlandson after G. M. Woodward | R. Ackermann, 101 Strand | Etching (hand-coloured) | Series (satire (society)) | Female | BM 2004,1130.40 |

Table 1.1 (*cont.*)

| No. | Date (range) | Title | Artist | Publisher | Medium | Genre | Gender | Source |
|---|---|---|---|---|---|---|---|---|
| 31 | 1802 | The Beggar Girl | Anon | Laurie & Whittle, 53 Fleet St | Mezzotint (hand-coloured) | Song illustration | Female | BM 2010,7081.835 |
| 32 | 1805 | The Enraged Politicians or Political Ballad Singers | C. Williams | S. W. Fores, 50 Piccadilly | Etching (hand-coloured) | Satire (politics) | Female (3) Male (2) | BM 1868,0808.7359 |
| 33 | 1806 | The Disabled Soldier | R. H. Heath after G. Morland | T. Tegg, 111 Cheapside | Etching, mezzotint | Subject | Female | BM 2010,7081.4374 |
| 34 | 1806 | Triumphal Procession of Little-Paul-The Taylor upon his new-Goose | J. Gillray | H. Humphrey, 27 St James's St | Etching (hand-coloured) | Satire (politics) | Female (2) | BM 1851,0901.1812 |
| 35 | 1806 | Untitled | R. Cooper after S. De Wilde | Unknown | Stipple, etching | Illustration (portrait) | Female | BM Ee,5.180 |
| 36 | 1807 | The Close of the Poll, or John Bull in high good humour | C. Williams | E. Walker, 7 Cornhill | Etching (hand-coloured) | Satire (politics) | Female | BM 1868,0808.7564 |
| 37 | 1808 | Bartholomew Fair | T. Rowlandson | R. Ackermann, 101 Strand | Etching, aquatint | Series (cityscape) | Female | The Microcosm of London, I:52 |
| 38 | 1808 | Covent Garden Market | T. Rowlandson | R. Ackermann, 101 Strand | Etching, aquatint | Series (cityscape) | Female | Ibid, I:209 |
| 39 | 1808 | The Cobler and Poet | I. Cruikshank | Laurie & Whittle, 53 Fleet St | Etching | Song illustration | Female | BM 1861,0518.1181 |

| No. | Date | Title | Artist | Publisher | Medium | Subject | Gender | Reference |
|---|---|---|---|---|---|---|---|---|
| 40 | 1808 | Triumphal procession of the hog in armour | S. De Wilde | S. Tipper, 37 Leadenhall St | Etching, aquatint | Satire (politics) | Male | BM 1867,0112.34 |
| 41 | 1809 | The Ballad Girl | J. Young after J. Rising | J. Young, 65 Charlotte St | Mezzotint | Subject | Female | BM 2010,7081.3573 |
| 42 | 1810 | Sketches of fairy land or a comparison between England & Lilliput Pl.1 | C. Williams after G. M. Woodward | T. Tegg, 111 Cheapside | Etching (hand-coloured) | Series (satire (society)) | Female | BM 1872,1012.4967 |
| 43 | 1812 | The Grievances of London | G. Cruikshank | Unknown | Etching (hand-coloured) | Satire (society) | Female | BM 1859,1012.926 |
| 44 | 1812 | Manchester Square cattle shew | C. Williams | Unknown | Etching (hand-coloured) | Satire (politics) | Female | BM 1868,0808.8011 |
| 45 | 1814 | Frost Fair on the River Thames | Anon | G. Thompson, 43 Long Lane | Woodcut (hand-coloured) | Landscape | Female (2) | BM 1931,1114.394 |
| 46 | 1817 | Untitled (Joseph Johnson) | J. T. Smith | J. T. Smith, 4 Chandos St | Etching | Book illustration | Male | Vagabondiana, 67 |
| 47 | 1817 | Untitled (blind beggar) | J. T. Smith | J. T. Smith, 4 Chandos St | Etching | Book illustration | Male | Ibid., 125 |
| 48 | 1817 | Untitled (Charles Wood) | J. T. Smith | J. T. Smith, 4 Chandos St | Etching | Book illustration | Male | Ibid., 133 |
| 49 | 1817 | Untitled (mock fiddler) | J. T. Smith | J. T. Smith, 4 Chandos St | Etching | Book illustration | Male | Ibid., 139 |
| 50 | 1819 | The funeral procession of the rump | G. Cruikshank | G. Humphrey, 27 St James's St | Etching (hand-coloured) | Satire (politics) | Female (2) | BM 1859,0316.1072 |
| 51 | c.1820 | Ballad Singer | T. Rowlandson | Unknown | Etching (hand-coloured) | Book illustration | Female | Rowlandson's Characteristic Sketches of the Lower Orders, plate 17 |

Table 1.1 (cont.)

| No. | Date (range) | Title | Artist | Publisher | Medium | Genre | Gender | Source |
|---|---|---|---|---|---|---|---|---|
| 52 | c.1820 | Last Dying Speech | T. Rowlandson | Unknown | Etching (hand-coloured) | Book illustration | Female | Ibid., plate 32 |
| 53 | 1820 | Billy Waters, the Dancing Fiddler | T. L. Busby | Baldwin & Co. | Engraving, aquatint | Book illustration | Male | Costume of the Lower Orders of London, 1 |
| 54 | 1821 | The Ups and Downs of Life in London | G. Cruikshank & I. Cruikshank | Sherwood & Co., Paternoster Row | Etching (hand-coloured) | Book illustration | Male | Life in London, front matter |
| 55 | 1821 | Tom and Jerry 'Masquerading it' among the cadgers in the 'black slums,' in the Holy Land | G. Cruikshank & I. Cruikshank | Sherwood & Co., Paternoster Row | Etching (hand-coloured) | Book illustration | Female | Ibid., 346 |
| 56 | 1822 | Butter Cups & Daisies a sketch from Low life | W. Heath & J. Gleadah | S. W. Fores, 50 Piccadilly | Etching, aquatint | Satire (society) | Female | BM 1935,0522.7.214 |
| 57 | 1828 | The March of Intellect | W. Heath | G. Humphrey, 27 St James's St | Etching (hand-coloured) | Satire (society) | Female | BM 2002,0519.1 |
| 58 | 1830 | Ballad Singer's [sic] | W. Heath | T. McLean, 26 Haymarket | Etching (hand-coloured) | Satire (politics) | 'Female' (transvestite) | BM 1868,0808.9207 |
| 59 | 1830 | The Orphan Ballad Singers | J. Romney after W. Gill | R. Ackermann, 101 Strand | Etching | Song illustration | Female (2) | BM 1917,1208.3122 |
| 60 | 1831 | Little Ballad Singer | W. Taylor after J. Jackson | J. Dickinson, 114 New Bond St | Lithograph | Subject | Female | BM 1878,0511.890 |
| 61 | c.1833 | Ballad singers. Any thing for an honest living | R. Seymour | W. Spooner, 259 Regent St | Lithograph | Satire (society) | Female (cat) | BM 1982,U.839 |
| 62 | 1837 | Jack Cartar | G. Cruikshank | J. S. Hodson, 112 Fleet St | Etching | Book illustration | Male | Streetology, no.5 front matter (preceding p.67) |

| No. | Date | Title | Artist | Publisher | Technique | Type | Gender | Reference |
|---|---|---|---|---|---|---|---|---|
| 63 | c.1839 | The Rose Shall Cease to Blow | Anon | Unknown | Lithograph (hand-coloured) | Subject (satirical) | Male | BM 1951,0411.4.51 |
| 64 | 1839 (pub.) | New Elegy | J. T. Smith | J. B. Nichols | Etching | Book illustration | Male | *The Cries of London*, 47 |
| 65 | 1839 (pub.) | Sprig of Shillelah and Shamrock so Green | J. T. Smith | J. B. Nichols | Etching | Book illustration | Male | Ibid., 67 |
| 66 | 1842 | Poet's Corner | Anon | Punch Office | Etching | Magazine illustration | Female (2?) Male (2?) | *Punch*, 2 (1842): 183 |
| 67 | 1844 | Sketches of Street Singers | George Scharf | N/A | Pencil drawing | Subject | Female (6) Male (5) | BM 1900,0725.41 |
| 68 | 1845 | Sketch of Street Singers | George Scharf | N/A | Pencil drawing | Subject | Male (2) | BM 1862,0614.971 |
| 69 | 1846 | The Ballad Singer | D. Maclise | N/A | Oil on canvas | Subject | Female | *Art Journal* (1865): 140 |
| 70 | 1847 | The English Serenader | E. Wild | Theatrical Journal | Etching | Magazine illustration | Male | *Theatrical Journal* 8 (1847): 161 |
| 71 | 1853 | The Ballad Monger | R. Dadd | N/A | Watercolour | Subject | Male | BM 1953,0509.2 |
| 72 | 1854 | The Ballad Singer | C. B. Leighton | J. Shepherd, Newgate St | Lithograph (hand-coloured) | Score illustration | Female | British Library H1296 (1) |
| 73 | 1854 | The Ballad Singer | Anon | J. Allen, 20 Warwick Lane | Etching | Score illustration | Female | British Library H2345 440 |

Table 1.2 *Woodcut ballad illustrations*

| No. | Date range | Publisher | Illustration to | Gender | Bod. Illustration no. |
|---|---|---|---|---|---|
| i | 1802–19 | J. Pitts | Arthur O'Bradley's Wedding | Male | 17746 |
| ii | 1813–38 | J. Catnach | Old Woman and her Cats | Female | 2170 |
| iii | 1837–38 | J. Catnach | Biddy the Basket Woman | Female (2) | 19173 |
| iv | 1838–45 | J. Catnach | Don't let me Die a Maid | Female | 1230 |
| v | 1860–83 | H. Disley | The Rambling Boys of Pleasure | Female | 6547 |
| vi | Unknown | Unknown | The Little Gipsy Girl | Female | 7473 |
| vii | Unknown | Unknown | The Dealers' Downfall | Female, Male (2) | 9221 |

Table 1.3 *Masquerades*

| No. | Date | Name | Venue | Type | Repertoire | Source |
|---|---|---|---|---|---|---|
| 1 | April 1801 | Mr Penn of Stoke Park | Mrs Methuen's, London | Male | | *Morning Post* 10195 (1 May 1801) |
| 2 | May 1802 | Lady Smith Burgess | Mrs Thellusson's, Foley House, London | Female | | *Morning Post* 10497 (28 May 1802) |
| 3 | June 1802 | Mr Simmons (actor) | Queen's Fête, Frogmore Gardens, Windsor | Crossed | 'a very droll song' | *Morning Post* 10514 (16 June 1802) |
| 4 | September 1802 | 'male and female' | Margate Theatre Royal | Couple | 'The Beggar Girl', 'The Post Captain' | *Morning Post* 10583 (4 Sep 1802) |
| 5 | May 1803 | Mrs Littledale | Miss Morgan's, Kensington, London | Female | | *Morning Post* 10797 (13 May 1803) |
| 6 | May 1805 | Captain Gordon | Mrs Dupre's, Grafton St, London | Male | | *Morning Post* 11424 (17 May 1805) |
| 7 | June 1805 | Lady Christiana Reade | Mrs Coke's, Hanover Sq., London | Female | 'Crazy Jane', etc. | *Morning Post* 11448 (14 June 1805) |
| 8 | July 1805 | Lady Honeywood | Countess Dysart's, Ham House, Richmond | Female | | *Morning Post* 11521 (20 July 1805) |

Table 1.3 *(cont.)*

| No. | Date | Name | Venue | Type | Repertoire | Source |
|---|---|---|---|---|---|---|
| 9 | June 1807 | Anon 'accompanied by her Husband, a disabled soldier' | Lady Stronge's, Grafton St, London | Female | | *Morning Post* 11827 (8 June 1807) |
| 10 | 1809 | Captain Kemble | Numerous | Male | | *Morning Post* 12275 (1 June 1810) |
| 11 | June 1810 | Captain Kemble | Mrs Boehm's, St James's Sq., London | Male | | *Morning Post* 12281 (8 June 1810) |
| 12 | June 1813 | Anon | Mrs Dottin's, Argyle St, London | ? | | *Morning Post* 13220 (3 June 1813) |
| 13 | February 1814 | Mr Joseph Birley | Preston Assembly Rooms | Male | | *Lancaster Gazette* 663 (26 February 1814) |
| 14 | February 1814 | Miss Elizabeth Hornby | Preston Assembly Rooms | Female | | *Lancaster Gazette* 663 (26 February 1814) |
| 15 | February 1815 | Anon | Mr Corri's, Edinburgh Concert Rooms | ? | 'selling ballads' | *Caledonian Mercury* 14539 (18 February 1815) |
| 16 | February 1815 | Anon 'with four infants' | Mr Corri's, Edinburgh Concert Rooms | Female | A high-pitched custom song | *Caledonian Mercury* 14539 (18 February 1815) |

| | Date | Performer | Venue | Gender | Songs | Source |
|---|---|---|---|---|---|---|
| 17 | June 1815 | Miss Rockwood, with 'Miss Clayton, an Old Fish-woman [and] Miss O'Donnell, an Orange-woman' | Lady Owen's, Argyll Rooms, London | Female | | *Morning Post* 13549 (25 June 1815) |
| 18 | September 1822 | Mrs Astley of Dukinfield, with sister | Preston Theatre | Female | 'several popular songs' inc 'Ye [bonny] banks and braes' and 'some French ballads' | *Liverpool Mercury* 590 (20 September 1822), *Morning Post* 16079 (26 September 1822), and *Lancaster Gazette* 1111 (28 September 1822) |
| 19 | June 1825 | Mr H | Argyll Rooms | Male | 'Green grow the rushes' | *Lancaster Gazette* 1253 (18 June 1825) |
| 20 | June 1825 | Lord — | Argyll Rooms | Male | 'Oh! 'tis love, 'tis love' | *Lancaster Gazette* 1253 (18 June 1825) |
| 21 | February 1844 | Mr Shand, with 'Mr Jopp as a ne'er-do-weel husband' | County Rooms, Aberdeen | Crossed | Songs | *Aberdeen Journal* 5014 (14 February 1844) |

# Interlude I
## 'Oh! Cruel'

Example I.1 'Oh! Cruel, A Comic Song', vocal reduction (Liverpool, 1810)[1]

Oh! cruel was the water, as bore her love from Mary,
And cruel was the fair wind, that would'nt [*sic*] prove contrary.
And cruel was the captain, the boatswain and the men,
As did'nt [*sic*] care a farthing if we never met again.

Oh! cruel was the splinter, as broke my deary's leg,
Now he's oblig'd to fiddle for it, and I'm obliged to beg,
A vagabonding vagrant, and a rantipoling wife,
We fiddle, limp, and scrape it, through the ups and downs of life.

[1] Reduction of melody, derived from BL Mus G809 b (52).

Oh! cruel was the engagement in which my true love fought,
And cruel was the cannon ball, as knock'd his right eye out,
He us'd to leer and ogle me with peepers full of fun,
But now he looks askew at me, because he has but one.

My love he plays the fiddle, and wanders up and down,
And I sing at his elbow through all the streets in town,
We spend our days in harmony, and very seldom fight,
Except when he's his grog aboard, and I get queer at night.

Then ladies all take warning, by my true love and me,
Tho' *cruel* fate shou'd cross you, remember constancy,
Like me you'll be rewarded and have all your hearts delight,
With fiddling in a morning, and a drop of gin at night.[2]

'Broadside balladry as a whole is not self-regarding', writes James Hepburn.[3]
Put differently: there are remarkably few ballads *about* ballad-singers – and
most of them feature in this interlude. Generally, singers – tawdry, mundane – were effaced from their own product, in favour of shipwrecks, ghosts,
satire, love, exotica, or erotica – anything to lift the plebeian imagination out
of the street. Of the few 'self-regarding' songs that did exist, 'Oh! Cruel' was
probably the most widespread and the most influential, spawning at least one
'answer', two reworkings, two parodies, and a retitling, published across
England.[4] As is typical of the sub-genre, it was originally written for the
stage, not the street, a setting in which the balladeer *was* a little exotic, and
therefore stands comparison with many of the genteel media discussed in
Chapter 1. It was printed in London by both George Pigott and Thomas
Evans, in editions noting its stage origin: for, as its earliest extant score from
1810 proclaims, 'Oh! Cruel' was 'A Comic Song, Written & Sung by
A Gentleman of Liverpool, in the Character of a Female Ballad Singer,
Accompanied by an Amateur, on the Evening of the Amateur
Performance, for the Benefit of the Poor, at the Theatre Royal Liverpool.'[5]
    This subtitle heavily conditions our expectation of how the song will
represent ballad-singers: they are to be made fun of. The melody helps this

---

[2] 'Oh! Cruel', Roud V1836. This edition by George Pigott, Old St, London: Bod. 2806
   c.18(220).
[3] Hepburn, *Scattered Leaves*, vol. 2, 480.
[4] 'Answer to Oh! Cruel' (London and Bristol), Bod. Harding B 11(81) and Bod. Firth
   c.12(205); versions from Workington and North Shields, Bod. Harding B 11(672) and
   Bod. Harding B 25(1396); parodies 'A Pretty Little Dear' (London), Bod. Harding B 16
   (214a), and 'Dr Shuffle' (Norwich), Bod. Johnson Ballads fol. 250; 'Tommy Strill'
   (Manchester), Bod. Harding B 25(1930).
[5] BL Mus G809 b (52).

end: it is in the simplest major key and, aside from in bars five and six, the ascending phrases of which may be intended to evoke the rowing motion of the 'little boat', it exerts little pressure upon the lyric. Structurally it is generic, unexceptional: the words are left to do their work. The writer of those words is clearly attempting a travesty, parodying the pathetic narrative songs of the day. Specifically, the words (but not the tune) are a parody of the widespread street song 'Winter's Evening' (itself a variant of 'The Maid in Bedlam'), in which the narrator observes a destitute mother and child dying in the winter snow, the mother's plaint beginning with the lamentation, 'Oh! cruel'.[6] The Liverpudlian parodist echoes the sentimental original in the first three verses, creating a tragic scenario – only to subvert it in the song's second half, which knowingly[7] reveals the song's ballad-singing narrator to be a lustful alcoholic. The song is written to mock rather than to sympathise with its subject, relying upon the circumstances of its stage performance to set up its reception as comic. It depends upon a shared assumption with the audience that plaintive street singers are more likely to be charlatans, and reinforces this with a disguise of its own: the first singer, as the subtitle makes clear, was cross-dressed, in a stage convention closely associated with low comedy. In the 1790s as before and since, performers such as Birmingham's John Collins would don the guise of a stage Irishman or Frenchman, or – as in this case – that of a low female. The intention was always derogatory, and would certainly have been construed thus by the audience.[8] There are at least two other songs representing ballad-singers that are similarly cynical, suggesting this trope was not uncommon.[9] In the Liverpool theatre, then – rather distastefully, we might think today, at a charity function 'for the Benefit of the Poor' – 'Oh! Cruel' was performed as a cynical and comic representation of ballad-singers, and was likely to be received as such.

Other representations that were circulated and performed among a relatively elite, musically literate sphere offered similarly small scope for interpretation, but tended to the sentimental rather than the cynical. These divided into two basic modes: those written and presented in a pastoral idiom, and those that adopted a tragic tone. The former mode – calling to mind the

---

[6] This song is numbered in the Roud Index, confusingly, as both V17586 and V20461. One of its earliest ephemeral editions was printed at Salisbury between 1770 and 1800: see Bod. Harding B 14(35).

[7] For an elaboration of nineteenth-century knowingness, see Chapter Six of Bailey, *Popular Culture*.

[8] Regarding which construction, see Gerald Porter on Roland Barthes, in *The English Occupational Song* (Umeå, 1992), 12. Or, as Booth puts it in *The Experience of Songs*, 11, 'Audiences are ready for their songs to say certain things in certain ways.'

[9] 'Number One', Bod. Johnson Ballads 2293; and the well-known 'Down by the Dark Arches', Bod. Firth c.17(285).

ancien régime trend for dressing as rustic shepherdesses – was consistent across our period, from Samuel Arnold's 'Little Bess the Ballad Singer' of 1794, to George Linley's 'The Ballad Singer' of sixty years later.[10] Both afford their female singer ample scope to perform the picturesque, as she sings of a carefree, idealised life on the road. Linley's score of 1854, availing itself of newly affordable technologies, reinforces this with a stunning full-page, full-colour illustration of the comely singer herself, tripping along a country lane, topped with the chorus line, 'Gaily I take my way'. A review in the *Lady's Newspaper* declared that 'The melody is pretty, light, and playful; and, as the words express, will cheer the youthful heart, delight the ears of age, and attract the gay and grave.'[11] Musically, this was worlds away from 'Oh! Cruel's conception of the balladeer: the song was written for Charlotte Dolby, a highly regarded concert contralto greatly admired by Felix Mendelssohn, and the epitome of respectable femininity.[12] In the second, tragic mode, at least four songs between 1800 and 1854 offered secure middle-class women similar opportunities to ventriloquise a pitiable and precarious female singer.[13] On the spectrum of feeling posited by Edmund Burke, these were written to prompt pity instead of empathy, 'where the beholder is pleased by the representation rather than the reality of suffering'.[14]

Though the reception of all these songs was of course subjective, their textual, material, and performative dimensions all militated in favour of a passive, complacent regard on the part of their genteel singers and audiences. In a different performance context, however, even so deterministic a song as 'Oh! Cruel' had the potential to be sung and heard altogether differently. To comprehend this mutability, I wish to consider two songs, the second of which is a very close relative of 'Oh! Cruel' itself.

The first is 'The Ballad-Singer's Petition', also known as 'With Lowly Suit', written for the 1790 Stephen Storace/Prince Hoare operatic afterpiece *No Song No Supper* mentioned in Chapter 1.[15] It is squarely in the sentimental mode, its rhymes of ditty/pity, beating/intreating [*sic*], and distressing/blessing emphasised by the tune's halting phrasings, as shown

---

[10] BL Mus G383 h (10) and H1296 (1), respectively.
[11] 'Literature', *Lady's Newspaper* 507 (1856): 166.
[12] John Warrack, 'Dolby, Charlotte Helen Sainton- (1821–1885)', *ODNB*, oxforddnb.com /view/article/24521.
[13] These are Andrew Cherry, 'The Beggar Girl', and his (with John Davy) 'The Wandering Beggar Girl' (1806); Reginald Spofforth, 'The Ballad Singer'; and Henry Russell and E. W. Tracy, 'The Ballad Singer' (1854): see *The Myrtle and Vine; or, Complete Vocal Library*, 4 vols. (1800), vol. 3, 170–1; BL Scores G.805 (18); Reginald Spofforth, *The Twelfth Cake, a Juvenile Amusement Consisting of Little Ballads* (1807), 14–15; BL Mus H2345 440.
[14] As in Chapter 1, see Lamb, *The Evolution of Sympathy*, 42.
[15] BL Mus H1653 j(39); Bod. Harding B 17(342).

Example I.2  Stephen Storace and Prince Hoare, 'The Ballad-Singer's
Petition' (Dublin, 1790), bars 14–18.[17]

in Example I.2, described by its librettist as 'that most touching and
simple of all melodies'.[16]

As in 'Oh! Cruel', the original stage performer, Nancy Storace, takes
the role of a ballad-singer, Margaretta. Yet the character Margaretta is
herself disguised within the play: after singing this song, she reveals that
she is no true balladeer: having turned down numerous wealthy mar-
riages, she is merely awaiting the (imminent) return of her beloved
Robin.[18] The pose of distress is therefore a double affectation, a role
within a role. This 'touching and simple' song therefore contained
within it a degree of deception, taken far further when the song was
interpolated by the playwright William Thomas Moncrieff into his
incredibly successful adaptation of Egan's *Tom and Jerry; or, Life in
London*, first staged at the Adelphi in 1821, and infamous as perhaps
the most knowing and cynical production of the age. Within this later
play, it is sung by a character, Sue, who is herself disguised as a 'beautiful
ballad-singer' in a den of fraudulent beggars.[19] She performs the song to
elicit, not charity, but sexual attention, from the titular Jerry, in
a theatrical episode reminiscent of the assumption, discussed in
Chapter 1, that a woman in want was a wanton woman. A 'touching
and simple' song ostensibly connoting sincere distress is thereby entirely
subverted to bawdy ends.

The second song, like 'Oh! Cruel', is an adaptation of the older
ballad 'Winter's Evening'. It occurs in another interpolation by
Moncrieff into his 1839 burletta *The Ballad Singer*, also discussed in
Chapter 1. The titular Ruth, in circumstances of great distress, is
moved to sing a single verse outside what turns out to be the house of
a benevolent magistrate:

---

[16] Hoare, *No Song No Supper*, vi.     [17] BL Mus H1653 j(39).
[18] Hoare, *No Song No Supper*, 17.     [19] Moncrieff, *Tom and Jerry*, 50–1.

O cruel was my mother that shut her doors on me
And cruel those who stood unmov'd & such a sight could see
And cruel is the wintry wind that chills my heart with cold
But crueller the fate that robb'd me of my friends of old[20]

The magistrate takes the performance, as Ruth means it, at face value, remarking: 'That voice tis sad and sweet ... what is it moves me thus ... I don't think I shall do my duty as a Magistrate if I was not to take her in.'[21] In this play, Ruth is by birth an heiress, but at this point both she and the audience believe her to be a true singer, and despite the verse's close similarity to the cynical 'Oh! Cruel', it is played here entirely straight. The context of performance was key to the song's interpretation.

These theatrical examples enjoin us, then, to move beyond the text to the performance, and especially to think of the songs' literal rather than represented singers, of their own motivations and circumstances. In the drawing room, such songs – whether comic, pastoral, or tragic – were all essentially forms of play, offering low-stakes opportunities for impersonation and ephemeral emotional thrills. Yet many of these songs, and none more so than 'Oh! Cruel' itself, were also published in street editions, leading us to consider their performance at point of sale in the street. Under these circumstances, the framework changed: the performance was no longer one of the ballad-singer as imitated by social superior, but of ballad-singer as performed by ballad-singer. In no other medium could singers thus take ownership of their representation – for even in autobiography, singers were relinquishing their identity as such in favour of other labels: political reformer, evangelist, or at the very least, writer. In performing these songs, singers asserted a voice denied them in other media.

This is a stranger prospect than it sounds. A ballad-singer singing 'I am a ballad-singer' from a sheet she was selling was not simply being herself, but consciously performing a persona that was in some respects less like herself than when she sang 'My name is Napoleon Bonaparte' or whatever the song may have been. The narrative voice prescribed features and emotions that may not have coincided with the singer's, yet were superficially so proximate – since both were ballad-singers – that the singer's actual self was more occluded than if she were ventriloquising, for instance, Robin Hood. However, the street singer retained control over what James Porter describes as 'the complex of experiential and subjective

---

[20] Moncrieff, *Ballad Singer*, f.286. The verse is a close paraphrasing of the second verse of 'Winter's Evening' as found in an 1837 edition: see Bod. 2806 c.17(315).
[21] Moncrieff, *Ballad Singer*, f.287. Moncrieff cannot quite resist a destabilising pun here: by 'take her in' the magistrate means into custody, and is reproved by his Indian servant, who declares it his master's duty to take her in 'as a man', that is, to give her shelter.

meanings the singer brings to the song.'[22] A genuinely destitute singer might profit financially by singing a song coincident with their own condition, while gaining comfort from this means of voicing their distress. An accomplished and therefore comfortable street performer could adopt the same pitiable persona and pull it off, convincing passers-by of their extreme distress – or indeed might fail to convince, thereby provoking the writers of sceptical songs such as 'Oh! Cruel'. Alternatively, a singer might revel in reappropriating 'Oh! Cruel' itself, charming customers with their roguish and knowing displays, exploiting rather than being exploited by the unflattering description in the later verses. Meanings located in performance need not be congruent with a writer's intentions. Take as example the classic beggar's song 'The Wandering Bard', which contains six verses detailing the singer's plight, the first of which ends:

> My lot is cast I am forced at last,
> To ask of you to buy

and the last of which closes:

> Now buy my song be it right or wrong
> It will help a wandering Bard.[23]

The song could easily be played straight, as a plea for pity. Yet equally it might be played for laughs, its successive description of items of second-hand clothing providing ample scope for physical comedy. Either interpretation made an asset out of the singer's presumably ragged attire, which in other aspects of life was a disadvantage.

This interpretative scope could even take on radical political potency. 'The Ballad Singer, A New Song' is, at face value, typically pathetic, bemoaning the singer's lot.[24] Yet, loudly voiced by a genuine ballad-singer, situated resentfully in the gutter or dominating a street corner, it could swiftly shed its pathos, becoming a form of bitter social commentary pitched to elicit guilt, shame, discomfort, from among its more prosperous auditors. In moving from a drawing-room realm of make-believe to the reality it describes, its maudlin lyric becomes an accusation:

> Gentle people as ye throng,
> List'ning to a beggar's song,
> Think ye mirth inspires the strain?

[22] James Porter, cited in David Atkinson, *The English Traditional Ballad: Theory, Method and Practice* (Aldershot, 2002), 6–7.

[23] Again, the song has two Roud numbers, 2687 and V3128. A representative edition is Bod. Firth c.21(3). The tune, however, is entirely unknown, so I have not recorded a version.

[24] *The Ballad Singer, A New Song* (c.1800). The tune is unknown.

Think ye joy and pleasure reign?
Ah! no, the strains that beggars chaunt,
Issue from the breast of want,
Ah! the strains that beggars sing,
Not from mirth but mis'ry spring.

... Need you gentlefolks be told
How hard it is when wet and cold.
And hunger round the minstrel cling,
How very hard it is to sing.

It is even possible that these highly subjective performances travelled full
circle and left their mark on the texts of songs, with printers adapting new
editions to reflect the interpretative choices made by successful singers.
Around the 1840s, a new glut of representational songs, all apparently of
low origin, enjoyed a run as popular broadsides and in chapbooks.
Characterised by satire, flash language, spoken 'patter' sections and,
above all, knowingness, these songs – 'Beggars and Ballad Singers',
'Anything to Earn a Crust' (tune unknown), 'The Dustman's Brother' –
glory in the compelling, disreputable character of the street singer.[25] The
first of these three proved uncommonly susceptible to variation, even by
the mutable standards of the broadside: chopped and changed, reordered
or abbreviated, with directions for new melodies often given mid-song.
The third, which started life as a parody of 'The Literary Dustman'[26] and
remained anchored by that comic song's melody, was rewritten several
times in the 1840s, becoming first 'The Bard of Seven Dials'[27] and then
'Billy Nutts, the Poet'[28] (a variant famous enough to be quoted in a new
edition of The Swell's Night Guide, a brothel handbook of 1846),[29] which
was in its turn rivalled in the 1850s by the riposte 'Jimmy Jumps the
Rhymer'.[30] These sequels also varied greatly between editions. In many
respects, these songs were the logical street successors to 'Oh! Cruel':
bawdy, scurrilous songs that gloried in presenting a disreputable but
highly proficient version of the street singer. It is no great stretch to
conjecture that the remarkable variation between editions of these songs
reflects a dialogue between printer and singer, the former responding to
the particular innovations and interpretations of the latter, and enabling

[25] For three variants of the first, spanning some fifty years, see BL Ballads 1606.aa.24 (42),
Bod. Harding B 28(259), and Bod. Firth c.21(2); Bod. Harding B 20(5); Bod. Harding
B 11(1264).
[26] A song of 1835 by a Mr Glindon, arranged by J. T. Craven: BL Scores I.530.i (19).
[27] Bod. Johnson Ballads 466.
[28] Bod. Firth c.21(4). For a fuller history of the song, see Hepburn, Scattered Leaves, vol. 2,
488–93.
[29] The Swell's Night Guide: or, a Peep through the Great Metropolis (New edn, 1846), 39.
[30] Bod. Firth c.21(7).

purchasers to buy the song as they had seen and heard it done by whichever seller had thus entertained them. Meanwhile, to a lesser street interpreter, the revised text provided a blueprint from which to construct a persona more successful than their own.

My point in this interlude is a simple one. Of all our source types, songs are perhaps the most open to interpretation. Only by attending to the contexts of their performance can we gain the insights necessary to speculate with any degree of security as to how they may have been received. If, then, the performance, not the original text, is where the ballad-singer may actually be found, then 'Oh! Cruel', the condescending elite creation, becomes as subversive and enabling a foundation as the street-authored, self-aggrandising 'Billy Nutts'. In a real singer's mouth, 'Oh! Cruel' could damn the navy; glamorise licentiousness; even trouble the world view of passing elites. Thus the represented singer lost her fixity, gaining the power to surprise, confound, or subvert. It is the crowning irony of 'Oh! Cruel' that this travestied depiction of a ballad-singer, by virtue of its form *as a song*, was susceptible to the destabilising agency of the very singer its writer sought to belittle.

# 2 Progress
## Ancient Custom in the Modern City

---

'The common people are to be caught by the ears as one catches a pot by the handle'[1]

'Curse those Ballad singers what a noise they make.' So speaks the caricature of Richard Brinsley Sheridan in Figure 1.8. This imagined version of Sheridan uses the standard vocabulary of respectable London – 'noise' – to condemn the singer behind him. As John Picker observes of a later generation: 'The most damning method of attacking street music . . . was to deny its very musicality.'[2] The same may be said of the song's lyrical content. Yet we, the caricature's viewers, can see that the singer's 'noise' is in fact highly articulate and even witty: she is singing a new song called 'Sherry done over'. Sheridan has just lost the Westminster election of May 1807, a defeat often attributed to William Cobbett's campaign against him in his *Political Register*, then a middling paper sold for ten pence.[3] Yet the caricature hints at a more demotic cause: the voting public has been influenced, not by the respectable press, but by the ballad-singer. As Douglas Jerrold wrote as late as 1840, this singer could serve as a 'loud-mouthed advocate of party zeal', every bit as crucial to the election as its more formal officials:

He takes temporary promotion at an election, merging the mendicant in the more honourable appointment of party-minstrel. He sings the merits of the new candidate, and exposes the frailties and venalities of his opponent, with a modesty and energy that sometimes reminds us of the House of Commons. The Ballad-Singer . . . is, indeed, a parliamentary agent of no small importance; he may take rank with the solicitor, the professional friend of the candidate; and, if his voice

---

[1] François VI de La Rochefoucauld, unattributed quotation in Charles Hindley, *Curiosities of Street Literature* (1871), frontispiece.

[2] John M. Picker, 'The Soundproof Study: Victorian Professionals, Work Space, and Urban Noise', *Victorian Studies* 42 (2000): 427–53, 442.

[3] A. Norman Jeffares, 'Sheridan, Richard Brinsley (1751–1816)', *ODNB*, oxforddnb.com/view/article/25367.

and style of singing have won a few votes for his employer, they have doubtless been as honestly obtained as many procured by the man of law[.][4]

In the interlude following this chapter, I will return (unlike Sheridan) to the Westminster elections, in pursuit of a party-political history of ballad singing that has only recently begun to be written.[5] Yet the parliamentary election was only one of many contexts in which singers exerted political, moral, or social influence, leading to the widespread belief – epitomised by this chapter's epigram and first discussed in this book's Introduction – that 'the common people' responded more to the messages in song than to those in sermons, pamphlets, and the statute book. And certainly, all these areas had their treatment in song. Charles Manby Smith, one of the medium's antiquarians, wrote that:

The popular ballad, Seven Dials born, treats of all popular subjects – it is political, warlike, amatory … it plunges into questions of moral[ity] and religion, of teetotalism, of sabbatarianism, of patriotism and legislation, and is diffuse and humanely indignant on the matter of wife beating.[6]

This all-encompassing topicality placed the singer – a figure whose personal status was beyond and beneath society – at the very centre of London life, her or his function being, like the fool of a medieval court, to articulate unlicensed commentary on current affairs. In this chapter I wish to explore this time-honoured role, coming to conceive of it as one that was increasingly seen as inimical to the programmes of modernity and improvement. Since the French Revolution in particular, fears of ballad singing's malign influence were usually structured around one of two themes: its effects in the moment of performance, primarily located in the physical realm; and its effects upon the subsequent behaviour of listeners, chiefly in terms of mentality and opinion – themes that, though argued separately by contemporaries, were closely related within an overarching framework of (non-radical) *progress*. By the nineteenth century, the ballad-singer represented an undesirably anachronistic way of negotiating issues within society, and it is this conflict between the traditional and the modern that lay at the heart of the ballad singing 'problem' in the city, more than that between high and low, or between order and chaos. In interrogating those two related themes of the balladeer's challenge to progress – first the immediate (embodied) and then the subsequent (moral, political) effects of ballad singing upon the urban and social order – I will demonstrate this inherently

---

[4] Jerrold, 'The Ballad-Singer', 294.
[5] See the following interlude for the existing literature, of which the most comprehensive treatment is Bowan and Pickering, *Sounds of Liberty*, esp. 140–64.
[6] Charles Manby Smith, *The Little World of London; or, Pictures in Little of London Life* (1857), 253.

*chronological* tension to be central not only to the social and political importance of the ballad-singer, but to the operation and development of nineteenth-century London. I move from defining and theorising elite concerns, to tracking these in practice, to an analysis of attempts to overcome this 'problem' and why they failed, before concluding with two paradigmatic case studies, one from each end of the period, in order to contend that the greatest foe of the potent, influential, and remarkably resilient ballad-singer was not simply the policeman, or the moral reformer, but the idea of progress itself.

### The Disreputable Singer

As discussed in Chapter 1, while much of the anxiety occasioned by the singer stemmed from the content of their songs and the manner of their performances, this also mapped on to the singer's body – in representation, but also in fact. As individuals, ballad-singers could offend propriety in their appearance and their character. This was the most basic level on which singers could be a barrier to progress: if, as individuals, they conspicuously embodied a state of unimprovement. In the first instance, singers were often assumed to be drunk.[7] There is some evidence for this: in 1841 a ballad-singer was killed when he was hit by an omnibus, the vehicle's driver being exonerated on the grounds that the singer had been lying drunk in the street for some time,[8] while in 1856 James Cookney, 'an itinerant ballad-singer', was sentenced to three months' hard labour for exposing himself indecently to passers-by, his defence being that he had 'met some gentlemen, who were so pleased with his singing that they gave him one pint of beer, and that made him drunk'.[9] But there was also an influential body of contemporary legal and medical thought that linked singing in public to inebriation, as singing was held to be symptomatic of a loss of self-control due to an exacerbation of the physical passions.[10] In the late eighteenth century this was particularly undesirable against a backdrop of revolution: public performers could not be permitted

---

[7] 'State of the Poor', *Morning Post* 18403 (5 December 1829).

[8] 'Police Intelligence', *Morning Post* 22123 (13 December 1841) and 22125 (15 December 1841).

[9] 'Police Intelligence', *Morning Chronicle* 27931 (2 July 1856).

[10] Penelope Gouk, 'Music and the Nervous System in Eighteenth-Century British Medical Thought', in James Kennaway (ed.), *Music and the Nerves, 1700–1900* (Basingstoke, 2014), 44–71; Aris Sarafianos, '"Subsiding Passions" and the Polite Arts of Healing: Music and Images of the Medical Profession in "Moderate Enlightenment"', ibid., 118–51. See also Penelope Gouk and Helen Hills (eds.), *Representing Emotions: New Connections in the Histories of Art, Music and Medicine* (Aldershot, 2005) and, for instances of the legal profession, POB t17830723-94, t17870221-29, t18010520-38, t18240114-128, t18420103-595, t18440205-798.

such excesses. In the nineteenth century, this form of excess was antithetical to a growing discourse of self-discipline, restraint, and even teetotalism.

In the second instance, singers were suspect due to their inherent mobility as denizens of the public highways. Some were long-distance itinerants, and even those who operated more locally were transgressive in their movements, constantly crossing between the jurisdictions of different parishes and corporations.[11] An 1841 parliamentary report on gaols emphasised the peripatetic nature of criminal singers, such as the 'wandering ballad singer that had been a sailor' executed for aggravated rape, and the seven 'strangers' and one 'foreigner', against one 'dweller in Sussex', in the category of 'Itinerant musicians and ballad singers' brought to trial in that county.[12] Their mobility not only resisted forms of jurisdiction founded on geographical boundaries, but threatened a society that privileged domesticity and order. When in 1829 'Elizabeth Smith, who is a ballad-singer about the streets', 'decoyed' and robbed two four-year-olds, having first 'enticed them from their homes, by giving them a number of her ballads', she transgressed the boundaries between the private and the public that were increasingly insisted upon by genteel city-dwellers.

## Impediments to Progress: The Crowd

In these respects, ballad-singers were posing the same challenges that they had for centuries, occasioning the same worries that Elizabethan burghers had entertained about 'masterless men'.[13] If the fear of the mobile and the disreputable was particularly heightened in this period, it was far from new, and singers were no more problematic in this regard than dustmen, beggars, or pedlars generally.[14] While the mobility of individual singers remained as problematic as ever, however, their activities caused a greater physical problem more specific to the advent of modernity: not of mobility, but of stasis. Successful ballad-singers, like the buskers that followed them, gathered crowds around them. And from the late eighteenth

---

[11] For much more on the movements of singers, see Oskar Cox Jensen, 'The *Travels* of John Magee: Tracing the Geographies of Britain's Itinerant Print-Sellers, 1789–1815', *Journal of Cultural and Social History* 11 (2014): 195–216.

[12] House of Commons Parliamentary Papers, 1841. Gaols. Copies of all reports, and of schedules (B.) transmitted to the Secretary of State . . . (1842), 185–6.

[13] See especially Hitchcock, *Vagrancy in English Society*, and Patricia Fumerton, *Unsettled: The Culture of Mobility and the Working Poor in Early Modern England* (Chicago, 2006).

[14] Brian Maidment makes these same points throughout his *Dusty Bob*.

century, the street crowd became reconceptualised as a significant threat, not to the political order, but to capital.

In generating crowds of idlers, ballad-singers committed a double sin against property. Most obviously, they were accused of aiding and abetting pickpockets. In 1816, the Lord Mayor of London asserted that:

[G]roups of persons were collected in the streets, particular in St. Paul's Churchyard, where, while a man or woman attempted to amuse the passengers, by singing ballads, the light-fingered gentry were no less actively engaged in picking pockets ... he had the fact from indubitable authority, that ballad-singers, and such persons, were leagued with, and in pay of, pick-pockets.[15]

It seems implausible that ballad-singers were systematically colluding with criminals. In seven trials between 1802 and 1856 (there must have been many more cases which, due to their mundane nature, never had their details made available to the public), men and women testified that they had been pickpocketed while standing to hear a ballad-singer.[16] Yet in only one case, in Holborn, 1853, was the Lord Mayor's assertion borne out and a connection proven between thief and singer.[17] The singer's offence was generally against the spirit, not the letter, of the law: the fault lay in gathering crowds at all, in causing otherwise industrious citizens to become so idle and distracted that they might allow their pockets to be picked.

Certainly, this was the rationale behind the singer's second sin: that by creating crowds they endangered, not merely the petty cash and handkerchiefs of passers-by, but the progress of capital *through* the modern city. Productive citizens, in idling, became unproductive, and by massing together in the street they impeded the flow of the traffic that underpinned London's commercial prosperity. The former point was emphasised by Jane Taylor in a morally didactic 1809 book 'for Good Children':

What a set of idle folks are gathered round that poor ballad-singer, listening to her silly songs! There is Betty the waiting maid, who was sent in a great hurry to the washer-woman's, while her mistress is waiting to go out; and Tom the porter, with a parcel for the Harwick Mail, that will set off in a few minutes; and Sam the foot-boy, who was sent post haste to the doctor's, as his master was taken very ill; and half a score more idle folks, who ought to be minding their business.[18]

[15] 'Police', *Examiner* 457 (29 September 1816): 623.
[16] POB t18020918-128, t18180114-124, t18350511-1339, t18420131-659; *Morning Chronicle* 15696 (20 August 1819); 'Police Intelligence', *Bell's Life in London and Sporting Chronicle* (19 June 1836); 'Police Intelligence', *Morning Post* 25650 (19 March 1856).
[17] 'The Police Courts', *Daily News* 2358 (10 December 1853).
[18] Jane Taylor, *City Scenes; or, A Peep into London, for Good Children* (1809), 41.

The scene Taylor critiques is the inverse of that idealised in later Victorian paintings of hypermodern industry, busyness, and circulation, such as George Elgar Hicks' 1860 *The General Post Office, One Minute to Six* or Ford Madox Brown's 1865 *Work*. The second and related point – that idle crowds compromised not only their own productivity but that of the wider commercial system – is hinted at in the eloquent construction of Georg Christoph Lichtenberg, a physicist and travel writer who visited London in the later eighteenth century, remarking upon 'the ballad singers who, forming circles at every corner, dam the stream of humanity which stops to listen and steal'.[19] While Lichtenberg's superficial concern relates to pickpockets, the phrase 'dam the stream of humanity' introduces the idea of obstruction, of blockage, in a road system increasingly reconfigured for constant progress.

In this regard, the 'nuisance' caused by singers represents nothing less than a collision of two worldviews. On the one hand – that of the singers and their audiences – a view that has now passed, rooted in a medieval and early modern conception of the public street as an extension of the marketplace: a space in which to linger; to conduct pleasure and, above all, business. For centuries, Londoners had been accustomed to do much of their shopping in the open street, buying groceries and services from street traders, socialising, and listening to and purchasing ballads. On the other hand, a view that (in the developed west) has triumphed: a modern reconceptualisation of the street as an unobstructed conduit for productive traffic, conveying goods and people, and organised to facilitate progress. Legislation to keep left was first applied to London Bridge – where commercial traffic was heaviest – in 1756; in 1835 it passed (not without opposition) into law across the country.[20] Proponents of improvement championed this new conception of the single-purpose street as a space of linear progress, likening it to the circulation of the blood in a healthy human body. Physical barriers were as objectionable as mercantilist regulations to Smithian free-market capitalists, and while much of the best recent scholarship on urban improvement has documented ideologically driven alterations to the *built* environment – such as market crosses, or, eventually, Fleet Street's Temple Bar – these went hand in hand with a programme of 'change to ways of ordering the urban population'.[21] The singer who gathered a crowd by a market cross was

[19] Cited in Robert Shoemaker, *The London Mob: Violence and Disorder in Eighteenth-Century England* (2004). Lichtenberg was writing in 1770.
[20] Mick Hamer, 'Left is Right on the Road', *New Scientist* (20 December 1986/ 1 January 1987): 16–17.
[21] Bob Harris and Charles McKean, *The Scottish Town in the Age of the Enlightenment, 1740–1820* (Edinburgh, 2014), 7. See also ibid., 103–34.

as much of an obstruction as that cross itself, and was consequently problematised – in a metaphorical language that owned its debt to William Harvey's circulatory theories – as a clot.[22] To the modern improver, then, the singer's crowd was not only undesirable, but anachronistic: a relic from an earlier mode of organising urban society that was antithetical to progress.

This definition of progress, based on the advancement of capital rather than of happiness, did not go unopposed by reformers of a more democratic stamp, to whom the ancient customs of the people were an inalienable foundation of English liberty. As such, this aspect of urban improvement was understood as part of a wider struggle, encompassing resistance to Pitt's Seditious Meetings Act of 1795 – which restricted the public right to assembly – and even the Peterloo Massacre of 1819. Indeed, two months after the latter event, the *Morning Chronicle* classed the dispersal of crowds assembled to listen to ballad-singers among the 'most wanton exercise[s] of authority' perpetrated by magistrates.[23] And in 1836, the radical *Examiner* launched an extensive tirade when a pair of 'very decently dressed' ballad-singers were brought before the Marlborough Street magistrate Mr Conant and 'charged with singing in the streets'.[24] Taking particular issue with the injunction to the singers that they must not 'collect crowds', the newspaper framed the issue satirically as one of class conflict:

To sing in the streets and to collect crowds is, in the worshipful opinion of Mr Conant, reprehensible as an idle mode of life; but in what material circumstance does singing in the streets to collect crowds differ from singing in the Opera House to collect crowds[?] Oh! the obstruction of a thoroughfare. And is there no obstruction of the Haymarket, of Charles street, and Waterloo place, every Tuesday night and Saturday night, nay, every Sunday morning? What obstruction did a street singer ever create to be compared with the throng of carriages and servants about the King's Theatre[?]

The journalist's rhetoric reconfigures the debate around the idea of a hypocritical elite, rather than contesting the necessity for free-flowing traffic. They conclude: 'Would it not be cheaper, as well as more humane, to empower the police simply to keep order and an open thoroughfare?' Fundamentally, then, the *Examiner* spoke for modernity. But the local

---

[22] See especially Richard Sennet, *Flesh and Stone: The Body and the City in Western Civilization* (New York, 1994), 256–71 and 323; Lynda Nead, *Victorian Babylon: People, Streets and Images in Nineteenth-Century London* (New Haven, 2000), 5, 163; and Joanna Hofer-Robinson, *Dickens and Demolition: Literary Afterlives and Mid-Nineteenth-Century Urban Development* (Edinburgh, 2018), 2–3.

[23] 'Warrington, Oct 27', *Morning Chronicle* 15757 (30 October 1819).

[24] 'Law for the Poor', *Examiner* 1481 (19 June 1836).

community involved in the case may have felt differently. 'A respectable person, living in the buildings, was quite sure that none of his neighbours would have considered their singing as a nuisance.' The locals did not object to the presence of the singers and their crowd, which posed no threat or inconvenience to those within the immediate area, but only to those attempting to move *through* the district.

In the issue of the crowd, then, we have our first intimation of variance between the attitudes of a community, accustomed to the activities of singers, and the concerns of legislators and the press, involved in a contestation over the form improvement should take but both committed to the basic principle of progress. While the politicisation of space was an extremely sensitive issue,[25] and the ballad-singing debate undoubtedly concerned freedoms of assembly and – as expanded upon throughout this book – of expression, the most pressing issue for authorities *at the moment of performance* was the jeopardisation of freedom of movement, caused by the generation of static, unproductive crowds. Thus the singer and her persecutors were separated by an irreconcilable gulf that was, at heart, chronological, between early modern and modern conceptions of civic order, in which the street was a space for either congress or progress. As we shall see, the fault lines along which this issue split were much the same when it came to the second – and perhaps the greater – realm in which the singer's actions were construed as an impediment to progress: that of the influence of their songs upon the people.

## Impediments to Progress: The Song

In this second, more substantial section of the chapter, I turn from the physical to the mental, beginning by identifying the fears of the establishment in the discourse on ballad-singers and the root cause of these concerns, before documenting why these fears were generally justified in both theory and practice. I examine the attempts of authorities to solve the ballad-singer problem, all of which – whether prohibitive or, more interestingly, co-optive – proved ineffectual – and, finally, I situate the explanation for that failure within the same framework of anachronism that characterised the physical nuisance posed by singers. Of course, the two issues – physical and mental – were frequently entangled, as becomes apparent when we examine the presence of ballad-singers on corners by St Paul's churchyard, a traditional haunt of balladeers in the City of London itself ever since the Tudor period.

---

[25] On which, the most comprehensive recent authority is Katrina Navickas, *Protest and the Politics of Space and Place, 1789–1848* (Manchester, 2017).

In April 1807, a contributor to the literary journal *The Director* found himself, with a companion, on just such a corner. '[A] number of people stopping for an opportunity to cross the way, a ballad singer and guitar player approached the crowd; and just as they were going to *strike up*, I found that I had been separated from my friend.'[26] This writer – an engaged, modern, educated individual committed to improvement – had fallen foul of the singer's obstructive crowd, of which he himself took no part. Physically, he had been inconvenienced. But his entitled sense of self precluded the possibility that he could be susceptible to a more pernicious danger: the corrupting influence of the singer's performance. To grasp this danger, we might go back a generation to John Raphael Smith's 1775 mezzotint of a ballad-singer stationed in the same position, on a street corner near St Paul's (Figure 2.1). Smith's print, after a painting by George Carter, is ostensibly a portrait of the aged singer John Massie, a sentimental image celebrating a known individual described by Jeroen Salman as appearing 'unassertive'.[27] Yet it may be read as presenting – however unintentionally – a more troubling encounter. The powerful singer looms forth from the shadows, towering over the listening nurse-maid and the curious boy, whose expression and posture appear to indicate either rapt attention or some debilitating illness. Perhaps (to recall the etymology of the word *influenza*) it is both, since the two states were linked in the rhetoric of disapproving commentators, who feared the contagious effect of street ballads upon the irrational and mentally deficient orders of the metropolis: that is, the lower orders, young women, and children.

To improvers, this mental influence was the gravest threat posed by singers. As one commentator wrote with bitter irony in 1812: 'Can any thing be more *moral?* How *improving* to the rising generation! How admirably calculated for *finishing* the youthful passenger's education! I wish these ... male-itinerant singers, with their "filthy tunes," were sent to thump hemp in Bridewell.'[28] From this perspective, Smith's dumbstruck boy in Figure 2.1 was symptomatic (the vocabulary of disease is pertinent here) of worries about respectable children in the street, either unaccompanied or chaperoned by equally irrational beings, where 'not a ballad-singer can escape their notice, and not unfrequently ballads are purchased by them to be read or sung at their own homes, by the nurses &c'.[29] Parents were advised to 'beware of [their children] loitering on their errands at any ... ballad-stall, where dangerous articles are put into the

---

[26] 'Rusticus', *Director* 2, no. 16 (9 May 1807): 101.     [27] Salman, *Pedlars*, 67–9.
[28] *Metropolitan Grievances; or, a Serio-Comic Glance at Minor Mischiefs in London and Its Vicinity* (1812), 104.
[29] C-RS, 'Ballad-Singers', *Scourge*, 7 (1814): 378.

Figure 2.1 John Raphael Smith after George Carter, 'The Old Ballad Singer', 1775.
Mezzotint. Heritage Image Partnership Ltd / Alamy

hands of our youths'.[30] Employers too were warned of 'the troops of ballad singers, who disseminate sentiments of dissipation in minds which should have been bred in principles of industry and sobriety',[31] while in the turbulent year of Peterloo, concerned activists founded the *Patriot: A Periodical Publication, Intended to Arrest the Progress of Seditious and Blasphemous Opinions, Too Prevalent in the Year 1819*, in part to

[30] 'Tradesman', *Advice to the Labourer, the Mechanic, and the Parent* (c.1800), 11.
[31] Cited in Roy Palmer (ed.), *A Touch on the Times: Songs of Social Change, 1770–1914* (Harmondsworth, 1974), 13.

denounce the activities of 'persons travelling in the garb of Ballad Singers' in spreading 'Seditious publications'.[32]

As theorised in this book's Introduction, contagion of this kind – like its physical counterpart – was believed to spread most easily in a crowd:

The effects of the fulsome, obscene, and improper songs that are sung to a surrounding *mob*, composed of people of all ages, who affect the sneering grin or fascinating look, when any thing ludicrous or infamous is expressed, must assuredly be stamped and riveted on the imagination, and ultimately corrupt the morals of the idle crowd.[33]

The most prominent voice of censure was Patrick Colquhoun, a London magistrate, administrator, and theorist, who lamented that: 'Ballad-singers are suffered often to insult decency and disseminate poison in every street in the Metropolis.'[34] Reinforcing the connection between message and medium – that is, between the singer's physical and moral transgressions – even their style of performance was figured as a corrupting influence. One evangelical writer spoke with horror of an otherwise respectable congregation: 'some of the girls … sung the praises of God just as if they had been ballads; and tossed their bonnets back, and let their cloaks hang about their shoulders as if they were ballad singers. It is a wonder that shame does not keep girls from doing such things!'[35]

These concerns recall the criminal transgressions with which we began: that the low character of the street could penetrate into the realm of middling domestic respectability. Singers operated in public space but the influence of their songs carried, like an infection, into the home, where – as with infection – the weakest were most at risk. In contemporary discourse, this meant children, women (especially young women), and the unlearned. In 1816, the influential pedagogue John Bigland neatly summarised the consensus in unusually optimistic language:

Popular songs are the species of poetry which, in every country, has the most powerful and the most extensive influence. They are diffused among all classes of the people: they animate the mariner on board of his vessel, the mechanic in his workshop, and the peasant in following his plough. The songs and ballads of a country influence the morals and manners, and even the principles of its inhabitants, as much, perhaps, as any adventitious circumstance whatever[.][36]

---

[32] *Patriot*, 6 (1819): 93–4.    [33] C-RS, 'Ballad-Singers', 378.

[34] Patrick Colquhoun, *A Treatise on the Police of the Metropolis* (6th edn, 1800), 349. See also Patrick Colquhoun, *A Treatise on the Functions and Duties of a Constable* (1803), 6.

[35] Anon., *Religious Tracts, Dispersed by the Society for Promoting Christian Knowledge*, 12 vols. (1800), vol. 12, 29.

[36] John Bigland, *An Historical Display of the Effects of Physical and Moral Causes on the Character and Circumstances of Nations* (1816), 308.

As attested by numerous court proceedings and tacitly acknowledged by Bigland, ballads were in fact heard, read, and bought by all levels of society, yet those who were in a position to contribute to the written discourse clearly considered themselves immune to the detrimental effects of song. Even contemporary dictionaries defined the ballad in relation to its influence on the lower classes of society.[37] In an age characterised by bids to widen the franchise and mobilise ever-wider spheres of public engagement with political and moral questions, the threat of the ballad-singer was perhaps greater than ever before.

### '[H]er too sensitive nerves': Influence in Action

Given the conditions in which these fears were formed – by a relative elite using a patriarchal set of prejudices as criteria by which to evaluate the susceptibility of their supposed mental inferiors – it might be worth taking seriously what it was that made the ballad-singer's song such an influential form of rhetoric. If contemporary theorists spoke of a 'magic power'[38] of song and took a condescending attitude towards the nervous systems and mental faculties of their fellows, then more recent writers have located the particular potency of song in its musicalised and performative elements. In performance – as discussed further in the Introduction and in Chapter 3 – the singer claimed a temporary monopoly on narration, vocabulary, and morality, to which listeners were to a lesser or greater extent in thrall.[39] Texts disseminated in this manner had substantial advantages over those read from the page, Richard Taruskin writing that 'it is the all but irresistible kinaesthetic response that music evokes that makes it such a potent influence on behaviour, thence on morals and belief'.[40] Bruce Smith develops this premise, asserting that 'In the first instance at least, ballads belong not on a broadside … but in lungs, larynx, and mouth, in arms and hands, legs and feet.'[41] His argument is one of amplification, of this bodily existence literalising and magnifying the text being sung, which 'interact[s] in highly volatile ways with the physical body, with soundscapes, with speech communities, with political authority, with the singer's sense of self'.[42] Booth stresses that: 'As opposed to speaking, singing of words joins the single self with its

[37] See, for example, POB t18040704-14, t18041024-43, t18151206-160; and George Gregory, *A Dictionary of Arts and Sciences*, 2 vols. (1806), vol. 1, 197.
[38] See the Introduction.    [39] See also Cox Jensen, *Napoleon*, 31, 33–4, 38–9.
[40] Richard Taruskin, 'The Danger of Music and the Case for Control', in his *The Danger of Music and Other Anti-Utopian Essays* (Berkeley and Los Angeles, 2009), 168–80, 169.
[41] Bruce R. Smith, *The Acoustic World of Early Modern England* (Chicago, 1999), 170.
[42] Ibid., 173.

community', elaborating that: 'Because song comes to us in a voice, without dramatic context, to pass through the consciousness of the listener, it fosters some degree of identification between singer and audience.'[43] Here he follows the pioneering if idiosyncratic ethnomusicologist Alan Lomax in stressing the formal *limitations* of song as being partially responsible for this effect, Lomax stating that: 'The high redundancy level of song has many consequences. Song is essentially louder and more arresting than speech. It shouts across social space and across human time as well, since its formal patterns are both emphatic and easy to remember.'[44] To Booth, this 'is the description of ritual. The individual member of the audience enters into a common pattern of thought, attitude, emotion, and achieves by it concert with his society.'[45] Smith does not construe this act on the part of the singer as a loss of self, however, writing that 'In singing the ballad alone, in performing it for others, even in performing it *with* others, the singer perforce becomes the titular hero.'[46] To Lomax, this was a defining feature of the British ballad-singer as an unlikely authority figure, akin to a lawyer, priest, or doctor as a (rather shabby) pillar of the community: 'His association with his audience is, in sociological terms, one of exclusive authority, a principal model for conduct in Western European culture.'[47]

In practice, this potency resulted in instances when ballad singing had direct and palpable consequences, usually construed as detrimental to the morality or social utility of those in the audience. Two separate contributors to *The Child's Companion*, an evangelical magazine with a large circulation, reported their observations of the pernicious effect of balladsingers upon the actions of specific groups of children.[48] In an evangelical memoir, an anonymous Clerkenwell printer recalls his own childhood 'corruption', dating his fall to 1823 when exposure to low ballads in the taproom of a public house led him into 'absurdity, profanity, and obscenity'.[49] Among the elite, meanwhile, the invasive effect of a song in domestic space, working to corrupt women and children in particular, is realised in the *Reminiscences* of Henry Angelo, who relates how as a child he was rated midshipman and 'intended for the sea; but here again the

[43] Booth, *Experience*, 19, 15.
[44] Alan Lomax, 'The Good and the Beautiful in Folksong', *Journal of American Folklore* 80, no. 317 (1967): 213–35, 219.
[45] Booth, *Experience*, 15.    [46] Smith, *Acoustic World*, 203.
[47] Alan Lomax, 'Song Structure and Social Structure', *Ethnology* 1 (1962): 425–51, 439–40.
[48] 'Ballad Singers', *The Child's Companion or Sunday Scholar's Reward* 9 (September 1824): 85; 'Hide and Seek', *The Child's Companion* 4 (April 1838): 98.
[49] Robert Maguire (ed.), *Scenes from My Life, by a Working Man* (1858), 25–6.

tenderness of a mother interposed, and her singing the favourite air in Thomas and Sally, "*For my true love is gone to sea,*" operating on her too sensitive nerves, frequently set her weeping; and my infantine sympathy making me do the like, the blue jacket ... was laid aside'.[50] Though no ballad-singer was involved upon this occasion, the sentimental song 'For My True Love is Gone to Sea' still worked its influence to the ultimate detriment of the state, diminishing the ranks of the Royal Navy by one.

Angelo's anecdote, steeped in a context of sentimental engagement with culture, is thoroughly of its time as a late eighteenth-century response to song. In the tragic case of Mary Bailey, however, the influence of the ballad-singer, and the spatial context of their performance, may be seen to typify a more early modern archetype: that of the female servant positioned in the liminal domestic space of the threshold, vulnerable to the destabilising influence of the street itinerant.[51] Note too (as this will be discussed further) that, while the lurid news item that formed the subject of the performance was one of national interest, it affected its individual auditor – Mary Bailey – by virtue of its explicit parallels to her own situation. On 26 July 1815, London was rocked by news of a controversial bloodletting. Not the battle of Waterloo, the full horror of which was already being subsumed into public celebrations, but the execution for murder of 22-year-old domestic servant Elizabeth Fenning, whose arrest, trial, and hanging ran roughly parallel to the Hundred Days and caused almost as much comment. As Hindley writes: 'Few cases ever excited greater interest in the public mind or caused more street-papers to be sold.'[52] Public opinion deemed her innocent; ten thousand attended her Bloomsbury funeral; her story continued to attract scholarly and literary interest throughout the century.[53] Vic Gatrell and Patty Seleski have each used the case to interrogate the development of public opinion and middle-class receptiveness to a radical narrative, in accounts centred on press discourse and prose pamphlets.[54] But its mediation by the

---

[50] *Reminiscences of Henry Angelo; With Memoirs of His Late Father and Friends*, 2 vols. (1830), vol. 1, 109. Many thanks to Joanne Bailey for directing me to Angelo. For the song, see BL Mus G.321.b (2), *The Overture with the Songs in Thomas and Sally As perform'd at the Theatre Royal in Covent Garden by Mr Beard, Mr Mattocks, Miss Brent and Miss Poitier. Compos'd by Dr. Arne* (1765), 7.

[51] Emma Whipday, *Shakespeare's Domestic Tragedies: Violence in the Early Modern Home* (Cambridge, 2019), esp. sub-section 'Liminality and Danger: at the Thresholds of the Home', 119–28.

[52] Charles Hindley, *The Life and Times of James Catnach* (1878), 79.

[53] Alsager Vian, 'Fenning, Elizabeth (1793–1815)', rev. J. Gilliland, *ODNB*, oxforddnb .com/view/article/9292.

[54] Vic Gatrell, *The Hanging Tree: Execution and the English People, 1770–1868* (Oxford, 1994), 339–40, 353–70; and Patty Seleski, 'Domesticity Is in the Streets: Eliza

ballad-singer proved every bit as influential, and rather more problematic to the ideals of progress.

On Tuesday, 8 August, two weeks after Fenning's execution, another 22-year-old domestic servant, Mary Bailey, was found dead in Kennington on the south side of the river. The *Morning Chronicle* gave this account of the subsequent inquest:

It appeared on the evidence of Mrs Tankerville, a washer-woman, and others, that the last time the deceased was seen alive was about eight o'clock on Tuesday morning. After having breakfasted she went and stood for a time at the street door listening to a ballad-singer, singing one of those doleful ditties composed on the death of Eliza Fenning; the deceased bought one, and sighed 'ah, poor Eliza!' She then went from the door, was missed shortly afterwards, and was not to be found.[55]

Bailey had in fact retired upstairs to cut her own throat with 'a large carving knife'. The inquest concluded that 'No cause appeared for her committing this rash deed, further than her master giving her warning to quit his service on the preceding night. Verdict—*Insanity.*' This verdict presumably allowed Bailey a Christian burial, while sparing her erstwhile employer the need to examine his conscience over her dismissal: a convenient result all round. But mad or not, one salient feature of the tragedy is Bailey's self-identification with Fenning, and the affective role of her encounter with the ballad-singer in shaping her mood, response, and – possibly – her fatal act of violence. The only surviving song on Fenning's execution, 'Lines on the Death of Eliza Fenning', published by John Pitts, might easily have influenced the susceptible Bailey if appropriately performed: its four brief, accessible verses make a martyr out of Fenning, extolling her white dress and 'lovely head', and concluding that 'angels bore her soul to heaven'.[56] Though the tune is not specified, any simple melody could have added a dangerous degree of pathos to the lines, resulting in a potent example to set a vulnerable servant.[57] Two young women, two and a half miles apart, linked perhaps causally by the singer's agency: a singer standing in the

Fenning, Public Opinion and the Politics of Private Life', in Tim Harris (ed.), *The Politics of the Excluded*, c.1500–1850 (Basingstoke, 2001), 265–90.

[55] 'Suicide', *Morning Chronicle* 14440 (15 August 1815).

[56] 'Lines on the Death of Eliza Fenning Executed at Newgate July 26 1815'. The lines are reproduced in Gatrell, *The Hanging Tree*, 353–4; the original is in Cambridge University Library's Madden Collection, London Printers 2, Item no. 466.

[57] The structure – an ABAB rhyme scheme with four stresses in each line – would fit many melodies, though interestingly *not* the only tune with a direct connection, the seventeenth-century 'The Ladies' Fall'. This is the tune specified for an earlier ballad featuring the same woodcut – eerily enough, a cautionary tale of a young woman's suicide. See Bod. Douce Ballads 1(87b). In the accompanying recordings I have chosen a melody by Charles Dibdin the Elder that laments another tragic death.

street but performing and selling to those in doorways, linking house, street, and city in a shared community of experience. In this case, a very traditional form of engagement with a news story resulted in the multiplication of a tragedy, the ballad-singer's act proving fatally detrimental to the rational, progressive operation of society.

## 'A Useful Minister in Rude Society'

In the face of this palpable threat, the obvious solution was prohibition. But Regency improvers were hardly the first to legislate against ballad-singers, who had been targeted by the statute book since the reign of Elizabeth. The fact that, in our period, it was found necessary to issue further directives against them is eloquent only of these directives' failure. In 1790, the Surrey magistrates sought to forbid 'all ballad singers without exception' as part of a crackdown on unlicensed musical performance, attracting the ire of the London press in the process.[58] In 1803, Colquhoun drew attention to the legal fact that 'it is further the duty of every Constable to detect and apprehend ballad-singers ... The punishment for such offences is *fine, imprisonment,* and the *pillory.*'[59] In 1817, Samuel Taunton, a Bow Street runner, was questioned on behalf of a parliamentary select committee: 'You have stated it to be the duty of beadles to patrol the streets in the daytime, and in the evenings, for what purpose? – To remove nuisances, such as ballad-singers'.[60] In 1839, the new 'Act for Further Improving the Police in and near the Metropolis' included in clause 57 provision for police constables 'to require any street musician to depart from the neighbourhood' on pain of a penalty not to exceed forty shillings.[61] In 1864, Michael Thomas Bass MP forced through the Street Music Act that is the subject of this book's conclusion. There are two clear inferences to be drawn from this series of official actions: first, that the powers of constables and the punishments they could enforce appear to have been circumscribed, rather than increased, over time; and secondly, the existence of such a series of measures can only indicate their failure to deal with the problem. Throughout the period, singers continued their activities more or less unchecked by the law.[62]

---

[58] Cited without attribution in Mary Thale (ed.), *The Autobiography of Francis Place (1771–1854)* (Cambridge, 1972), 81.

[59] Colquhoun, *Treatise on the Functions,* 6.

[60] *New Police Report for 1817. The Second Report of the Select Committee* (1817), 594.

[61] *An Act for Further Improving the Police in and Near the Metropolis: (17th August 1839)* (1839), 12.

[62] Due in part to their peripatetic nature, habitual poverty, and the impracticality of long terms of incarceration for such minor offences, singers were almost impossible to regulate against. See Henry Mayhew, 'Labour and the Poor', *Morning Chronicle* 25009

Contemporaries were well aware of this, Colquhoun himself acknowledging that singers 'cannot be suppressed',[63] and they frequently evolved a pragmatic response: if the ballad-singer's power could not be curbed, then it might be co-opted so as to serve, rather than to impede, the smooth progress of society. Given that the singer's influence was held to be a consequence of the innate irrationality of the wider populace, persons more effectively swayed by song and sentiment than by legislation and reason – and in that sense embodying the power of traditional *custom* – then might not that populace be susceptible to good governance, and even improvement, if such campaigns were carried out by means of ballad-singers? Such was the position ultimately propounded by Colquhoun:

Even the common Ballad-singers in the streets might be rendered instruments useful under the control of a well-regulated Police, in giving a better turn to the minds of the lowest classes of the People. – They too must be amused; and why not, if they can be amused innocently? – If through this medium they can be taught loyalty to the Sovereign, love to their Country, and obedience to the Laws, would it not be wise and politic to sanction it ... in language familiar to their habits[?][64]

Though never adopted as policy by City or state, this pragmatic model of improvement was pursued by a number of interest groups. Chronologically it is where this book begins, in response to the French Revolution.[65] As a female member of John Reeves' Association for Preserving Liberty and Property against Republicans and Levellers proposed in 1792, 'through the medium of popular ballads surely much instruction might be convey'd and much patriotic spirit awakened'.[66] As amateur composer William Gardiner later recalled in rather sardonic style, 'Ballad-singers were paid, and stationed at the ends of streets, to chant the downfall of Jacobins, and the glorious administration of Mr. Pitt.'[67] In early 1795, Hannah More commenced her own well-documented campaign to reform the masses' morals through street literature; by 1798, she and Henry Thornton had conducted extensive

(15 December 1849); Alfred W. Tuer, *Old London Street Cries* (1885), 51–2; Audrey Eccles, *Vagrancy in Law and Practice under the Old Poor Law* (Farnham, 2012), 184–6.
[63] Patrick Colquhoun, *A Treatise on Indigence* (1806), 74.
[64] Colquhoun, *Treatise on the Police*, 348. This advice was later cited approvingly in the *Satirist* (May 1808): 242.
[65] See the opening pages of the Introduction.
[66] Cited in Mark Philp, 'Politics and Memory: Nelson and Trafalgar in Popular Song', in David Cannadine (ed.), *Trafalgar in History: A Battle and Its Afterlife* (Basingstoke, 2006), 93–120, 94.
[67] William Gardiner, *Music and Friends: or, Pleasant Recollections of a Dilettante*, 2 vols. (1838), vol. 1, 222.

research into singers as a preliminary to engaging their services as vendors of their *Cheap Repository* tracts; by the turn of the century, the movement was in full swing.[68] Decades later, when the ballad-singer was in terminal decline for reasons discussed towards the end of this book, Douglas Jerrold wrote approvingly of these efforts to employ singers in what he saw as the national interest:

> How many times has the Ballad-Singer, with voice no softer than the voice of Cyclops, set the nation's heart dancing! . . . He has been the poor man's minstrel, satirist, historian; nay, at certain seasons, he has been invested with almost sacerdotal gravity to prosperous men. . . . We have seen him a useful minister in rude society.[69]

Yet Jerrold's was a lone voice. For the most part, both contemporaries and subsequent historians have judged these attempts as failures – from John Clare, William Hone, and John Thomas Smith in the early nineteenth century, to scholars including Jacky Bratton, Robin Ganev, and Andrew Noble.[70] Though ballad-singers were used to sing and to distribute moralist and loyalist songs in vast numbers, their impact was judged to have been, relatively, negligible. To understand these failures, we must return to our overarching theme of chronology – for such schemes had been tried, and had failed, before.

### Andrew Fletcher's Maxim

In our period as before and after, writers who considered the possibility of harnessing the power of ballad-singers invariably quoted the same maxim in support of their position. As the poet, collector, and customs official William Allingham put it in *Household Words* in 1852, 'Any didactic essay on ballads might fairly be expected to commence with the remark that a wise old writer has said, "Let me make the ballads of a nation, and who

---

[68] Of particular interest is More's correspondence in Georgiana Chatterton (ed.), *Memorials, Personal and Historical of Admiral Lord Gambier, G.C.B.*, 2 vols. (1861), vol. 1, 274–5, 349; Leslie Shepard, *John Pitts, Ballad Printer of Seven Dials, London, 1765–1844* (1969), 32; see also Oskar Cox Jensen, 'The Ballad and the Bible', in James Grande and Brian Murray (eds.), *The Bible and Musical Culture in Nineteenth-Century Britain* (Oxford, forthcoming).

[69] Jerrold, 'The Ballad Singer', 292–3.

[70] Philip Connell and Nigel Leask (eds.), *Romanticism and Popular Culture in Britain and Ireland* (Cambridge, 2009), 29; William Hone, *The Reformists' Register and Weekly Commentary* (1817), 391–2; Smith, *Vagabondiana*, 29; Jacky Bratton, *The Victorian Popular Ballad* (1975), 140–1; Robin Ganev, *Songs of Protest, Songs of Love: Popular Ballads in Eighteenth-Century Britain* (Manchester, 2010), 201, 206; Andrew Noble, 'The Languages of Resistance: National Peculiarities, Universal Aspirations', in John Kirk, Andrew Noble, and Michael Brown (eds.), *United Islands? The Languages of Resistance* (2012), 1–33, 20. See also Cox Jensen, '*Travels*': 211–12.

will may make the laws." This saw … is somewhat rhetorical in form, and exceedingly musty'.[71] And indeed, the maxim Allingham references with unusual self-awareness is employed with total confidence in: a Dublin reference work of the start of the nineteenth century; the cleric and moral reformer James Plumptre's *Collection of Songs* of the same period; a Mancunian account of street hawkers narrowly post-dating Allingham's quip; an 1868 survey of international street song; two early twentieth-century ballad studies; and in a work of modern historical scholarship from 1997.[72] The 'wise old writer' in question was Andrew Fletcher of Saltoun, an important political theorist of the early Enlightenment era.[73] The maxim comes from his last published work, *An Account of a Conversation Concerning a Right Regulation of Governments for the Common Good of Mankind*, printed in Edinburgh in 1704: a 'letter' in the form of a recalled Socratic dialogue between Fletcher, the Earl of Cromarty, and two Tory politicians, Sir Christopher Musgrave and Sir Edward Seymour.[74] In putting the frequently abstracted and paraphrased dictum back into its original context, we may begin to perceive why the possibility it points to – for ballads to do the work of laws among the people – was invariably undermined in practice.

Fletcher's work was, formally speaking, a piece of classical political philosophy. He situates the four speakers in his text – himself, an earl, and two Tory knights – in a set of rooms in Whitehall, from where they command 'a full view of the Thames and city of London'. From this position of privileged metropolitan omniscience, Sir Christopher Musgrave observes that:

Even the poorer sort of both sexes are daily tempted to all manner of lewdness by infamous ballads sung in every corner of the streets. One would think, said the Earl, this last were of no great consequence. I said, I knew a very wise man so much of Sir Chr[istopher]'s sentiment, that he believed *if a man were permitted to make all the ballads, he need not care who should make the laws of a nation.* And we find that most of the antient legislators thought they could not well reform the

---

[71] William Allingham, 'Irish Ballad Singers and Irish Street Ballads', *Household Words* 94 (January 1852), reprinted, Hugh Shields (ed.), *Ceol* 3 (1967): 2–16, 15.

[72] *The Encyclopaedia of Anecdote* (Dublin, *c.*1800), 291; James Plumptre, *A Collection of Songs Moral, Sentimental, Instructive, and Amusing* (*c.*1803), 2; 'F. Folio', *The Hawkers and Street Dealers of Manchester and the North of England* … (Manchester, 1858), 117; 'Street Songs and their Singers', *The London: A First-Class Magazine* 3 (1868): 226–38, 234; Harold Simpson, *A Century of Ballads, 1810–1910, Their Composers and Singers* (1910), frontispiece; William Henderson (ed.), *Victorian Street Ballads: A Selection of Popular Ballads Sold in the Street in the Nineteenth Century* (1937), 9; Murray G. H. Pittock, *Inventing and Resisting Britain: Cultural Identities in Britain and Ireland, 1685–1789* (Basingstoke, 1997), 115.

[73] John Robertson, 'Fletcher, Andrew, of Saltoun (1653?–1716)', *ODNB*, oxforddnb.com/view/article/9720.

[74] Later collected in *The Political Works of Andrew Fletcher, Esq.* (1737), 365.

manners of any city without the help of a lyrick, and sometimes of a dramatick poet. But in this city ... the ballad-maker has been almost wholly employed to corrupt the people, in which they have had most unspeakable and deplorable success.[75]

Two points appear to me to be particularly significant. Firstly, Fletcher makes three choices – his literary form, his four speakers, and their physical situation – that all acknowledge the vast gulf between his elite discourse and the plebeian reality under discussion. Secondly, Fletcher's argument is as pessimistic as any nineteenth-century commentator. He laments the existing state of affairs, and holds out little hope of things changing: the bulk of ballads corrupt, rather than improve. Fletcher's maxim, thus contextualised, is not a formula for progress, but simply one more comparison of present corruption with the idealised past of the classical city-states of Greece and Rome.

Writing at the tail end of a period noted for both its moral and political turbulence, Fletcher possibly had a specific case in mind when he concluded his account so pessimistically. In 1684, the Tory publisher Nathaniel Thompson, printer of a white-letter anthology of 120 Loyal Songs, claimed to have succeeded where Colquhoun, Reeves, and More would later fail, writing in the anthology's prefatory material that:

Among the several means that have been [employed] of late years to reduce the deluded Multitude to their just Allegiance, this of BALLADS and LOYAL SONGS has not been of the least influence. ... these flying choristers [i.e. ballad-singers] were asserting the Rights of Monarchy and proclaiming Loyalty in every street. The mis-inform'd Rabble began to listen; they began to hear to Truth in a SONG, in time found their Errors, and were charm'd into Obedience. Those that despise the Reverend Prelate in the Pulpit, and the Grave Judge on the Bench; that will neither submit to the Laws of God or Man, will yet lend an itching Ear to a New SONG, nay, and often become a Convert by It, when all other means prove ineffectual ... it cannot be imagined how many scatter'd flocks this melodious Tingling hath reduced ... [to the] discipline of Obedience or Government.[76]

However, Angela McShane's extensive analysis of the case gives the lie to Thompson's boast. She concludes by contrasting Thompson's songs – printed in progressive white-letter, didactic in tone and awkward in composition, in many ways alienating to a demotic audience and only ever lasting for a single impression – with those of his competitors such as Philip Brooksby, who were more used to the ballad market: 'really excellent songs, written by some of the top songwriters of the period, and set to popular theatre tunes'.[77] Crucially, rather than advancing a moral message,

[75] Ibid., 372–3. Emphasis added to highlight the line so often paraphrased.
[76] Cited in McShane, 'Drink, Song and Politics', 184.    [77] Ibid., 185.

these black-letter ballads, many of which ran to several impressions, couched their political advocacy in sympathy with, rather than in opposition to, the disreputable practices of their context. Thus 'the highly commercial, mass-produced, mainstream market held its own values, choosing to publish only those songs and messages that would be attractive and acceptable to a nationally and socially broad popular market'.[78] Idealists such as Thompson and his later successors, however many songs they printed, could not hope to influence the masses if they did not compromise. The result, as Fletcher himself observed, was that 'unspeakable and deplorable success' remained the preserve of those songs figured by improvers as essentially corrupting in their content.

### The Unreformed Singer

We should be wary of intellectual slippage here. Most of both the contemporary and the scholarly discourse that has condemned improvers' efforts as failures has focused, not on ballad-singers, but simply on ballads. By this reasoning, it was the songs – mere versified sermons, alienating and unenjoyable – that were at fault, manifestly unfit for consumption as entertainment. So far as it goes, this argument is a convincing one, and it is one I have discussed at length in regard to the loyalist propaganda wars against the French Revolution and Napoleon towards the beginning of our period.[79] Yet it remains merely half the story without an equal attention to the role of the ballad-singers, since it was they who mediated these songs and had the greatest influence over their reception by audiences.

None of the numerous ideological campaigns sought to change the means of dissemination. To reformers as to loyalists, it was the ballad-singer's influence that was the attraction, hence the desire to co-opt existing methods for what they perceived as the public interest. Reeves' Association, the Cheap Repository Tracts movement, teetotallers, all sought to disseminate reformist songs by means of unreformed singers. But as we have seen in the first section of this chapter, it was not merely the balladeers' songs that were inimical to improvement, it was their persons and their actions as well. The essentially self-defeating irony of entrusting an improving message to unimproved singers did not go unobserved by those involved in the ballad trade. The mid-nineteenth-century ballad 'Anything to Earn a Crust' took this irony as its subject, featuring as its narrator (to be voiced by the singer) an amoral songwriter happy to turn his hand to 'sarmonizing' or impersonating a 'teetotal spouter' in

---

[78] Ibid., 185.    [79] Cox Jensen, *Napoleon.*

order to earn the titular crust.[80] Its message is plain: knowing singers would happily be subsidised by reformers and disseminate their songs. But that act could not carry the faintest trace of conviction: the nature of the mediator undermined the message.

At least in part, the tension here was chronological. Itinerant, unruly, employing the street as a space of congress, the ballad-singer was increasingly construed as an anachronism unsuited to voicing the ideals of the day. The most extensive contemporary treatments of ballad-singers were all by antiquarians. John Thomas Smith's *Vagabondiana* situated its subjects within a prefatory account of their Tudor heyday. Mayhew's 'Of Ancient and Modern Street Ballad Minstrelsy' borrowed heavily from Joseph Strutt's 1801 *Glig Gamena Angel-Deod, or, the Sports and Pastimes of the People of England*, which identified the modern 'mere singer of ballads' as an Elizabethan relic.[81] Sabine Baring-Gould's *Strange Survivals* of 1892, which included forty-one pages on ballad singing, replicated this story, while all of the above owed a debt to an essay on minstrels from Thomas Percy's 1765 *Reliques of Ancient English Poetry*.[82] Even Jerrold's 1840 essay, part of a collection celebrating and satirising modern London, is wholly saturated with nostalgia for the singer's early modern roots.

In drawing attention to this chronology, in the course of which they frequently invoked both Shakespeare and Queen Elizabeth, writers were negotiating their own modernity, creating a thoroughly national narrative in the process. This is why – to return explicitly to politics – when modernising advocates of working-class enfranchisement sought to contest their reputation as credulous, irrational, and susceptible to the influence of singers (as discussed extensively earlier), they repeatedly claimed that this anachronistic culture of ballad singing *had* been improved in the nineteenth century – and improved, not from above, but by modern, respectable working-class communities. The radical tailor Francis Place famously contended, in Vic Gatrell's words, 'that one measure of how far both he and his class had travelled was the improved character of the people's songs'.[83] In 1819, Place prepared a manuscript concerning 'Specimens of Songs and parts of Songs, (from memory) sung about the streets within my recollection and without molestation', introducing the

---

[80] Bod. Harding B 20(5).
[81] Mayhew, *London Labour*, vol. 1, 226, 274; Joseph Strutt, *Glig Gamena Angel-Deod, or, the Sports and Pastimes of the People of England* (1801), 215, and see also 142. This narrative is critiqued in Gerald Porter, 'The English Ballad Singer and Hidden History', *Studia Musicologica* 49 (2008): 127–42, 129–32.
[82] Sabine Baring-Gould, *Strange Survivals: Some Chapters in the History of Man* (1892, 2nd edn, 1894), 180–221.
[83] Gatrell, *The Hanging Tree*, 126.

work with the remark that 'It will seem incredible that such songs should be allowed but it was so.'[84] He argued that

the taste for them subsided. I have no doubt at all [that] if ballad singers were now to be left at liberty, by the police, to sing these songs[,] that the people in the streets would not permit the singing of them. Such songs as even 35 years ago produced applause would now cause the singers to be roll'd in the mud.[85]

In 1835, he made the same argument before the Select Committee on Education: that 'The whole of this is materially changed, the songs have all disappeared and are altogether unknown to young girls.'[86] His argument explicitly differentiated between the propensies of the disreputable singer, and the enforcement of new standards of decency by self-improving communities. It is an argument predicated on chronology: the singer stands for 'then', the bad old days, opposed to the deserving people who were 'now' fit to be entrusted with the franchise.

At mid-century, Mayhew argued much the same thing in the articles that became *London Labour and the London Poor*, carefully presenting interviews in which virtuous, reformed ballad-singers refused to perform indecent material, preferring the songs of teetotallers, or reflecting on the 'wickedness' of a former age.[87] And in 1861, Charles Hindley maintained in the *National Review* that

The temper of the ballads on such questions as strikes and lock-outs has struck us as singularly fair and moderate, and very creditable to the streets ... The contrast between the spirit and temper of the ballads of the present day on the questions as to which one would expect the most bitter feeling to prevail, and those of fifteen or twenty years ago, is certainly both remarkable and encouraging ... proof of a very much better state of things.[88]

The cumulative effect of these arguments, reiterated across the century, is a little unconvincing. The fact that each generation of working-class advocates disavowed the respectability of their immediate predecessors in order to advance their own cause hardly lends the narrative credibility – yet the very same consistent stress on the chronological dimension is surely of significance. Ballad-singers were acknowledged by contemporaries to be relics of a pre-modern society that, considered in terms of progress, was undesirable. A political engagement that was

[84] Francis Place, 'Notes on Grossness in Publications and Street Songs; 1705–1795', in Francis Place, *Collections Relating to Manners and Morals*, 6 vols. (BL Add MS 27825–27830, n.d.–1846), vol. 1, ff. 2–169, f. 143. Original emphasis.
[85] Ibid., ff. 144–5.
[86] Thale, *The Autobiography of Francis Place*, 57; see also xxv–xxvi.
[87] Mayhew, *London Labour*, vol. 1, 278–80.    [88] 'Street Ballads', 412, 413.

mediated by the enflamed passions, rumours, scandals, and nuisances that ballad singing entailed was held to be incompatible with the vote in an extended franchise.

## The Limitations of an Imagined Community

The chronological crux here was not the content of songs, but the conventions of their performance. Alcohol, domestic violence, faith, the monarchy, party – all these subjects had formed part of the ballad repertoire since their inception, though the paramount idea of the nation state and the British Empire represented a new imagined community less immediately accessible than anything ballad audiences had been asked to relate to in the sixteenth and seventeenth centuries. Yet the modes of performance that had mediated these subjects in the early modern period were increasingly out of step with modern ideologies. As John Street has written of 'popular' song culture in general: 'What it affects or reinforces are the politics of the everyday. Its concerns are with our pleasures and our relationships, and the intuitions that inform both.'[89] Unlike the national newspaper or the Church of England service, ballad-singers were not part of a larger institution: their performances and their individual concerns functioned at the level of the individual and relied upon human interest. It is no coincidence that the bestselling ballads of the century concerned not foreign wars, but local murders,[90] their affect generated on a personal level (remember, again, Mary Bailey); nor is it a coincidence that, when major political events did cause a sensation, they did so by accentuating the 'ordinary' aspects of their drama. Consistently, this meant that these performances were at odds with the establishment interpretation of events. Thus the single greatest stir was caused by the Queen Caroline affair, when an unprecedented volume of ballads was sold in support of the injured wife of an abusive husband.[91] A generation later, ballad-singers demonised the visiting Austrian general Julius Jacob von Haynau, not as the suppressor of revolutions, but as 'the fellow that flogged the women', while the 1850 restoration of the Catholic hierarchy was contested through the knock-about construction of 'The Pope and Cardinal Wiseman', one such performance prompting a 'skrimmage'

---

[89] Street, *Rebel Rock*, 3.

[90] Contemporary sources are unanimous on this point. See, for example, Hindley, *Curiosities*, 159.

[91] Anthony Bennett, 'Broadsides on the Trial of Queen Caroline: A Glimpse at Popular Song in 1820', *Proceedings of the Royal Musical Association* 107 (1980–1): 71–85; John Gardner, *Poetry and Popular Protest: Peterloo, Cato Street and the Queen Caroline Controversy* (Basingstoke, 2011), 159–217.

between English and Irish auditors.[92] This was how politics had been cast in ballads since their beginning – with irreverence, pathos, and bathos, conducted at the level of everyday experience.

It is easy enough to trace this approach within the texts of ballads approved of by singers. Mayhew relates a case he presents as comical that in fact epitomises this preference for the vernacular perspective:

One chaunter, who was a great admirer of the 'Song of the Shirt,' told me that if Hood himself had written the 'Pitiful Case of Georgy Sloan and his Wife,' it would not have sold so well as a ballad he handed to me, from which I extract a verse:

'Jane Willbred we did starve and beat her very hard
I confess we used her very cruel,
But now in a jail two long years we must bewail,
We don't fancy mustard in the gruel.'[93]

Hood's 'Song of the Shirt', first published in *Punch* in 1843, was a sensation among London's literary circles, yet Mayhew's 'chaunter' expresses a preference for an altogether more rooted domestic tragedy whose suffering female is, crucially, *named*, in a tightly constructed verse boasting strong internal rhymes and emphatic rhythm but above all articulating an idiomatic, censorious response to the domestic abuse of a servant.[94]

We can even trace these preferences from texts to performance practice. In his memoirs, the celebrated ballad-singer David Love, discussed in Chapter 1, gives the following account of his first successful performance:

To the fair I went, got a stool, mounted, and thus began my harangue: – 'Good people, here are two excellent new songs never before printed, composed by myself, your humble servant. One is "The Pride and Vanity of Young Women, with advice to Young Men that they may take care who they marry." And that the young women may not be offended, I have another which may serve as an answer, "The Pride and Vanity of Young Men, with advice to the Maids, to beware of being ensnared by their flatteries, and enticing words."' I soon drew hundreds about me, where I boldly stood, and there I sang aloud, before a gaping crowd: I sold all my songs the first day of the fair, and was sorry that I did not bring two thousand more songs with me; the people bought them so fast, that I could not deliver them so quick as they wanted; sometimes a dozen of hands holding out for them at once, the men buying the songs concerning the women, and the women that of the men.[95]

---

[92] Mayhew, *London Labour*, vol. 1, 226–8. As the tune is wholly unknown I have not recorded a version.
[93] Mayhew, *London Labour*, vol. 1, 220. Once again, no tune is known for this song.
[94] For the full song, see Bod. Firth c.17(107).
[95] Love, *Life, Adventures, and Experience*, 32–3.

I think we may broadly trust Love's account, especially as he represents his conduct as shameful rather than to be boasted of. He presents us with a compelling example of community formation, creating two traditional identity groups among his audience in a performance built on knowingness, low observational comedy, and a shared perception of experience and the gendered social order. This accords with the practice of later nineteenth-century *kobi* in Kolkata, who 'routinely mobilised the collective interests of the listening public by playing to different sub-sets at different points during the performance – women, lovers, office-workers and the socially less privileged'.[96] Rather than seeking to improve or instruct his audience, Love's success – like the conservative *kobi* – is predicated on a common understanding, and helps to perpetuate rather than reform social conventions.

In giving voice to such perspectives, ballad-singers were mediating an unenfranchised, demotic public sphere that eschewed both the vocabulary and the ostensibly rational codes of conduct of polite political discourse, relocating authorised opinion from the informed, classically educated orator to the affective, musicalised, idiomatic singer: an inherently subversive act equally alienating to both major parliamentary parties. In 1843, the maverick socialist botanist Johann Lhotsky recorded how he:

met two men of the tribe of ballad-singers. Instead of 'Black-eyed Susan' and the usual stock in trade of a similar class, they were chanting a duet of political conundrums; one uttering the 'Why?' the other the 'Because.' Amongst the rest they said, 'Why is Sir Robert Peel like a counterfeit shilling?' Which was responded to by the other with, 'Because he's a precious bad *Bob*.' Bob being the cant phrase for a shilling. 'Why are the Whigs and Tories like a stale fish and a stinking fish?' 'Because one is *very bad*, and the other a great deal worse.'[97]

As the *National Review* reluctantly conceded two decades later, 'the ballad-singer handles the names and doings of those who sit in high places with a familiarity scarcely equalled by Mr. Punch himself' – an admission that, while marking the 'absence of reverence' characteristic of the medium, also accorded singers an implicit equivalence with the foremost satirical organ of the respectable press.[98] Phil Eva contends that this 'amounted to a "counterculture" of industrial society, an implicit rejection of the culture of improvement and respectability, embodied by the street singers who sang and sold the broadsides'.[99] The singer's role was to provide, in the

---

[96] Ghosh, 'Singing in a New World', 120.
[97] Johann Lhotsky, *Hunger and Revolution* (1843), 29, 30.    [98] 'Street Ballads', 407.
[99] Eva, 'Home Sweet Home?', 148.

words of Patrick Joyce, 'a moral commentary [that] privileged certain views of the world and denied others' – a role 'which in turn represented rather old and long-established ways of seeing the social order'.[100] Karl Bell concurs that 'ballad conventions expressed long-established modes of imagining the social order in older, moralised contrasts'.[101]

Rather than constituting a convenient mouthpiece for established authority, then, the ballad-singer arrogated that authority to herself, and in so doing fundamentally recast the terms of political discourse, not in order to deny the existing order, but to claim a place within it. Unlike the arguments of Place or Mayhew, this was a claim to informal rather than formal enfranchisement, framed by reference to older ideas of custom. The same *National Review* article mentioned earlier concluded that: 'on the whole, the ballad-singer is a Liberal, though of an old-fashioned kind, and loses no opportunity of telling the Tories that he, for his part, does not look upon them as the men whom he desires for his rulers.'[102] Joyce writes of this culture that:

The crown is positively, even fulsomely, regarded, yet the ballads very characteristically tend to humanise the mighty by presenting them in the guise of ordinary people. In a sense the subject of such ballads is not the monarchy at all but 'ordinary people' themselves. The people were [thereby] held to be a part of the great world, their exaltation stemming from inversions of the established order which involved their inclusion in the company of their equals, the mighty, or in the great traditions of the nation.[103]

According to Mayhew this audacity in humanising, even embodying, the monarchy must have been taken quite literally by some singers, as he records one ballad performance with the refrain 'My name is Victoria the Queen', and another as being 'sung by Prince Albert in character' – two quite remarkable instances that far exceeded in their temerity anything licensed for performance on the stage.[104] In August 1856, one W. H. Smyth sent a ballad collector of his acquaintance a single slip entitled 'Gallant Cambridge Jumping Over Prince Albert', accompanying the song with a letter describing its performance one evening on Albemarle Street by a singer who 'warbled' it – to the tune of an Irish love song named after a seventeenth-century rebel – to a large 'circle' of 'unwashed' or 'gardes-noir' (literally 'blackguards').[105] This singer,

---

[100] Joyce, *Visions of the People*, 234–5, and see also 243.
[101] Karl Bell, *The Magical Imagination: Magic and Modernity in Urban England, 1780–1914* (Cambridge, 2012), 211.
[102] 'Street Ballads', 411.    [103] Joyce, *Visions of the People*, 244.
[104] Mayhew, *London Labour*, vol. 1, 227, 276.
[105] BL Ballads HS.74/1251 (222). Smyth's letter is inserted on the page preceding the ballad sheet.

described, in a phrase that the subsequent 150 years have loaded ideally for our purpose, as a 'man in the street', regaled his listeners with verses delighting in the Duke of Cambridge's promotion at the expense of the Prince Consort. Importantly and entirely typically for the medium, this major political appointment was treated in extremely colloquial, familiar terms, privileging the judgement of 'John Bull' and describing Albert's reaction thus:

> Oh crikey good gracious on last Monday night
> Bonny Albert lay down kicked and cried to his wife
> He trembled and shook like a stale cabbage leaf
> Saying I was ^not^ made a Commander-in-chief[106]
>
> Albert bawled stand at ease and he danced round the room
> He knocked down the saucepan and shouldered the broom
> He pipe-clayed his breeches and grant no reliel [sic]
> To fight for the place of Commander-in-chief

Of course, ballads on such subjects cannot always have been this irreverent towards their monarchs and masters. Yet the very fact of their performance constituted a highly contentious political statement founded in an anachronistic conception of the social order. For, as Bruce Smith writes of ballad singing in the early modern period:

Implicit in both senses of the verb *to ballad* is the idea of taking an event or a person and performing it: giving it a voice, giving it a body, appropriating it by *becoming* it. ... From the standpoint of authorities, ballads were dangerous not only for *what* they might say but for *how* they might say it. To ballet a subject was to commandeer the subject.[107]

Unregulated and unimproved, in engaging with major political and social questions, ballad-singers were reinforcing a pre-modern perspective that was inherently inimical to progressive constructions of patriotism or self-discipline. It was not until the rise of the music hall as the dominant medium of everyday culture that these ideologies could truly take hold among the populace.[108] Though the halls were on one level a direct evolution of the ballad-singer's art, on another they represented its antithesis: licensed, indoors, ticketed, subject to oversight, and their well-dressed, well-spoken star performers – the 'swells' – perfect exemplars of the capitalist system, encouraging consumption and self-betterment rather than standing for nuisance and makeshift. It was only in such

---

[106] The emendation 'not' is added by hand to the printed verse.
[107] Smith, *Acoustic World*, 188, 196.
[108] The seeds of this argument may be traced in the thesis of Bratton, *The Victorian Popular Ballad*, while the wider context for what follows is best treated in Bratton, *Music Hall*.

a system, aligned with the interests of modernity and the state, that the modern virtues could be successfully inculcated.

## The Last Dying Speech

In order to substantiate this rather broad chronological contention, we might consider the particular case of the execution ballad and its singers. By the nineteenth century, the public hanging had itself become something of an anachronism. The location most fabled in song, Tyburn Tree, was last used in 1783, after which executions were relocated to just outside Newgate Prison itself, where the condemned were incarcerated, reducing the degree of pageantry involved. By the end of our period, in the late 1860s, hangings were removed from public space altogether, carried out within the privacy of the prison. This progression from public display to private act, so symptomatic and well-known a part of the modernising tendencies of bureaucracies everywhere, was in large part a response to the challenge posed to the state by a public execution. It was the ultimate test of authority – the question being, in James Epstein's unsurpassable construction, 'whose show was it?'[109] In theory, the execution was the monarch's show – the crown being technically the injured party – and by extension the state's: it was their justice that was seen to be done; their power that was shown to be invincible. This is familiar territory, theorised most famously by Michel Foucault, and historicised most extensively by Gatrell.[110] By performing this spectacular ritual in public, the modern state became vulnerable even in the reassertion of its strength, its sovereign justice exposed to the opinion of the crowd – which is where the ballad-singer enters the story.

That crowd constituted the ballad-singer's largest single audience: an unrivalled captive market to whom she could sing and sell what purported to be the condemned prisoner's last dying speech and testament – a statement heard, read, and repeated by vastly more people than the actual speech, if any, given from the gallows. Of course, these works were not in fact penned or dictated by the prisoner, nor were they prescribed by the judicial authorities, who might thereby have effected a partial oversight of what was sung. Instead they were written by printers' hacks and even by singers themselves: Mayhew credits one interviewee with writing numerous 'Newgate' ballads.[111] John Morgan, a Seven Dials ballad

---

[109] James Epstein, *In Practice: Studies in the Language and Culture of Popular Politics in Modern Britain* (Stanford, 2003), 87.

[110] Michel Foucault, *Discipline and Punish*, trans. Alan Sheridan (2nd edn, New York, 1995), 43–69; Gatrell, *The Hanging Tree*.

[111] Mayhew, *London Labour*, vol. 3, 195.

writer interviewed by Hindley, was responsible for several of the most successful.[112] Usually written in the first person, the performance of these ballads granted the ballad-singer a hugely influential role in the reception of each execution.

One of Morgan's death songs was laboriously picked apart by a troubled Hindley in his *History of the Catnach Press*. The antiquarian took pains to render the narrative bathetic, resorting to rules of grammar in order to delegitimise the work:

After almost lawyer-like particularity as to dates and places, the poem begins with an invocation from the murderer in *propria personae*.

> 'Oh! give attention awhile to me,
> All you good people of each degree;
> In Newgate's dismal and dreary cell,
> I bid all people on earth farewell.'

Heaven forbid, say we, that *all* the people on earth should ever get in Newgate, to receive the farewell of such a blood-thirsty miscreant.[113]

Hindley's joke is a feeble one, while his criticism of the 'almost lawyer-like particularity' betrays his unease: the balladeer has become too much a part of a learned legal process. He continues in his criticism:

> 'John William Marchant is my name,
> I do confess I have *been to blame*.'

And here we must observe that the poet makes his hero speak of his offence rather too lightly, as if, indeed, it had been nothing more than a common misdemeanour.[114]

His censure acknowledges the moral weight of the singer's role: the song constructs, not a felon, but a 'hero' who risks being absolved rather than vilified by the crowd. Hindley concludes that Morgan should 'not make his heroes die grumby' – that is, a last dying speech should centre on pious repentance, not the airing of grievances: justice is at risk of being perverted after the act.

By ventriloquising the individual criminal, who was already lent the glamour of public attention, the ballad-singer relocated much of the authority on display at the execution from the abstracted ideal of the monarch and state to the folk-hero of traditional culture. Her method of performance, intimate and idiomatic, was lent additional affect by its musical component, as singers could derive gravitas, even sacral authority, from their choice of tune: Mayhew mentions an execution song of

---

[112] Charles Hindley, *The History of the Catnach Press* (1887), xii–xiv.
[113] Ibid., xii. There is no indication of a tune for this song.     [114] Ibid., xiii.

1812 set to the melody and opening with the first line of the Old
Hundredth psalm, much as in the seventeenth century such songs were
generally sung to the tune of 'Fortune My Foe'.[115] But authority was
contested irrespective of content: even if the song featured a thoroughly
contrite, repentant sinner, the crowd was still enabled to take ownership
of the judgement, invested with an omnipotence and moral authority that
the modern state ideally reserved for those appointed within the courtroom. Justice was relocated from the seat of power to the emotive,
volatile, irrational street or square, a carnivalesque and unreformed environment. In a last dying speech, a ballad-singer might be articulating
a conventional moral message, aligned with the court's judgement. Yet
to do so was far from deferential, for by operating, for once, on the side of
the law, the singer appropriated the law's authority.

### A Neighbourhood Voice

Far from existing only as outcasts, as marginal figures of negligible
importance to the societies that shunned them, ballad-singers in fact
appear to have exercised a remarkable amount of authority. This authority was derived, not from any legal or even social standing, but from less
tangible sources: from centuries of custom and the charisma of performance. It was exerted at an intimate affective level through appeals to
sentiment, emotion, and self-identification, and conducted in the vernacular language and rhetorical gestures of the everyday. Because of this
peculiar form of authority – granted to singers *in performance* on account
of their function, not their persons – ballad-singers were most instrumental in influencing the actions and opinions, not of large-scale modern
institutions such as the nation state, but of small-scale communities,
above all the neighbourhood. Individually peripatetic, it may seem
strange that singers played a part in the ordering of behaviour in known,
local communities – but once again, this was because of the singer's
function and practice, not their specific identity. Of course, many singers
*were* known locally – but it was more important that their singing constructed and mediated identity and conduct at the neighbourhood level.
By these means, local communities attempted to order the conduct of
their constituent members at a time of unprecedented mobility and
migration, using mechanisms developed in the early modern era to preserve the integrity of their neighbourhoods within the modern city.

Specific instances endorse this interpretation. Two months into
Victoria's reign William Arnold, a young Guildford man who had

---

[115] Mayhew, *London Labour*, vol. 1, 283; Marsh, *Music and Society*, 300–2.

immigrated to Camden, North London, as a beer-seller, was indicted for
bigamy, having lived with a wife on a farm before marrying Elizabeth
Hardiman, the fourteen-year-old daughter of a greengrocer across the
street.[116] When cross-examined as to whether she had heard that Arnold
was already married, Hardiman admitted: 'Yes – not from my mother,
but from the neighbours – it was a current report in the neighbourhood,
and I heard of it – I know there was a song printed about his being
a married man.' Here the transgressive economic migrant was subjected
to first the surveillance and subsequently the censure of his new community, by means of ballad singing. I think that we may also view in this light
the ostensibly subversive practice described by the hack writer George
Parker to his scandalised middling readership: that 'If you have a mind to
have a ballad on a treasonable subject, or one which injures the peace of
Society, you have but to apply at this House with seven-and-six-pence,
and you may hear it sung in the course of three hours from your time of
payment in St. Paul's Churchyard, or the Corner of Fleet market.'[117]
While Parker figures this practice as antisocial, in practice it may more
often have been the means of exercising rough justice on the part of a self-
policing community: the age-old practice of *charivari* perpetuated in
modern London by means of the ballad-singer.

To close this chapter, I would like to consider two incidents in particular
London neighbourhoods, one from either end of our period. Though
removed from each other in space and time, the two cases share significant
characteristics, each typifying this 'neighbourhood' model of the ballad-
singer's authority and influence. The first, in modernising Whitechapel in
the 1770s, sees the ballad-singer employed to shame members of a local
neighbourhood for their unorthodox behaviour – and running foul of a cen-
tralised legal system in the process. The second, in suburban Wandsworth in
the 1860s, sees the ballad-singer celebrate a thoroughly vernacular love
story, agitating crowds, and once again incurring the wrath of the state.
Taken together, the two case studies encapsulate the contentions of this
chapter, affirming the ballad-singer's influence in asserting pre-modern
social values, and demonstrating their defiance in the face of progress.

### Whitechapel, 1779

The first case opens with a prosecution, the first charge of which is so
eloquently worded for our purpose that I must give it in full. In 1779,
Robert Wright, a butcher, 'was indicted for that he with a loud voice and
in a publick open manner did sing, say, speak, utter, and pronounce divers

[116] POB t18370814-1867.    [117] Parker, *A View of Society*, vol. 2, 59.

false, scandalous, infamous, malicious, and obscene songs and matters of
and concerning Elizabeth the wife of Joseph Orpwood and Elizabeth the
daughter of the said Joseph reflecting on their character and reputation', and
on further counts of procuring and publishing the said songs.[118] It is telling
that the charge opens by emphasising the 'loud voice' and 'publick open
manner' of the singing, which took place in the marketplace of Whitechapel,
an area of east London beyond the City limits with a strong local identity.
Yet it transpired that, rather than singing the songs himself, Wright engaged
John Cooley, presumably an established ballad-singer, to 'sing them up and
down the market' on his behalf. Wright, the prosecution contested, was
injuring the reputation of Orpwood and his family in the most influential
manner possible: by hiring a ballad-singer.

David Kennerley, who has studied the case, points out that Orpwood,
who brought the prosecution, was an extremely prosperous master
butcher, and that Wright had until recently been his apprentice.[119] The
offence, Orpwood argued, threatened his livelihood by undermining his
reputation, causing 'a great deal of prejudice among my customers'. The
official court convened at the Old Bailey some two miles away evidently
agreed, as Wright was found guilty in the eyes of the law. Yet the case
admits of another interpretation, in which Orpwood was the guilty party
and Wright the aggrieved prosecutor, pursuing a public form of justice by
means of the ballad-singer. Kennerley's reading is that Orpwood (the rich
old master and father familiar from so many early modern plays) had
blocked the marriage of Wright, his apprentice, to his own daughter
Elizabeth – it emerged that the two were known to have been courting
during Wright's apprenticeship – and that Wright, thwarted and dismissed, was seeking to avenge his perceived wrongs.

Wright's strategy may have been economic, aimed at undermining
Orpwood's business and attracting the scandalised customers to his
own butcher's stall. But his *tactics* were far more personal, for the song
in question targeted Orpwood only indirectly through his daughter and
wife. Opening with the classic 'come-all-ye' invitation to the market's
patrons, the song proceeds to narrate the scandalous sexual indiscretions,
first of Elizabeth the daughter, and then of Elizabeth the wife, and is
largely performed in the persona of the younger Elizabeth. This form of
ventriloquism imaginatively exposed her person and conduct to the

[118] POB t17790707-48.
[119] I am much indebted to Kennerley, both for bringing the case to my attention, and for
effectively handing it over to me, following his paper 'A Tale of Two Butchers:
Contesting the Urban Soundscape of Whitechapel Market, 1779' (British Society for
Eighteenth-Century Studies Annual Conference, St Hugh's College, Oxford,
6 January 2012).

community, which was invited to imagine the wanton young woman before them, performatively laying bare these alleged private transgressions to the surveillance of the neighbourhood. For the sake of interest, I replicate the verses here as they were transcribed in evidence at the trial, beginning 'Good people, I pray, to these lines now attend': sadly, the tune is unknown, though it fits the conventional meter and rhyme scheme of songs such as 'King John and the Abbot of Canterbury', to which it is set in this volume's accompanying audio files.

Good people, I pray, to these lines now attend,
And listen a while to these lines I've penn'd;
It is of a young damsel I mean for to sing,
Who has long time been pleas'd with a delicate thing.
    Tol lal lal lol, &c.

A waggish young lass I protest she has been;
And by this time our neighbours are near of a kin.
It is reported for truth that a young man she pris'd;
So attend to what follows, and be not surpris'd.

Says she, my dear, I hope you'll be so kind,
You shall ever enjoy me when you are inclin'd;
Tho' I'd have you take care; for if we are found out,
It will certainly cause a most terrible rout.

My dear, such a scheme I have got in my head;
Which, if follow'd, will lead you secure to my bed;
And whenever I give you the nod, wink, or smile,
Then I mean to retreat to my chamber a while.

You must know that I lie near the top of the house,
Where there's none to molest us, no, not so much as a mouse;
In at the garret window you easily may get.
Then into my room you I quickly will let.

Where we safely may lie, and fulfil our designs,
And none to suspect us or rifle our minds;
No girl half so happy or joyous as she,
And wish'd that such frolicks ne'er ended might be.

But her father has lately found out their fun,
By which I'm persuaded, his daughter's undone.
Her mother cries, Hussey, how could you do so?
And Betsy says, Mammy, you very well know,

When you was in your youth you the like game did play,
Then be not so angry, dear mother, I pray;
It is said that one P— in the Borough did dwell,
A man that you loved most wonderous well.

It is well known that you both to a tavern did hie,
And call'd for a bed there all night for to lie;
And after you had revell'd the night unto day,
P— gave you the bag, left the reckoning to pay.

Since then, my dear mother, your frolicks are known,
I hope you will always be ready to own,
That all have their failings, tho' a difference in crimes;
And you've had your tail-n-gs some hundreds of times.

And now to conclude, I have only to say,
It is a fatal disorder that will have its sway;
But since it[']s found out, it is a folly to pine,
Since your case is my case, and my case is thine.

It is discomforting to sympathise with Wright, whose song is both prurient and misogynistic. Yet many Whitechapel residents clearly did so: Cooley 'bought' the songs from Wright as a saleable commodity, rather than being paid to sing them, indicating a ready audience. This included one of the two witnesses in the published trial record, fellow butcher Thomas Gamble, who enquired 'if he [Cooley] had got any of those songs about Betsy Orpwood', and bought a copy in the Bull's Head alehouse. Considered from this perspective, Wright's action becomes an archetypal shaming ritual, justified as exposing private misdeeds to neighbourhood surveillance and censure: an assertion of social norms with regard to women's conduct rather than a self-interested act of slander. Cooley the ballad-singer embodied an articulate form of *charivari* or rough music, targeted at the morally transgressive Orpwoods. Rather than driving Orpwood out, Wright's song was designed to make him a laughing stock (it is fundamentally a comic song) – for as Henri Bergson observes, 'it is the business of laughter to repress any separatist tendency'.[120] The 'twenty or thirty' listeners who assembled to hear the song apparently made no attempt to silence Wright: it was the state that did that. The spaces of the song's performance – the open market, the Bull's Head, and even Orpwood's own doorstep – speak of a construction of neighbourhood community that insisted upon the unity of communal life, rather than the evolving bourgeois separation of the private domestic realm: an issue especially fraught in contemporary Whitechapel, which as Kennerley notes was then in the throes of rapid urbanisation.[121] Doorstepping, neighbourhood surveillance, public shaming: these were

---

[120] Henri Bergson, *Laughter: An Essay on the Meaning of the Comic* (1911), 77, 98.
[121] Kennerley draws upon Jon Sygrave, 'Development and Industry in Whitechapel: Excavations at 27–29 Whitechapel High Street and 2–4 Colchester Street, London E1', *Transactions of the London and Middlesex Archaeological Society* 56 (2005): 94.

all ways of ordering urban communities most characteristic of the early modern period, as of course was the master–apprentice system leading to (in this case prevented) matrimony that began the dispute.[122] In pursuing justice via ballad singing, Wright proved that such methods remained relevant in the face of modernisation.

### Wandsworth, 1865

One interesting detail of the Whitechapel case is that, while Wright was convicted, the actual singer, John Cooley, was not even charged. Nearly a century later, the reverse was the case, as the opportunistic ballad-singer George Scrorfield was arrested and fined a shilling for his part in what the magistrate described as the 'nine hours' wonder' of the marriage of George Smith and Alice Crosse.[123] The background to this arrest is rather involved: though well worth reading in full, I can only give the briefest précis here.[124] Crosse, twenty years old and therefore not of age, was the daughter and sole heir of a wealthy clergyman at Ockham near Woking in Surrey, southwest of London. She eloped with Smith, an eighteen-year-old groom recently employed by her father, and the pair made their way to London, arriving at Waterloo station via Weybridge. Thwarted in their application for a wedding licence, they took lodgings in Wandsworth, a semi-rural suburb familiar to Crosse, where Smith was arrested and charged with abduction. Crosse was temporarily housed with the police inspector Mr Lovelace, and Smith was released on bail. Crosse's father located his daughter and the case came to trial, but immediately collapsed for lack of evidence. The father now granting his consent, the marriage took place at Wandsworth church, at which point:

An extraordinary scene took place. The fact becoming known, the people thronged the streets leading to the church. Every window was filled, and many spectators were on the housetops ... Everywhere the most unmistakable expressions of sympathy were given as the bride and bridegroom passed along, and they appeared to be the least excited of the many who were present. The police had to clear a way through the crowd up to the church ... Cries of 'Well done, George!' and 'Hurrah for the groom!' were frequent. When the ceremony had been

---

[122] Laura Gowing, *Domestic Dangers: Women, Words and Sex in Early Modern London* (Oxford, 1996), 98; Whipday, *Shakespeare's Domestic Tragedies*, esp. 119–29.

[123] 'The Popular Wedding and the Ballad Singer', *Evening Standard* (15 September 1865): 5.

[124] See ibid., but primarily, 'The Aurora Floyd of Real Life', *Empire* 4 (Sydney, 28 November 1865): 2. This extensive report is available at www.nla.gov.au/nla.news-article63240145. The article's title is an allusion to Mary Elizabeth Braddon's sensational novel *Aurora Floyd* (1863), the sequel to her more famous *Lady Audley's Secret* (1862).

concluded, and the couple came from the church door, the enthusiasm of the people appeared to know no bounds.[125]

The excitement persisted throughout the day, fuelled by a later speech from the newly married Smith, and by the evening it was reported that 'the police had great trouble to prevent a complete riot'.[126] Here Scrorfield the ballad-singer enters the proceedings. The *Evening Standard* stated that: 'Police-constable Bellow, 336 V, said [that] at seven o'clock last night he was on duty in the High-street, when he found the prisoner drunk and singing a ballad, surrounded by a large crowd of persons.' Inspector Lovelace testified that 'there was a collection of several hundred persons there … the object of taking the prisoner into custody was to prevent a disturbance, as there was great excitement in the town … the prisoner's singing caused a complete obstruction of the street'.[127] Lovelace's testimony recalls the elite anxieties of the early part of this chapter: the singer as agent of disorder, causing volatile crowds and preventing free movement. The singer's own evidence meanwhile revives a different concern: the singer as ungovernably mobile. 'Mr Dayman [the magistrate] inquired of the prisoner where he obtained the songs, and he replied at Seven Dials, and that he was not in Wandsworth till past one o'clock in the day. He came down by train.'[128]

Mention of the train – the same technology that had enabled the initial elopement – seems almost incongruously modern, a world away from the eighteenth-century Whitechapel of the previous case study. Presumably Scrorfield walked the half-mile from Seven Dials (specifically, from the print shop of Henry Disley at 57 High Street, St Giles's) to Charing Cross, the nearest terminus, and changed at Victoria, where trains ran to Wandsworth via Clapham Junction. Having once arrived, however, Scrorfield played a central part in a thoroughly early modern drama.

Wandsworth itself in 1865 still looked like a self-contained village neighbourhood, surrounded by fields, with St Anne's church literally around the corner from the courtroom, some four minutes' walk along the High Street and St Anne's Hill.[129] By fuelling what apparently became tantamount to a riot on that high street, Scrorfield was contributing to an unimproved atmosphere of carnival, and seeking to profit in the process, though once his initial purchase at Disley's, his rail fare (unless he dodged it), and his fine are taken into account, he would have had to sell to a significant proportion of his admittedly large

---

[125] 'The Aurora Floyd', 2.     [126] Ibid.     [127] 'The Popular Wedding', 5.
[128] 'The Aurora Floyd', 2.
[129] An exactly contemporary Ordinance Survey map is available at maps.nls.uk/view/ 102345976.

audience. The song in question was presented in court: 'Inspector
Lovelace produced a bundle of papers, and said "These are the kind of
things he had." ... Mr Dayman alluded to one part of the song as being
coarse, but supposed, however, that it suited the tastes of those persons
who bought them.'[130] As in the previous case study, I reproduce the entire
song, 'Blooming Beauty of Surrey and her Father's Servant Man', most
probably sung to the tune of the blackface minstrel song 'Lucy Neal'.[131]

> There was a beauty bright.
> At Woking she did dwell,
> Her father had a handsome groom,
> And his daughter loved him well.
> They used to trot away,
> Conversing on the land,
> Oh! Alice Caroline dearly loved
> Her father's servant man.
> > Alice loved her father's groom,
> > She longed to take his hand,
> > No one can seperate [sic] her
> > From her father s [sic] servant man.
>
> She is twenty years of age,
> As blythe as e'er was seen,
> And George, the groom, was a youth in bloom,

---

[130] The Aurora Floyd', 2.

[131] Cambridge University Library, Madden Microfilm collection reel 7:4738. As the text
gives no tune indication, the process of determining the melody was a long one. The
song had two subsequent editions: 'Marriage of the Blooming Lady and the Groom', in
Hindley, *Curiosities*, 132; and 'The Bonny Blooming Lady and her Father's Servant
Man', Bod. Harding B 11(399). Five years earlier, another song was printed with
a markedly similar title and theme, with the same meter and rhyme scheme, and an
almost identical last line of the refrain. This was 'The blooming lady worth £500,000
and her footman', Bod. Firth b.27(386). It concerns the sensational elopement of a Mrs
Gurney, the wife of Henry John Gurney MP, with her groom, a younger man, and both
the song and the newspaper report share many details with the later case of Smith and
Crosse: clearly, this song was the model for the 1865 song sold by Scrorfield. For an
account of the affair, see 'Elopement of Mrs Gurney', *Bell's Life in Sydney, and Sporting
Reviewer* (5 May 1860): 4. Though this song also gives no tune indication, it appears to
be based in its turn directly on a song printed by Birt in Seven Dials around a decade
earlier: 'Jenny Lind, the Singing Bird', Bod. Harding B 13(171), with which it shares its
meter, rhyme scheme, and most significantly its opening line concerning the 'blooming
lady' that is the opening motif of all these songs. This song on Lind is, like its successors,
deeply prurient concerning its young female subject and her romantic attachments.
Though the wording of its chorus suggests the writer has become confused with the
similar blackface minstrel song 'Lucy Long', the ballad sheet gives the tune as 'Lucy
Neal', and indeed it fits the latter, another early blackface minstrel song also introduced
to England by the Ethiopian Serenaders, exactly. If the song's textual persistence is
anything to go by, the use of 'Lucy Neal', a famous and popular melody well into the
1860s, may well have been preserved as the subject changed, and thus I have postulated
'Blooming Beauty of Surrey' as still being sung to this tune.

Is aged but eignteen [*sic*].
She dearly loved her George.
She by his side would stand,
She vowed no one should part her,
From her father's servant man.

George and Caroline would toy,
Each other they would please,
Each other they would kiss,
And tiddle each other's knees.
They swore by all above,
Did together fondly plan,
To dear each other. lovely [*sic*]
Alice and her servant man.

From Woking they set out,
Thinking 'ere theyfar [*sic*] had got,
A lovely chance they'd have
To tie the lovers' knot.
They disappointed was,
And they amazed did stand,
Then young Alice went to Wandsworth
With her father's servant man.

The banns they did put up,
Alice and her father's groom,
And in Love Lane, in Wandsworth,
They together took a room :
Saying they were man and wife.
As the young lady blythe did stand,
Vowed she would lose her life,
Or wed her father's servant man.

But mark! young men and maids,
Sad was the lovers' fate ;
They were by her father took
Before the magistrate ;
Alice boldly faced them all,
As she at the Bar did stand,
And swore she ran away
With her fathet's [*sic*] servant man.

Have her Georgy Smith she would
For he had gained her heart ;
No power in the world,
She and he[r] groom should part,
Like a maiden in despair,
She would wander through the land,

If they would not let her wed,
Her father's servant man,

May they both united be,
And live a happy life,
May the pretty sweet Miss Crosse,
Be a kind and loving wife ;
And may she ne'er regret
She did at the altar staud [sic],
By the side of Georgy Smith,
Her father's servant man.

You Weybridge pretty girls,
You Chertsey lads and lasses gay,
Can you blame me 'cause from Woking
With my love I run away?
You girls of Guildford town,
Together we will trill,
To see the pleasant fair,
At the place called Catharine Hill.

This lovely pretty maid,
The parson's daughter all in bloom,
Declares she'll never have another man,
Unless she has her groom,
She loves him as her life,
May her belly soon get big,
And may she have a little boy,
Marked with a parson's wig.

The song itself affords several telling indications of what was at stake. As
the magistrate observed, the song is a little 'coarse', at least in the third
verse (imagine a singer pausing suggestively before 'knees' in the fourth
line), and irreverent at the very end, speaking not in the sensational
language of the newspaper report, but with the customary familiarity of
the ballad vernacular. The litany of local place names in the penultimate
verse constructs a known locality, in which groups among the audience
are defined as girls or young lovers tied to nearby towns. A series of
typographical errors unusual even for a ballad, corrected in later editions,
attests to the speed of its production, as do several missed opportunities:
the double meaning of 'groom' and the aptness of 'Love Lane' would
surely have been better exploited by a less hurried writer. Even so it can
scarcely have been composed, as its narrative claims, after the wedding, as
Scrorfield was on the spot selling copies as early as one in the afternoon.
Indeed its narrative, which includes a defiant verse in the voice of Crosse,
constitutes a strong endorsement of the couple's actions, its principles of

romance and custom taking precedence over the marginalised figures of official authority. As such – and as sung on the scene to an impassioned crowd – it evokes the spirit of the execution ballad in relocating judgement from the modern institution of the county court to the lovers and their adoptive community. At the same time it is highly prurient, never questioning its right of surveillance over the body and conduct of its young female heroine, whose belly and knees it imagines and whose titular 'blooming' or fertile beauty it reiterates. Its difference from Wright's misogynistic libel and slander is one of valence rather than attitude, as both cases led to a male ballad-singer both ventriloquising and objectifying a young woman before a deeply interested neighbourhood. If anything, that objectification was compounded in this case by the probable tune 'Lucy Neal', one of several early minstrel songs based upon the 'comic' exploitation of black female bodies.

Scrorfield may have caught a train to Wandsworth. But the social order he was reinforcing by doing so predated that railway by centuries. In arresting him, the officials were at least in part acknowledging the potency of the voluble street itinerant as a figure of influence and authority, able to affect public discourse and to lay claim to public space. Far from diminishing that stature, his drunkenness only added a further insult to the injury – an affront, above all, to the ideals of progress. Throughout our period, the presence of the shabby hat or dirty red shawl of the ballad-singer was a blemish on the façade of public buildings; the sound of that stentorian voice a provocation in the shadow of the gallows; that articulate melody the reminder of an unimproved past still present in the modern, ordered city.

# Interlude II
## 'Lord Viscount Maidstone's Address'

You, gen-tle-men of West-min-ster, would doubt-less know my rea-son, For

com-ing as a Can-di-date so ve-ry late in sea-son; No great names in the field I see, to

rep-re-sent your glo-ry, So of-fer mine—whose great re-nown tre-men-dous is in sto-ry.

Good folks, go Poll for me, and don't you vote for a-ny thing that's low.

Example II.1 'Lord Viscount Maidstone's Address', vocal reduction adapted from Charles Morris, 'Sit Down Neighbours All. Bow Wow Wow' (1783)[1]

I'm told that you Electors disapprove of the facility
Of promises from Candidates who shew their own servility,
By telling you they'll overturn our habits, institutions,
In favour of Reforms as bad almost as Revolutions.
  Oh dear, oh! I hate Reform and every thing that is so horrid low!

[1] Tune from 'Sit down neighbours all. Bow Wow Wow' (1783), BL Mus G.806.f.(72). Words from Bod. Johnson Ballads fol. 61.

I've no right to refuse a *great and influential party*;
So here am I, a DERBYITE, upright, downright, and hearty—
A Viscount, too, remember *that!* you'll be lucky if you get me,
*I* wouldn't tax the people's food—*because* they wouldn't let me.
    O no! no! We'll try to do it by and bye—just now 'twould be 'no go!'

I'm standing now not very far from the bugbear throne of *Wiseman*,
And I'm resolved to play the part of Protestant Exciseman;
*Tho' you may think of foes within, who take the Church's pelf, sirs.*
*There's more to guard against by half, than from Old Nick himself, sirs!*
    Right! right! right! Old England needn't mind the Pope—but
    *confound the Puseyite!*

I disapprove of Parliaments *triennial*, and because
It takes M.P.'s at least a year to learn to make new laws—
Another year is swallowed up in '*Constituent*' orations—
Take two from three, there is but one that we can call the nation's!
    One—two—three! The Chancellor himself might study 'figures'
    under me!

The Ballot I don't like at all—a nasty mean contrivance,
That takes away from Candidates all '*Constitutional connivance!*'
A pretty thing for *me* to go and fill a fellow's belly—
And then *he* go and ballot both for EVANS AND FOR SHELLEY!
    No! no! no! *That* won't suit at any price—'THE BALLOT-BOX
    WON'T DO.'

Some people think Conservatives were only born to 'job,'
And that, *by Nature*, Derbyites were all inclined to rob;
I assure you they're mistaken—we're not such greedy elves,
We only want a *little* of the 'plunder' for ourselves.
    Still I *say*, Retrenchment and Economy's the *watchword of the day.*

Do send me into Parliament—give Derby a majority;
For what can he or 'Dizzy' do, while they're in a minority?
But let them have the reins a bit; if HUME kicks up a riot,
Or COBDEN says a crooked word—why, we'll soon make 'em quiet.
    Oh! oh! oh! Support us then—for after us, THE DELUGE! ho!
    ho! ho!

Now having neatly touched upon the topics of the day
In a manner quite original, do vote for me, I pray;
I place my fortunes in your hands, for '*what I mean I say*,'
And '*what I say I mean*'—that, *in general*, is my way.
    O yes! yes! And *so* says *good* Lord Derby—as the Yankees say,
    I GUESS!

I've nothing more to add, except a word of good advice—
You've other Candidates, you know, so don't be over nice;
If *me* you want, why *have* me; I shall not care a pin,
If you only 'keep your tempers,' who may lose or who may win.
    Poll then, poll! For me, a jolly Tory, of the 'good old English School!'

Though incredibly common (the Bodleian alone holds 635 of them), election ballads of the eighteenth and nineteenth centuries remain understudied, especially when compared with the healthy interest in political ballads in general, and their performances have attracted still less attention.[2] Recent decades have seen periodic attention from several notable scholars of British politics in minor journals that have generally viewed them in terms of written texts, while their treatment within a chapter by David Vernon on 'Power, Print, and the Public Sphere' is by far the thinnest section of an otherwise brilliant analysis of orality, visual culture, and space.[3] A dedicated treatment in Kate Bowan and Paul Pickering's *Sounds of Liberty* has emphasised their role in political culture, while arguably the single best consideration of election ballads as performed song is restricted to two pages within an edition of Newcastle-under-Lyme broadsides by Hannah Barker and David Vincent.[4] The interest from scholars is undoubtedly there, but the songs appear to resist sustained, fruitful analysis.

This may be in part due to their lyrics, which are so full of references and in-jokes as to resist easy comprehension without extensive study of individual elections. For, unlike the generality of discourse on political ballads, which generally assumes a truly mass audience, election ballads were relatively unusual in being directed at an electorate that, up to and during this period, was necessarily propertied and, for the most part, educated. They were, in short, aimed at swaying an informed minority opinion. One effect of this, unremarked by contemporaries, was that it afforded a rare opportunity for subaltern, disreputable, unenfranchised singers to perform songs specifically to their supposed betters, when hired

---

[2] ballads.bodleian.ox.ac.uk/search/themes/Parliamentary%20elections. For political songs more widely, see discussion in the Introduction and Chapter 2. Recent monographs in this area and period include Kate Horgan, *The Politics of Songs in Eighteenth-Century Britain, 1723–1795* (2014); my own *Napoleon and British Song*; and Bowan and Pickering, *Sounds of Liberty*. With David Kennerley, I have co-edited a forum on 'Music and Politics in Britain, c.1780–1860', as a special forum of *Journal of British Studies* 60, no. 3 (2021).

[3] Frank O'Gorman, 'Coventry Election Broadsides, 1780', *Yale University Library Gazette* 67 (1993): 161–9; Richard A. Gaunt, 'Cheering the Member: Gladstone Election Songs at Newark', *Transactions of the Thoroton Society of Nottinghamshire* 114 (2010): 159–66; Barbara Crosbie, 'Half-Penny Ballads and the Soundscape of Eighteenth-Century Electioneering', *Publishing History* 70 (2011): 9–32; David Vernon, *Politics and the People: A Study in English Political Culture c.1815–1867* (Cambridge, 1993), 105–60, esp. 127–31.

[4] Bowan and Pickering, 'Votes for a Song', in their *Sounds of Liberty*, 140–64; Hannah Barker and David Vincent (eds.), *Language, Print and Electoral Politics, 1790–1832: Newcastle-Under-Lyme Broadsides* (Woodbridge, 2001), xxxv–vi.

on behalf of a candidate, as was common practice.[5] In this these songs differed too from the party-political songs performed privately between equals, at dinners for or meetings of party members, which were very much preaching to the choir.[6] Though election ballads ostensibly engaged with national issues, they were intensely local in character, designed to support, and often denigrate, specific individuals known to the songs' audiences, written with references to the personal and the particular, and exclusively performed, for obvious reasons, within the physical spaces of the constituency concerned – street, square, market, fairground, public house, and tavern. They may therefore be seen as exemplary of the themes of community and neighbourhood addressed in Chapter 2.

It is in this context that I wish, for the third and final time, to draw attention to Sheridan's contestation of the Westminster elections, in which he was blighted by ballad-singers – elections notable for their disputed, even violent soundscapes. On that occasion, the radical candidate James Paull engineered an unprecedented radical turnout of local residents, employing literal volume of support as a populist electoral strategy. '"From the noise the people made it was supposed half Westminster was coming to the poll", recorded [Francis] Place.'[7] In the following decade, radicals supporting Henry Hunt and John Cartwright also 'hired ballad singers to praise their two candidates and musicians to stir up crowds'.[8] This riotous, demagogic mood endured well into the mid-century,[9] and was certainly a feature of the General Election of 9 July 1852, from which the song 'Lord Viscount Maidstone's Address' dates. As the *Spectator* reported the next day:

The nomination was at hustings in famed Covent Garden, on Wednesday; in presence of a vast crowd, who, notwithstanding the sweltering heat of the sun, maintained the old privilege of the place for physical struggle and uproar. ... Scarcely a word of the candidates was heard[.][10]

---

[5] According to one of Mayhew's informants, Lord John Russell paid ballad-singers 'very poorly' when he stood as a candidate in the City of London: see Mayhew, *London Labour*, vol. 1, 227. The general practice is attested in Jerrold, 'The Ballad-Singer', 293; and in 'Explanation of the Prints of Hogarth, Called the Election', *Belle Assemblée* (December 1811): vii.

[6] Of these, the best-known are perhaps the songs written and performed by the Whig activist Captain Charles Morris, on which Ian Newman has written extensively. See especially his *The Romantic Tavern: Literature and Conviviality in the Age of Revolution* (Cambridge, 2019), 113–48.

[7] Cited in Marc Baer, *The Rise and Fall of Radical Westminster, 1780–1890* (Basingstoke, 2012), 23, 102.

[8] Ibid., 166.

[9] Ibid., 10. See also Vernon, *Politics and the People*, 108, for the wider sensory context of hustings.

[10] 'Westminster', *Spectator* (10 July 1852): 2.

This, then, was a very familiar form of English party politics: one in which, quite literally, the loudest voices often prevailed.

To appreciate the song in question, a few contextual details are necessary. The Westminster electorate was voting to return two MPs. Candidates ran campaigns from local headquarters, which until 1883 could be public houses as well as private residences. Crowds had rioted as recently as 1841, and there were perhaps a hundred men of the Covent Garden police division on standby.[11] The vote was open, as touched upon in verse six, the secret ballot not being introduced until 1872. The election had been called by the Tory premier Lord Derby, a recurrent figure in the song, who was struggling to govern with a parliamentary minority.[12] Its two chief issues, especially as seen in Westminster and addressed in verses three, four, and seven, were protectionism and the Catholic question: at the time of the song, Cardinal Wiseman was presiding over the first provincial synod of Westminster, making the greatest theological question of the day a key local issue.[13]

The Liberal candidates, General Sir George de Lacy Evans[14] and Sir John Shelley[15] – whose names are trumpeted in verse six – had looked like shoe-ins until William Coningham stood in the radical interest, threatening to split the Liberal vote and thereby affording the Conservatives a shot at the second seat.[16] George James Finch-Hatton, Viscount Maidstone and heir to the earldoms of Winchilsea and Nottingham, obtained the Tory nomination. Coningham's approach relied heavily upon sonic and performative devices: he packed the hustings with 'thousands' of voluble supporters including Irish Catholics, and 'entered Covent Garden in an open carriage at the head of [a] procession, "with flags flying and music playing, and was most vociferously cheered"'.[17] By contrast, Maidstone was almost inaudible at the hustings, proving himself incapable of mastering the complexities of nineteenth-century public oratory, preferring

[11] All from Baer, *Radical Westminster*, 119, 103, 116, 120, 78.

[12] Angus Hawkins, 'Stanley, Edward George Geoffrey Smith, fourteenth earl of Derby (1799–1869)', *ODNB*, oxforddnb.com/view/article/26265. Although Derby formed the resultant government, another minority, he was forced to resign on 17 December 1852.

[13] Richard J. Schiefen, 'Wiseman, Nicholas Patrick Stephen (1802–1865)', *ODNB*, oxforddnb.com/view/article/29791.

[14] Edward M. Spiers, 'Evans, Sir George de Lacy (1787–1870)', *ODNB*, oxforddnb.com /view/article/8960, and Edward M. Spiers, *Radical General: Sir George de Lacy Evans, 1787–1870* (Manchester, 1983).

[15] historyofparliamentonline.org/volume/1820-1832/member/shelley-john-1808-1867.

[16] Bruce Kinzer, Ann Robson, and John Robson, *A Moralist in and Out of Parliament: John Stuart Mill at Westminster, 1865–1868* (Toronto, 1992), 22; Spiers, *Radical General*, 140; Baer, *Radical Westminster*, 31–2.

[17] Spiers, *Radical General*, 140; 'Westminster', 2; Baer, *Radical Westminster*, 170.

instead to publish his address in the Tory mouthpiece the *Morning Post* rather than get his points across in public, and to run his campaign from a dilapidated but secluded townhouse at 71 Jermyn Street.[18]

Besides the glosses that 'Hume' refers to the radical politician Joseph Hume,[19] and 'Dizzy' to Benjamin Disraeli, the song requires no further annotation, as its subtitle is surprisingly truthful: it *is* a 'versified' version of Maidstone's address as published in the *Morning Post*, occasionally paraphrased but mostly quoted verbatim. This original address, a full thousand words, was also subjected to a laborious critique in the Liberal *Daily News* two days after its publication, a lengthy paragraph-by-paragraph rejoinder.[20] By contrast with this anxious, pedantic article, the song is a masterpiece of rhetorical economy. It deals with the threat of Coningham by ignoring his existence. None could mistake it for a genuine endorsement of Maidstone – it has clearly been produced on behalf of the Liberal campaign – yet its potency derives from the deployment of Maidstone's own words. The writer was perhaps inspired by this paragraph from the genuine address:

I have been explicit ... because I have found that the slightest ambiguity of expression is perverted, in the hands of ingenious and unscrupulous political opponents, into any shape which best suits their own purposes; and I have no mind to concede to them, thus early, my chance of being heard with attention on other points of vital importance.[21]

In response, Maidstone's expressions have been left to stand for themselves – with the crucial augmentation of a changing refrain that consistently ironises the quotations – and only the fourth line of verse three and the bulk of verse seven directly 'pervert' Maidstone's statements within the sixteen bars of the verse structure.

Two factors are responsible for the song's devastating satirical effect: the choice of tune, both for its associations and for the melopoetic complexity it allows; and the very fact of its performance by a balladsinger. The tune, as indicated by the title, is 'Bow Wow Wow'. We may assume that, despite the ostensibly intimidating amount of text (which in any case might be abridged at the singer's discretion), the song was indeed sung, and to this tune: a performance of all ten verses would take

---

[18] 'Westminster', 2; 'To the Electors of Westminster' and 'Lord Maidstone for Westminster', *Morning Post* 24509 (29 June 1852); 'A Passing Sketch, or the "Symbolic Action" of Toryism', *Reynold's Newspaper* 100 (11 July 1852). See also 'London', *Daily News* 1906 (1 July 1852); and 'Maidstone for Westminster', *Era* 719 (4 July 1852). See Vernon, *Politics and the People*, 117–24, for the oratorical context.

[19] V. E. Chancellor, 'Hume, Joseph (1777–1855)', *ODNB*, oxforddnb.com/view/article/14148.

[20] 'London'.  [21] 'To the Electors of Westminster'.

at most five and a half minutes; Marc Baer – by no means a scholar preoccupied with music – repeatedly attests to the aural use of song in these elections, sometimes to the assaulted ballad-singer's cost; and who, by this stage, can doubt the singer's capacity to make themselves heard in a crowd?[22]

The tune itself is repeatedly referred to in other media as a fixture of nineteenth-century street repertoire.[23] Moreover, 'Bow Wow Wow' was a distinctively political air. Written by the Whig raconteur Captain Charles Morris and first sung by the Vauxhall Gardens composer James Hook, the original song 'Sit down Neighbours all. Bow Wow Wow' was a savage satire on Pitt the Younger and Henry Dundas, debuting at a gathering of the Anacreontic Society in around 1783.[24] The song was endlessly reprinted in both score and broadside until the end of the nineteenth century – by which time it had become a standard in the United States – and its parodies and repurposings were almost invariably political. 'Dunkirk Races' attacked the Duke of York's failed 1790s campaign in Flanders;[25] 'The Barking Barber' and both William Shield's and Mr Johannot's 'Bow Wow Wow' were social satire;[26] 'New Fasions' [sic] took a swipe at Edmund Burke's comments about the 'swinish multitude';[27] there were at least two parodies about Thomas Paine;[28] 'Paddy, the pointer' concerned the Irish rebellion of 1798;[29] three parodies of 1803–5 ridiculed Napoleon;[30] a comic political version on 'Guy Fawkes' was in turn borrowed for demagogic purposes by the Anti-Vaccination society;[31] a Lancashire variant from the second half of

[22] Baer, *Radical Westminster*, 70, 87, 115, 164–5; 141.
[23] *Metropolitan Grievances*, 104; Patrick Spedding and Paul Watt (eds.), *Bawdy Songbooks of the Romantic Period*, 4 vols. (2011), vol. 1, *passim*; Charles Hindley, *A History of the Cries of London: Ancient and Modern* (1881, repr. Cambridge, 2011), 181.
[24] BL Mus G.806.f.(72). See also *The New Vocal Enchantress* (1788), 134–8, and, for Morris, Patrick Waddington, 'Morris, Charles (1745–1838)', *ODNB*, oxforddnb.com/view/article/19300. See also footnote 6 of this Interlude. The Anacreontics were swift to parody their own song, Thomas Goodwin penning 'Mew mew mew' for Hook to sing: BL Mus H.1652.pp (15).
[25] Bod. Harding B 22(71).
[26] BL 1347.m.8 and BL Mus H.2818.(17); BL Mus G.426.ww.(1); Bod. Harding B 22(26).
[27] Bod. Harding B 2(56).
[28] 'Pour commencer, Tom, the bodice-maker', Bod. Firth b.22(f.85a); 'The Jacobine journey, or Mad-Tom and the devil', Bod. G. A. Warw. b.1(929).
[29] BL no shelfmark (Dublin, *c*.1800).
[30] 'Crocodile's Tears; or Bonaparte's Lamentation', Bod. Curzon b. 12(62); 'Bonaparte', *The Yorkshire Irishman* (Belfast, *c*.1803), 6–8; Thomas Best, 'Done Over' (1805), in John Holloway and Joan Black (eds.), *Later English Broadside Ballads*, 2 vols. (1975), vol. 2, 190–1.
[31] Bod. Johnson Ballads 2539; 'Vaccination', *National Anti-Compulsory-Vaccination Reporter* 2 (1877): 20.

the century disputed 'the strikes & rises of the present day';[32] and all three
US variants postdating the Civil War were political.[33] Most pertinently of
all, by 1852 'Bow Wow Wow' had been used in at least six (and probably
many, many more) parliamentary elections, including the Westminster
election of 1796.[34]

'Bow Wow Wow', then, was a tune that had strong political overtones,
connoting satire and ridicule. Its conventional nonsense chorus of 'Bow,
wow, wow, fal lal di iddy iddy, bow, wow, wow' is in this instance replaced
by non-recurring text, yet the familiar words will have been present,
ghostlike, to the 1852 audience, shading their replacements with a sense
of the absurd. The tune's consistent use for political expression goes
deeper than its associations, however: few melodies have ever been so
well suited to the voicing of precise political sentiment. Baer stresses the
crucial importance of specific vocabularies and semiotics to these election
campaigns as bearers of both ideology and affect, and the volatile soundscape of Covent Garden necessitated a song that could convey such words
both clearly and memorably.[35] 'Bow Wow Wow' is that song. Its verse is
practically recitative – lines one, two, and four open as measured speech
(bars 1–3, 5–7, 14–16) – thereby maximising comprehensibility, yet all
four lines end on a distinctive, lingering, falling cadence, giving these end-
words, which also bear the rhyme, a marked and memorable rhetorical
emphasis. This potential is best realised in verses three (if you get me /
wouldn't let me), six (contrivance / connivance), and seven (job / rob),
when Maidstone is ventriloquised rather than quoted, with especially
damning words placed in 'his' mouth. The earworm refrain, rather than
providing an opportunity for communal participation, is here repurposed
to emphasise or undercut each preceding verse, refrains two and three in
particular imputing to Maidstone a craven, duplicitous character.

Nothing, however, can have been so injurious to Maidstone's character
as the song's performance, in character, by the ballad-singer. If we are to
give any credence to Mayhew, then it appears singers were known to 'dress
up to the character' for certain topical songs – and certainly Westminster

[32] Bod. Firth c.16(265).
[33] Eugene T. Johnston, 'The War is over now' (Boston, 1865), BL RB.23.b.7019.(96);
Francis Eastlack, 'The great Know Nothing song' (Philadelphia), Bod. Harding
B 18(216); John Zieber, 'Change. a song of the present times' (Philadelphia), Bod.
Harding B 18(79).
[34] Barker and Vincent, *Newcastle-under-Lyme Broadsides*, 17–19, 77 (1790 and 1792);
'Admiral Gardner for ever, huzza.' (1796), BL HS.74/1986(15); 'A new song, to an
old tune' (Coventry, 1802), Bod. G. A. Warw. b.2(143); '1822. Salop county election'
(Salop, 1822), Bod. Harding B 32(46); 'A new hunting song' (Honiton, 1832), BL 1853.
d.9(75); 'A new song', Bod. Johnson Ballads fol. 298.
[35] Baer, *Radical Westminster*, 78–9, 81, 164.

elections were famous for their use of visual iconography.[36] A male impersonator of Maidstone would be comical enough, a female doubly so. The electorate had apparently seen, but not heard, the real Maidstone; many would have read or heard about his address in the *Post* – yet their only experience of the two together, both body and address, took the form of this low comic burlesque.

Sadly we have no account of specific performances by singers during elections beyond the information that singers would stand on stools to gain attention,[37] the nearest evocation being a passage in an exemplary tale by Harriet Martineau, herself a seasoned political activist and songwriter.[38]

A crowd was slowly making its way along the middle of the street. At first we thought it was a fight; but there was no scuffling... Sir H. Withers's carriage came along the street, and the crowd being obliged to give way to let it pass, we saw in the midst a ballad-singer – a youth with tattered dress and a bundle of papers. As the carriage passed, he raised his voice in song ... 'It is about Sir Henry Withers!' cried my brothers; and they were running off to hear more[.][39]

Martineau concludes that 'The light and giddy sang the ballad daily and hourly when they had once caught the tune' of the song, composed by a Mr Carey in order to satirise Sir Henry Withers in just the same manner as 'Lord Viscount Maidstone's Address'.[40]

Martineau's tale illustrates a common practice, whereby part of the crowd's excitement and sense of frisson is caused by the close physical proximity of the song's real subject and his impersonator. We might extrapolate that, to the enfranchised and unenfranchised alike, this juxtaposition was especially thrilling because it conferred on the knowing audience an unparalleled degree of inclusiveness: they were party to every aspect of a political discourse, rather than the passive consumers of a text commenting on matters removed from them by both space and status. In thereby 'becoming' Lord Maidstone, the ballad-singer not only reduced the patrician to the level of the street: she or he temporarily elevated both self and audience to the heart of the political nation. We may therefore see the election ballad, even if written by a journalist or politician, as fundamentally empowering for both singer and audience, because of its embodied performance within a political community of neighbourhood.

---

[36] Mayhew, *London Labour*, vol. 1, 276.
[37] Thomas B. Howell (ed.), *A Complete Collection of State Trials*, 21 vols. (1816), vol. 20, 1286.
[38] Harriet Martineau, *Illustrations of Political Economy: No. III, Brooke and Brooke Farm: A Tale* (3rd edn, 1833).
[39] Ibid., 22–3.    [40] Ibid., 27–8.

In one sense, Maidstone – by virtue of his title and his reactionary politics – was a very traditional sort of politician. Yet he ran his campaign from a private headquarters, rather than a tavern or alehouse; he was parachuted in as the candidate of a national party, not as a local figure; and he published his address in that most nineteenth-century of mass media, the newspaper, rather than engaging with the localised forms of speech, parade, and ballad. By employing the last of these means to mock him, Westminster Liberals were turning to a far older form of political discourse, and voicing it on the open streets of a neighbourhood community. Recall once more Fletcher's old saw from 1704, quoted in Chapter 2: 'If a man were permitted to make all the ballads, he need not care who should make the laws of a nation.' Maidstone's political career was quashed by the election result, in which he finished in a tame third place. He never had the chance to make the nation's laws, at least in part because he failed to make its ballads.

# 3  Performance
## The Singer in Action

---

> When I, to London, first came in,
> How I began to gape and stare!
> 'Fresh lobsters – dust – and wooden-ware!'
> The cries they kept up such a din –[1]

The singer had to contend with more than the artist's pen, the watchman's truncheon, and the magistrate's gavel. As so many print series have depicted, the ballad-singer was just one of the numerous Cries of London. The extract here is the opening of a comic drawing-room song of 1800, 'London Cries', which fills three long verses with contemporary Cries. Six decades later, George Augustus Sala invites us to accompany him – at 5am – from Billingsgate market to the offices of *The Times*, counselling us, as we walk west towards Blackfriars and Fleet Street, to:

Never mind the noises of dogs barking, of children that are smacked by their parents or guardians for crying, and then, of course, roar louder; of boys yelling the insufferable 'Old Dog Tray,' the abominable 'Keemo Kimo,' the hideous 'Hoomtoomdoodendo,' and rattling those abhorrent instruments of discord, the 'bones;' of women scolding, quarrelling, or shrieking ... of men growling, and wagon-wheels rumbling, and from distant forges the yell of the indignant anvil[.][2]

In 1832, neatly bisecting these dates, the amateur composer William Gardiner published a remarkable, five-hundred-page book on *The Music of Nature*, in which he records numerous Cries, set to musical notation – yet informs us that: 'As the noise of the carriages, and the din of traffic increased, these intonations have died away, and are scarcely heard, but in the quiet of the morning in the most solitary parts of the town.'[3]

Allowing for the amplifying effects of satire, hyperbole, and nostalgia, these three sources make a simple point, one that recurs endlessly in contemporary discourse: London was loud; getting louder; and not all

---

[1] Opening lines of 'London Cries', *The Myrtle and Vine; or, Complete Vocal Library*, 4 vols. (1800), vol. 1, 130.

[2] George Augustus Sala, *Twice Round the Clock; or the Hours of the Day and Night in London* (1861), 25.

[3] William Gardiner, *The Music of Nature* (1832, New edn, Boston, 1841), 300.

sounds could coexist. And yet, in amongst Sala's pandemonium of human and industrial noise, three songs may still be heard. According to Gardiner, this was the very reason that the commercial Cries of London were first set to music: because 'musical sounds are heard at a greater distance than others more noisy. As such it is the object with him who cries to choose a word upon which he can pour out the whole force of his voice'.[4] The ballad-singer, like other vendors, employed music in a crowded, contested soundscape, as an aid to the sale of physical wares. Other street-criers were her competitors for both coin and auditory attention: more so even than modern buskers, ballad-singers had to work to make themselves heard.

Singers were not above giving as good as they got – in 1818, two employed by Jemmy Catnach were tried at Bow Street for disturbing the peace of a Chelsea morning with their 'most tremendous noise' – yet, as this very example reminds us, theirs was an occupation attended by greater risks than those faced by the seller of watercress or the bawling cab-driver.[5] In 1835, a second pair of singers was dragged into Hatton Garden police station. Inspector Oakley of E Division reported that, though they appeared to be a married couple, the husband was – biologically speaking – nothing of the kind:

I have known her at least ten years, and she always appeared in a dress similar to the one she now wears, namely, a hat, smock-frock, trousers, or knee-breeches, and until last night I always supposed her to be a man. She is known all over England as a ballad-singer. ... She travels the country with a woman named Isabella Watson, and they are both known at every race-course and fair as ballad-singers, and considered to be man and wife.[6]

Though reported rather pruriently as an 'extraordinary case', and whatever their private motivations may have been (I have no wish to deny the validity of a queer historical perspective here), the most *pragmatic* explanation is that Watson and her companion adopted their trans disguise as a pre-emptive defence against the harassment two itinerant, singing females might expect to suffer on the road – and yet even so, this act of self-protection ultimately resulted in persecution.

---

[4] Ibid., 306–7. It is certainly true that musical sound, when recognised as such, is more penetrative than non-musical, hence the campaign against street music led by Charles Babbage in the 1860s, discussed in Interlude IV. Anecdotally: as I write these lines, the words 'Do you believe in life after love?', as sung by a workman across the street more or less to the tune of Cher's once-ubiquitous hit 'Believe', have just interrupted my train of thought, emerging from an often far louder background of London traffic and the shouts and clatter of the workman's crew.
[5] Shepard, *John Pitts*, 54.    [6] *The Dens of London Exposed* (1835), 78–9.

The ballad-singer clearly had much to contend with in the pursuance of her trade, from sonic competition to detention and abuse – and all this to be overcome before an audience could be assembled, an audience that would then have to be transformed, by the singer's craft, into paying customers. In this chapter I will follow singers' attempts to engage with, overcome, and exploit their environments, in a succession of narrowings of focus: from the broadest concerns of topography and time; to the particularities of site-specific performance; to a breaking down of the constitutive elements of those performances – voice, body, audience engagement, and their relationship with the physical commodity of the song sheet itself – in order to establish both the craft, and the art, of the ballad-singer at work.

## Time and Place in the Big City

In 1830 a long article appeared in the *National Magazine*, reprinted the following year in Dublin, Edinburgh, and London, describing the ballad-singers of Dublin.[7] Its author, Samuel Lover, adopts the attitude of a (tongue-in-cheek) connoisseur, directing his readers to the streets where they will hear the best singers: High Street, Cornmarket, Cutpurse Row, St Thomas Street (these comprising a cluster of streets just south of the Old Bridge), and, further south beyond the Cathedral district, Fumbally's Lane and St Kevin Street. By contrast Merrion Square, in the elegant east end beyond Trinity College, is dismissed as being 'far too genteel'. Lover, clearly delighting in his travesty of a respectable guide, also informs us that the singer 'prefers the evening for his strains', enabling Lover to construct an exotic, titillating 'after-hours' tour critiquing the standard of entertainment on offer, parodying accounts of theatrical and concert life. He admits that: 'Ballad-singers, to be sure, may be heard at all times of the day, making tuneful the corners of every street in the city, and moving the vocal air "to testify their hidden residence"', yet he also maintains that: 'No ballad-singer of any eminence, in his or her profession, ever appears until the sun is well down; your she ballad-singers in particular are all "maids that love the moon"'.

There are obvious parallels with London in this account, both geographical and literary, the nearest corollary being William Harvey's 1862 reminiscence of 'Street Music of London Fifty Years Since', which takes readers on a tour of the City from Temple Bar eastwards, imagined as

[7] Samuel Lover, 'National Minstrelsy: Ballads and Ballad Singers', *National Magazine* 1, no. 2 (August 1830): 193–204. See also John Moulden, 'Ballads and Ballad Singers: Samuel Lover's Tour of Dublin in 1830', in Atkinson and Roud, *Street Ballads*, 127–46.

occurring at 8pm on a Saturday in October 1812.[8] Lover's Dublin, mirroring Harvey's London, is only half a city, restricted to its south bank and the hours of darkness, a conceit at odds with his admission, above, of the singer's temporal and geographic ubiquity. Undoubtedly, individual singers would have favoured certain times and sites. But another parallel account from a third major city, Manchester, suggests this was less a case of singers en masse favouring certain areas, but rather a case of singers systematically varying their location:

[T]he professional street singers who sell ballads know what subjects will suit certain neighbourhoods, and 'work' accordingly. In the districts where weavers most abound a song upon anything or anybody connected with the loom finds its best market, and by the same rule Irish songs are sung and sold where they are sure to be appreciated.[9]

This is corroborated by first-hand accounts from London. The narrator of the lightly fictionalised *Surprising History of a Ballad Singer* notes that 'We were also careful to vary the scene, that our voices might not become too common in any one neighbourhood.'[10] In 1814 the once-peripatetic Scottish singer David Love, driven from Nottingham to London by fear of a rumoured bill of repatriation, 'took an empty room at No. 42, Fleet Lane, so that I might have an equal distance to go round the City and Suburbs, to get home in good time each evening.'[11] In 1795 William Brown exercised a different form of discretion in choosing his pitch, writing: 'In the evening I took my station at the end of several streets . . . in the dark', using the dim light to sell scraps of newspapers that passers-by were convinced, by his singing, were copies of 'The Arethusa'.[12] After he had sold 'about forty' in 'a quarter of an hour', an angry resident declared that he would call the watch – whereupon Brown simply relocated and 'sold about twenty more'. The author of *Streetology* claimed that regular singers 'generally commence business about three or four o'clock in the afternoon', while adding that 'those who are not fortunate enough to obtain a situation or standing in some frequented thorough-fare, or market-place, generally travel about from street to street'.[13] By contrast, John James Bezer, singing in 1838, restricted his performances

---

[8] 'In Aleph' (William Harvey), *London Scenes and London People* (1863), 343–53.
[9] 'F. Folio', *The Hawkers and Street Dealers of Manchester and the North of England Manufacturing Districts Generally* (Manchester, 1858), 118–19. By 'Irish Songs', the author means songs from Ireland rather than 'stage-Irish' numbers.
[10] *The Surprising History*, 14.
[11] David Love, *David Love's Journey to London, and His Return to Nottingham* (Nottingham c.1814), 4.
[12] William Brown, *A Narrative of the Life and Adventures of William Brown* (York, 1829), 13.
[13] 'Rag', *Streetology*, 83.

to the working day – yet he too varied his pitches within a single week from Brixton in the extreme south to Islington and Holloway in the far north, and from Wilderness Row in east-central Clerkenwell to Chelsea in south-western suburbia.[14]

Faced with such variation, it becomes impossible to trace any wider patterns. In the course of this research I plotted a map of specific reported performances by singers across the period, yet I soon realised that it was not worth the pixels it was drawn in, recording as it did a mere twenty-eight separate instances, when there must have been hundreds across London on any given day in the first few decades of the nineteenth century. This map revealed no trends over time, despite spanning some eighty years. The fact that most performances occurred north of the Thames may in part reflect population density, yet it is more plausibly a function of the data's selectivity: half the instances came from Old Bailey trials, which principally cover the City and Middlesex, both north of the river. Most of the points it plotted were primarily residential districts for the middle and lower classes, besides several more public, central spaces with a high footfall, and a few major arterial roads to the east and south where singers performed to crowds returning from fairs such as Greenwich and Camberwell. More of these locations fell outside than within the City limits, and from the later 1830s the former, peripheral region benefited from the replacement of granite streets with tarmacadam, which was noted at the time for 'the noiselessness of the traffic'.[15] We might also contrast these relatively amenable streets with the 'perfect dust-mill' of the outer suburbs, a region scarcely represented.[16] However, much of the map's data predated this change in the road surface – and it is moreover madness to infer anything from an absence of data when the total sample size is so minuscule. Analysing the data by time rather than space, I found every month of the year represented, as well as all times of day, from 'morning' and 8am, to 12am and 'night'.

There are two considerations that we might attempt to rescue from this sketchy impression of ubiquity. That singers performed at all times and all seasons underlines that, for many, this was an occupation driven by necessity, a ceaseless attempt to stave off hunger and, for the luckier singers, to stave off homelessness. To say that singers were always to be heard is to say that there was always deprivation among those people who might turn to ballad singing. Yet there is also a suggestion of agency here. Singers were not tethered to their place of abode or origin, nor to the

[14] 'The Autobiography of One of the Chartist Rebels of 1848', repr. in David Vincent (ed.), *Testaments of Radicalism: Memoirs of Working Class Politicians 1790–1885* (1977), 179–84.
[15] Mayhew, *London Labour*, vol. 2, 182.    [16] Ibid., 188.

printers in Seven Dials, but were able to traverse what was to them a highly legible city, choosing their pitches in order to take advantage of specific opportunities: a crowd of potential theatre-goers prevaricating in Drury Lane;[17] revellers returning from Camberwell Fair;[18] customers patronising Clare Market.[19] This mobility will have aided the sale of specific songs, especially topical compositions – as singers could seek out fresh audiences – and will have helped singers evade unwanted attention from the authorities. Yet far from being forced to the margins, or being pushed to the East End over time, singers also colonised locales of high entertainment (Drury Lane; Leicester Square),[20] the elite West End (Cavendish Square; Chelsea; The King's Road),[21] public monuments (St Paul's Cathedral; the Tower of London),[22] and areas of remorseless urban improvement (Holborn).[23] My abandoned map itself constituted something of a failure, yet the story it suggests is one of success.

## Taking a Stand

When historicising popular music, writes Vic Gammon, 'Not only are the immediate social relations of musical production important, but so [too] is the physical environment. We must ask how it was defined as social space and in what ways did interaction take place in the environment.'[24] In contrast to the representations discussed in Chapter 1, where singers were often drawn against a blank background or a depopulated street, this environment was defined in the first instance by people: by the relation of singer to auditors (if a singer performs in an empty street, does she make a sound?). Twenty years before our period of enquiry, the Hessian writer and natural philosopher Georg Christoph Lichtenberg described his experience of the London streets to a colleague at Göttingen, remarking in passing that 'I have said nothing about the ballad singers who, forming circles at every corner, dam the stream of humanity which stops to listen

---

[17] POB t18091101-45.
[18] Small news item, *Morning Chronicle* 15696 (20 August 1819).
[19] Hindley, 'Street Ballads', 398.    [20] POB t18020918-128.
[21] Benjamin Silliman, *A Journal of Travels in England, Holland, and Scotland, and of Two Passages Over the Atlantic, in the Years 1805 and 1806*, 2 vols. (2nd edn, Boston, 1812), vol. 1, 166–7; POB t18171029-137; POB t18310630-14.
[22] *Director* 2, no. 16 (9 May 1807): 101; POB t18420131-659.
[23] *Daily News* 2358 (10 December 1853).
[24] Vic Gammon, 'Problems of Method in the Historical Study of Popular Music', in David Horn and Philip Tagg (eds.), *Popular Music Perspectives: Papers from the First International Conference on Popular Music Research, Amsterdam, June 1981* (Göteborg and Exeter, 1982), 16–31, 22.

and steal.'[25] Michael Bywater describes this practice as the creation of 'liminal spacetime': walkers are seen as having a transitional status, and the singer must use music to convince them they are therefore outside measurable time, free of temporal imperatives and thus at leisure to stop and participate in the performance. Once created, it is not individual listeners that the singer seeks to maintain, but rather 'the crowd in aggregate', the members of which will necessarily come and go.[26]

The creation of this 'liminal spacetime' was no easy task. Writing of the three decades after 1800, Alison O'Byrne posits a change in modes of street walking and 'a greater sense of social segregation'. She notes that numerous 'texts and images proclaim that walking in London requires one's absolute attention regarding where to place one's feet, when to cross the road, and how to avoid carts, people, umbrellas, and sewage ... the focus is on crime, dirt, personal safety, and personal space'.[27] Didactic-cum-humorous publications for the aspirational reader portrayed the street as an aggressive, busy environment.[28] The Philadelphian topographer and engraver James Peller Malcolm went so far as to inform his readers that: 'The English walk very fast: their thoughts being entirely engrossed by business, they are very punctual to their appointments, and those who happen to be in their way are sure to be sufferers by it: constantly darting forward, they jostle them with a force proportioned to their bulk and the velocity of their motion.'[29] This impression deviates from Penelope Corfield's view of the eighteenth-century street as 'a coherent and lively arena for social peregrination, perception, challenge, and engagement', and is also at odds with other accounts more or less contemporaneous with Malcolm.[30] Hannah More's archetype of the young urban proletarian is anything but single-minded: 'If a blind fiddler, a ballad-singer, a mountebank, a dancing bear, or a drum were heard at a distance – out ran Jack'.[31] Far from encountering indifference or hostility when working its streets in 1814, Love found that: 'The people in

[25] Cited in Shoemaker, *The London Mob*, 2.
[26] Bywater, 'Performing Spaces', 118. See also Tia DeNora, *Music in Everyday Life* (Cambridge, 2000), 8, 132–3.
[27] Alison O'Byrne, 'The Art of Walking in London: Representing Pedestrianism in the Early Nineteenth Century', *Romanticism* 14 (2008): 94–107, 95, 97.
[28] For example, P. D. Stanhope, *Chesterfield Travestie: or, School for Modern Manners* (1808), 1–6.
[29] James Peller Malcolm, *Anecdotes of the Manners and Customs of London during the Eighteenth Century*, 2 vols. (1808; new edn 1810), vol. 1, 393.
[30] Penelope Corfield, 'Walking the City Streets: "The Urban Odyssey in Eighteenth-Century England"', *Journal of Urban History* 16 (1990): 132–74, 133.
[31] Hannah More, *The Two Shoemakers. In Six Parts* (n.d.), 9.

London are good natured, and charitable, especially to strangers; I have found more kindness, love and tenderness, than any place in England.'[32] Such discrepancies in characterisation of London's walkers may be down to chance, class, change over time, or authorial motivation – yet their conflicted impression is, I think, a useful one, as it presents us with the ballad-singer's plight: how to arrest the tide of walkers, to siphon off the idlers and the inquisitive; in short, how to 'dam the stream of humanity'.

The first step was to choose a pitch. As long as singers were mobile, they had some agency in this regard, for even if circumstances required them to work continually on the streets, they could occupy different spaces at particular times of the day. Love is despondent when he notes that: 'One Saturday, being very cold, I got very little to put over Sunday. I went out in the evening to Fleet-market, and took a few pence, the cold being very severe.'[33] Yet though poverty and poor weather forced his hand, he was still able to go where he knew there would be people with money to spend. Indeed, Love put great thought into his choice of urban space, going so far as to consider which attributes of London's bridges made them more or less conducive to sustaining an audience, paying particular attention to shelter, comfort, and light:

Westminster Bridge is the finest, and the strongest I ever saw, and seats on both sides at the top of every arch where people may sit dry and comfortable in a storm, being well covered above with Arched hewn stone, and each of them has a large lamp on the top; there is another bridge between that and Blackfriars, where foot passengers pay a penny. Blackfriars bridge is a very strong one, but not so many seats nor so well covered . . . London bridge, where you pass to the borough, is also very strong, nothing inferior to Westminster, in seats and lamps.[34]

Considerations such as these demonstrate a high degree of pragmatism echoed in more recent discourse on busking. Billy Bragg, perhaps the leading 'vernacular' singer of our own time, advising on a choice of pitch for busking, is similarly practical:

Look for a pedestrian area with plenty of space and not too many cars. Outside a station or shopping centre is good because you'll have a stream of people going past – and if you play at the bottom of an escalator people have time to see you. Avoid larger public areas as the crowd will be too spread out.[35]

We might add, try to select a space whose physical properties complement or even amplify your performance. An 1844 account of Greenwich Fair, which was itself an unpromising soundscape of 'organs, bells, trumpets, drums,

---

[32] Love, *David Love's Journey*, 5.    [33] Ibid., 7.    [34] Ibid., 6.
[35] Billy Bragg, 'How to Busk?', *Guardian* (21 March 2014), http://theguardian.com/lifeand style/2014/mar/21/billy-bragg-how-to-busk?

and stentorian voices', gives us one such strategy, whereby a singer situated just outside the fair's limits could capitalise on the large number of potential customers without being overwhelmed: 'The change from this scene of uproar to the comparative silence and the delightful scenery of the [adjacent] park is strikingly effective. The rich lawn is ornamented with numerous groups of well-dressed people: here a ring is formed round ... a ballad singer, bidding "old men beware"'.[36] According to Bruce Smith, St Paul's – a haunt of singers for several centuries – afforded two distinct spaces for performance; not merely the churchyard itself, but also the space directly in front of the cathedral doors, where visibility was wedded to the acoustic potential of a resonant soundboard at one's back.[37]

One of Mayhew's supposed interviews raises a further possibility: though stood in the street, a singer might direct a rendition at a ready-made gathering via an open window. 'Excepting when we needed money, we rarely went out till the evening. Then our pitches were in quiet streets or squares, where we saw, by the light at the windows, that some party was going on.'[38] If the singer was good, then revellers could enjoy the entertainment without sacrificing their comfort, even inviting the singer inside, where they might receive not only halfpennies, but – according to Mayhew's ostensible source – 'many a Christmas dinner'.

This sonic potential to transcend – or transgress – the boundary between street and home was not the only spatial tactic at the singer's disposal. As in the exploitation of the doors of St Paul's, the singer – a marginal, subaltern figure – could situate herself amid respectable public space and derive both attention and authority from that temporarily possessed position (as Bywater notes, 'in a sort of Newton's First Law of performance and liminality, the space also acts upon the performer').[39] Jessica Sack's practice-based research into street performance highlights the extent to which musicians theatricalise urban space, so that stairs or trees become stage properties, architecture serving to 'frame' the performer.[40] Such actions on the part of ballad-singers were inherently provocative, even political, leading us to reassess the power relations between them and the civic authorities, reinforcing the anxieties palpable in official discourse seen in Chapter 2.[41] There is a visual parallel to this practice in John Leighton's mid-century London Cries & Public Edifices,

[36] 'A Trip to Greenwich at Whitsuntide', Penny Satirist 372 (1 June 1844): 1.
[37] Smith, Acoustic World, 168.    [38] Mayhew, London Labour, vol. 3, 195–6.
[39] Bywater, 'Performing Spaces', 108; see also 103, 107.
[40] Sack, 'Street Music', 14, 19, 23.
[41] See also Barclay, 'Singing, Performance, and Lower-Class Masculinity', esp. 755–62.

wherein each street character is depicted in a prominent position before a well-known landmark, so that a bellows-mender dwarfs the Tower, and a Turkish rhubarb-seller strides, a giant, before East India House.[42] These images are intentionally troubling, apparently designed to problematise the vast gulf between wealth and poverty, yet admitting of more subversive readings of the contestation, even the appropriation of public space.

The Connecticut chemist Benjamin Silliman, resident in London in the summer of 1805, describes singers involved in just such an act:

> Returning home, about 10 o'clock at night, I observed one of those little circles which are very common in the streets of London; I allude to the audiences which gather around the ballad singers. These are usually poor women, or little girls, with every appearance of extreme poverty, who collect a few pence by singing ballads at the corners of the streets, under the bow-windows of shops, and the porticoes of public buildings. Although their voices are usually harsh from being so often exerted, and their performances, in every respect indifferent, they immediately draw a circle around them and detain them a long time.[43]

In this account, the singers' demonstrable success in creating (and profiting from) 'liminal spacetime' is due, not to their 'indifferent' voices, but to their exploitation of time and space. They choose to perform at a time of evening when aural competition is minimal, yet pedestrians are numerous, as they – like Silliman – return home from an evening's employment or recreation. The time of year – June – presumably makes the evening clement enough that people are happy to linger. Most significantly, the singers take their stands in prominent locations. Street corners maximise their field of visibility and audibility, while bow windows and porticoes create a framed space – a proscenium arch in miniature – while also providing shelter should the weather take a turn for the worse. These architectural features belong to commercial and state interests – yet for the duration of the performance, they are appropriated by the singers, thereby conferring a vicarious legitimacy, and even the thrill of subversion, upon that performance. Once drawn by such techniques, a 'circle' of auditors becomes self-sustaining, as the crowd is itself both a source of interest and a guarantee of worthwhile entertainment to further passers-by: a successful performance space has been created, and even Silliman is caught long enough to note its details.

### To Beg the Question

In closing the circle of a performative space, a crowd of listeners distinguished the singer from that closely related category, the beggar. Both Sack and

---

[42] John Leighton, *London Cries & Public Edifices. By Luke Limner Esq.* (1847).
[43] Silliman, *Travels*, 166–7.

Bywater have found modern street performers keen to observe that distinction, the former recording that performers received less money when they were perceived as beggars rather than musicians, the latter observing similarly that: 'Although busking apparently places the performer in the role of mendicant or petitioner, these performers would rather present it as a public display of – or investment in – their cultural capital, with the intention of receiving financial interest.'[44] The true beggar, by contrast, does not entertain a crowd, but rather seeks to establish a connection with the individual.[45]

Ballad-singers cannot always have succeeded in drawing a crowd, and it was at these times – alone, vulnerable, seeking rather than sustaining attention – that the line between singer and mendicant was at its most blurred. A beggar could always become a ballad-singer, and vice versa. In 1833 James Chasty testified at the Old Bailey that: 'I have been troubled with the severest poverty for two years; it was in a moment of urgent distress; I had not a place to lay my head – I have even gone to ballad singing to get bread'.[46] The first official Mendicity Commission heard from Reverend William Gurney that: 'There are others who are continually begging from house to house; they go through a great number of streets in the day, occasionally taking a ballad or a bunch of matches'; heard from Sampson Stephenson that one 'nimble young man' would travel 'without a hat, with a waistcoat with his arms thrust through, and his arms bare, with a canvass [sic] bag at his back; he begins generally by singing some sort of a song, for he has the voice of a decent ballad-singer', and that one Thomas Shepherd 'goes about singing ballads, and goes almost naked' to solicit sympathy; and heard from George Henry Malme of James Barratt, who 'has a club foot, and generally passes about the street singing'.[47] In 1814 William Reeve, co-proprietor of and composer for Sadler's Wells, found a young boy 'singing Ballads in the Street . . . and questioned him, concerning his Parents, and how he came to sing in the Streets'. The boy answered that his father 'had turned him into the Street; where by begging, he obtained enough money to buy a few Ballads, and between begging and Ballad singing he had supported himself'.[48]

In pursuing the connection between 'Beggars and Ballad Singers'[49] I am seeking neither to impose a hierarchy of occupations, nor to apply a dismissive value judgement to the former category. The work of Tim

---

[44] Sack, 'Street Music', 66; Bywater, 'Performing Spaces', 101.

[45] For a lucid sociological account of the 'emotional micropolitics' behind such interactions, see Candace Clarke, *Misery and Company: Sympathy in Everyday Life* (Chicago, 1997).

[46] POB t18331017-61.     [47] *Report from Committee*, 26; 52; 59; 67.

[48] George Speaight (ed.), *Professional and Literary Memoirs of Charles Dibdin the Younger* (1956), 109–10.

[49] See Interlude I and this chapter.

Hitchcock in particular has demonstrated how begging was a complex phenomenon deeply imbedded in the social fabric, and that 'the underlying cultures of obligation at the heart of these exchanges have been unreasonably ignored by historians'.[50] Reading against the grain of official discourse, Hitchcock reasons that beggars possessed 'the ability to construct in words and symbols a sophisticated and undeniable claim to the alms of men and women ... [and] to deploy fragments of a series of cultures of obligation that cut across the condemnation of begging found on the statute books'.[51] This was especially impressive in a culture where, in the words of Martha Stoddard Holmes, 'the truly deserving never ... "obtrude" themselves', so that 'what is at stake for a person telling his or her story is not only to tell the truth but also to tell it plausibly enough to generate support'.[52] Hitchcock's findings have wider ramifications, if we concur that 'London was more welcoming and more charitable, more orderly and more forgiving, than historians have allowed. It also suggests that the eighteenth-century poor were creative and imaginative actors in their own lives, and in the life of this metropolis.'[53] If ballad-singers augmented their performances by drawing upon related codes of social obligation, it is as indicative of their resourcefulness as of their desperation. Moreover, evidence of such practices persisting into the nineteenth century, particularly within the context of an act predicated on the rational exchange of goods (the song) for money, is highly suggestive of the persistence of early modern structures of society into the Victorian era, just as Chapter 2 found with regard to the self-regulation of neighbourhood order.

Such evidence exists in abundance right across the period. In 1808 a writer for the *Lady's Monthly Magazine* confessed that: 'A troop of merry Savoyards – a warbling ballad-singer – or the more specious gratification of a charity play, draws the money readily from the pocket', suggesting that sentiment, rather than desire to purchase the ballad, was the motivation.[54] And in 1846 we find a parallel case in the *Ladies' Cabinet*, where the writer assigns 1,300 words to describing the sentiments generated by a lone female singer, ending: 'when the sound of song struggles with

[50] Tim Hitchcock, 'Begging on the Streets of Eighteenth-Century London', *Journal of British Studies* 44 (2005): 478–98, 479.
[51] Ibid., 496.
[52] Martha Stoddard Holmes, 'Working (with) the Rhetoric of Affliction: Autobiographical Narratives of Victorians with Physical Disabilities', in James C. Wilson and Cynthia Lewiecki-Wilson (eds.), *Embodied Rhetorics: Disability in Language and Culture* (Carbondale and Edwardsville, 2001), 27–44, 36–37. See also Martha Stoddard Holmes, *Fictions of Affliction: Physical Disability in Victorian Culture* (Ann Arbor, 2004).
[53] Hitchcock, *Down and Out*, xvi.
[54] 'The Busy Body', *Lady's Monthly Museum* 4 (June 1808): 275.

the sigh of sinking hope, and the voice falters on the accents of broken melody[,] Pass not by ye manly readers and gentle dames, a ballad singer such as this!'[55] To take another parallel across time: in 1795 the author of *The Observant Pedestrian* discoursed for a chapter on an encounter with 'The Ballad Singer', who is described as 'a real object of compassion', exciting simultaneous feelings of disgust and obligation: 'thrice I determined to inquire his woe-fraught story, but my feelings instantly shrinking, repelled the wish'.[56] And in the early 1860s, Charles Allston Collins confessed to a similar conflict of sentiments, acknowledging the moral force of mendicancy: 'It is a dreadful thing to be begged of . . . Is there any one who has not quailed when he has seen the beggar-woman thus waiting for him, or, still worse, crossing over the street higher up, ready to attack him as soon as he gets within fire?'[57] A third generic pairing may be found in the 'serio-comic' grumbler of 1812 who makes an exception amid a wider attack on balladeers for 'the grunting, bellowing, lame and blind *warblers*, who really merit pity and benevolence'[58] and the cynic in *The English Gentleman* of 1845, moved to obey those codes of obligation despite himself: 'As for the ballad-singer, as a general rule, the policeman should be referred to, yet one sometimes hears a female voice, which distress and cold have not entirely ruined, proceeding from a thin and wasted form . . . it is impossible to refuse her your charity.'[59] Such was the singer-beggar's challenge: to overcome disgust and suspicion in order to forge a sympathetic, and ultimately profitable, connection.[60]

A fourth coupling of commentators brings out a common thread in the accounts above: the role of the singer's voice, generally considered a property of their commercial and musical performance, in appealing instead to charity. In a discussion of listening, Gardiner notes that 'we yield to sympathy what we refuse to description. There is a moving tone of voice, as Mr. Burke observes, an impassioned countenance, and agitated gesture, which affects [us] independently of the things about which they are excited'.[61] Jerrold gives us an imagined context for this effect:

At times we come upon ballad-singing that has its plaintiveness; a pathos, independent of the words and air, though the ballad shall be sweetly sung. May such

[55] 'The Italian Boy', *Ladies' Cabinet of Fashion, Music, and Romance* (1 September 1846): 156–66, 160.
[56] *The Observant Pedestrian; or, Traits of the Heart: in a Solitary Tour from Cærnarvon to London*, 2 vols. (1795), vol. 2, 211–12.
[57] Charles Allston Collins, 'Beggars', *Macmillan's Magazine* 5 (1861–1862): 210–18, 210.
[58] *Metropolitan Grievances*, 105.    [59] 'Beggars', *The English Gentleman*.
[60] Besides Clarke and Stoddard Holmes, referenced earlier, see also Paul K. Longmore, *Telethons: Spectacle, Disability, and the Business of Charity* (Oxford, 2016), esp. 94–6.
[61] Gardiner, *Music of Nature*, 55.

singing be seldom heard; may the passenger be rarely stopt [*sic*] when hurrying on a winter's night homewards, by the low, sweet voice of some thinly-clad woman, hugging her child, for whom and it may be for others, her wretched minstrelsy is to buy a supper. We have heard such singing; and the tune of the minstrel, the intonation of the words, told a tale of misery; declared that she had suffered many rubs of fortune; that she was not born to sing the requiem of her own lungs in November's fog and January's blast.[62]

Here it is a specifically musical voice that conveys sentiment by tone and timbre. Yet voice is further allied, in both accounts, to physical appearance and gestures both more commonly associated with begging than singing. We may conclude that it is unhelpful to place these elements in opposition: rather, a singer's signs of distress – plaintive voice, poor clothing, dependent infant – may all be considered as properties of performance. To suggest that singers exploited these signifiers of distress in order to play upon their audience's feelings is not to deny that these signifiers could be genuine. Singers simply made use of whatever assets they possessed – which included a demonstrable lack of material assets. One of the most popular ballads of the mid-century was 'The Wandering Bard of Exeter', each verse of which consists of a winning, even witty tale of how the singer-narrator came by their makeshift, disreputable apparel, thus making stage properties out of coat, hat, handkerchief, waistcoat, shirt, breeches, and shoes, exploiting their mismatched and shabby appearance – it is, in short, the perfect vehicle for the destitute singer.[63] In the first verse, the singer is compelled by poverty to 'either sing or cry', the verse concluding with the couplet: 'My lot is cast I am forced at last / To ask of you to buy' – a request repeated in the song's final lines: 'Now buy my song be it right or wrong / Twill help a wandering Bard.'

There is a knowingness in 'The Wandering Bard''s performance of mendicancy. As Hitchcock puts it, 'ballad-singers . . . seem to have built on the insecurity and excitement of the street, rather than trying to escape from it'.[64] Elizabeth Kathleen Mitchell makes the excellent point that the tendency for female singers to be accompanied by a pitiable infant, though a play for charity so common that these children had a 'flash' or slang name – 'King's mots' – was also a function of the occupation's practicality.[65] 'Pregnant women and those minding their small children could do this work more readily than other jobs. The trade required no special equipment aside from perhaps a basket, sturdy pocket, or an apron

---

[62] Jerrold, 'The Ballad Singer', 295.
[63] Bod. Harding B 25(1997). See Interlude I. As mentioned there, the tune is unknown.
[64] Hitchcock, *Down and Out*, 65.    [65] *Swell's Night Guide*, 123.

to carry the prints.'[66] Thus a happy marriage (whatever the singer's own domestic situation) was made between the performance of need, and the relative convenience of child minding while singing.

In 1817, a twenty-six-year-old singer named Ann Lee took this phenomenon to its extreme logical consequence, when she was convicted of kidnapping the two-year-old daughter of Mary Moseley, a resident of Chelsea.[67] Moseley 'received information, and found the prisoner with my child at the Royal Hospital public-house – it had two songs in its hand – the prisoner also had songs', a story corroborated by both the waterman Thomas Chittle, and one of the pub's patrons, Mary Pearce. Pearce 'went into the Royal Hospital public-house to get some beer, and saw the prisoner come in with the child, offering her songs for sale. I gave the child a halfpenny, seeing the woman in distress.' Lee, it transpired, had appropriated another woman's infant in order to make her performances as a ballad-singer more profitable by appealing to the sentiment of customers like Pearce. In the short term, this strategy was a demonstrable success. In the longer term, Lee's gamble failed to pay off: she was sentenced to seven years' transportation.

### Vocal Performance

Whatever the commercial gains afforded by drawing upon the techniques of mendicancy, the comparison with begging was one more way for the forces opposed to singers to deny their musicality. Nowhere is this denigration more apparent than in descriptions of the singer's voice. It should be made clear that, for all these claims of unmusicality, we are discussing *singing* rather than chanting, declamation, or recitation: my subject is not Mayhew's 'long-song sellers' or 'patterers' but the ballad-singer, and though scholars such as David Atkinson have (quite rightly) averred from setting too much store by the 'talismanic' status of the term 'oral', arguing that ballad texts could easily be separated from melody, and that many broadsides may have been read more than they were sung, my concern is those *who sang*.[68] To settle any doubts, we might cite a letter from W. J. Barrett of 2 Scott Street, just off North Street on the Whitechapel Road, given in Mayhew's own 'Answers to Correspondents' section in 1851:

Seeing in your periodical an account of street Ballad-singing, I have ventured to pen a few remarks relative thereto. I have often stood to listen to the rude music of

---

[66] Elizabeth Kathleen Mitchell, 'William Hogarth's Pregnant Ballad Sellers and the Engraver's Matrix', in Patricia Fumerton and Anita Guerrini (eds.), *Ballads and Broadsides in Britain, 1500–1800* (Farnham, 2010), 228–47, 233.

[67] POB t18171029-137.

[68] David Atkinson, 'Folk Songs in Print: Text and Tradition', *Folk Music Journal* 8 (2004): 456–83, 457–8.

those ditties, and it struck me they were not disagreeable, and, being a student of music, I committed to memory the tunes and wrote them on paper; if your correspondents, therefore, should feel desirous of obtaining the music (of any street ballad) they can by communicating with me.[69]

Though we cannot consult Barrett ourselves, it is a heartening sign, not only that singers *did* sing, but also that their performances were not universally derided among the literate. Given Barrett's address – between Whitechapel and Bethnal Green, just north of the Brady Street Jewish cemetery – and our understanding of the readership of Mayhew's original journalism, Barrett's letter may constitute a practically unique instance of working-class description of ballad singing. As with the multimedia representations of Chapter 1, Barrett is evidently performing her or his distinction: 'rude music' and 'not disagreeable' look like positioning strategies to convey Barrett's respectable status in this public sphere. Nonetheless, the legible musicality of the singers referred to is irrefutable. Even in the condescending account of W. H. Smyth, mentioned later and in Chapter 2, Smyth recognises the melody as 'a sort of Rory O More' – while he deprecates the circumstances, he acknowledges the music.[70]

We should not simply dismiss the raft of elite indictments of balladsingers' voices. When the presumably disinterested Oliver Goldsmith employs the analogy 'bawling for fair play, with a voice that might deafen a ballad singer', we may reason that, situated in a noisy streetscape, singers would naturally have sung extremely loudly to make themselves heard.[71] This accords with Bragg's busking advice on voice: 'You're competing with the noise of the street, the traffic, and you're trying to get the attention of people who are in a hurry. My test is – could a passing lorry driver hear me? If they can, then the people walking past can too.'[72] W. H. Smyth describes the voice of the male singer he encounters as 'though inferior in compass to [the world-famous Swedish soprano] Jenny Lind's, … a precious deal louder than mine or Parker's'.[73] Other accounts more suggestive of tone than volume – full of screechings, raspings, thin and reedy voices or hoarse and coarse voices – should lead us to accept that many singers possessed very poor vocal tone, but also to attribute some of this perception of unmusicality to the difference between a formally trained and an untrained voice: akin today to the difference between a 'classical' and a 'folk' singer.[74] There is of course an awkwardness in what Marsh calls 'reading such

[69] 'Answers to Correspondents' 23 (17 May 1851), cited in Taithe, *The Essential Mayhew*, 157.
[70] BL Ballads HS.74/1251 (222).     [71] Goldsmith, *Vicar of Wakefield*, 56.
[72] Bragg, 'How to Busk?'     [73] BL Ballads HS.74/1251 (222).
[74] Both the distance and the connection between these worlds is in evidence on the bass singer Joel Frederiksen's *Requiem for a Pink Moon: An Elizabethan Tribute to Nick Drake*

evidence against the grain', seeking clues to musical performance in descriptions that strive to deny that status.[75] In Marsh's own exhaustive survey of the early modern period, he can turn up only a single positive first-hand reception account of a singer's voice – yet it is a good one: that of Roger North, a Restoration-era lawyer and writer whose 'dominant passion' was music, and whose many writings on that subject were, according to the musicologist Jamie C. Kassler, highly innovative.[76] North includes ballad-singers in his discussions *On Music*, writing of 'a loudness that downs all other noise, and yet firme and steddy. Now what a sound would that be in a theater, cultivated and practised to harmony!'[77] This is perhaps the single most convincing description we have: loud but untrained, sufficient to its purpose, which was to render audibly and accurately the primarily modal street melodies of North's time.

It is worth pausing on this putative dichotomy of the trained (theatrical) voice and the untrained (street). As I discuss in Chapter 4, a high proportion of ballad tunes were theatrical in origin. We know that singers from the theatre or even the opera could sink to, or supplement their salaries with, street ballad singing.[78] Nor was the reverse trajectory out of the question. The child singer quizzed earlier by Reeve, known as 'Master Demar', was taken on at Sadler's Wells and had a successful season, being 'generally encored', before running away with the house silver: Charles Dibdin the Younger writes of his 'very sweet, strong, and flexible voice'.[79] Two years later in 1816, the *Morning Post* ran two articles about 'A Mr. J. King, who is said to have been a working goldsmith, and who, from the pressure of the times, was compelled to take up the humble profession of a street ballad-singer'.[80] He was heard by the managers of Covent Garden, and appeared that December in the part of 'Blind Beggar', the *Post* reporting that: 'His voice has great clearness and variety, and some of his tones are remarkably fine. He was rapturously *encored*', and that: 'His voice embraces three entire octaves, and is so full, rich, and harmonious, that it astonished all the musical Professors.' These considerations should guard us against a crude binary of

---

(CD: Harmonia Mundi, 2012); compare Frederiksen's interpretations with Drake's originals.
[75] Marsh, *Music and Society*, 239–40.
[76] Mary Chan, 'North, Roger (1651–1734)', *ODNB*, oxforddnb.com/view/article/20314.
[77] John Wilson (ed.), *Roger North on Music* (1959), 215, cited in Marsh, *Music and Society*, 245.
[78] These include George Demery Archer of Drury Lane and the Opera House (POB t17950520-47), and 'two women … that formerly sung at Sadler's Wells' (t17770910-21).
[79] Speaight, *Professional and Literary Memoirs*, 109.
[80] 'Drury-Lane Theatre', *Morning Post* 14326 (20 December 1816) and 14332 (27 December 1816). Let us hope that Mr J. King's first name was not Joe.

two unrelated vocal traditions, suggesting a more nuanced world where ballad-singers, though largely untrained, may often have possessed the musicality necessary to perform complex theatrical melodies – yet may also have operated within a vernacular musical idiom based upon different vocal conventions to the stage or the concert hall.

In this light, even the negative accounts afford insights. An 1852 article by William Allingham in *Household Words* mocks an Irish ballad-singer of around thirty-five thus:

[H]is vocal excellence consists in that he twirls every word several times around his tongue, wrapt in the notes of a soft, husky, tremulous voice. In this style of gracing – which is considered highly artistic, and for which, I believe, 'humouring' is the country phrase – the words are delivered somewhat as follows:

> This pay-air discoo-ooeyoor-cèrced with sich foo-oocy-oorce o' ray-
>     ayizin,
> Ther may-aynin they ay-apee-ayx-esprayss'd so-hoo-o-o clearrrr,
> That fau-hor to lae-ssen too-oo ther caw-aw-he-on-vairsay-ay-ashin,
> My ehe-ee-in-clinay-aheeay-ashin was for too-oo-hoo-hoo draw-aw-
>     haw-ee-aw-a-neerrrrr.[81]

Yet we find similarly absurd phonetic renderings in descriptions of concert singers. Gardiner, in discoursing on the proper manner of attacking syllables, continues:

The following slovenly expressions from a bass singer of eminence will be in the recollection of many.

> *Doo-ark-ness* shall cover the earth.
> The *Gen-te-oyles* shall come to thy *le-oyt*,
> The *she-had-dow* of death.
> The wings *oo-hof* the *woo-inde*.
A soprano of eminence,
> Bid me *dis-ke-orse, de-ance* and play.[82]

The comparison leads us to take more seriously Allingham's preamble, and to draw an analogy between vernacular 'gracing' and the syllabic extensions of the respectable stage. This relativism continues: a few pages later, Gardiner's description of the famous operatic star Catalani's singing as 'offensively loud to those who were placed near her' becomes a reminder of how ballad-singers were criticised for their own loudness – whereas in fact both Catalani and the balladeer must have painstakingly cultivated their delivery so as to be heard across a busy street or from the back of a crowded auditorium. In Gardiner's own words, 'volume and force of voice are essentially necessary in a public singer'.[83] Even his

---

[81] Allingham, 'Irish Ballad Singers', 4.    [82] Gardiner, *Music of Nature*, 72.    [83] Ibid., 76.

instructions for amateur singers, designed to promote better vocal technique, conjure up the image of the stock ballad-singer discussed in Chapter 1:

The first and most important operation is to open the mouth so completely, that the voice may meet with no obstruction in its course. To do this, the head must be thrown a little back, while standing in an erect posture, opening the mouth so as to admit three fingers set edgewise between the teeth[.][84]

This is not to say that there were not bad ballad-singers, but that it was an art with the potential to be performed well or badly. One of Mayhew's interviewees is quoted as opining that: 'It would puzzle any man, even the most exactest, to tell what they could make by ballad-singing in the street. Some nights it would be wet, and I should be hoarse, and then I'd take nothing.' To be clear: he did not 'take nothing' because the night was wet, but because the rain made him 'hoarse' – not only could one singer be good or bad, and aware of the fact, but in admitting that poor singing did not pay, the singer implies that successful singers *sang well* and were rewarded for it.[85] Bezer, in his brief spell as a street singer in 1838, thought as much: 'Whether it was my singing loudly – for I had a good strong voice at that time, – or my peculiar earnest manner, I know not, but, when I counted up my gains at about six o'clock, they amounted to six shillings, and, I think, fourpence.'[86] This is of course to speak of subjective judgements on the part of passers-by, who cannot all have been as harsh as those who denigrated singers in print: given that most singers were unaccompanied, it is hard to believe that the average auditor condemned them out of hand as tuneless in an age before the standardisation of musical pitch.

Having resolved to rescue the ballad-singer's voice from its critical exile as 'noise', the challenge becomes whether we can say something meaningful about their vocal performances. Frustratingly, modern writing on the subject suffers from inadequate referencing – Leslie Shepard, for instance, makes unsubstantiated claims for the 'uncanny power' of certain vocal inflections – yet contemporary evidence may be found to bear out this and similar assertions.[87] Allingham's comic account underpins

<hr/>

[84] Ibid., 28.     [85] Mayhew, *London Labour*, vol. 3, 196.     [86] Vincent, *Testaments*, 180.
[87] Leslie Shepard, *The Broadside Ballad: A Study in Origin and Meaning* (1962), 38. One notable exception is Ó Madagáin, 'Functions of Irish Song', yet the focus here is explicitly on singing in Ireland, in Irish, so that its findings cannot in all conscience be applied to Irish ballad-singers in London.

more recent discussion of Irish ballad-singers, stressing the high regard of street audiences for 'supplementary syllables' and extensive gracing, which was apparently much praised.[88] Earlier in his narrative, Allingham also gives the following description:

[A] ballad-singer, a young woman in old plaid cloak and very old straw bonnet, strikes up, with a sweet Connaught lisp, and slightly nasal twang, 'The Sorrowful Lamentation of Patrick Donohoe' – with the words 'Come all you tender Christians!' – and soon summons around her a ring of listeners. She will sing *da capo* as long as the ballad appears to draw attention and custom[.][89]

Besides seeming to give us evidence of the 'vernacular' voice – note the lisp and 'slightly nasal twang' – the woman's practice in 'summoning' a crowd around her with her opening words is highly reminiscent of the following interview conducted by Alan Lomax in the mid-twentieth century:

When I asked a bluff old lumberjack . . . what made a good bunkhouse singer, he was equally emphatic. 'Why, a feller that has a loud, clear voice so you can hear him – a man that can speak his words out plain so you can understand what he's singing about – and a fellow that remembers all the words.' Such is a folk definition of the underpinnings of the come-all-ye style that has dominated balladmaking in Britain and America for the last three centuries.[90]

This gives us other performative frames for the voice: loudness for the sake of inclusivity, and clarity for the better communication of text, which was, after all, the singer's primary function if they were to sell their wares.

There is, in these two accounts, an approximation of Lawrence Kramer's ideal of 'Songfulness' – a vocal delivery neither too technically proficient nor too virtuosic, informed by the (in this case entirely mercenary) consideration that 'the addition of voice to a melody activates a set of human relationships that an instrumental performance can only signify'.[91] Kramer's concept is admittedly problematic – in his own words, 'Being so Protean, songfulness seems not only to elude but also to resist critical or analytical understanding' – yet there is certainly a suggestion that the successful performances of Allingham's Connaught lisper, Mayhew's informant, Bezer, and the lumberjack's ideal singer might all be classed as 'songful'.[92]

---

[88] Neilands, 'Irish Broadside Ballads', 219–20.    [89] Allingham, 'Irish Ballad Singers', 3.
[90] Alan Lomax, 'The Good and the Beautiful in Folksong', *Journal of American Folklore* 80 (1967): 213–35, 214.
[91] Lawrence Kramer, 'Beyond Words and Music: An Essay on Songfulness', in Walter Bernhart, et al. (eds.), *Word and Music Studies: Defining the Field* (1999), 303–19, 306.
[92] Ibid., 307.

The songful ideal, self-consciously devoid of artifice, is clearly at odds with the apparent praise of gracing, and further contrasts a series of assertions found in Edward Lee's *Music of the People*, in which Lee states that: 'The tone of the street-singer appears to have been much broader, with a heaviness of technique well suited to the sentimentality which we have already noticed in much of the nineteenth-century urban song.' Lee quotes Cecil Sharp's observation that balladeers 'like to sing in as high a pitch as possible, and will often apologise for not being able, on account of age, to sing their songs high enough', placing it in conjunction with Albert Lloyd's dictum that: 'The street singers commonly pitched their songs about a fifth higher than their voice would really take, and they used voice breaks, slides, and high rasping wails, and in that way lines which look on paper merely sad and tearful become as thrilling as an Indian war whoop.'[93] Though unsubstantiated, this accords with repeated contemporary observations of the shrillness or high pitch of singers, and in particular with Jerrold's memory of the first ballad-singer he ever heard, singing 'Listen to the Voice of Love':

Billy had a rich *falsetto* . . . he would murmur, preludise a few low notes, then rush into it, and, once there, he knew too well his own strength to quit it on small occasion. Billy's *falsetto* was his fastness, where he capered and revelled in exulting security. We hear it now; yes, we listen to his 'love' whooping through wintry darkness – proudly crowing above the din of the street – shouting triumphantly above the blast – a loud-voiced Cupid 'horsing the wind.' Was it a fine cunning on the part of the musician – we trust it was – that made him subdue into the lowest mutterings all the rest of the song, giving the whole of his *falsetto*, and with it all his enthusiasm, to the one word 'love?' If this were art, it was art of the finest touch . . . we have known a worse *falsetto* than his ten thousand times better paid[.][94]

Between Lloyd's enthusiastic valorisation – 'thrilling as an Indian war whoop' – and Jerrold's ironical sketch, we may detect traces of plausible sound: high, keening, even – to borrow the ubiquitous idiom of the period – electrifying. There is clear consonance here with both later 'folk' traditions, especially in eastern Europe, and (as Jerrold hints) the high registers of contemporary trained singers; writing at the end of the nineteenth century, the musicologist Francis Cunningham Woods declared himself astonished at both the extensive gracing and the staggeringly high pitch of songs that were 'popular' a century earlier.[95] Yet within Jerrold's parenthetic asides we find vocal style married to pragmatism – 'crowing above the din of the

---

[93] All from Edward Lee, *Music of the People: A Study of Popular Music in Great Britain* (1970), 120.
[94] Jerrold, *The Ballad Singer*, 296.
[95] Francis Cunningham Woods, 'A Consideration of the Various Types of Songs Popular in England during the Eighteenth Century', *Proceedings of the Musical Association* 23rd Session (1896–1897): 37–55, 40.

street – shouting triumphantly above the blast'. We are returned to the considerations of noise with which this chapter began: a difficulty that singers appear to have met, not only by singing loudly, but by singing high, pitching their voices to the treble register of their auditors' ears so as to be distinguished from the lower sounds of traffic, conversation, and other street vendors.

Considered, then, in their totality, singers' vocal performances appear to have exhibited a range of evolved responses to the challenges of the street, within which different musical styles may be distinguished. Each of these techniques was at once cultivated to aid the sale of their songs, and each may be read in negative, from volume, to pitch, to gracing, in the accounts of their detractors. Yet time and again, it appears these vocal techniques were condemned, if only subconsciously, not for running in opposition to those of trained stage and concert vocalists, but for running in parallel. The successful ballad-singer was manifestly musical.

## Embodied Performance

'Whatever else music is "about," it is *inevitably* about the body'.[96] The relevance of Richard Leppert's axiom is striking: from their visual representation to their physical presence in the thoroughfare or before a prominent building, the singer's body was a vexed issue, central to both status and performance. Already in this chapter and the last, we have observed how singers could conversely attract custom by dressing up as royalty, or else exploit the trappings of penury, turning rags, wounds, infants, into stage properties in order to elicit greater sympathy from passers-by. Such techniques were taken a stage further by Joseph Johnson, to whom the next interlude is devoted: Johnson, a black disabled ex-seaman, turned bodily markers of marginalisation to palpable advantage in his years as a ballad-singer around 1815. It is important to note that the singer's body was more than a mannequin upon which to hang visual signifiers, however: for while artists consistently represented singers as static figures, rooted mulishly to the spot, more detailed accounts indicate that singers were as mobile within their performances as they were in their lives as a whole.

In Peter Bailey's account of indoor singing in the 1830s, the performers' use of dance is linked to the practice of the ballad-singer, via a quotation from Blanchard Jerrold:

The performer had to capture the attention of a large and increasingly anonymous crowd otherwise engaged in the rival attractions of eating, drinking, conversing,

---

[96] Richard Leppert, *The Sight of Sound: Music, Representation, and the History of the Body* (Berkeley and Los Angeles, 1993), xx. See also ibid., esp. xxi–ii, 64.

gazing, posing, lounging, flirting and promenading. The most effective technique was a cross between singing and shouting accompanied by various forms of stage business and a high degree of physicality, from 'winks and gesticulations', to 'the jerk (of the body) at the beginning of each line, in true street style'.[97]

In search of this 'true street style', we encounter John Badcock's rejoinder to Pierce Egan, *Real Life in London*, in which there is a characteristic sendup of an Irish ballad-singer. This 'Irish paddy' begins his song, not by clearing his throat, but by 'hitching up the waistband of his breeches', prior to his song 'to the tune of "Morgan Rattler," accompanied with a snapping of his fingers, and concluded with a something in imitation of an Irish jilt ... By this time a crowd was gathering round them'.[98] The incident is fictional, but appears based on actual performance – if not witnessed by Badcock, then at all events gleaned from the pages of John Thomas Smith. Smith's *Vagabondiana* takes note of several outré ballad-eers, one of whom 'accompanied his voice by playing upon a catgut string drawn over a bladder, and tied at both ends of a mop-stick'; another, Matthew Skeggs, 'played a concerto upon a broomstick', while one of Smith's etchings depicts another singer playing a 'fiddle' composed of two long tobacco pipes, one to represent the instrument, the other its bow.[99] These 'accompaniments', with the possible exception of the cat-gut, have nothing to do with music and everything to do with gesture, ironical and embodied; 'play' in its truly ludic sense. This was one advantage enjoyed by the ballad-singer over their rival street musicians: freed from the necessity of manipulating an instrument, they had hands and body free to 'add value' to their performances (always assuming that they could remember the words to the song in question). It is easy to imagine the singer of comic songs catching the eye, and thereafter the ear, of an audience with such strategies: certainly they caught the attention of Smith. Badcock's dancing Irishman bears still more resemblance to another of Smith's subjects, Thomas McConwick, an Irish singer immortalised in Smith's *Cries of London*. 'McConwick sings many of the old Irish songs with excellent effect, but more particularly that of the "Sprig of Shillelah and Shamrock so green," dances to the tunes, and seldom fails of affording amusement to a crowde[d] auditory.'[100] Smith interviewed McConwick, reporting the singer's view that 'the English populace were

---

[97] Peter Bailey, *Popular Culture and Performance in the Victorian City* (Cambridge, 1998), 131.
[98] John Badcock, *Real Life in London; or, the Rambles and Adventures of Bob Tallyho, Esq. and his cousin, the Hon. Tom Dashall, through the Metropolis*, 2 vols. (1821), vol. 1, 124.
[99] Smith, *Vagabondiana*, 45, 139.
[100] John Thomas Smith, *The Cries of London: Exhibiting Several of the Itinerant Traders of Antient and Modern Times* (1839), 67 and facing plate XXII.

taken with novelty, and that by either moving his feet, snapping his fingers, or passing a joke upon some one of the surrounding crowd, he was sure of gaining money'. Such is the performance of 'Irishness' found in Badcock; a knowing exploitation of the mood of the London crowd, effected as much by movement and gesture as voice or repertoire.

It may be significant that we have no corresponding accounts of female singers making use of their bodies in physical action, suggesting perhaps that street decorum precluded such a degree of free and playful movement. Certainly, with the exception of the 'extraordinary case' brought before the police at Hatton Garden, there were no breeches roles on the London street, restricting the scope of female performance relative to the respectable stage. For there is a definite theatrical parallel here: like their more celebrated counterparts, ballad-singers had to act as well as sing – they seem to have favoured low comic roles – and of necessity provided their own costumes. Unlike in the theatre, however, the all-important commercial transaction occurred at the end of the singer's act, rather than as its necessary precursor. Singing was evidently a multi-sensory, embodied activity, the common thread to which was the central imperative alluded to by McConwick: to create first of all an audience, and second, paying customers.

### Playing the Crowd

Bailey's description of the 'pub-singer' here acknowledges a debt to 'the well-practised techniques of the street ballad singer, whose craft of some centuries persisted among the hawkers or chaunters still contesting the hubbub of the modern street in their assertive appeals to a less than captive audience'.[101] Though a theatrical audience could be restive, it had nonetheless paid up in advance and was ostensibly there to see the show, whereas a street audience could move on without payment, and the wealthier its constituent members, the more likely they were to have somewhere else to be. As concertina player Lea Nicholson told Michael Bywater in 2004, 'when you're busking, they're not the audience. That's not what they've come out to be. They've got other things on their mind, and your job is to make them *be* an audience for a bit'.[102] As seen above, the ballad-singer had various tactics available to draw attention, at the centre of which remained their single greatest asset: that, as Tia DeNora has remarked, 'by anatomical design, the ear is "always open"'.[103] Yet attention does not necessarily generate either interest or sympathy. To

[101] Bailey, *Popular Culture*, 131.    [102] Bywater, 'Performing Spaces', 99–100.
[103] DeNora, *Music in Everyday Life*, 132–3.

sell their songs, singers had to establish a relationship with the mobile crowd sufficiently strong to generate committed auditors and, subsequently, purchasers.

This was of course a bilateral phenomenon and relied upon the crowd as much as the singer. If great events were afoot, citizens of London would be more likely to accord a singer time if they thought the song likely to be of topical relevance. As Charles Manby Smith wrote in the aftermath of the Crimean conflict: 'The song-trade is always most flourishing in periods of public excitement, and there is nothing more conducive to its prosperity than a stirring and popular war.'[104] David Love 'got more in a day than I do in a week now' at times when the fleet was docked and sailors were bent on making merry ashore.[105] Yet he was also well equipped to take advantage of such situations, having 'studied many curious songs, some on love, others on war, or whatever happened on any thing of note, such as a merry wedding, or pitched battle, &c.' so as to be ready to compose and perform new songs on these subjects when the occasion demanded – such as 'The Wanton Widow of West-gate, or the Coachman clapped in Limbo', which he had printed in haste at Berwick-upon-Tweed.[106] He recalled: 'I sold them very quick. I said, here is a new song, a song that is funny, well worth your money, concerning the wanton widow and the coachman; and that I might lose no time, a boy brought them to me, by three or four quires as I sold them; I made a very good night's work of it, and the next day I sold them well.'[107]

Here we see Love responding to a situation not merely by writing a song, but by taking pains to convince a putative audience of its interest – as new, funny, worthwhile, and topical. Rather than confine himself to his text, he actively promoted it to listeners. As Sack writes, 'when a performer recognises the audience and even moves into its space, the critical distance of performer and audience is broken, and the audience is further drawn into the performance. This "trick" is crucial for a musician to make money.'[108] This was a knack Love exhibited from his very first performance, described in Chapter 2, wherein he 'got a stool, mounted, and thus began my harangue'.[109] Note both the use of a prop to take control of his physical space and increase his prominence, and the term 'harangue', in an address that began with the salutation 'Good people' and continued by fashioning his motley audience into two colluding interest groups: young men wishing to buy songs about proud and vain

---

[104] Smith, *Little World of London*, 255.
[105] Love, *The Life, Adventures, and Experience*, 67.
[106] As with all of Love's own songs, the tune is unknown – as also, in this case, are the words!
[107] Ibid., 38.    [108] Sack, 'Street Music', 10.
[109] Love, *The Life, Adventures, and Experience*, 32–3.

young women, and young women intent on the reverse. Love profited by transcending the anonymity and heterogeneity of the situation, recasting himself as a keeper of special knowledge, and by constructing two special interest groups desirous of that knowledge.

This returns us to the argument of Chapter 2: though singers stood outside and indeed beneath society, in performance they became integral to both the workings and the identity of that society. By a single rhetorical stroke Love made each listener sensible of their normative gender role and its ensuing motivations, to his ultimate profit. Similarly, one 'chaunter' of Mayhew's described 'the ladies' as 'our best customers'[110] and gave the following account of his disingenuous technique in 'working' potential female customers, which, though perhaps overwritten by Mayhew, is at least indicative of the practice of constructing a 'type' of audience by flattering preparatory patter:

[I]f I see a smart dressed servant girl looking shyly out of the street-door at us, or through the area railings, and I can get a respectful word in and say, 'My good young lady, do buy of a poor fellow, we haven't said a word to your servants, we hasn't seen any on 'em,' then she's had, sir, for 1d. at least, and twice out of thrice; that 'good young lady' chloroforms her.[111]

Love's account of his first success brings home another key point about listening to a ballad-singer: though one listened and bought the song as an individual, listening was also a highly social and sociable act, and to become a member of a ballad-singer's crowd was to participate in a specific sort of social encounter that placed one in dialogue, not only with the singer, but with other members of that crowd. Such is the message of the essayist William Shenstone's recollection, that: 'The ways of ballad-singers, and the cries of halfpenny-pamphlets, appeared so extremely humourous [sic], from my lodgings in Fleet-street, that it gave me pain to observe them without a companion to partake.'[112] This consciousness of being one of many listeners was denounced by the *Scourge* as part of the ballad-singing problem, as their writer described the 'surrounding *mob*, composed of people of all ages, who affect the sneering grin or fascinating look, when any thing ludicrous or infamous is expressed'.[113] By this reading, a form of peer pressure was exerted by participation in the crowd that reinforced the influence of the singer, to the detriment of collective morality. In short, as Simon Frith argues, '"listening" itself is a performance'.[114] It is this communal

---

[110] Mayhew, *London Labour*, vol. 1, 228.     [111] Ibid., 227.
[112] William Shenstone, *Essays on Men and Manners* (Ludlow, 1800), 85.
[113] C.-R. S., 'Ballad-Singers', 378.
[114] Simon Frith, *Performing Rites: On the Value of Popular Music* (Oxford, 1996), 203.

performativity that Jerrold ironises when he discusses both the magnetic pull one singer exerted over his crowd, and the social relations between self-conscious listeners – one of whom is forced to defend her own raptness:

> A short time since, we paused to listen to the mud-notes wild of a street-singer [whose audience] stood in a ring of five or six deep about the slanderer, mutely, hanging upon the fellow's words . . . in the face of one creature we saw the growing anger spot: 'Infamous! he ought to be taken up, come away!' and she urged a matronly companion, who placidly replied, 'Not yet, Mary Anne – let's wait, only just to hear how far the fellow's impudence will carry him.'[115]

All this added up to make the experience of ballad singing far more than the communication of a song from mouth to ear. Singers were faced with restive, knowing, self-conscious crowds that had to be worked, fashioned, warmed up, if they were to buy the song. There is an implication in *Streetology* that singers spent almost as much time between recitations engaged in talk and transaction as they did in actually singing.[116] In the first half of the nineteenth century, this appears to have led to a great evolutionary step in ballad singing, one that was to transform the practice irrevocably. Singers had always, it seems, been able to preface a song with patter – the 'come-all-ye' touch described earlier by Lomax – and in 1789, George Parker even parodied this practice in his description of 'The Ballad Singer in the neighbourhood of St. Giles's', wherein the singer both begins and ends in supplication dressed up in highly 'flash' language, wheedling at the end: '*What*, no *copper clinking* among you, my hearties? No one to give me hansel? What, have you got *red-hot heaters*, in your *gropers*, that you're afraid to thrust your daddles in them? It won't do I say, to stand here for *nicks* – all hearers and no buyers – what, will none of you drop your loose *kelter?*'[117] By the middle of the nineteenth century, this spoken patter had developed further, becoming encoded *within* the performance of individual songs, wherein sung verses were interspersed with prose skits, as in the case of the pair of singers encountered by Lhotsky and described in Chapter 2, who: 'Instead of "Black-eyed Susan" and the usual stock in trade . . . were chanting a duet of political conundrums.'[118]

---

[115] Jerrold, 'The Ballad Singer', 294–5.
[116] The passage reads: 'As the time they are occupied in singing a song is not more than a few minutes, they chaunt about six or seven times within the hour, selling from two to half-a-dozen songs each time . . . they keep at it for four or five hours'. Reckoning a song at five minutes, that leaves nearly half an hour for the business side of things – which may or may not have helped preserve the singer's voice, depending on how committed they were to their patter! 'Rag', *Streetology*, 84.
[117] Parker, *Life's Painter*, 124.    [118] Lhotsky, *Hunger and Revolution*, 30.

Mayhew goes further, his description of pairs of 'chaunters' and 'running patterers' constituting almost a whole new trade – though one still rooted in the sale of printed ballads:

[W]ithin these few years the running patterers, to render their performances more attractive, are sometimes accompanied by musicians. The running patterer then ... takes his stand with the chaunter in any promising place, and as the songs which are the most popular are – as is the case at many of the concert-rooms – sometimes 'spoken' as well as sung, the performers are in their proper capacity, for the patterer not only 'speaks,' but speaks more than is set down for him, while the chaunter fiddles and sings.[119]

Twenty years later, Charles Hindley spoke of this development as a well-established practice:

To 'work a litany' in the streets is considered one of the higher exercises of professional skill on the part of the patterer. In working this, a clever patterer – who will not scruple to introduce anything out of his head which may strike him as suitable to his audience – is very particular in his choice of mate, frequently changing his ordinary partner, who may be good 'at a noise' or a ballad, but not have sufficient acuteness or intelligence to patter politics as if he understood what he was speaking about.[120]

We should exercise caution in taking Mayhew and Hindley on trust, especially given their predisposition to categorise, to inscribe legible order upon what must have been a heterogeneous and informal set of practices. Yet the parallels are telling: both describe spoken improvisation, and a double-act akin to that familiar from the music halls of the nineteenth and indeed much of the twentieth centuries. Mayhew explicitly links the practice to that of the 'concert-rooms', by which he has in mind, I think, the emerging halls rather than Hanover Square. The 'patter song' had featured on stage since at least the 1790s, when Charles Dibdin the Elder introduced many in his solo entertainments, and there is certainly a sense here that the nineteenth-century ballad-singer was evolving along the lines of the one- or two-man show. It is likely, as discussed in the final section of this book, that this was a response to the declining *musical* capital of their performances: as competition from organ-grinders, brass bands, and a legion of other instrumental and vocal buskers increased, singers may increasingly have drawn upon their extra-musical potential as eloquent street characters, working elements of stand-up comedy and soap-box politics into routines still based upon the sale of song sheets.

This evolution may be detected, as suggested paradoxically by Mayhew's 'speaks more than is set down for him' and Hindley's 'introduce anything

---

[119] Mayhew, *London Labour*, vol. 1, 226.     [120] Hindley, *Curiosities*, 52.

out of his head', in the printed songs themselves. 'Anything to Earn A Crust' is the witty 'confession' of a street performer on the make, recounting his past 'fakements' in verses broken up by five prose sections that in turn parody: the sale of a 'Last Dying Speech and Confession'; a beggar's pleas for charity; a hawker's patter; a Grub Street poet's bluster; and a paper boy's promotion of a murder story.[121] Similarly, 'Billy Nutts, the Poet' is interspersed with five spoken introductions to successive comic verses, each of which gives the lines a witty, informal frame of reference, punning in prose on the subject of the verse to come.[122] These prose sections begin as conversational segues, linking otherwise unconnected verses, the metre of which is highly variable. The effect is that of an original comic routine, all written out ready for the singer to recite and, crucially, to *elaborate upon* for the amusement of the crowd – members of which could thereafter recreate the act for an indulgent familial or social circle.

'Jimmy Jumps the Rhymer' is written as a direct riposte to this last song, beginning:

> Oh, you've heard talk of Billy Nuts,
> That great distinguished Poet;
> But people say I him outcuts,
> And very soon I'll show it.[123]

It includes directions for both spoken prose and poetry, as well as sung verses and a chorus, the whole constituting an elaborate, knowing, self-referential collage of street showmanship, wherein the self-aggrandising performer is in effect acting the part of himself – but not *her*self, for both these songs are highly gendered, and it is no coincidence that such extroverted *braggadocio* was framed as masculine. Even the oldest such song, which is ostensibly a duet for man and wife, was designed to be performed by a single male, employing by turns a 'gruff' and a 'squeaking' voice.[124] 'Beggars and Ballad Singers' was an infinitely adaptable song, endlessly reprinted with new arrangements of both sung and spoken sections. First performed in 1806 by John Bannister at Drury Lane (and thus plausibly written by Thomas Dibdin, who wrote many songs for Bannister, though the tune dates back to the mid-eighteenth century), the song appears in playbills as the preserve of a male entertainer – a Mr Braint performed it at Leeds in 1826 – whose solo imitation of a married couple doubtless generated much of the comic effect.[125] It was repeatedly

[121] Bod. Harding B 20(5).    [122] Bod. Firth c.21(4).    [123] Bod. Firth c.21(7).
[124] William Oxberry, *The Actor's Budget* (1811), 287.
[125] *The Songster's Museum of Celebrated Modern English, Irish, and Scotch Songs, for the Year 1807* (2nd edn, 1806), 8–12; Leeds Theatre playbill (20 December 1826), www.leodis.net/playbills/item.asp?ri=2003616_23333376.

printed on broadsides and presumably sung in the street, perhaps even by
pairs of singers, who might perform their own assumed identities, with
spoken interjections ranging from 'Look down with an eye of pity on an
unfortunate seaman. I lost my precious leg with gallant Nelson, God bless
him! and I value the loss of my pin no more than a bit [of] old mouldy
biscuit', to the mock-cantankerous exchange preceding a chorus:

Vy this an't a bad halfpenny, Doll, what the ge'man giv'd you. – 'Why, it is.' – Vy,
it an't, I say. – 'Why then you lie.' – Lie! if you say as how I lie, I'll punch your
pimpkin. 'You, you fellow you! why, if you offer to touch me, I'll break your fiddle
about your head, I'll shew you I don't care that for your nor your
    Fol loll, &c.[126]

One spoken skit even echoes Mayhew's chaunter above, who would
address serving girls as if they were mistresses: 'I address every old
maid, for I am sure to know them by their vinegar countenances, by the
title of "Most beautiful lady;" – a raw awkward fellow of a recruit, "Most
noble captain;" – any person in a carriage, "Right honourable;" – and so
on.'[127]

Whether such songs reflected practice, created new forms of it, or
indeed exerted a form of control or sanitisation over street performance –
turning genuinely subversive figures into Mockney self-caricatures – they
testify to a particularly nineteenth-century phenomenon whereby the
final generations of ballad-singers developed newly composite forms of
performance, in bids to remain relevant and appealing in a competitive
market for street entertainment. If nothing else, the ability to mix song
and drama, jokes and repartee, remained one of the singer's last great
assets in their attempts to play the crowd.

### Performing the Ballad

Whether a comedian, actor, demagogue, the ballad-singer still remained
literally defined by her text, the physical ballad sheet – slip, broadside,
songsheet, garland – of which, in order to secure anything like a living
wage once the printer was paid off, she had to sell many dozen copies
every day. Whatever else constituted her performance, above all else she
had to communicate – more or less accurately – that text, and do so in
such a way that listeners would not simply move on, satisfied, but would
seek to obtain a copy for themselves. Sources that enable us to consider
this ultimate dimension of performance are scarce. There is, however, one
substantial anecdote that serves as a fascinating starting point for most

---

[126] This phrasing comes from variant BL 1606.aa.24 (42).    [127] Bod. Firth c.21 (2).

aspects of this relationship. It comes – probably – via Hindley, who had, he claims, a friend who:

[N]ever would complete his purchase until he had heard the whole ballad sung at least once through. He maintained that the flavour was much improved for ever after if this rule had been rigorously adhered to at the time of purchase. One Saturday afternoon, as he was walking near the Old Kent Road, the familiar sounds caught his ear; he followed, and was soon close to a ballad-singer, a middle-aged, middle-sized, slightly dilapidated person, with no great strength about him but his voice. Our friend pulled up, and walked slowly along the pavement by the side of the singer, who was just beginning his stave again. He sang two stanzas with his eye on the new comer, and then offered him the sheet; but our friend shook his head. After one more stanza, the offer was repeated, and again declined. 'Presently,' our friend said, 'presently.' The man upon this continued singing, keeping his eye, however, restlessly on his apparently unwelcome companion; and after selling one or two sheets, and coming to the third stanza, again he stopped short. He looked again full at our friend, and then, seeing no sign of his moving on, dashed his old hat more firmly on his head with one hand, clutched his bundle of ballads with the other, and rushed into the nearest public[-house], exclaiming, 'There be lots more verses; but they be so 'nation cutting, I can't sing 'em!'[128]

The closing phrase, '[dam]nation cutting', is ambiguous: a straight reading after the *OED* definition of 'cutting' as 'That [which] acutely wounds the mind or feelings' would see this ballad-singer – who is, after all, not strong – overwhelmed with distress at the sadness of the narrative he sells.[129] A more euphemistic interpretation might infer that the verses grow scandalous or indecent. In either case, what must have been a common tactic is exposed: singing only the early verses of a longer song, so that a curious audience would be forced to buy in order to find out the rest. At a stroke, the persistence of the centuries-old model of many-versed songs becomes far more understandable in practice: it made commercial sense for singers. Marsh informs us of early modern performances that lasted up to an hour: certainly a possibility in the alehouse or home, but impractical in a busy street.[130] As Bertrand Bronson observes, the texts of songs did not grow radically shorter until the twentieth century and the era of radio – and though the songs were long on the page, we might conceive of singers' performances, especially if they had multiple texts for sale, as constituting a form of radio programming, with songs abridged at the singer's discretion.[131] An article of 1825, discoursing on the singer Ned Friday (active *c*.1805), remarks of his 'Jemmy Dawson' that 'to those who seemed more than usually interested in the sad record, he gave the full narrative'. Clearly Friday's common practice

---

[128] Hindley, 'Street Ballads', 410.    [129] www.oed.com/view/Entry/46407.
[130] Marsh, *Music and Society*, 286–7.    [131] Bronson, *The Ballad as Song*, 204.

was to sing the first part, then shut up and sell – but he would oblige with the full account if further remuneration appeared probable.

There is more to be gleaned concerning songs' strophic organisation in the light of Hindley's friend's apparently eccentric view that to hear the whole song through 'improved the flavour' thereafter. It is no easy matter to make numerous verses, often poorly typeset and poorly written, all scan to the same tune. While the first verse of most songs adhered fairly accurately to the metre, subsequent verses could stray far from the path, requiring substantial editing to fit to the correct notes and rhythm – the extending of some syllables, the cutting of others, or the mangling of certain common phrases, leading to such idiomatic constructions as 'for to hear'. Working with classically trained modern singers, I have found they often struggle with making their latter verses scan, even when given the luxury of writing out the 'underlay' below the notated melody. How much harder, then, to undertake this sophisticated poetical-musical labour in one's head on a street corner? Singers must have deployed considerable skill and experience in this matter, and a prudent purchaser wishing to hear the song through could both obtain guidance in how to do likewise, and ascertain whether the song remained singable all the way through!

Not all street songs were long, strophic ballads – but most of them were, even those deriving from the theatre. The latter had the benefit of distinctive melodies, but many more were written out as words only, to one of several common metres. While these might specify a well-known tune to which they should be sung (an instruction the singer could follow or ignore), most did not: it is notable that, while the majority of seventeenth-century ballads recommended a tune, by the nineteenth century, this had become exceptional.[132] This lack of prescription both challenged and empowered the singer, who was not only at liberty, but required, to choose a suitable melody. As Mayhew records:

I was told, on all hands, that it was not the words that ever 'made a ballad, but the subject; and, more than the subject, – the chorus; and, far more than either, – *the tune!*' ... To select a tune for a ballad, however, is a matter of deep deliberation. To adapt the ballad to a tune too common or popular is injudicious; for then, I was told, any one can sing it – boys and all. To select a more elaborate and less-known air, however appropriate, may not be pleasing to some of the members of 'the school' of ballad-singers, who may feel it to be beyond their vocal powers; neither may it be relished by the critical in street song, whose approving criticism induces them to purchase as well as to admire.[133]

Mayhew appears to be speaking of ballad-writers as well as singers here, yet the same problem applied to both: to be sufficiently musical and

---

[132] Marsh, *Music and Society*, 248.      [133] Mayhew, *London Labour*, vol. 1, 275.

melodious to entertain, without alienating an audience incapable of replicating one's own vocal dexterity. According to music semiotician Gino Stefani, melodies in this happy middle ground tend to have, as one might readily imagine, 'ranges limited to about an octave, conjunct motion, periodic durations of breath, and syllabic setting of text … making songs with such qualities more singable, and perhaps more singalongable' – qualities that add up to a fair description of many recorded ballad tunes.[134] Mayhew also draws attention to the notion of the 'appropriate' – a question of melodic fitness I have discussed extensively elsewhere.[135] There was one aspect increasingly common to many song texts, however, which could reconcile this distance between singer and audience: the chorus.

To speak of a chorus as opposed to a refrain is to mark a subtle qualitative shift between the early and late eras of ballad singing: a creeping shift from a preference for single repeated lines, or a repetition of the last line of each verse (though there were of course exceptions to this), to a fully fleshed-out chorus of two to four lines. As Mayhew protests: 'I was corrected … by a street chaunter for speaking of this burthen as a jingle. "It's a chorus, sir," he said. "In a proper ballad … there's a four-line chorus to every verse; and, if it's the right sort, it'll sell the ballad."'[136] One constant across the centuries, however, was the prevalence of 'nonsense' in these repeated sections: the '*derry downs*, and *toll de rolls*' that clergyman James Plumptre considered 'merely an apology for noise and riot'.[137] Plumptre's condemnation contains the seed of these choruses' strength as an aspect of the ballad-singer's performance: they provided an opportunity for the audience to participate, irrespective of their familiarity with the theme of the song. This was the case, for example, at the funeral of the boxer Tom Sayers, in Camden High Street, 1865: 'A little way off was a ballad singer chanting in praise of the deceased hero, and gathering halfpence from the throng. The ditty being set to a popular tune, many of the people about joined in the chorus'.[138] In the words of literary theorist Richard Blackmur, such practices are 'the lyric gesture of recognition and the emphatic gesture of identity. The ballads are full of it'.[139]

---

[134] Gino Stefani, cited in Alisun Pawley and Daniel Müllensiefen, 'The Science of Singing Along: A Quantitative Field Study on Sing-along Behaviour in the North of England', *Music Perception* 30 (2012): 129–46, 131.
[135] Cox Jensen, *Napoleon*, 20–2, 47, 56, 151.
[136] Mayhew, *London Labour*, vol. 1, 275.     [137] Plumptre, *A Collection of Songs*, 12.
[138] 'The Burial of Tom Sayers', from the *Pall Mall Gazette*, cited in *John Bull* 2345 (18 November 1865): 756.
[139] Richard P. Blackmur, *Language as Gesture: Essays in Poetry* (1954), 21. See also ibid., 13–22; and Kramer, 'Beyond Words and Music', 312.

Nor is the word 'gesture' – an aspect also developed by Edward Cone with regard to nonsense choruses – of relevance merely in a poetic or metaphorical sense.[140] As Andreas Haug has written: 'The creation of such a refrain is not primarily an aspect of compositional form, but of performance', tellingly tracing the refrain's origins to 'songs which accompanied or underscored motion'.[141] We are returned – via Haug's analogy of 'dance songs', Plumptre's talk of 'riot', and also Bruce Smith's etymological linking of the words 'ballad' and 'ballet' in its sense of dance – to an understanding of performances as more than vocal, instead constituting embodied, communal acts, including both participation and movement.[142] Thinking again of the choosing of tunes, it is far from coincidental that many *topical* ballads took their tunes from fiddle dances, with the chorus often fitted to the dance tune's B-section. We might very plausibly recall our vision of the all-action singer – itself a far cry from the static, stolid figure in contemporary images – and place it in dialogue with an audience also in motion, tongues and toes (or even hands and hips) contributing to the totality of the performance. Musicologists have conjectured that 'by joining its participants in a relatively unison activity, singing along facilitates the formation of temporary neo-tribes in leisure contexts, where mostly strangers are brought together socially to form a tribe, and then are instantaneously released from the tribe once the event is over'.[143] As a model for the formation of singers' crowds, this makes a strong case for the 'magic' influence ascribed to song, and the potential power of songs for influencing mass opinion, as discussed in the previous chapter.

Very often, the physical iteration of the ballad included not only text, and either a specified melody or a suggestive metre, but also an image – normally a woodcut – at the head of each song, as discussed at the end of Chapter 1. Recent and ongoing research by early modernists has moved well beyond the old assumption that these were paired with songs more or less at random, and it is possible that, in performance, the singer may have made use of these images.[144] Sadly the evidence for the

[140] Edward T. Cone, *The Composer's Voice* (Berkeley and Los Angeles, 1974), 162–3.
[141] Andreas Haug, 'Ritual and Repetition: The Ambiguities of Refrains', in Nils Holger Petersen, et al. (eds.), *The Appearance of Medieval Rituals: The Play of Construction and Modification* (Turnhout, 2004), 83–96, 86.
[142] Smith, *Acoustic World*, 170.
[143] Pawley and Müllensiefen, 'The Science of Singing Along', 130.
[144] Christopher Marsh in particular has published extensively on this issue. See his '"The Blazing Torch": New Light on English Balladry as a Multi-Media Matrix', *The Seventeenth Century* 30 (2015): 95–116; 'A Woodcut and its Wanderings in Seventeenth-Century England', in Fumerton, *Living English Broadside Ballads*: 245–62; and 'Best-Selling Ballads and their Pictures in Seventeenth-Century England', *Past and Present* 233 (2016): 53–99.

later period is silent on any explicit link between image and performance. In several of the artistic representations also detailed in Chapter 1, the singer's sheaf of copies, and sometimes the slip in their hands, is arranged so that the heading illustration is visible to the hypothetical audience, albeit usually upside down. It is unclear whether this is an artistic device, the better to indicate that the papers *are* songs – undeniably the connection between image and ballad was understood by artists and public alike – or representative of actual practice. It is easy to imagine singers drawing attention to unusual or striking images as an asset of a particular song for sale, the better to secure a purchase. This must have been especially true of more 'collectible' broadsides such as Christmas carols, which featured a more extensive – and often rather striking – degree of illustration, and were often coloured and sold at double price.[145] More resourceful singers might even have used certain well-matched images as cues to imaginative performance, the pictures helping them to inhabit a particular role.

All this achieved, only one moment remained: that of the successful financial transaction. This was most famously described in verse a century earlier, from the singer's perspective:

> [I] Begin to sing. The people soon
> Gather about, to hear the tune –
> One stretches out his hand, and cries
> Come, let me have it, what's the price?
> But one poor halfpenny, says I,
> And sure you cannot that deny.
> Here, take it, then says he, and throws
> The money. Then away he goes,
> Humming it as he walks along,
> Endeavouring to learn the song.[146]

It was no great feat to remember or to pick up a song – bear in mind that melodies were relatively short and repeated with each verse – and recent research has endorsed the view that even the most unmusical listener can quickly recognise and retain an entire tune.[147] Nor is there a great conceptual leap from hearing to repeating a song. In an era before recorded sound, this was entirely normal. As Nicholas Cook writes, 'to hear any

---

[145] For examples, see http://ballads.bodleian.ox.ac.uk/search/themes/Christmas%20carols. See also Cox Jensen, 'The Ballad and the Bible'; Smith, *The Cries of London*, 48; and Hindley, *History of the Catnach Press*, xvi.

[146] *Weekly Register* (9 January 1731).

[147] Matthew D. Schulkind, et al., 'Musical Features that Facilitate Melody Identification: How Do You Know It's "Your" Song When They Finally Play It?', *Music Perception* 21 (2003): 217–49.

music as form is then to hear it as repeatable, and hence as independent of its realisation in sound on any particular occasion'.[148] As to why one would decide to purchase a song: for the most part, the desire to have entertaining material to perform and to fill one's leisure time must constitute much of the explanation. Lyrics might reward rereading; the material object was moreover useful for adorning walls with cheap imagery, and thereafter as wrapping or even lavatory paper. But what of baldly topical songs, containing news rather than emotional or aesthetic value? If nothing else, 'purchasing a song … allows one to "own" the song', in a more than literal sense.[149] As Booth writes of early modern ballads telling of new-found sea monsters:

Once one has heard the song itself, it is idle to pretend that one buys the ballad to learn about the strange fish. Buying shows the buyer's desire not merely to learn the facts but to take possession of them. Owning the ballad confers certain proprietary rights and opportunities. The new owner can, for example, take it back to the tavern with him and amaze a circle of listeners.[150]

Furthermore, ownership also conferred 'the right to suspend disbelief and riot in credulity. Why would your own ballad lie to you?' This sort of circular self-affirmation may have been at play, reinforcing the potency of the bought song. Still, it was no concern of the ballad-singer's, whose vocation was founded upon the security that tomorrow, there would be a new song – or a new old song – to master and to sell.

### A Saturday in 1812

In 1862, retired journalist William Harvey looked back on his youth in 'Street Music of London Fifty Years Since', when he had been a lad of sixteen. This account – a stroll through the City eastwards at 8pm on a Saturday in October – combines descriptions of an implausible number of musicians with a suspect degree of rhetorical embroidery and nostalgic sentimentality, yet the ballad-singing performances it describes tally precisely with the findings of this chapter.[151] Peter Links draws 'a great crowd in Salisbury-square', in anticipation of which he has 'wisely mounted on a stool, to give his voice more freedom'.[152] The next 'thick gathering' encountered is 'at Waithman's corner' – a significant crossing point between Fleet Street and Ludgate Hill and thus an excellent place

[148] Nicholas Cook, *Music, Imagination, and Culture* (Oxford, 2002), 36.
[149] Paul Charosh, 'Studying Nineteenth-Century Popular Song', *American Music* 15, no. 4 (1997): 459–92.
[150] Booth, *Experience of Songs*, 107.    [151] Harvey, *London Scenes*, 343–53.
[152] Ibid., 347.

for a pitch. This singer, Martha Hart, has a voice that 'is low, but clear and sweet'; she performs an old heraldic ballad, which is 'highly relished, and applauded as it deserved, for that soft, low voice was very winning' – songful, perhaps? – thereby allowing her (though she is already forty in 1812) to be 'heard in London streets till 1830'.[153] A far cry, this, from the shrill caterwauling of contemporary condemnation.

Continuing eastwards, 'The Arethusa' is sung 'at the Fleet Prison gate', a prominent civic landmark in a nautical part of town – an appropriate location also for the 'youth, gentlemanly in appearance, and with a rich tenor voice', who sings the 'Death of Nelson' nearby.[154] A 'comic artist' impersonates a Yorkshireman, as did the West End comedian John Emery; another imitates the 'brogue' of the stage singer John Henry 'Irish' Johnstone.[155] Still others fit their appearance to their parts, from 'a one-legged individual, in the militia dress, roaring forth his version of the "British Grenadiers"', to 'a pair of masquerading sailors' who sell 'The Bay of Biscay' and 'The Storm', and the singer of a hunting song who has donned 'a tattered red coat ... and a hunting-whip' in order to caricature 'a master of the hounds'.[156] A genuine crippled sailor chooses a suitably piteous number – 'A tar, with only a left arm, is rehearsing the praises of "Poor Tom Bowling"' – indeed, so apt are the various pairings of singer and song that one is tempted to put the whole lot down to invention rather than recollection.[157] Yet whether or not Harvey's reminiscences are drawn directly from life, his account is a valuable aid in imagining a variety of performances that deploy a range of techniques, from the spatial to the gestural, the visual to the vocal, in order to secure a paying audience in a highly contested streetscape. Harvey's singers, observed at the safe distance of half a century, can actually sing rather than croak or squeal: they can also act, raise a laugh, or extract a tear as well as a halfpenny. Such are the singers we have observed at work: skilled practitioners exploiting the commercial opportunities of a largely hostile environment, fashioning, from their tiny corners of the London street, spaces not only for gain, but for artistry.

---

[153] Ibid., 347–8.    [154] Ibid., 348–9.    [155] Ibid., 349.    [156] Ibid., 351.    [157] Ibid., 352.

# Interlude III
## 'The Storm'

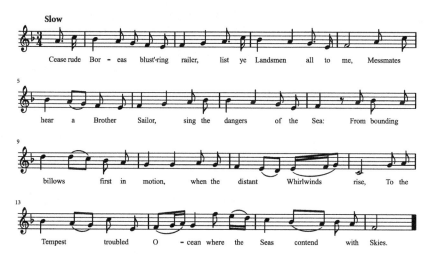

**Slow**

Cease rude Bor - eas blust'·ring railer, list ye Landsmen all to me, Messmates

hear a Brother Sailor, sing the dangers of the Sea: From bounding

billows first in motion, when the distant Whirlwinds rise, To the

Tempest troubled O - cean where the Seas contend with Skies.

Example III.1  George Alexander Stevens, 'The Storm' or 'Cease Rude Boreas. A Favorite Song, Sung by Mr. Incledon', vocal reduction (1795)[1]

Hark the boatswain hoarsely bawling by top-sail sheets and haul-yards stand,
Down top-gallants quick be hauling, down your stay-sails, hand boys hand,
Now it freshens at the braces, now the top-sail sheets let go.
Luff boys luff, don't make wry faces, up our top-sails nimbly clew.

A later and lengthier version of this interlude has been published as 'Joseph Johnson's Hat, or, The Storm on Tower Hill', in *Studies in Romanticism* 58 (2019): 545–69.
[1] Author's own copy. Stevens' version dates from around 1770, the year of the earliest extant score (BL Mus H.1994.a (202)). This is in agreement with Gerald Kahan, *George Alexander Stevens and the Lecture on Heads* (Athens, Georgia, 2008), 35. It is rarely easy to date the origin of Stevens' pieces: see James Sambrook, 'Stevens, George Alexander (1710?–1784)', *ODNB*, oxforddnb.com/view/article/26422.

Now all you at home in safety sheltered from the howling storm,
Tasting joys by heaven vouchsafe ye of our state faint notions form
Round us roar the tempest louder think what fear our minds
    enthralls [sic],
Harder yet it yet blows harder now again the boatswain calls

The top-sail yard points to the wind boys see all clear to reef each
    course.
Let the fore sheet go don't mind boys tho' the weather should be
    worse,
Fore and aft the sprit sail-yard get reef the miz[z]en see all clear,
Hands up each preventer brace man the fore-yard cheer lads cheer.

Now the dreadful thunder roaring peal on peal contending clash,
On our heads fierce rain falls pouring in our eyes blue lightnings flash,
One wide water all around us all above us one black sky,
Different deaths at once surround us, hark! what means that dread-
    ful cry.

The foremast's gone! cries every tongue out o'er the lee twelve feet
    'bove deck,
A leak beneath the chest tree's sprung out, call all hands to clear the
    wreck.
Quick the lan-yards cut to pieces, come my hearts be stout and bold,
Plumb the well the leak increases four feet water in the hold,

Whilst o'er the ship wild waves are beating, we for wives and children
    mourn.
Alas! from hence there's no retreating, alas! to them there's no return.
Still the leak is gaining on us both chain pumps are choak'd [sic] below,
Heaven have mercy here upon us, for only that can save us now.

O'er the lee beam is the land boys let our guns o'er board be thrown,
To the pump come every hand boys, see our miz[z]en mast is gone,
The leak we've found it cannot pour fast we've lightened her a foot or
    more,
Up and rig a jury fore-mast she rights she rights boys we'er [wear] off
    shore.

Now once more peace round us beaming, since kind heaven hath sav'd
    our lives.
From our eyes joy's tears are streaming for our children and our wives.
Grateful hearts now beat in wonder to him who thus prolongs our days.
Hush'd to rest the mighty thunder every voice breaks forth his praise.[2]

---

[2] The text inevitably varies across editions. This edition comes from a broadside printed by
R. Harrild, 20, Great Eastcheap, between 1809 and 1821 (Bod. Johnson Ballads fol. 303),
the likeliest text for the performance under discussion, which – like most broadsides –
condenses the text by half, making one line from every two for reasons of space, hence the
lack of punctuation in the middle of each line above.

In the immediate aftermath of the Napoleonic Wars, 'Cease, Rude Boreas', commonly known to contemporaries as 'The Storm', had been in circulation for more than forty-five years, though its tune was still older. Previously associated with the nautical titles 'The Sailor's Complaint' and '[Admiral] Hosier's Ghosts', it was set by Handel as the sixth of his twenty-four *English Songs* as 'Come and Listen to my Ditty'.[3] The song given here, however, appeared first in George Alexander Stevens' solo show *Lecture on Heads*, then in domestic score and street broadside, before being revived on London and regional stages in the 1790s by the Cornish tenor (and ex-naval seaman) Charles Incledon.[4] Set Incledon to one side, however – he will reappear in due course – for this interlude is concerned with one particular performance, or set of performances, of the song: those by the ballad-singer Joseph Johnson. Indeed, in homage to Timothy Brook's inspirational study, this section might almost be called, not Vermeer's, but Johnson's hat.[5]

Johnson, who is well documented, is therefore a necessarily remarkable figure, given a place in Smith's *Vagabondiana*, a long section of the 1825 'London Ballad Singers' article in the *Mirror of Literature*, and the anti-quarian John Timbs' rather later (and rather derivative) compendium, *Curiosities of London*.[6] In *Vagabondiana* itself, Smith draws particular attention to Johnson's singularity by according him a full-page etching (see Figure III.3) to accompany his account of Johnson's performative strategies:

[I]n order to elude the vigilance of the parochial beadles, he first started on Tower-hill, where he amused the idlers by singing George Alexander Stevens's 'Storm.' By degrees he ventured into the public streets, and at length became what is called a 'Regular Chaunter.' But novelty, the grand secret of all exhibitions, from the Magic Lantern to the Panorama, induced Black Joe to build a model of the ship Nelson; to which, when placed on his cap, he can, by a bow of thanks, or a

---

[3] See http://tunearch.org/wiki/Annotation:Hosier%27s_Ghosts. The Handel setting is the sixth of his twenty-four *English Songs*: HWV 228[6]. A recording may be heard at http://yo utu.be/BjNGHaFduwU. My thanks to Berta Joncus for her immense kindness in alerting me to the Handel setting and the tune's wider history.
[4] 'Incledon, Charles Benjamin 1763–1826, singer, actor', in P. H. Highfill, K. A. Burnim, and E. A. Langhans, *A Biographical Dictionary of Actors, Actresses, Musicians, Dancers, Managers, and Other Stage Personnel in London, 1660–1800*, 16 vols. (Carbondale, 1973–1993), vol. 8, 86–99. Incledon is also endowed with a remarkably thorough Wikipedia entry.
[5] Timothy Brook, *Vermeer's Hat: The Seventeenth Century and the Dawn of the Global World* (2008).
[6] Smith, *Vagabondiana*, 33; 'London Ballad Singers', 42; John Timbs, *Curiosities of London* (1855, New edn 1867), 10–11.

supplicating inclination to a drawing-room window, give the appearance of sea-motion. Johnson is as frequently to be seen in the rural village as in great cities; and when he takes a journey, the kind-hearted waggoner will often enable him in a few hours to visit the market-places of Staines, Rumford, or St. Albans, where he never fails to gain the farmer's penny[.]

Smith's biographical sketch exceptionalises its subject, marking him out from the masses as a person worthy of special consideration. Yet in the case of Johnson, it also serves to demystify and de-exoticise, attributing a pragmatic economic motive to his remarkable headgear, and presenting a narrative common to many performers and petty traders in the London street, whose acts were attributable first and foremost to a legal technicality by which they could evade official persecution if they sold or performed rather than begged.

Smith also situates Johnson and his performances in tangible spaces: Tower Hill, 'the public streets', and the marketplaces of satellite towns. The second of these was, as the previous chapters have established, the ballad-singer's usual home, a mixed commercial space with heavy footfall; the first and third spaces, however, invite closer attention. To take the latter first: Staines, Romford, and St Albans boxed the compass on three sides, lying west, east, and south of London on a radius approximating to today's M25 ring road. We may suppose Johnson to have visited on market days, involving a more rural audience in his performances. His presence may not have been altogether dissonant. Staines marketplace, for instance, features an imposing Georgian public house called 'The Blue Anchor', that would have constituted a suitably maritime backdrop for the ex-sailor. Johnson also took the sea with him: by bobbing and weaving to make his model 'sail', he thereby fashioned a seascape out of any surrounding crowd, in a *coup de théâtre* that transformed those around him into unwitting nautical scenery.[7] Besides, the late Georgian marketplace still carried connotations of the fair, with its attendant traces of carnival: the singing sailor from London knew what he was doing in soliciting 'the farmer's penny'.

Tower Hill, meanwhile, referred to the open space immediately west of the Tower of London, a prominent spot used until late into the previous century for executions and the pillory, now thronged with tradespeople and promenaders. Though hemmed about by both ancient and modern bastions of the political and commercial state in the Tower and the newly erected Mint, the Hill itself afforded an open space for genteel recreation and thereby custom for the singer, as idealised in Robert Bremmel Schnebbelie's illustration for Hughson's *Depiction of London* (1810),

---

[7] With thanks to Matthew Ingleby, whose incisive questioning provoked this observation.

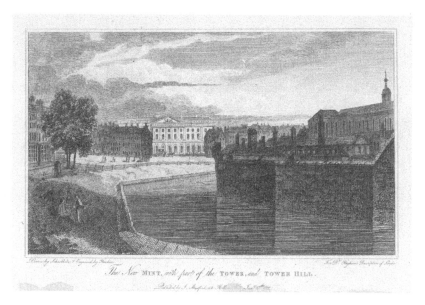

Figure III.1  W. Hawkins after Robert Bremmel Schnebbelie, 'The New
Mint, with part of the Tower, and Tower Hill', 1810.
Engraving. Yale Center for British Art, Paul Mellon Collection

reproduced as Figure III.1 – an image from which minority figures such as
Johnson are predictably excluded.

This urban-pastoral take on the London landmark was not the only form in
which it might be represented, however, as evidenced in a satirical print by
Charles Hunt (Figure III.2). Tower Hill marked the boundary between the
City of London and the insalubrious – though commercially crucial – East
End. From its heights, Johnson's auditors had a view over the Thames, its
docks, and its staggering volume of shipping. This gave the area a marked
nautical as well as mercantile character that, in the years of depression
following the end of the Napoleonic Wars, made for a decidedly mixed
message. Hunt's caricature places Tower Hill in conversation, not only
with the navy, but with the alehouse and the pawn shop, the crooked can-
non/bollard a bathetic echo of the midshipman's own career, now equally
askew.

While Hunt's superannuated midshipman is reduced to blacking
boots, Johnson's chosen employment was ballad singing. Tower Hill,
where he began, lay two miles east of Seven Dials, home of the
leading ballad printers, from whom he might be expected to source
his physical wares. However, there was a printer of ephemera,

Figure III.2  Charles Hunt, 'A Mid on Half Pay. Tower Hill', 1825.
Aquatint (hand-coloured). © The Trustees of the British Museum

R. Harrild, located a few streets away from the Tower at 20 Great
Eastcheap, who is known to have stocked Johnson's signature song
'The Storm' at around this date.[8] Besides 'The Storm', known works
in Johnson's repertoire were 'The British Seaman's Praise' and 'The
Wooden Walls of Old England', as well as 'the best of Dibdin's
songs', presumably meaning those on nautical themes.[9] Johnson him-
self had been a sailor in the merchant marine, rather than a true Jack
Tar, and his choice of ballad stock exploited this association.[10] 'The
Storm', like those later nineteenth-century stalwarts 'The Sea' and 'A
Life on the Ocean Wave', is not a *naval* but simply a *nautical* song,

[8]  See Edward G. D. Liveing, *The House of Harrild, 1801–1948* (1949).
[9]  *Vagabondiana*, 33; 'London Ballad Singers', 42. Charles Dibdin the Elder's posthumous
     reputation rested almost exclusively on his 'sea songs'. See Oskar Cox Jensen, David
     Kennerley, and Ian Newman (eds.), *Charles Dibdin and Late Georgian Culture* (Oxford,
     2018), throughout but especially the Introduction and chapters 7 and 11.
[10]  *Vagabondiana*, 33.

Figure III.3  John Thomas Smith, 'Joseph Johnson', 1815. Etching on
paper. Author's own copy

its manly maritime character enough to confer the stamp of patriotism upon its singer. Johnson's choice of songs, besides carrying a
personal significance to him based on his professional background,
was well judged to resonate with his sites of performance, from
Staines to Tower Hill, and helps us begin to make sense of his
most captivating attribute: the vessel on his head (Figure III.3).

   This headgear warrants extensive consideration. For both Kwame Dawes
and Mark Stein, the image of 'the ship' on a black man's head necessarily
recalls the slave trade, and the forcible migration of people. For Dawes, it is
'the badge of his immigrant status – his sense of alienation and difference',
while for Stein, 'this hat is *doubling* Johnson's blackness ... [it] confronts
white guilt by making it more explicit ... it turns Johnson into a spectacle of

otherness'.[11] While a perfectly valid reading, representing one plausible association for Johnson himself, this seems unlikely to have been a strong association for most Londoners – perhaps unlike their Bristolian and Liverpudlian compatriots – who, circa 1815, were likelier to have leapt to more comfortable frames of reference: profitable trade in non-human commodities, and above all, naval supremacy, thereby conflating state and commercial incarnations of patriotism in similar manner to the monuments of Tower Hill and the public houses of market towns. Model ships were often made by British sailors, and also featured, famously, in contemporary effusions of metropolitan theatrical patriotism: on-stage at Sadler's Wells, or on the Serpentine, as part of the Prince Regent's 1814 victory celebrations.[12] Significantly, Smith calls Johnson, not an ex-slave, but an ex-sailor, before proceeding – erroneously – to refer to his headgear as a model of 'the ship Nelson'. This mistake, echoed in an otherwise astute reading by art historian Eddie Chambers,[13] was corrected in both Timbs and the 1825 journal article, each of which speaks of 'the brig Nelson' – for Johnson's model, to judge by its hull and rigging, was a brig, not a ship, since the latter had to have three square masts.

This distinction is important if we are to invest meaning in the specific identity of the vessel constructed by Johnson. I think this is worth attempting if we wish to think ourselves into Johnson's act: contemporary Londoners were often astonishingly well versed in naval matters and were practised at making significant distinctions between vessels, both as a matter of course and in relation to major political and theatrical events.[14] As one of those Londoners and, moreover, an antiquarian, curator, and architectural artist, I think we can trust the fidelity of Smith's image. Thus the model cannot be, as Chambers suggests, *HMS Nelson*, a 126-gun first rate launched in 1814, nor the East Indiaman *Lord Nelson* (1799), as both were substantial ships.[15] Conversely, three hired armed cutters all named *Lord Nelson* (1798,

---

[11] Kwame Dawes, 'Negotiating the Ship on the Head: Black British Fiction', *Wasafiri* 14, no. 29 (1999): 18–24, 18; Mark Stein, *Black British Literature: Novels of Transformation* (Ohio, 2004), 103–4.

[12] For particularly colourful first-hand accounts, see, respectively, Speaight, *Professional and Literary Memoirs*, 87; and Charles F. Lawler (pseud. Peter Pindar), *Lilliputian Navy!! The R–t's Fleet; or, John Bull at the Serpentine* (1814).

[13] Eddie Chambers, 'Black British Artists: Celebrating Nelson's Ships', available at http://theibtaurisblog.com/2014/07/02/black-british-artists-celebrating-nelsons-ships/.

[14] I discuss this in far greater detail in Oskar Cox Jensen, 'Of Ships and Spectacles: Maritime Identity in Regency London', *Nineteenth Century Theatre and Film* 46, no. 2 (2019): 136–60.

[15] Chambers, 'Black British Artists'; Brian Lavery, *The Ship of the Line*, 2 vols. (2003), vol. 1, 187; Rowan Hackman, *Ships of the East India Company* (Gravesend, 2001), 148.

1803, 1803) were smaller one-masters.[16] This leaves the obscure Nova
Scotia privateer *Nelson* (1799),[17] and the armed survey vessel *Lady
Nelson* (1798), this last being the nearest visual fit and enjoying a distinguished record of Antipodean exploration.[18] Though unlikely, it is
tempting to make a connection to the final vessel's Australian adventures, if only to underscore the truly global discourse in which one East
London singer was participating.

The practical application of the model in performance is plain
enough, combining potent iconography linked to song and space with
both visual interest and extra height, helping Johnson draw and entertain a curious crowd. Yet it remains unclear how anyone knew by name
exactly which brig Johnson had constructed: did he tell them? Did the
identity – purported or exact – matter to performer and audience; to the
antiquarians; or was 'Nelson' merely a detail invented after the fact for
the sake of posterity? Given the recent (2017) controversy engendered
by that admiral's unsavoury views on race and slavery, it is of no small
irony that his name became attached to Johnson's model, raising the
tantalising possibility that this was a case of a black subaltern voice
appropriating the cultural capital of the 'white supremacist' Nelson.[19]
Was Johnson, in calling his vessel 'Nelson', bidding for a share of
reflected glory in defeating the French and Spanish? If so, his act of
self-fashioning was close to that of his more famous theatrical contemporary and fellow ethnic outsider, the composer, tenor, and theatre-
manager John Braham, born John Abraham, whose own success story in
the face of anti-Semitism owed much to his signature patriotic song,
'The Death of Nelson'.[20]

The London theatre scene, of which Braham was at this date becoming
such an integral part, was itself a circum-Atlantic institution, and

[16] Rif Winfield, *British Warships in the Age of Sail 1793–1817* (Barnsley, 2008), 389–94.
[17] Mentioned at http://threedecks.org/index.php?display_type=show_ship&id=12745.
[18] Winfield, *British Warships*, 337. A contemporary model of the *Lady Nelson* is held by the *National Maritime Museum*, object SLR0601, viewable at http://collections.rmg.co.uk/collections/objects/66562.html, and a plan of its rigging may be viewed at http://ladynelson.org.au/ship. As the *Lady Nelson* never returned home from Australia, it is unlikely, though still not impossible, that Johnson had been among its crew. Though destroyed in 1825, a replica *Lady Nelson* sails to this day.
[19] See, for example, http://theguardian.com/commentisfree/2017/aug/22/toppling-statues-nelsons-column-should-be-next-slavery.
[20] For the latest account of this transformation, see Susan Rutherford, 'John Braham and "The Death of Nelson"', in Newman, *Song and the City*: 525–43. 'The Death of Nelson' remained iconic for at least a century, coming nearest Johnson in an uncannily relevant reference in James Joyce's *Ulysses*, where it is sung by a street beggar who also happens to be an ex-sailor with a disabled leg. My thanks to Daniel Karlin for drawing this later allusion to my attention: Karlin's further observations may be found in his *Street Songs: The Clarendon Lectures 2016* (Oxford, 2018).

nowhere are these connections clearer than in the case of Matthew Gregory 'Monk' Lewis: playwright for the Haymarket theatre, Gothic novelist – and slave owner. On 1 January 1816, one year after Smith's preparation of *Vagabondiana* and one year before its publication, Lewis had his first sight of Jamaica. He records in his journal that:

> the sudden sounds of the drum and banjee called our attention to a procession of the *John-Canoe*, which was proceeding to celebrate the opening of the new year at the town of Black River. The John-Canoe is a Merry-Andrew dressed in a striped doublet, and bearing upon his head a kind of pasteboard house-boat filled with puppets, representing, some sailors, others soldiers, others again slaves at work on a plantation, &c. … the John-Canoe is considered not merely as a person of material consequence, but one whose presence is absolutely indispensable. Nothing could look more gay[.][21]

Five days later he met the houseboat's maker, John Fuller, who 'had made every bit of the canoe with his own hands … And indeed it was as fine as paint, pasteboard, gilt paper, and looking-glass could make it!'[22] Twenty-one years later, this populated, intricate houseboat had become the sturdier model depicted by the Sephardic Jewish painter Isaac Mendes Belisario (Figure III.4). Belisario was the London-trained creator of a 'taxonomic' series of Jamaican prints modelled on London Street Cries who, in another intimation of circum-Atlantic circularity, had undoubtedly studied Smith's *Vagabondiana* prior to making his own studies.[23] By contrast, as Susan Valladares has noted of native-born English audiences in general in an excellent study of the subject, Smith was understandably ignorant of 'John-Canoe', or Jonkonnu, the only recorded appearance of which in England prior to Johnson seems to have been as a burlesque representation in John Fawcett's pantomime *Obi; or Three Finger'd Jack*, set in Jamaica, which debuted at the Haymarket on 2 July 1800, wherein the character of 'Jonkanoo' was 'equipped with a ludicrous and enormously large false head' rather than a model boat.[24] It seems reasonable to identify in the performance of Johnson, an itinerant black sailor, a form of Jonkonnu, and to surmise a Jamaican heritage (the practice itself has been traced backwards, perhaps via Dutch Guinea, to Nigerian and

---

[21] Matthew Lewis, *Journal of a Residence among the Negroes in the West Indies* (1845, repr. Stroud, 2005), 33.

[22] Ibid., 45–6.

[23] Gillian Forrester, 'Mapping a New Kingston: Belisario's *Sketches of Character*', in Tim Barringer, Gillian Forrester, and Barbaro Martinez-Ruiz (eds.), *Art and Emancipation in Jamaica: Isaac Mendes Belisario and His Worlds* (New Haven, 2007), 65–87, esp. 74–81.

[24] Peter P. Reed, *Rogue Performances: Staging the Underclasses in Early American Theatre Culture* (New York, 2009), 101. Quotation from the *Dramatic Censor*'s reviewer Charles Dutton, cited ibid., 115.

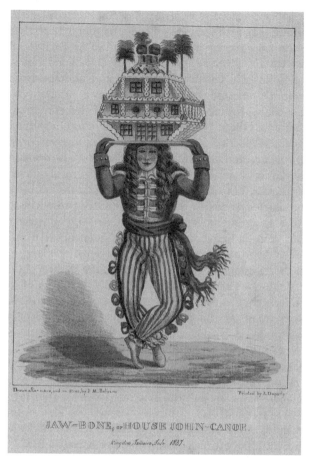

Figure III.4  Isaac Mendes Belisario, 'Sketches of Character: Jaw-Bone, or House John-Canoe', Jamaica, 1837–8.
Hand-coloured lithograph. Yale Center for British Art, Rare Books and Manuscripts: Folio A 2011 24

Congolese tribes) or to conclude, as Peter Reed does, that Johnson visited Jamaica in his career as a sailor.[25]

[25] Ibid., 118, and Robert Farris Thompson, 'Charters for the Spirit: Afro-Jamaican Music and Art', in Barringer, *Art and Emancipation*, 89–101. The connection with Johnson is also asserted in Barbaro Martinez-Ruiz, 'Sketches of Memory: Visual Encounters with Africa in Jamaican Culture', ibid., 103–19, 114. Peter Reed, '"There Was No Resisting John Canoe": Circum-Atlantic Transracial Performance', *Theatre History Studies* 27 (2007): 65–85, 80. Susan Valladares, 'Afro-Creole Revelry and Rebellion on the

Understandably, modern scholarship has emphasised the function of
Jonkonnu among Jamaican slaves as an enabling tool of resistance, insub-
ordination, carnivalesque inversion, and even the appropriation of traditional English ritual.[26] Reed concurs, recalling Dawes and Stein earlier in
his view that 'Johnson's costume embodies and perhaps criticises the
systems of labour discipline that impelled his own circulations and left
him unemployed in the metropolitan centre of the empire.'[27] Yet as
Elizabeth Maddock Dillon observes, echoing Simon Gikandi's analysis,
'Jonkonnu wears two faces' – it 'operates in dual registers of Europeanized
and African culture, and of play and resistance'.[28] It is a stimulating
thought that, under a mask of patriotism, Johnson may have been in
some sense 'mocking' (Gikandi's term)[29] the dominant culture in which
he now found himself, invoking what Dillon calls 'a presencing of something else – of both a remembered African culture and an Africanization,
or an indigenization of the colonial ground'.[30] Transposed from Jamaica
to London, his performance may thus be read as an exhilaratingly anti-
colonial act, creating a non-western space in the centre of a western
metropolis. We might also take seriously the idea that both of Johnson's
'two faces' were genuine: since Johnson had been a British sailor, his
patriotic display may also have been a sincere act – especially as this
gesture of assimilation was in his direct personal interest. Kathleen
Wilson has written convincingly of the extreme difficulty of overcoming
'cultural ideas about race and racialised notions of nation' in Britain at a
time when 'rationality, nationality and physical difference become inter-
twined, and where acquired cultural characteristics are transformed into
innate ones, the intangible inheritance of "blood."'[31] This ethnic articulation of Britishness – for which Wilson would have us read 'Englishness'
– became 'difficult, if not impossible, to acquire or naturalise'.[32]

Returning to Smith's depiction of Johnson, we immediately perceive
this barrier: as Dawes notes, Smith 'gave him [Johnson] stereotypical
features such as thick lips, bulging eyes and a broad nose, marking him
as a splendid specimen of curiosity.'[33] Yet it was in the face of such

British Stage: Jonkanoo in *Obi; or, Three-Fingered Jack* (1800)', *Review of English Studies*,
New Series (2018): 1–21, 5–6.
[26] Kathleen Wilson, *The Island Race: Englishness, Empire and Gender in the Eighteenth Century*
(2003), 164; Reed, *Rogue Performances*, 117–20; Barringer, *Art and Emancipation*, 1,
31, 72.
[27] Reed, 'There Was No Resisting John Canoe', 81.
[28] Elizabeth Maddock Dillon, *New World Drama: The Performative Commons in the Atlantic
World, 1649–1849* (Durham and London, 2014), 203.
[29] Simon Gikandi, *Slavery and the Culture of Taste* (Princeton, 2011), 273.
[30] Dillon, *New World Drama*, 204. Dillon borrows the term 'indigenization' from Sylvia
Winter.
[31] Wilson, *The Island Race*, 12.    [32] Ibid., 14.    [33] Dawes, 'Negotiating the Ship', 18.

difficulties that Johnson assembled his potent markers (songs, headgear) of nation and, via his indisputable identity as a seaman, of *belonging*. That this was achieved by recourse to a West Indian slave tradition presumably unknown to the vast majority of his audience, thereby enabling him to claim one identity by the secret assertion of another, makes his a doubly ingenious form of circum-Atlantic performance.

This meeting of British maritime iconography and Jonkonnu was far from a reconciliation of opposites. Attention has been drawn to the spiritual dimension of the latter,[34] which one could apply equally to the patriotic triumvir of Church, King, and constitution as reified in the British ship or brig – especially when named Nelson! Indeed, the 1816 Jonkonnu documented by Lewis had itself absorbed references to Britannia and Waterloo, even featuring '"Nelson's car," being a kind of canoe decorated with blue and silver drapery, and with "Trafalgar" written on the front of it'.[35] More prosaically, the percussion in Jonkonnu celebrations appears, to judge from Belisario, to have been performed on British army drums[36] – far from surprising in an age when many military bands featured black musicians – and thus constituting another blurring of cultural registers. There is even a wearisome parallel between Jamaica and the London street in the language of condescension employed by our sources, since Belisario's critique of the singing that accompanied Jonkonnu is indistinguishable from contemporary accounts of London ballad-singers: 'These songs, are chanted at the top of their voices, with an accompaniment of instruments, for the most part out of tune, and played by musicians, rather carelessly dressed … . It would appear, that *sound*, without the slightest attention to *harmony*, delights these personages.'[37] The comparison endorses Makdisi's argument, discussed in Chapter 1, that elite rhetoric racialised the London underclass, making a colony out of its grubbier streets: the singing of Jamaican slaves and metropolitan balladeers was equally unbearable in the rhetoric of elite commentary.[38]

---

[34] Thompson, in Barringer, *Art and Emancipation*, 92; Martinez-Ruiz, ibid., 105, 479.

[35] Lewis, *Journal*, 35, 37, 48. As Stephen Banfield observes, these imperial elements were almost certainly the result of 'coercive' or co-optive' oppression 'by its white patrons'. Stephen Banfield, 'Anglophone Musical Culture in Jamaica', in Barringer, *Art and Emancipation*, 137–49, 144, 147.

[36] Kenneth Bilby, 'More Than Met the Eye: African-Jamaican Festivities in the Time of Belisario', in Barringer, *Art and Emancipation*, 121–35, 127; Banfield, ibid., 141.

[37] Verene A. Shepherd, 'Work, Culture, and Creolization: Slavery and Emancipation in Eighteenth- and Nineteenth-Century Jamaica', ibid., 27–39, 28, and ibid., caption to 'Jaw-Bone, or House John-Canoe' (unpaginated; plate three).

[38] Makdisi, *Making England Western*.

Figure III.5 'Coëffure à la Belle Poule', Paris, c.1778.
Engraving (hand-coloured). Bibliothèque Nationale de France, Hennin
9728

Returning to Johnson's own performance of 'The Storm', we find yet
another unlikely parallel in a maritime context that drew its lines of
belonging and difference along national rather than racial lines. I wish
to suggest a secondary analogue for Johnson's headgear: the court of
Versailles in 1778. Though a direct influence on Johnson is extremely
unlikely, the headdresses worn by Marie-Antoinette and other court
ladies, à la Belle Poule and à la Frégate la Junon (Figure III.5 is one of
many examples), correspond far more closely to the model in
Vagabondiana than does Belisario's houseboat.

The Belle Poule and the Junon were French frigates, each celebrated in
1778 for single-ship actions wherein the former bested the larger, heavier

*HMS Arethusa* and the latter took the 28-gun *HMS Fox*. The coiffure *à la Belle Poule* featured 'ingenious … sails of gauze' and 'riggings of silver and gold threads', while that *à la Junon* went into small-scale production as 'a hat on which is represented a vessel with all its apparatus and tackle, having its cannons in formation', which 'could be purchased from the *marchande de modes* Mademoiselle Fredin at the sign of *L'Écharpe d'Or* on the rue de la Ferronerie'.[39] The latter's construction cannot have been dissimilar to Johnson's *Nelson*, just as both have been dismissed as 'novelty' while actually being freighted with meaning, while the coiffure *à la Belle Poule* boasts a second connection to Johnson's performance, as they share an unlikely common acquaintance: the Cornish tenor Charles Incledon.

Although the *Belle Poule* dismasted and evaded her larger opponent *HMS Arethusa*, Admiral Keppel's dispatch framed the engagement as a British success, leading to its simultaneous celebration on both sides of the Channel. Yet it was not until eighteen years later in 1796 that Prince Hoare penned 'The Arethusa', arranged by William Shield to the 1730s tune 'The Princess Royal', and sung by Incledon in the part of Cheerly in the farcical afterpiece *Lock and Key*.[40] The song proved a tremendous hit, its shilling score advertised 'as Sung with great applause by Mr. Incledon'; we have already seen how the young ballad-singer William Brown capitalised on its popularity.[41] It was at precisely this mid-nineties moment that Incledon was also reviving 'The Storm', described by his biographer as 'a dramatic work, said to have astonished the great French tragedian Talma'.[42] Like Johnson, Incledon had been a sailor, serving before the mast; like Johnson – and indeed the song's writer Stevens before him – Incledon performed the song in solo entertainments, dressed in character. While a painting by Joseph Ayton is the more striking depiction of Incledon as sailor on stage, foot-lit before a backdrop of stormy waves striking the white cliffs of England's southern coast,[43] it is Figure III.6, drawn by Incledon's friend and fellow actor John Emery, that leads us back to Johnson's own performances.

---

[39] *Journal politique* and *Journal des modes de Paris*, both quoted in Kimberly Chrisman-Campbell, *Fashion Victims: Dress at the Court of Louis XVI and Marie-Antoinette* (New Haven, 2015), 161, 162.
[40] 'New Lights upon Old Tunes. "The Arethusa"', *Musical Times and Singing Class Circular*, 35, no. 620 (1894): 666–8.
[41] BL Mus H.1653.b (28); Brown, *A Narrative*, 13.
[42] BL Mus G.424.pp (1) (*c*.1795); John Rosselli, 'Incledon, Charles (*bap.* 1763, *d.* 1826)', *ODNB*, oxforddnb.com/view/article/14377.
[43] After Joseph Ayton, 'C. Incledon as he appeared singing the storm' (1826). Lithograph, National Portrait Gallery D36441.

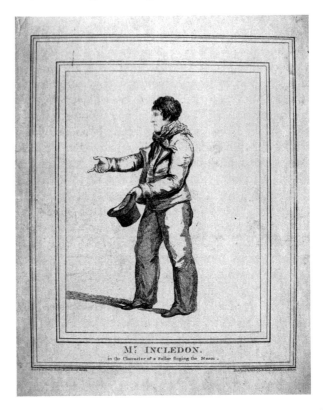

Figure III.6 Piercy Roberts after John Emery, 'Mr Incledon in the Character of a Sailor singing the Storm', *c*.1800. Etching. © The Trustees of the British Museum

This character portrait shows Incledon appropriately dressed for the rough weather of the song – yet his supplicatory pose indicates that this 'Jack Tar' is not figured as enduring the storm of which he sings, but rather the unforgiving climate of the London streets. Emery sketches Incledon cap-in-hand, in a gesture evocative, not of the song's latter verses, but of its first: 'Messmates, hear a brother sailor'. As Stein notes of the Johnson sketch, 'In his hand the beggar carries another hat, which he hopes to fill with money' – and it is this, Johnson's *second* hat, that links him most obviously with Incledon's stage act.[44]

While mendicant sailors had long since been a feature of London's streets, their numbers swelled significantly after the General Peace of

----

[44] Stein, *Black British Literature*, 102.

1814, at which point many naval vessels formerly employed in convoy duty or the blockade of French ports were decommissioned. The situation was worst for those sailors, like Johnson, who had been incapacitated in the course of their duties, many of whom were, again like Johnson, refused a pension and reduced to a life in the streets. The situation grew endemic, exhausting the sympathies of even the playwright Douglas Jerrold, whose 1829 melodrama *Black-Ey'd Susan* argued so passionately on behalf of the ordinary sailor. Jerrold grew weary of the beggar who 'attacks our sympathies with one arm and a wooden leg', or roved in groups, 'executing, as they pick their way, "Ben Bowline," or at times plunging with one accord into the "Bay of Biscay"' – two famous nautical songs of the day.[45] The journalist William Harvey, with a cynicism typical among his contemporaries, documented just such a scene as taking place in 1812, a short walk west of Johnson's first haunt of Tower Hill:

Let us mount the hill, and take our chance for something fresh at Newgate and Giltspur-street Compter. A pair of masquerading sailors hold those posts, and are violently rendering in harsh accents – which are neither speaking [n]or singing – 'The Bay of Biscay,' and 'The Storm' – then immensely relished by the London operatives[.][46]

Around 1820, Thomas Rowlandson included a scene along just these lines in his *Characteristic Sketches of the Lower Orders*, reproduced as Figure III.7.

While the sailor on the left is depicted as shamming by the ever-cynical Rowlandson – note the conspicuously bare left foot with the shod right tucked up behind out of sight of his target – there is no denying the wooden leg of the central figure, nor that their open mouths indicate that they are probably singing, in an attitude identical to both Incledon's persona and Johnson's actual practice. This figure pulls a cart on which stands – what else? – a model ship, perhaps a 74-gun man of war, fully rigged and as tall as his shoulder. This underscores the point that, while Johnson's animated headgear may have been indebted to Jonkonnu, the combination of model vessel and beggar's hat drew on iconography common to white British sailors, intended to evoke positive patriotic associations among London audiences. It is likely that Rowlandson was drawing from life, as an almost identical and far more sympathetic depiction appears in a book of moralising lessons for children by the poet Jane Taylor.[47] The latter image is accompanied by a poem written from the

---

[45] Jerrold, 'The Ballad Singer', 295.    [46] Harvey, *London Scenes*, 351.
[47] Anon, 'Sailors and Ship' (1808). Plate 20 of Taylor, *A Peep into London*.

DISTRESSED SAILORS.

Figure III.7  Thomas Rowlandson, 'Distressed Sailors', c.1820. Plate 52 of Rowlandson, *Characteristic Sketches of the Lower Orders*. Etching with stipple (hand-coloured). By permission of the British Library

perspective of the 'poor sailors, lame and blind' that stresses the global backdrop to this call for charity: for besides two references to storms, Taylor conjures up voyages 'Far, to east or western shore', a shipwreck on 'a desert coast', and travels 'Round and round the world' that perfectly prefigure Johnson's own narrative, 'Come to beggary at last'.[48]

---

[48] Ibid., 16–17.

These images remind us that Johnson was marked out by more than his skin: he too was disabled, requiring two crutches, and like so many other ballad-singers he made an asset of this injury by appealing to his audience's charity, those crutches as potent a symbol of both his merit and his authenticity as dress, hat, or song. Yet his self-fashioning was a complex and conscious act, and I do not wish to see him simply as a beggar, but rather – a decade before Ira Aldridge's London debut as Oronooko – as a successful black performer whom we should take seriously; a sophisticated, theatrical singer on the London street. He even received a highly favourable, belated notice, in the 1825 article 'London Ballad Singers'. Allowing for the condescending tone and the customary disparagement of vocal technique, the account is invaluable, and worth quoting in full.

But who is there, old or young, among the busy population of Tower-Hill, that does not bear in mind, and will not lend a kind word towards commemorating, that ornament of the profession, Joe Johnson! Joe was wont to wear, on days of business, a model (and an elaborate miniature it was) of the brig Nelson on his hat. She was full-rigged, had all her masts set, and looked for all the world as if she scudded before a gale of wind. The district just mentioned used to be called, and will be reported in traditions, no doubt in technical phraseology, 'Black Joe's Pitch.' The man was lame, or, as he himself used to say, was damaged in his cock-pit – but in bust, in mien, and with his swarthy, bony face, half concealed by black, frizzy curls, and crowned by a ship in full sail; he had the bearing of an Atlas. He was conversant with the best of Dibdin's songs – and in the 'British Seaman's Praise,' and the 'Wooden Walls of Old England,' he approved himself the Incledon of the highways. But these, in point of excellence, stood in relation to Joe's 'Storm,' as the best of his contemporaries was to Joe in his other songs. Incledon had voice and science – Joe's deficiencies in these particulars were compensated by rude strength (the song is peculiarly susceptible of vocal force) and by pantomime. This ballad-singer not only described, he demonstrated – he lowered the top-gallants, then the stay-sails, and as soon as the time came for the breeze to freshen, Joe was seen to set the braces with a nimbleness and success that would have extorted praise in the great world of a man of war. Successively you were stunned with the boatswain's bawl and the cheer of the crew. Next of all he looked like a man possessed with a raging demon, as he darted from place to place in mimic fury, cutting down masts, casting guns overboard, and gathering all hands to the pump. Here was an improvement on that difficult grace of poetry, making the words an 'echo to the sense.' Joe acted the song – he passed you through all the perils of the tempest, snatched you from the imminent wreck, without uttering a note. Never shall we forget the shout of satisfaction with which he consigned every bitter remembrance to oblivion, as he fervently cried, 'She rights, she rights, boys! wear off shore.'[49]

Most interesting here, perhaps, are the aside 'as he himself used to say', which accords Johnson a certain dignity and autonomy of expression; the

[49] 'London Ballad Singers', 42.

emphasis upon the skilful creation and manipulation of the model *Nelson*; and of course the repeated comparison to Incledon. We may detect a degree of irony here: but why not take the comparison seriously? The dismissal of Johnson's voice in preference to focus on his body may in fact reflect astute choices on the part of the singer. For all that the tune could be said to admit of a solemn, hymnal beauty – particularly in the final cadence, which begins rather remarkably by leaping a minor seventh – it is objectively slow and short, and unlikely to sustain a street audience's interest through eight subsequent repetitions without some theatrical embellishment of the narrative. Indeed, the 1825 account – closing with 'wear off shore' – suggests that Johnson chose to omit the song's ninth and final verse, an artistically satisfying decision that focuses both attention and affect upon the struggle at sea, rather than dissipating the emotions involved with a detached final moral. Finally, the term 'pantomime' appears to be used with precision, the subsequent assertion that 'Joe acted the song' further indicating that this was an act of elaborately choreographed theatre: theatre that combined multiple circum-Atlantic devices, from Afro-Caribbean Jonkonnu, to Anglo-French militaria, to 1770s nautical balladry, in order to enrich its mixed medium of pantomime.

We might productively recall the gesture depicted in Figure III.6: rather than enact one of the stock theatrical attitudes of the day, later delineated in Leman Thomas Rede's manual for actors, Incledon is striving instead for verisimilitude, adopting the supplicatory pose of the beggar.[50] To judge by the 1825 account, Johnson similarly favoured a realistic enactment that appears to have captivated the reviewer – in this case a realisation of his former status as sailor, not his current status as mendicant. For like Incledon, Johnson's particular authority as a performer of this song derived, not from the stage, but from personal experience: he could execute the song's actions as Stevens, its writer, or Dibdin, the contemporary benchmark of nautical performance, landsmen both, never could. His was a language of theatrical gesture taken directly from 'the great world of a man of war'. The result was an eloquence of performance that reconciled, at least in the moment, both his own otherness and the transatlantic world of the sailor to the local context of the London street or satellite town.

This transcendental feat was still, in essence, merely theatrical: it could neither cure Johnson of his disability nor make him eligible for the pension that would rescue him from the streets. It was a particularly cruel irony that, due to their design and the strain placed upon them, the

---

[50] Leman Thomas Rede, *The Road to the Stage* (1836).

asymmetrical crutches Johnson mastered in order to move so dexterously would within a few years exact an inexorable price, exacerbating rather than ameliorating his injuries. Yet I would rather spotlight Johnson's limited success than make him into an unwitting tragedian. For his audience, attracted and prepared by both his headgear and his crutches, it was Johnson's body – ostensibly, by Wilson's reading, a symbol only of difference – that, by virtue of its enacting a series of exact, seamanlike gestures, confirmed both his ownership of the song and his active, participatory place within the British nation. By his performances of 'The Storm' – a song narrated, let us not forget, by a 'brother sailor' to the imagined listener – Johnson not only made himself a living; he made himself a home.

# 4   Repertoire
## Navigating the Mainstream

---

Come, my lucky masters, here's a choice collection of songs, that have been sung at Drury-lane, *Common Garden*, Sadler's Wells, the *Uproar House, Fox-Hall*, and other places, out of the most *famoustest roratorios*.[1]

These words of George Parker are manifestly not taken verbatim from a real singer, but are instead of a piece with a low literary vogue for flash language and crude imitations of street culture at the turn of the century. Parker's litany of malapropisms seeks, in its condescension, to represent the singer and by extension his audience (in this case the singer is male) as comically unfamiliar with the spaces of respectable culture from which his songs stem. This policing of cultural capital was echoed two decades later in the 'Fine Arts' column of the fledgling *Edinburgh Annual Register*, whose writer observed that 'The subject most easily understood will always be most popular; and a ballad-singer in the street can attract greater crowds, by chaunting the comic songs of a Sadler's Wells burletta, than he would draw together by repeating the text of Macbeth.'[2] Both commentaries betray the same essential truth: that singers were wholly accustomed to songs that originated in social spaces not meant for them – spaces that were by no means limited to the minor theatres.

Derek Scott has observed that 'street singers ... had bourgeois songs in their repertoire', adding that 'the printing of drawing-room ballads as broadsides shows that an interest existed in working-class environs'.[3] When turning to evidence of these repertoires, however, we are confronted with a gulf between the rich collections of ephemeral print that now exist, and the scant scraps of documentation concerning their dissemination and performance. Vic Gammon's proposition that 'broadside ballad collections may give us little insight into what was actually performed and need to be compared with full repertories of singers when

---

[1] George Parker, 'The BALLAD SINGER in the neighbourhood of ST. GILES's', in Parker, *Life's Painter*, 124.
[2] 'Fine Arts', *Edinburgh Annual Register* 1 (January 1808): 326.
[3] Scott, *The Singing Bourgeois*, 183.

these are available' seems, in this light, to be defeated by the difficulty of its own caveat.[4] On the subject of 'popular music' more broadly, Gammon is more sanguine, writing with Sheila Gammon of 'the eclecticism of lower-class musical culture. This culture drew its repertory from a wide range of available sources, including oral tradition, ballads, psalms, popular songs, popular church music, military music, and popular dance tunes'. This repertory they characterise as cohering into what they term 'the "plebeian musical tradition"'.[5] Yet singers also derived their material from non-'plebeian' musical registers: from Handel to the Christy Minstrels, from early modern court composers to contemporary *Grand Opera*, and above all from the theatres and pleasure gardens of the capital itself.[6] From high to low, from ancient to modern, street repertoire found a space for everything. In 1807 J. F. Herling, writing in the *European Magazine*, maintained that 'many of the favourite ballads' of the sixteenth and seventeenth centuries 'are still chaunted by vagrant musicians about our streets'.[7] Fifty years later, Charles Manby Smith uncovered three centuries of canonical lyricists 'on turning over a massive bundle' of ballads, 'from the works of Shakspeare [*sic*], Herrick, Suckling, Rochester, Burns, Byron, Moore, Dibdin, Russell, Eliza Cook, and a number of other names well known in literature' – always remembering that Manby Smith's list is not evidence of a *performed* repertoire, but rather of a published one.[8] Discussing actual performance, an 1868 journalist claimed continued street popularity for theatrical and society writers of the past 150 years, including John Gay, David Garrick, Andrew Cherry, Thomas Campbell, Thomas Moore, and the remarkable aristocratic Irish sisters Lady Dufferin and Caroline Norton, concluding that 'one cannot fail to be struck with the diversity of style and value of the street songs'.[9] The later antiquarian William Henderson asserted that several notable Child ballads, such as 'Lord Bateman', 'The Outlandish Knight', and 'Sir Patrick Spens', had all been in vogue on the Victorian

---

[4] Vic Gammon, 'Problems of Method', 18.
[5] Vic Gammon and Sheila Gammon, 'The Musical Revolution of the Mid-Nineteenth Century: From "Repeat and Twiddle" to "Precision and Snap"', in Trevor Herbert (ed.), *Bands: The Brass Band Movement in the 19th and 20th Centuries* (Buckingham, 1991), 120–44, 121.
[6] See too Georgina Bartlett (*née* Prineppi), 'From the Stage to the Street: Theatre Music and the Broadside Ballad in London, 1797–1844' (Oxford University D.Phil. thesis, 2020), and published work by Bartlett that may appear subsequent to this book.
[7] J. F. Herling, *European Magazine* 51 (1807): 109.
[8] Smith, *Little World of London*, 253.
[9] 'Street Songs and their Singers', 226–33. Several of these songs, attested as being among the most popular street songs of the mid-century, are included in the accompanying audio files.

street.[10] Perhaps in preference to the Gammons' 'plebeian musical tradition', we might substitute the dictum of Richard Middleton: that 'There is no pure popular music; rather, the voice of the people is always plural, hybrid, compromised.'[11]

This plurality is evident in two extensive repertoires that were allegedly performed, given in the first volume of Mayhew, of which this is the second:

'Ye Banks and Braes o' Bonnie Doun,' with (on the same sheet) 'The Merry Fiddler,' (an indecent song) – 'There's a good Time coming, Boys,' 'Nix, my Dolly,' 'The Girls of —shire,' (which of course is available for any county) – 'Widow Mahoney,' 'Remember the Glories of Brian the Brave,' 'Clementia Clemmins,' 'Lucy Long,' 'Erin Go Bragh,' 'Christmas in 1850,' 'The Death of Nelson,' 'The Life and Adventures of Jemmy Sweet,' 'The Young May Moon,' 'Hail to the Tyrol,' 'He was sich a Lushy Cove,' &c. &c.[12]

We cannot ignore the possibility of Mayhew's editing of this list, just as we cannot neglect the extent to which it distorts through omission as much as inclusion. It is a motley collection, containing obscene and seditious songs, old favourites and topical numbers, genuine and 'stage' Irish productions, settings as disparate as the Alps and the slave plantations of America, elite compositions such as Braham's 'Death of Nelson' and generic hackwork such as 'The Girls of —shire'.[13] At the very least, this enriches and supports the view that street repertoire was heterogeneous and wide-ranging. It reinforces the impression that ballad singing operated on a basic principle of miscellaneity, a hallmark of the Georgian era that gradually gave way at higher social levels to a Victorian taste for specialisation and categorisation.[14] Thinking generically, we might even position nineteenth-century ballad singing as a hybrid cultural form, offering a highly miscellaneous medium that was conceived of as

---

[10] Henderson, *Victorian Street Ballads*, 19.    [11] Middleton, *Voicing the Popular*, 23.

[12] Mayhew, *London Labour*, vol. 1, 279. See also ibid., 221. A similarly dense and varied repertoire may be found in 'Rag', *Streetology*, 87, ranging from the ancient to the topical, the musically simple to the ornate, originating in London, Scotland, America, from obscure rural poet or famed composer, and spanning all genres from the comic to the supernatural, via love, patriotism, adventure, and satire.

[13] As the sociologist Paul Charosh has observed of such repertoires: 'It would be convenient for scholars if there were sharp, consistent discontinuities between the ages of these songs, their subjects and structures, the musical idioms and devices employed in their setting, and the institutions associated with their dissemination and consumption, but this is not the case.' Charosh, 'Studying Nineteenth-Century Popular Song': 467.

[14] William Weber, *The Great Transformation of Musical Taste: Concert Programming from Haydn to Brahms* (Cambridge, 2008). See also the Introduction to Cox Jensen et al., *Charles Dibdin and Late Georgian Culture*.

a spectrum of evolving sub-categories: the comic, the sentimental, the sporting, and so on. That is, while *songs* were perceived as belonging to strict generic categories, *song* as mediated by the ballad-singer was a promiscuous mingling of these categories – a practice taken further in the second half of the century by music hall programming.

In this chapter I will pursue, not the programmatic, but the pragmatic and the problematic dimensions of ballad-singers' repertoires, looking at the agency that took individual songs from the point of authorship to that of street dissemination, and situating these journeys within a broader cultural context: that of the mainstream. By 'mainstream' I mean simply the usual, current usage of a term rarely applied to centuries before the twentieth – indeed a term that, following Peter Burke, one might hesitate to use for periods predating the media technologies of film, radio, and television. In the context of late-eighteenth and nineteenth-century London, however, I think that it possesses a good deal of figurative energy, lacking the historiographical baggage of 'popular' or, worse still, 'mass'.[15] In this analogy, London is a great river delta of disparate cultural influences, with its various streets, squares, and public houses (rather than the Thames itself) constituting the central flow, while the ballad-singer is our shabby ferryman or -woman. In the sections that follow I shall move from various sources of derivation, to the means by which these songs were taken into the street, to how the mainstream was thereby created and how it might best be characterised, before ending with a consideration of the ultimate consequence of this historical process: the creation of a (primarily *musical*) current too strong for the ballad-singer to navigate beyond the middle of the nineteenth century.

### Where Did Songs Come From?

For William Makepeace Thackeray, surveying the lyricists that might be found on Catnach's ballads, the remarkable thing was not that respectable authors abounded, but rather that they kept such miscellaneous company:

They come from all sources, – Tom Dibdin, Tom Moore, Bailey (Tom and F.W.N.), Praed, F. Fitzgerald, Barry Cornwall, Horace Twiss, Ditto Smith, James Smith, James Crow, Hook, Hood, Reynolds, Hannah More, Coliseum Sloman, Lord Byron, and others, have all contributed to the collection now in our possession. The old ballad-writers have likewise been put in requisition; and along with them the

---

[15] Meredith McGill, however, opts for 'mass' in her astute discussion of 'a larger media ecology' in which 'the ballad . . . offered much-desired access to an emergent, multimedia mass culture'. McGill, 'What Is a Ballad?', 157.

actual nameless scribes of modern Grub Street, who furnish satires and ballads *de circonstance*, chastising the follies, or chronicling in playful verse the events of the day. A collection more curious cannot be easily imagined[.][16]

The collection's 'curiousness' comes, less from the profusion of famous lyricists of the past fifty years, than their pairing with Grub Street and gutter hacks past and present, in a blurring of literary registers discussed at length by Hepburn in *A Book of Scattered Leaves*.[17] By his estimate, at least half of all ballad lyrics were not originally written for a street audience,[18] a consideration equally applicable to the tunes. Here, Bennett's pragmatic verdict, now a generation old, still stands:

[T]he explosive vitality of this burgeoning song culture was confined almost entirely to its texts. In terms of new music it had virtually no life of its own, and the reasons are not hard to see. While the texts of songs were available in print to the popular market, their tunes had still to be transmitted orally, and the age-old practice of writing new words to existing tunes inevitably continued.[19]

Bennett's research turns up a list of composers comparable to Thackeray's lyricists: Purcell, Leveridge, Hook, Shield, Charles Dibdin the Elder, Reeve, Blewitt, and Bishop.[20] Their music was written for the theatre and the drawing room rather than the street. In the words of the 1868 journalist: 'Street songs ... may first appear in an opera, and then at once be heard at a street corner; or they may slide down from drawing-room to concert-hall, and then on to the streets.'[21] Bennett's own construction gives a greater sense of agency, however, writing that: 'their tunes were *taken* second-hand, with or without the addition of new words, into popular consciousness'.[22] Such bottom-up appropriations happened without the consent or even, quite often, the knowledge of their original authors: while Dibdin resented street piracies, as described in more detail later, an anecdote concerning the poet Thomas Campbell has him:

passing one evening through the streets of London with a friend, and being attracted by a crowd eagerly listening to a street singer. Pausing for a little, 'I think I know that song,' said Campbell. 'Of course you do,' said his friend; 'it is your own "Exile of Erin."' 'Ah!' rejoined the author ... 'I have not heard it these twenty years; this is popularity indeed.'[23]

[16] Thackeray, 'Horae Catnachiane', 409.
[17] Hepburn, *Scattered Leaves*, vol. 1, 39, 62–5.    [18] Ibid., 63.
[19] Anthony Bennett, 'Music in the Halls', in Bratton, *Music Hall*, 1–22, 2.
[20] Ibid., 2–3.    [21] 'Street Songs and Their Singers', 227.
[22] Bennett, 'Music in the Halls', 3. Emphasis added.
[23] 'Street Songs and Their Singers', 226.

Tracing these appropriations at the level of the individual song can be both diverting and rewarding. In 1840 Arthur Armitage, a contributor to *Heads of the People*, archly observed that: 'The Spitalfields Weaver ... laughs immoderately at comic songs, especially those which touch upon donkeys and itinerant vendors of greengrocery, and he joins in the chorus cordially and lustily.'[24] One such song is 'The Green-Grocer's Lament', a supremely silly narrative of what might happen to a man's ass;[25] another is 'Gee Ho Dobbin'.[26] The latter, an explicitly bawdy affair, became the inadvertent subject of a trial for theft in 1801 when a milkman's son had his pocket picked, for his money was wrapped in a copy of the song.[27] The prosecutor was sidetracked when he heard that 'the tune was Geho Dobbin', enquiring:

> Q. Is there any print at the top of it? –
> A. Yes, three men; it is about the butchers and the bakers, and
>    forestallers and farmers.
> Q. Do you know if the word shufflers was wrote under the picture? –
> A. Yes; the three shufflers.

Perhaps initially suspicious of indecency, the lawyer quickly detects that the song was in fact a parody called 'The Shufflers', a subversive but not actually seditious political lyric printed by Pitts.[28] This was an up-to-the-minute working-class polemic, penned by an unknown hand – yet its tune, conversely, was hallowed by inclusion in William Chappell's anti-quarian collection *Popular Music of the Olden Time*, wherein both its ancient origins as polite dance music and a literary mention by Oliver Goldsmith are noted, along with its revision into 'the popular form' when, in 1762, 'it was introduced in *Love in a Village*' by the composer Thomas Arne (of 'Rule, Britannia!' fame).[29] We are left with an impression of a thoroughly entangled mainstream culture, wherein anonymous agitators could overwrite scurrilous verse, to a respectable and even venerable tune, for the enjoyment of milkmen's boys and weavers, and to the consternation – but not the incomprehension – of sharp-eared lawyers.

Both Hindley and Mayhew give us a similar picture of songs as old as the sixteenth century remaining in circulation alongside topical pieces that are 'written, and then sung in the streets ... in little more than an hour.'[30] Hindley, 'Jack Rag', and Jerrold further emphasise the seasonal importance of the respectable carol to the ballad-singer's economy:

---

[24] Arthur Armitage, 'The Spitalfields Weaver', *Heads of the People*, vol. 1, 268.
[25] The tune, alas, is unknown.   [26] Bod. Harding B 18(221); Bod. Harding B 45(20).
[27] POB t18010415-82.   [28] Bod. 2806 c.18(286).
[29] William Chappell, *Popular Music of the Olden Time*, 2 vols. (1855–1859), vol. 2, 690–1.
[30] 'Street Ballads', 400; Mayhew, *London Labour*, vol. 1, 275.

'the Christmas-carol; the homely burden sung two centuries ago: the self-same words, too, that Shakspere in his childhood may have lain and listened to'.[31] Thinking along similar lines of chronological entanglement, the third component of many song sheets was of course the woodcut image at the sheet's head, the aesthetic of which was by this time self-consciously, picturesquely antiquated. We should, however, guard against overemphasising the predominance of the antique, especially where melody is concerned. When Dickens' song 'The Ivy Green' of c.1840 received a street parody as 'The Cabbage Green', the new lyrics were of a style that could have been penned at any point in the last three centuries – yet the tune called for, probably that composed by Henry Russell, clearly anticipated the stamp of the coming music hall in its rhythms, phrasings, and modulations.[32] Yet whether the music was old or new, from the London stage or further afield, we have zero evidence of the composition of tunes in and for the metropolitan street. As far as I can tell, there were no street composers. Indigenous lyricists, however, were known both in the aggregate and in particular.

All accounts of 'chaunter culls' and ballad-mongers – of Joseph Clinch, John Martin, Richard Lyon, George Brown, the writers in Mayhew and, most famously, the songwriter John Morgan – give a strikingly similar impression of a hand-to-mouth existence 'of the lowest grade',[33] wherein writers were stranded between the authority of the printer and the agency of the singer, rarely receiving more than a shilling per composition (Parker quotes 7s 6d, but that was for a custom commission, and in any case comes in a rather implausible account).[34] This low flat rate (rather than a royalty) was invariably attributed to widespread piracy, which precluded any economic arrangement based on intellectual property rights. Hindley speculates that: 'Something more like bread-and-butter might be made, perhaps, by poets who were in the habit of singing their own ballads, as some of them do', and elsewhere describes the writer/printer transaction as implying the same dual function on the part of the writer: 'If one of the patterers writes a ballad on a taking subject, he hastens at once to Seven Dials, where, if accepted, his reward is "a glass of rum, a slice of cake, and five dozen copies," – which, if the accident or murder be a very

---

[31] 'Street Ballads', 417; 'Rag', Streetology, 88; Jerrold, 'The Ballad-Singer', 293.
[32] Bod. Harding B 11(509).
[33] William West, Fifty Years' Recollections of an Old Bookseller (Cork, 1835), 68.
[34] George Parker, A View of Society and Manners in High and Low Life, 2 vols. (1791), vol. 2, 58–9; John Caulfield, Blackguardiana: or, A Dictionary of Rogues (c.1793), 54; Charles Manby Smith, The Cries of London (1839), 97; Mayhew, London Labour, vol. 1, 279–80; vol. 3, 196–7; Smith, Little World of London, 254–6; Hindley, History of the Catnach Press, xii–xxvi; Hepburn, Book of Scattered Leaves, vol. 1, 23, 39, 43–6.

awful one, are struck off for him while he waits.'[35] There were obvious benefits to being, like David Love at the start of the century, simultaneously writer and singer: benefits both commercial and artistic, for a singer who could convincingly claim authorship of her or his pieces thereby gained a degree of performative authority. Alternatively, a writer and a singer could develop a working partnership, though this entailed its own risks, as an 1843 proceeding at the Westminster Court of Requests demonstrates.

The case – a claim for 10s 6d – was brought by Edward Julian Morten, a songwriter, against Alexander Sadgrove, a street singer, for whom Morten had 'expressly' written several songs: 'the "Queen of the Sea" and "Father Mathew's Teapot" in particular.[36] He was to have paid me 3s. 6d. a piece, and he owes me for the two I have mentioned and another'.[37] The price per song is extremely high, which may be why Sadgrove struggled to reimburse Morten:

Commissioner: Well, how will you pay it?—Defendant: That's exactly what I don't know, sir. The fact is that I got the plaintiff to write these songs for me and had them printed at my own expense to sing and sell about the streets, but it was a bad speculation.—Commissioner: Oh, you are a ballad singer?—Defendant: That's all, sir—only a poor fellow who has to sing for his dinner every day, and seldom gets it more than once a week.

The case has clearly been written up so as to entertain – yet it points, like Hindley's details of the rum and cake, to a creative and disseminatory practice run on trust, individual relations, and petty economies of makeshift: a personal form of production conducted on intimate, neighbourly lines. The songs in question are also significant: along with other titles attributed to Morten – 'Dorothy Douse, or the Cold-water Cure', and 'The Bluebottle buzzing', written about the New Police ('Queen of the Sea' concerned Victoria) – they suggest a writer penning, not lyrics on the latest news as such, but songs addressing aspects of a broader topical modernity, couched in a vernacular idiom. Sadgrove, the singer, could if he chose perform anything from the latest theatrical and poetic hits to centuries-old standards. But he determined to anchor his repertoire in fresh material addressing contemporary issues – and was able to enter into business relations, however unstable, in order to facilitate this specialisation. In nineteenth-century London, the ballad-singer had little problem sourcing material.

[35] Hindley, *History of the Catnach Press*, xiv; *Curiosities of Street Literature*, 118.
[36] These songs, like Morten's other compositions listed below, are now entirely lost.
[37] 'Court of Requests, Westminster', *Lloyd's Weekly Newspaper* 45 (1 October 1843).

## Songs in Circulation

In 1806, a writer for the *Belle Assemblée* observed in passing that: 'The orchestra of the opera, which is confined to the metropolis, hath diffused a good style of playing over the other bands of the capital, which is, by degrees, communicated to the fidler [*sic*] and ballad-singer in the streets', concluding rather unusually that Londoners in general were therefore more tuneful than country dwellers.[38] This top-down view of musical distribution combines a conventional mode of condescension with a rare acknowledgement that different social registers of music-making were on some level connected – yet the manner of that connection is left obscure, reduced to the empty passivity of 'diffused'. Scholarly accounts, more nuanced in their understanding of high and low, have similarly neglected (on the reasonable grounds of time, focus, and lack of information) the issue of human agency in this 'diffusion'. E. P. Thompson, for example, notes that 'a culture is also a pool of diverse resources, in which traffic passes between the literate and the oral, the superordinate and the subordinate, the village and the metropolis', without enquiring into the nature of that traffic.[39] Mark Philp, drawing in part on Simon McVeigh, writes more perceptively of the 'considerable commerce between traditional ballad singing, country dancing tunes, the performances in Vauxhall Gardens, and the concert performances in St James, in the sense that players, tunes and musical styles traversed the terrain with relative ease'.[40] This takes us further, though we lack a sense of direction. One obvious model for circulation is the top-down engagement with plebeian culture posited by Emma Griffin: 'that music, particularly the music of high culture, did not simply float into the lives of the poor; it was taken there'.[41] This is a model that I have discussed at length elsewhere[42] – one that might be summed up by the radical William Hone's 1817 complaint that: 'This very week, when tens of thousands in London are out of work, a ballad is hawked about the streets, written by Miss HANNAH MORE, to the tune of "a cobler there was, and he liv'd in a stall," … This is the dull lying consolation offered to the half-starved and the miserable.'[43] Primarily, this practice involved the circulation of new lyrics, relying upon

[38] 'Experiments and Observations on the Singing of Birds', *Belle Assemblée* 1, no. 9 (October 1806): 462.
[39] E. P. Thompson, *Customs in Common* (1991), 6.
[40] Mark Philp, Introduction to 'Music and Politics, 1793–1815', in Mark Philp (ed.), *Resisting Napoleon: The British Response to the Threat of Invasion, 1797–1815* (Aldershot, 2006), 173–204, 173.
[41] Emma Griffin, 'Popular Culture in Industrialising England', *Historical Journal* 45 (2002): 619–35, 630–1.
[42] Cox Jensen, *Napoleon*, 16–17, 20–6.
[43] William Hone, *The Reformists' Register and Weekly Commentary* (1817): 391–2.

a set of tunes familiar to writer, singer, and audience. This theoretical model has only one major flaw: it wholly fails to account for the spread of new *music*. The following description is presented by Mayhew as stemming from 'one of the class' of 'ordinary street ballad-singers', and may be taken as indicative of general practice.

When any popular song came up, that was our harvest. 'Alice Gray,' 'The Sea,' [etc] . . . these were all great things to the ballad-singers. We looked at the bill of fare for the different concert-rooms, and then went round the neighbourhood where these songs were being sung, because the airs being well known, you see it eased the way for us. The very best sentimental song that ever I had in my life, and which lasted me off and on for two years, was Byron's 'Isle of Beauty.' I could get a meal quicker with that than with any other.[44]

Whether the erroneous attribution to Byron was the mistake of a genuine interviewee, or a rhetorical touch of Mayhew's, is less significant than the real origins of 'Isle of Beauty', its words written by Thomas Haynes Bayly and its tune by 'his friend Charles Shapland Whitmore', and incidentally a song that coined the phrase 'absence makes the heart grow fonder'.[45] Though the score could be purchased for 2*s*, it is unthinkable that this was the ballad-singer's point of access: it is far likelier that the tune was learnt by ear at the St James's Theatre or the Haymarket, where Bayly's productions were staged. As Mayhew observes regarding this account: 'The tunes are mostly picked up from the street bands, and sometimes from the cheap concerts, or from the gallery of the theatre, where the street ballad-singers very often go, for the express purpose of learning the airs.'[46] This practice is corroborated in the fictionalised autobiography *The Surprising History of a Ballad Singer*, whose author claimed 'to select popular theatrical songs, and to learn the true air. We used to go three or four times to the house where it was brought out; and I in general remarked, we were most fortunate with those produced by the summer theatres, especially Sadler's-Wells'; her favourite singer to learn songs from was Dorothy Jordan.[47] The practice was also known among sex workers, the *Swell's Night Guide* recording of a Miss Merreton that 'she visits the side-boxes very frequently, which puts it in her power to oblige the admirers of her voice with most of the modern songs'.[48] For a ballad-singer, attending a theatre even for the second half only, in the cheapest

[44] Mayhew, *London Labour*, vol. 3, 195–6.
[45] John Russell Stephens, 'Bayly, Nathaniel Thomas Haynes (1797–1839)', *ODNB*, oxforddnb.com/view/article/1768; BL Mus G.805.c (54); http://oed.com/view/Entry/64 5, P2.
[46] Mayhew, *London Labour*, vol. 3, 196.    [47] *Surprising History*, 14–15.
[48] *Swell's Night Guide*, 96.

seats, would have represented a substantial outlay of funds and thereby constituted a form of speculation, requiring an ear good enough both to learn a tune and to gauge the likelihood of its success when transposed to the streets. John Thomas Smith relates a less costly alternative, whereby ballad-singers would eavesdrop on rehearsals, a practice achieved more easily at outdoor venues such as Bermondsey Spa in 1795, where the manager was wary of 'people in the road (whose ears were close to the cracks in the paling to hear the song)'.[49] By such means, even the poorest ballad-singer could obtain new melodies.

'Obtain' is itself a mealy-mouthed term for what many even then denounced as piracy. Charles Dibdin the Elder complained in 1803 that: 'I have already been under the very unpleasant necessity of commencing prosecutions against fourteen persons who have pirated my productions', while his son and namesake, suffering the same abuse, was warned off prosecutions by his own printer, who advised that 'you'll get damages awarded you no doubt, but you'll have your own expenses, £60 perhaps, to pay; for the People that publish these things are too poor to pay damages or your expenses'.[50] Even the legal situation was ambiguous. While sheet music had been protected by copyright law since 1777, single sheets such as broadsides and slips were only defined in law as 'books' from 1809 – a precedent set in relation to scores but made applicable to all single sheets, and one that does not appear subsequently to have been tested.[51] The resultant statute prohibited the replication of an author's name or signature without permission, yet remained equivocal on whether their lyrics could be reproduced anonymously.[52] In any event, the risk – itself vanishingly small – was run only by printers, and not by the singers: without the reproduction of musical notation in print, there existed no concept of legal ownership of a tune transmitted orally. The only barrier, then, to the appropriation of new music by ballad-singers, was the price of a venue's admission – or, in the case of parks and gardens like Bermondsey, the width of a fence.

Personal familiarity with a new song might be enough for a busker; the ballad-singer also needed physical copies in order to operate. Again, this required an initial outlay of capital as, in the words of Charles Manby

---

[49] John Thomas Smith, *A Book for a Rainy Day* (1845), 137.
[50] Charles Dibdin, *The Professional Life of Mr. Dibdin*, 4 vols. (1803), vol. 1, vi; Speaight, *Professional & Literary Memoirs*, 47.
[51] John Small, 'The Development of Music Copyright', in Michael Kassler (ed.), *The Music Trade in Georgian England* (Farnham, 2011), 233–386, 380–1. See also Paul Watt, 'The Prefaces to Songsters: The Law, Aesthetics, Performers and Their Reputations', in Watt et al., *Cheap Print*, 32–46, 35–7.
[52] *The Statutes of the Realm*, 11 vols. (1810–1828), vol. 5, 430.

Smith: 'Credit ... is a word unknown in the Dials'.[53] Individual singers paid printers up front for their copies, yet apparently kept 'as profit four-fifths of [their] receipts' – this presumably being the net profit, rather than a formal arrangement whereby a singer had to return twenty per cent of their takings to the printer. The singer's margin of profit, on which she or he lived, derived from the economy of scale made by buying wholesale: though the printers of Seven Dials operated out of their own shops, they clearly relied upon singers for the bulk of their distribution. Pitts and Catnach, the two printers who all but monopolised the London ballad trade in the first third of the century, had well-established methods for this distribution. Accounts of these methods are however couched in anecdote and legend, creating an impression of sub-Dickensian idiosyncrasy: the great man sitting in state, a fiddler by his side, humming and hawing over each new lyric that a hopeful hack presented and selecting a likely tune, or else seeking out ancient airs from Ireland or the English countryside, brought within his hearing by newly arrived bumpkins.[54] Much of this business was said to be done in public houses, particularly the Crown and Clock Tower in Great St Andrew Street, owned by Pitts' friend William Neats, and the Rose and Crown, formerly known as the Beggar's Opera, in Church Lane.[55]

In assessing this evidence, we must balance this tempting specificity of place against the doubtful practicality of auditioning new material in a raucous pub, unless the aim was to test a song in situ. The assertion that singers went to public houses in order to obtain new stock is more convincing: conviviality suited a business reliant on intimate, informal networks, in which word-of-mouth must have played a central part in selecting what was likely to sell. One account of this practice from 1825 is clearly an exercise in flash picturesque, embroidered for literary purposes – yet the impression it creates is too vivid entirely to dismiss:

Bat Corcoran, Pitt's great ballad factor, ... held his weekly market at the Beggar's Opera ... Thither flocked in each Saturday night the unnumbered brothers and sisters of the profession, to purchase, to pay, to exchange, to bleed a tankard, to fathom a rowley-poley, and blow a cloud. Ah, the glorious confusion of those festivals! Who that has heard, will ever forget the mingling contributions of the hundred voices, exercising themselves in the respective pastimes of singing, scolding, swearing, roaring, &c. Above the various chorus swelled the deep tones of Bat Corcoran. But let us see Bat amidst his customers – see him riding

[53] Smith, *Little World of London*, 264–5.
[54] *The Life of Old Jemmy Catnach, Printer* (1878, repr. Penzance, 1965), 8; Sabine Baring-Gould, *Strange Survivals: Some Chapters in the History of Man* (2nd edn, 1894), 212–13.
[55] Shepard, *John Pitts*, 52–3.

the whirlwind – let us take him in the shock, the crisis of the night when he is despatching the claims of a series of applicants. 'I say, blind Maggie, you're down for a dozen "Jolly Waterman," thirteen to the dozen. – Pay up your score, Tom with the wooden leg, I see you are booked for a lot of "Arethusas." – Master Flowers, do you think that "Cans of Grog" can be got for nothing, that you leave a stiff account behind you. – Sally Sallop, you must either give back "The Gentleman of England," or tip for them at once. – Friday, my man, there are ever so many "Black-eyed Susans" against you. – Jemmy, get rid of the "Tars of Old England," if you can; I think "Crazy Janes" are more in vogue. What say you to an exchange for "Hosier's Ghost?["]' This was Bat's way.[56]

There is much in this depiction that is simply preposterous, while the figure of the controlling genius is something of a trope, anticipating Dickens' Fagin. Still, the idea that singers in a single district coordinated their activities, taking different songs rather than competing, deserves our consideration as highly plausible. We might also set against this predictable impression of the all-knowing ballad patriarch, a typical male gatekeeper, the knowledge that most of the great nineteenth-century London printers were succeeded by women: Pitts by his housekeeper Elizabeth Hodges; Catnach by his sister Anne Ryle; and Thomas Birt by his widow Mary.[57] We should also widen our conception of the printer–singer relationship beyond the confines of Seven Dials. John Harkness, a Preston (and, later, Blackburn) printer in operation from 1838 onwards, took advantage of the developing railway networks to dispatch large numbers of his songs to London, where singers would collect them from Euston station. Unlike the songs he printed for sale in the northwest, Harkness omitted his imprint from these 'SEC' sheets, thereby infiltrating the metropolitan market anonymously: perhaps he feared the taint of provincialism.[58] Songs circulating in the London street might not only have originated elsewhere, they might even have been *printed* outside the metropolis.

This external origin applied still more to the singers themselves, who surely cannot have been as subservient as the 1825 account above suggests. David Love, who cultivated close relations with at least five printers over the course of a long and peripatetic career, seems sometimes to have been formally employed – as by Steed of Gosport, with whom he was 'in good agreement, and I got large quantities of Books on trust, till I sold them' – and sometimes, as at Dumfries in Scotland, to have entered into

[56] 'London Ballad Singers', 54–5.    [57] Hepburn, *Book of Scattered Leaves*, vol. 1, 34.
[58] Gregg Butler, 'John Harkness: Reflecting the Northwest and making a living out of it', paper given at *Broadside Day* conference, Chetham's Library, Manchester, 20 February 2016.

temporary partnerships.[59] In Berwick-upon-Tweed, to aid his same-day circulation of 'The Wanton Widow of West-gate', which he had written about an incident he had just witnessed, Love managed to have a printer's boy deliver fresh batches of the song 'as I sold them', so 'that I might lose no time'.[60] When first in London, where he spent three years, Love 'composed many poems, and Mr. Evans printed them for me' – this can only have been John Evans of Long Lane, Southwark, a major ballad printer operating from 1780 until 1828.[61] Just as notable as Love's agency is the degree to which he epitomises a larger body of singers from across Britain who at some point visited or immigrated to London, bringing regional influences with them. Prior to his move to the metropolis, for example, Love had 'travelled through most parts of Scotland in the same line of business, and composing songs on any thing remarkable'.[62] A second spell in London later in his career involved a journey from Nottingham via Leicester, hitchhiking on the country's new network of canals.[63] I have written elsewhere of this itinerant phenomenon, focusing on the sometime ballad-singer John Magee, an Irish rebel who travelled to London from Glasgow via the entire eastern sea-board from Newcastle southwards.[64] London could be as much a destination as a place of origin for printed song, and while we cannot ignore the capital's influence on regional print culture, neither should we neglect the certainty that the influence flowed in both directions, enmeshing the metropolis within a wider reciprocal song culture, rather than privileging it as an almighty machine of dissemination.

Just as song repertoires were above all else mixed, their physical circulation was also subject to variation, from the long-distance peregrinations of Love or Magee, to the smaller radius worked by Joseph Johnson, who based himself around London's Tower Hill but, by hitching lifts with waggoners, spent market days in Romford, Staines, or St Alban's: market towns all within a few hours' travel of a central point.[65] The author of *Surprising History* relates that: 'We frequently went many miles from home; attended the installations, and all manner of public fetes: sometimes we repaired to sea-ports; and once we made a pedestrian excursion as far as Margate, subsisting on the road by singing a fashionable song of Grimaldi's in every town or village through which we passed.'[66] Thomas McConwick, by contrast, restricted himself to 'the western streets of

---

[59] Love, *Life, Adventures, and Experience*, 65–6, 39. See also ibid., 31.     [60] Ibid., 38.
[61] Ibid., 76.     [62] Ibid., 16.     [63] Love, *David Love's Journey*, 3–4.
[64] Cox Jensen, '*Travels*'.     [65] Smith, *Vagabondiana*, 33. See Interlude III.
[66] *Surprising History*, 14.

London'.[67] Yet even this more localised practice was far from insular: when we remember that Johnson hailed from the Caribbean, that the anonymous author here came from Scotland, and that McConwick was an Irishman who 'sings many of the old Irish songs with excellent effect', we might do better to think, even in sleepy market towns or the north Kent estuary, of a form of vernacular cosmopolitanism. An 1818 survey of London's 'vagrants' conducted over nine months determined that, of 3,284 cases, just 720 came from London parishes: nearly a thousand each came from the English countryside and Ireland, a small proportion from Scotland and Wales, and more than an eighth from beyond the British Isles. Meanwhile, more than a quarter of this total were located in the parish of St Giles's, the home of the great ballad printers, reinforcing the association between the dissemination of song and geographic diversity.[68] Even Samuel Milnes, a London-born ballad-singer 'who used between the years of 1835 and 1842 to visit Fetter Lane every Thursday with the newest and most popular ballad of the day', and was still singing in the Strand as late as 1869, spent much of his time at Brighton, and reported that 'I have travelled all over England – all over it I think – but the North's the best – Manchester, Liverpool, and them towns; but down Bath and Cheltenham way I was nearly starved'.[69] Perhaps the most eloquent expression of this relentless mobility may be found in the song 'The Wandering Bard', printed across the century in London, Birmingham, Manchester, Liverpool, and Glasgow.[70] The first line, which the singer could of course alter to fit their own circumstances, stated the narrator's place of origin: 'I'm the wandering bard of ...' – usually followed by 'Exeter', sometimes by 'Manchester', and even by 'Italy', the chief consideration being that the place should have three syllables with the stress on the first. In the dissemination and performance of this song, life and art must have imitated each other, the itinerant singer constructing an itinerant narrative voice in order to suit audiences across the British Isles.

The result of this heterogeneous circulation was a populace well versed in a wide array of songs of all ages and origins, whether or not those listeners were located in London – a promiscuity that predictably enraged the ballad revivalists of the end of the century, Sabine Baring-Gould writing that: 'The ballad-vendor, who vended his broadsheets, did much to corrupt the taste of the peasant', and Cecil Sharp endeavouring

[67] Smith, *Cries of London*, 67.
[68] *The First Report of the Society Established in London for the Suppression of Mendicity* (1819), 14–16.
[69] Hindley, *History of the Catnach Press*, viii–ix.
[70] See http://vwml.org.uk/roudnumber/2687.

to prove that: 'A broadside version of a ballad is ... a very indifferent one, and vastly inferior to the genuine peasant song.'[71] Fifty years earlier, collectors had known better than to believe in 'genuine peasant song', James Dixon noting of 'The Bold Pedlar and Robin Hood' that: 'An aged female in Bermondsey, Surrey, from whose oral recitation the editor took down the present version, informed him that she had often heard her grandmother sing it, and that it was never in print; but he has of late met with several common stall copies.'[72] In fact, Catnach had previously sold the song in question, as did Henry Such, decades after Dixon's own investigations.[73] Catnach, along with various regional printers from Truro to Hull, had also published 'The Tars of the Blanche',[74] a song Dixon recognised as 'a street-ballad, and written by some unknown author', yet which he finally determined to include in his *Ancient Poems, Ballads, and Songs of the Peasantry of England* due to 'its popularity, as well as from its poetical merit'. Notwithstanding its urban origin, he records that:

The first time we heard it sung was by a charcoal-burner in the New Forest. It was a hot sultry summer's day in 1835, and tired with pedestrianing, we had just entered a small inn when our ears were regaled with the Tars of the Blanche. The swarthy songster gave it with great spirit, and the chorus was well sustained, by five or six fine-looking fellows of the like occupation with himself.[75]

The tune 'Tars of the Blanche' was subsequently stipulated for several unconnected songs printed by Swindells of Manchester, linking that fast-growing, northern, urban centre of the Industrial Revolution, with reclusive forest-dwellers of the south.[76]

Perhaps the best single example of this fluid, interconnected culture is that of Henry Burstow, a labourer in Horsham, Sussex, born in 1826, whose *Reminiscences of Horsham* have been studied by Vic Gammon. Burstow was an 'eclectic' local singer:

In his repertory we find old songs rubbing shoulders with new songs, broadside ballads with sentimental Victorian songs, and classic 'folk songs' with 'nigger minstrel' pieces. Among composers and authors represented are Henry Russell, Charles Dibdin, Henry Clay Work, Stephen Foster, Fred Weatherby and M. G. Lewis. Burstow gives us a good account of where and how he learned his

---

[71] Both of these famous quotations may be found in a wider discussion by Roy Palmer, '"Veritable Dunghills": Professor Child and the Broadside', *Folk Music Journal* 7 (1996): 155–66, 156–7.

[72] James H. Dixon (ed.), *Ancient Poems, Ballads, and Songs of the Peasantry of England* (1846), 71.

[73] ballads.bodleian.ox.ac.uk/search/roud/333.

[74] Sadly, the tune of this is unknown, though its Roud number is 4583.

[75] Dixon, *Ancient Poems*, 236–7. [76] http://ballads.bodleian.ox.ac.uk/search/roud/4583.

songs. His father had a repertory of nearly two hundred, many of which Burstow learned; he also got songs from his mother and brother-in-law, from fellow workers and bellringers, from 'Country Wills' heard in local pubs. About the rest he is quite specific: 'The remainder I learnt from ballad sheets I bought as they were being hawked about at the fairs, and at other times from other printed matter'[.][77]

Many songs in Burstow's repertoire may be found elsewhere in this book: 'Isle of Beauty', 'Old Dog Tray', 'The Storm', 'Black-Ey'd Susan' and many more, songs originating in Ireland, Scotland, England, and America, in the Georgian theatre and the Victorian music hall.[78] Burstow even remembers that a local village personality, Charlotte Venn, was known on account of her notoriety as 'Cherry Ripe', in testament to the cultural resonance of Eliza Vestris' signature song of the late Georgian stage (for more concerning which, see later).[79]

Burstow also records transactions with individual ballad-singers, as in the following anecdote:

I remember, when quite a boy, buying for my mother of a pedlar, as he sang in the street, the old ballad 'Just before the battle, Mother.' This was her favourite song because, I think, her brother, their mother's favourite boy, after having fought in many battles, had deserted and fled and was never more heard of.[80]

If Burstow was 'quite a boy', we must date the incident to, at the very latest, the 1840s, yet the song does not appear to have been published before the 1860s – among many others, Harkness of Preston was one of the first to print it as one of his 'SEC' ballads designed for a London audience – and the first extant sheet music editions, from 1866, associate it with the US Civil War and the American songwriter George Frederick Root.[81] Yet Burstow speaks of it as 'the old ballad', which is less surprising when we remember that his recollections date from the early twentieth century. Rather than attempting to correct Burstow's chronology, we might do better to reflect on the mechanisms that could take a song from America to England and from the urban north (Preston) to the rural south (Horsham); the means by which an artefact accessed by modern technologies of print, railway, and Sunday school education might come to be conceived of as 'the old ballad'; and the universalising narratives that enabled a country boy to purchase a song from a singing stranger, because of its generic appeal to his sorrowful mother. It is, in

[77] Vic Gammon, '"Not Appreciated in Worthing?" Class Expression and Popular Song Texts in Mid-Nineteenth-Century Britain', *Popular Music* 4, 'Performers and Audiences' (1984): 5–24, 19.
[78] Henry Burstow, *Reminiscences of Horsham* (Horsham, 1911), 115–19.   [79] Ibid., 60.
[80] Ibid., 108.
[81] http://ballads.bodleian.ox.ac.uk/search/roud/4263; BL Mus H.2706 (2).

passing, likely that the ballad-singer came from outside Sussex: in 1841, when Burstow was fifteen, nine 'itinerant musicians and ballad singers' were brought to trial in Sussex, only one of whom was native to the county, while seven were 'strangers' and one a 'foreigner', meaning non-British.[82]

Even Chappell, the great antiquarian of the mid-century and a firm believer in the national differentiation of songs, was aware of the practical mobility of this culture, recording that 'I have heard [the song] [']Early one morning['] sung by servants, who came from Leeds, from Hereford, and from Devonshire, and by others from parts nearer to London.'[83] There is further evidence here to confound theories of distinctive traditions of national song, so prevalent at the time, Derek Scott observing that 'many blackface minstrel songs and pseudo-Celtic songs came to be accepted as the authentic cultural expression of black Americans and of Irish and British Celts'.[84] Londoners of all classes exhibited a strong appetite for 'Scotch song' across this period, and frequently allowed themselves to be deceived on this account.[85] Yet as Chappell admitted: 'The mixture of English and Anglo-Scottish with the genuine Scottish music has been gradually increasing ... the Scotch have themselves been deceived into a belief in their genuineness.' Elsewhere in his compendium of songs 'Illustrative of the National Music of England', Chappell calls a song now generally considered as Irish to be 'one of the common street ballad tunes of London'; claims two famous Irish and Scottish airs as 'mere modifications' of an English original; and, while attempting to construct four distinct categories of 'the characteristic airs of England', ends his analysis of melodic structure by conceding that: 'I attached formerly greater importance than now to the termination of tunes as national characteristics; for, although certain closes may prevail over others in a nation, it is very difficult to assign an exclusive right to any.'[86]

Chappell's dilemma is primarily a musicological one, yet the actions of travelling ballad-singers in spreading a thoroughly mixed song culture, or in selling the 'Longsheets issued by printers from the 1830s [that] mixed English and Irish songs indiscriminately', cannot be neglected as part of

[82] House of Commons Parliamentary Papers, 1842 (63): *1841. Gaols. Copies of all reports, and of schedules (B.) transmitted to the Secretary of State, pursuant to the 24th section of the 4th Geo. IV. cap. 64, and 14th section of the 5th Geo. IV. cap. 12. (Counties, ridings, or divisions.)*, 186.
[83] Chappell, *Popular Music*, vol. 2, 735.      [84] Scott, *Singing Bourgeois*, 81.
[85] See, for example, the testimony of a credulous listener, George Byrne, in POB t17800510-9, and the confession of a writer of artificial 'Scotch songs', in Robert Anderson, *The Poetical Works of Robert Anderson*, 2 vols. (Carlisle, 1820), vol. 1, xxiv–xxv.
[86] Chappell, *Popular Music*, vol. 2, 610; 730; 770; 792–3.

this narrative.[87] To more refined observers, intellectually invested in rigid musical and racial hierarchies, this could produce instances of dissonance that:

stand high in offensiveness ... whilst the ear of musical taste, or classical correctness, is assailed and tortured so as to make discord ring in it long after the noise has been heard. Fancy to yourself, harmonious reader, the horrifications which 'Blue Bonnets,' from a black beggarman, mumbling bad English, must occasion.[88]

The combination of 'black' and 'bad English' suggests the former is a racial designation, the writer's horror being located therefore in hearing a 'Scottish' song performed by a person considered racially both inferior and exotic. Yet, as Joseph Johnson's success in particular and the spread of such a heterodox variety of songs in general so amply demonstrate, most listeners evinced no such scruples when participating in such a mixed – and even in a sense cosmopolitan – song culture.

These conclusions are by no means unprecedented. As long ago as 1950, Bruce Millar observed of our period that: 'The old ballads that they found in manuscripts and printed collections, like the Percy Folio and the Pepys Collection, were exactly like (or even exactly the same as) those they saw being hawked in the streets or country roads around them, and the ones the city dwellers sang were often the same as those of the rustics.'[89] Bennett, though speaking primarily of the later nineteenth century, concludes that: 'The evidence of songs printed in London and elsewhere points to a huge central repertory common to all these classes; and if this is true of songs, it must mean that an even greater proportion of tunes was held in common: a national repertory rather than a popular one.'[90] Ballad-singers and their audiences alike were invested in the sharing of a repertoire of songs that was in every conceivable way a mixed repertoire, and that act of sharing was itself facilitated by an equally fluid mode of circulation. Though the origin of a song or indeed its performer might be elite or in some way exotic, though it might be distinguished as supremely topical or hallowed by antiquity, or its sales boosted by association with a celebrity performer such as Grimaldi, Jordan, or Vestris, once incorporated into this common repertoire the song became, quite simply, part of the mainstream. It was this mainstream that singers made it their job to navigate and to control.

[87] Eva, 'Home Sweet Home?', 135.    [88] 'The Italian Boy', 156.
[89] Millar, 'Eighteenth-Century Views', 125.    [90] Bennett, 'Music in the Halls', 4.

## Charting the Mainstream

In writing of the 'mainstream' I make no claims for the word's historicity. Rather, I am drawn to its explanatory potential regarding a song culture held in common by all classes both in London and across much of Britain: and it is worth noting here that, while various regions also enjoyed a less porous indigenous song repertoire, rooted in specifically nuanced dialect or a host of idiomatic references, which was *not* shared nationally, London seems to have had no such secondary reserve of songs: the songs of London, however cockneyfied or localised, were necessarily also the songs of the nation. I am attracted by the metaphorical aptness of 'mainstream', locating its central current in London's streets, with the tributaries of stage, pleasure garden, immigrant communities, itinerants, all pouring in. It fits the thing it describes, unlike the better uses of 'popular culture' to describe what is, effectively, a mainstream. For instance, Peter Bailey writes: 'Popular culture is conceived of here as a sprawling hybrid, a generically eclectic ensemble or repertoire of texts, sites and practices that constitute a widely shared social and symbolic resource … that allows for a more volatile mix of players, real and imaginary, than those of the self-enclosed working-class neighbourhood'.[91] Fundamentally, I am persuaded that the typical answer of the person not greatly interested in music, when questioned concerning their musical taste, may have been as prevalent in the past as it is today: 'oh, I like a bit of everything'.

While musicologists in particular have invested a great deal of energy in investigating the appropriation of what is usually termed 'folk' song by elite composers and audiences in the eighteenth to twentieth centuries, very little has been said of the reverse – the appropriation of more or less elite music by those of lower social status – while even fewer attempts have been made to elucidate a culture that cannot be reduced to a flow of influences either up or down a social spectrum, but instead sustained a repertoire that was held in common, however tacitly, across social classes and spaces. Work in the latter area has concentrated on a period postdating recording and the radio – the age of Cole Porter rather than the *colporteur* – when the great social and technological changes of the twentieth century made it far more natural to conceive of a song culture that might be shared across a nation, on both ideological and pragmatic grounds.[92] At no stage has anyone suggested, nor would I wish to suggest, that this mainstream precluded other modes of

---

[91] Bailey, *Popular Culture*, 10–11.
[92] The best single case study might be that of the Netherlands, in José van Dijck, 'Record and Hold: Popular Music between Personal and Collective Memory', *Critical Studies in*

musical consumption: participants in mainstream culture need neither have acknowledged the fact, nor need they have neglected additional niche musical interests.

In the latest, 2009 edition of Peter Burke's great thesis, in which a 'striking' similarity is noted between the broadside ballad and that most contentious of twentieth-century designations, 'mass culture', we still find the conclusion that: 'By 1800 . . . the clergy, the nobility, the merchants, the professional men – and their wives – had abandoned popular culture to the lower classes'.[93] There are three aspects of this claim with which I would take issue, the first being the extent to which an attention to material culture, in the form of the broadside as a printed object, may be something of a red herring: not only, as we have seen earlier, did elites continue to buy these ephemeral items, but more importantly we should not conflate the printed object with the song it represents. Although a cheap slip, a bound songbook, or an autographed presentation copy of a score all mediate the perception of a song in different ways, they still give access to what is fundamentally the same composition: the fact that a song may be found on a ballad sheet need not consign that song to the prescriptive category of 'mass culture'. Second, Burke cites in support of his position on British song, in an uncharacteristically egregious act of outdatedness, the opinion of the nineteenth-century folklorist Francis James Child, rather than any more recent view, such as that advanced by Dave Russell of: 'the complexity and variety of popular repertoire and taste, demonstrating that Italian opera and oratorio as well as music hall song and parlour ballad flourished quite happily alongside each other in nineteenth-century popular musical culture, often within the same household'.[94] Third, and most problematic in relation to song culture, is the directional construction of Burke's argument: that the agency lay solely with the middling and elite groups who were 'abandoning popular culture, or more exactly the common culture that was coming to be viewed as popular'.[95] I would maintain that, in the case of London and the case of song, this was a culture whose artefacts continued to be held *in common*, and that it made no difference how vulgar certain elites professed ballads and their singers to be,[96] if the lower orders independently persisted in appropriating the songs that were written for more exclusive settings, and

---

*Media Communication* 23 (2006): 357–74. I may as well also own up that the Cole Porter/ *colporteur* joke is about as old as the man himself.

[93] Peter Burke, *Popular Culture in Early Modern Europe* (3rd edn, Farnham, 2009), 347, 366.

[94] Ibid., 367; Dave Russell, 'The "Social History" of Popular Music: A Label without a Cause?', *Popular Music* 12 (1993): 139–54, 143.

[95] Burke, *Popular Culture*, 368.    [96] Ibid., 375–6.

incorporated them within that mainstream.[97] Burke's thesis only holds because he accepts the songs that are 'rediscovered' by antiquarians and their view of these songs as the productions of a 'folk' culture, as constituting the reality of the 'popular' culture that these elites had supposedly withdrawn from a century earlier.[98] This neglects, above all, the role of the theatre as a technology for the mixing of songs, audiences, and influences, so that a respectable audience at the Princess's Theatre on Oxford Street in 1864 – a venue that veered in its own repertoire between grand opera, Shakespeare, promenades, and melodrama – might be convinced to applaud a production of Dion Boucicault's *The Streets of London* primarily because it was 'Furnished with a lively overture by Mr. Charles Hall, introducing all the street tunes of the time'.[99] By attending to the practical operation of a mainstream musical culture, we may sidestep any distractions offered by the 'folk' and come to a more nuanced understanding that, while rifts and distinctions undoubtedly obtained, Londoners of all walks of life were continuing to listen, at least some of the time, to a shared, common, mainstream repertoire.

Perhaps the most convenient way of assessing the operation of this mainstream and the role of the ballad-singer within it is to focus upon three of its most successful and enduring songs. Gammon observes that: 'When [songs] move from one social milieu to another we can look at the way a song changes in response to the move, but we can also legitimately ask what there is in the song that has appeal in spite of changed conditions of performance and reception.'[100] While I agree with this, my ultimate concerns are centred, not on the songs themselves, but on what these songs reveal of the culture in which they were shared. We might consider first 'Black-Ey'd Susan'.[101]

An early eighteenth-century lyric by John Gay with at least two common tunes, the better-known (see Example 4.1) said to have been composed by Handel (but generally attributed to the bass singer Richard Leveridge), it is perhaps *the* archetypal English ballad-opera

---

[97] Burke may have done better in this regard to turn to Gramsci rather than Bakhtin for a theoretical perspective. Mike Pickering and Tony Green observe that 'Gramsci pointed out that even though most songs are written "neither by nor for the people", people nevertheless selectively and creatively adopt and adapt particular songs', in their introduction 'Towards a Cartography of the Vernacular Milieu', in their edited collection, *Everyday Culture: Popular Song and the Vernacular Milieu* (Milton Keynes, 1987), 1–38, 3.
[98] Burke, *Popular Culture*, 385–6.      [99] Review article, *Era* 1350 (7 August 1864).
[100] Gammon, *Desire, Drink and Death*, 12.
[101] Since the time of writing, I have become aware of a superb article by Andrew Gustar that forms an incredibly detailed case study of this song: see his 'The Life and Times of Black-Ey'd Susan: The Story of an English Ballad', *Folk Music Journal* 10 (2014): 432–48.

Example 4.1  Richard Leveridge and John Gay, 'Black-Ey'd Susan',
vocal reduction adapted from an arrangement by William Chappell[102]

song, with a correspondence between the worlds of court, theatre, and
street, evident even in the circumstances of its first assembling. It is
strophic, it relates a sentimental narrative of two parted lovers (versions
of the text are easily accessible online), and its second, more famous
tune, given here, is a simple minor-key composition with highly distinctive melodic cadences, especially in its B section. Though never out
of circulation, 'Black-Ey'd Susan' enjoyed a particular revival at the
turn of the century when sung by Charles Incledon at Covent Garden,
and it was frequently marketed as such on sheet music copies.[103] As an
1804 court case makes clear, the song could be (and was!) bought from
cheap booksellers, such as Ann Read's establishment off the
Tottenham Court Road.[104] In 1829 it formed the basis of Jerrold's
sensationally successful melodrama of the same name, a piece that
went on to play at theatres of all ranks, but that was first introduced
in a double bill with another of Jerrold's short dramas, *Sally in Our*

---

[102] This version of the better-known of the song's melodies is based on that given in William
Chappell (ed.), *A Collection of National English Airs, Consisting of Ancient Song, Ballad, &*
*Dance Tunes*, 2 vols. (1840), vol. 2, 27, which is itself a nineteenth-century setting of the
melody 'by Handel', that is, Leveridge's, found in the next footnote, with the rhythm
altered, apparently to reflect nineteenth-century performance practice.
[103] For all of the above, see BL Mus H 1860 ww (21).    [104] POB t18040215-76.

*Alley*, also based upon a century-old ballad (the titular 'Sally in Our Alley'), and performed at the Surrey Theatre on 8 June.[105] Though the Surrey was a minor theatre, the first printed playtext was 'Dedicated, by permission, to his Royal Highness the Duke of Clarence'.[106] Clarence, soon to become William IV, was closely associated with the Royal Navy: the pairing of the plays, the use of the original songs, and the playtext's dedication all affirm Jerrold's deft manipulation of patriotic pride and national history, which in this case was required to buttress what was in fact a subversive radical political argument pursued across the two plays, only three years before the passing of the Great Reform Bill.[107] To return to our central purpose, the juxtaposition of the two plays closely resembles the publishing strategies of both Pitts and Catnach, when they reissued their own editions of 'Black-Ey'd Susan' on broadsides. One Pitts edition from between 1819 and 1844, on a large horizontal sheet, appends two 'answering' ballads to the first, resulting in a sheet that closely resembles in composition if not in typeface the old black-letter broadsides of the seventeenth century: evidently Pitts was marketing the song on a nostalgic premise.[108] Elsewhere, Pitts paired the song with 'Rule, Britannia!', while Catnach similarly published multiple versions paired with 'The Storm', which as discussed in Interlude III was another of Incledon's most successful sea-songs; both printers were positioning 'Black-Ey'd Susan' as iconic of seafaring patriotic pride, the better to sell an old song.[109] These associations demonstrably stuck: Harvey's 1862 retrospective, discussed at the end of Chapter 3, mentions '"The Storm" – then immensely relished by the London operatives, and as often whistled at their work as "Black-eyed Susan" or "Sally in our Alley"', in an aside that evokes both Jerrold's and Catnach's pairings, while Chappell's list of 'national favourites' includes, sequentially, 'Black-eyed Susan, Rule Britannia, &c.'[110] The missing figure in this story is supplied in an 1806 account from the *European Magazine*, discussing a disreputable beggar: 'I took note, also, of her success in picking of pockets . . . and squeaking out the history of Robin Goodfellow, or singing the ballad of Black-eyed Susan.'[111] We have here a song that was carried

[105] Douglas Jerrold, *Black-Ey'd Susan: A Drama, in Three Acts* (1829); Douglas Jerrold, *Sally in Our Alley. A Drama, in Two Acts* (1829).
[106] Jerrold, *Black-Ey'd Susan*, frontispiece.
[107] For example, on the frontispiece of *Sally in Our Alley* Jerrold declared that 'The Design of this Piece is to beat down Pride, Inhumanity, and Presumption; to show that "A man's a man for a' that!" however low his Estate.'
[108] Bod. Harding B 1(12).
[109] Bod. Harding B 11(307); there are at least three editions of the Catnach pairing extant, catalogued consecutively as Bod. Harding B 11(3672) to (3674).
[110] Harvey, 'Street Music', 351; Chappell, *Collection of National English Airs*, v.
[111] 'The Adventures of a Pen', *European Magazine* 50 (1806): 280.

back and forth for a century between street and stage, for the enjoyment of high and low, accruing a nautical, national resonance that was assiduously promoted by ballad printers, and appropriated by a radical Bohemian playwright – but that maintained, as its lowest common denominator, a facility to be performed by the most negligible of ballad-singers.

It is precisely this sort of early eighteenth-century stalwart that one essayist of 1800 had in mind when they wrote of the 'compositions that will last as long as taste and judgement shall preside among us; or while sound and sense continue to give pleasure to a well-tuned ear, or a sound understanding' – a rhetoric notable for its stress upon a cultivated, refined taste, that disingenuously belies the social mobility of a song like 'Black-Ey'd Susan'.[112] Yet, despite the conservative tone adopted by this author, new songs were continually finding a place in mainstream repertoires. One such was the William Shield and John O'Keeffe composition 'The Wolf' of 1798, written for a comic opera, which the essayist above deemed exceptional:

The last modern songs which bear the strongest marks of sterling ability, in respect to musical composition, are Dr. Arnold's 'Flow, thou regal purple stream;' and that of Shield's Wolf Song, in 'The Castle of Andalusia.' – There is a stamina about the above songs which will be a lasting credit to the genius and judgement of the composers, and the means of holding up their reputation to a vast longevity.[113]

Though 'The Wolf' resembled 'Black-Ey'd Susan' in its sphere of origin, it is a very different sort of song, as is evident from Example 4.2. Through-composed rather than strophic, moving from a 'Siciliana' in 6/4 to an *Andante* tempo in common time, and cycling through further tempi and key changes before resolving in an extended and truly operatic coda in 3/4, there is no way in which it might be described as a 'ballad'. It calls for impressive vocal range and proficiency, and features several chromatic passages that would surely tax an untrained singer. And yet both Harvey, speaking of 1812, and Mayhew, presenting a later generation, attest to its popularity among ballad-singers.[114]

The Scottish man of letters Alexander Molleson, writing in 1806, opines in a footnote that: 'Mr. Shield is one of those composers who have sacrificed least to the rage of fashion, and most cultivated expressive easy melody. Accordingly, his strains are deservedly popular; and will no

---

[112] 'Remarks on the Science of Singing', in Charles Wilson, *The Myrtle and Vine; or, Complete Vocal Library*, 4 vols. (1800), vol. 1, 38–44, 42.

[113] Ibid., 42.    [114] Harvey, 'Street Music', 347; Mayhew, *London Labour*, vol. 3, 195.

Example 4.2  William Shield, 'The Wolf', vocal reduction adapted from an edition for domestic performance (1820)[115]

---

[115] This vocal reduction is based on an 1820 edition published for voice and piano, though with orchestral parts indicated within the piano score: BL Mus H.3400.f (7).

Example 4.2 (cont.)

doubt long outlive many extravaganzas of the day.'[116] In the case of 'The Wolf', we might take 'easy melody' to refer to the listener's perception

[116] Alexander Molleson, *Miscellanies in Prose and Verse* (Glasgow, 1806), 92, *fn*.

rather than the singer's. Even so, to accept Molleson's explanation is to move no further than an idea that catchy, 'tuneful' songs were popular – a position simultaneously self-evident and impossible to argue on an objective musicological level. More recently, Scott has sought to rationalise the appeal of this 'war horse of the Victorian drawing room', a song that 'held a place throughout the nineteenth century as one of the half-dozen best-known bass songs'.[117] His analysis, though rooted in a mode of close reading I have generally tried to avoid, prompts us to consider the song's appeal to a dramatic performer:

[W]hy did the song survive musically? . . . [S]ome of its features, for example, the excessive use of sequence (the repetition of a melodic phrase at a different pitch) borrowed from *opera seria*, would have sounded routine and old-fashioned in the nineteenth century. The principal explanation for its continued musical fascination would seem to be the possibilities it offered for a melodramatic rendition. The tempo moves from a gentle, rocking rhythm for the sleepy world, to a slightly quicker, atmospheric section for the prowling wolf, to a vigorous final section for the robbing and plundering.[118]

In turning to the street rather than the drawing room, I might offer one further material reason for the song's longevity: though its rendition takes upwards of five minutes, in print it consists of a mere twelve short lines, due to the high degree of lyrical repetition involved – a characteristic shared, for example, with the John Braham standard 'The Beautiful Maid'.[119] If a London printer desired to bulk it out to a full column length to sell it as a single slip, they could simply include the repetitions, as John Sharp did around 1845, topping off his production with a gruesome skull-and-crossbones for an appropriately Gothic visual appeal.[120] Yet its potential physical brevity meant it could also be included as a makeweight on a larger sheet, evening out an irregular length of columns, or adding extra value at little material cost, and it was in this manner that both Pitts and Catnach tended to produce 'The Wolf' – a characteristic that lent itself to the increasing trend for larger compilation sheets containing dozens of songs, and that may have done much to ensure the song's longevity in print as the century progressed.[121] To thrive in the mainstream, however, 'The Wolf' had to suit singers as well as printers. The use of sequence mentioned by Scott was here an asset rather than a drawback; without a score, those repeated phrases at different pitches would have done much to fix both the lyrical repetitions and the tune itself in a singer's memory. Its bass register also offered something different

[117] Scott, *Singing Bourgeois*, 7.    [118] Ibid., 7–8.    [119] BL Mus G.250 (10).
[120] Bod. Harding B 16(312a).
[121] See numerous examples at ballads.bodleian.ox.ac.uk/search/roud/V5485.

for those male ballad-singers incapable of singing at the high pitch discussed in Chapter 3. This low, growling quality offered great sonic potential when combined with the 'melodramatic' possibilities that Scott notes – remembering too that melodrama was fast becoming the dominant theatrical mode of the age. This potential is realised in the recollection given by Harvey: whether we take or leave his ironical tone, the following account demonstrates how an ostensibly difficult song such as 'The Wolf' need not be delivered with great precision to be fit for purpose as entertainment:

Yes, there is a great crowd in Salisbury-square, and you may easily recognise the tones of Peter Links, the wonderful London bass, who has a standing engagement from the mobility. What an animated circle of eager listeners, not in full dress, certainly, but well able to contribute their coppers. Notice that slatternly woman, with a child perched on her shoulder, the youngster crowing with delight, and mamma heartily sympathising. Don't get too near; beware of your pockets. Links is beginning, and we are fortunate, for he will give us his favourite song. Links is a broad-shouldered, portly man, rather vulgar, and very dirty; perhaps he sometimes practises as the burglar he is about to describe. He begins, having wisely mounted on a stool, to give his voice more freedom:–

> 'When the wolf in midnight prowl,
> Bays the moon with hideous howl,
> Howl, howl – '

the last word being indefinitely prolonged, and clouding over the advent of the robbers, up to the climax –

> 'Locks, bolts, and bars soon fly asunder;
> Then to murder, pillage, plunder;'

and this brilliant passage gradually falling into the original 'prowl' and 'howl,' which, after vociferous applause, led to a double encore, a liberal shower of pence, and my companion's loss of his bandana. Better move on; Links's friends are not so orderly to-night as might be wished.[122]

Every part of this account, from the titillating warning to 'beware of your pockets' onwards, suggests the experiential thrill on offer, irrespective of the listener's social status. What began as an elite cultural object has, by virtue of both its musical properties and its subject matter, been thoroughly and successfully appropriated from below so as to embody a vernacular or even an underworld milieu. There is an appeal here different to that of the sentimental, strophic, narrative ballad, yet equally open to repurposing and imaginative engagement across time and space.

The final song I wish to consider is 'Cherry Ripe' (Example 4.3), a song that might at first appear less mobile due to its indelible association with

---

[122] Harvey, 'Street Music', 347.

Example 4.3 Charles Edward Horn and Richard Herrick, 'Cherry Ripe', vocal reduction (c.1820)[123]

[123] This vocal reduction is based on a score from c.1820: BL Mus G 425 oo (11).

a single singer, Eliza Vestris.[124] Of the three figures central to its production, the most easily overlooked is its composer, Charles Edward Horn (though not by his contemporary Thomas Attwood, who unsuccessfully sued Horn for plagiarism over the melody), an oversight hinted at by Horn's biographer Clive Brown when he notes that 'Cherry Ripe', which was technically described as a cavatina, 'almost attained the status of a folk-song' – a telling if anachronistic turn of phrase gesturing to the song's wide and long-lasting success, continuing into the twentieth century and across a host of other media, which left its writer behind in the process. Horn, a singer and string player with links to the court, had a career that wove between grand opera, the founding of the New York Philharmonic Society, and theatre management, yet he remained associated with accessible song in spite of himself, the *Athenaeum* reflecting near the end of his life that he was 'the best of our ballad composers ... who, if trained under a better dispensation might have done much for English music'.[125] The song's lyricist Robert Herrick was, by contrast, immune to such criticism, having died in 1674: Horn's setting, for an 1825 production of *Paul Pry*, was of a text written by someone who had grown up in the sixteenth century.[126] As Hindley remarked: 'What a tribute to the fine old poet ... to have had the principal streets and dirty lanes of London, two hundred years after his death, made vocal with his words that seemed to gush from his heart like the nightingale's song.'[127] Though the lyric's antiquity may have appealed to those of Hindley's stamp, it is unlikely that most listeners were aware of this derivation: the poem's conceit is that it ventriloquises a street seller's cry, a practice little changed by Vestris' day. Above all, it is Horn's setting of that cry itself, in imitation of the short melodic phrases used by street vendors,[128] that is at the heart of the song's identity, as seen in Example 4.4.

The composition is based around this earworm – and while the somewhat improbable modulations in the song's later passages are unlikely, shorn of their harmonic accompaniment and consequent

---

[124] The authoritative account of this relationship, and of Vestris herself, is David Kennerley, *Sounding Feminine: Women's Voices in British Musical Culture, 1780–1850* (New York and Oxford, 2020).

[125] *Athenaeum* 20 (15 May 1847): 1226, cited in Clive Brown, 'Horn, Charles Edward (1786–1849)', *ODNB*, oxforddnb.com/view/article/13781.

[126] Tom Cain, 'Herrick, Robert (*bap.* 1591, *d.* 1674)', *ODNB*, oxforddnb.com/view/article/13092.

[127] Hindley, *History of the Cries of London*, 13.

[128] See, for example, Gardiner, *Music of Nature*, 311–21. As Gardiner points out (319), another trace of these cries as appropriated in song comes in 'One a-penny, two a-penny, hot cross buns', a tune still familiar in England today, let alone in 1832.

Example 4.4  Extract of Herrick, 'Cherry Ripe', single bar

logic, to have been replicated by street singers, its central hook is
indelible. That short phrase encapsulates the imaginative appeal of
the song, ostensibly one of romantic love, but in fact carrying highly
licentious and promiscuous implications. As discussed in Chapter 1,
the established trope of the female street seller advertising wares open
to salacious interpretation – cherries, primroses – could appeal, however surreptitiously, across different levels of society.

In this context, the close association with the original singer, Vestris –
an association advertised on early broadside editions from Pitts, Birt, and
Catnach – served primarily to reinforce this permissive message: Vestris,
an assiduous businesswoman, cultivated a risqué stage persona based
around her success in breeches roles, in more than one of which she
sang 'Cherry Ripe'.[129] Yet London printers were unusually keen to target
as wide an audience as possible, with both Pitts and Birt including the
following direction on their sheets:

> Where my Julia's lips do smile,
> There's the land of cherry isle.★
>
> ★ When sung by a lady—
> Where the sun-beams sweetly smile,
> There's the land of cherry isle.

This emendation may have had less to do with the performer's sex
than with propriety: Vestris in a breeches role was of course still
a woman, but not necessarily a 'lady', and by including an innocuous, pastoral alternative, printers were attempting to have their cake
and eat it (perhaps even with a cherry on top). The result was a song
accessible to all, to be sung by either sex, with or without a sexualised
intention.

In 1841, Charles Mackay recalled that:

About twenty years ago London resounded with one chorus, with the love of
which everybody seemed to be smitten. Girls and boys, young men and old,
maidens and wives, and widows, were all alike musical. There was an absolute

---

[129] Bod. Harding B 11(342), Harding B 25(367), and Johnson Ballads fol. 29.

mania for singing, and the worst of it was, that ... they seemed utterly unable to change their tune. 'Cherry ripe!' 'Cherry ripe!' was the universal cry of all the idle in the town. Every unmelodious voice gave utterance to it; every crazy fiddle, every cracked flute, every wheezy pipe, every street organ was heard in the same strain, until studious and quiet men stopped their ears in desperation, or fled miles away into the fields or woodlands, to be at peace. This plague lasted for a twelvemonth, until the very name of cherries became an abomination in the land.[130]

Mackay writes of this 'plague' lasting a 'twelvemonth', yet the records of cheap print, sheet music, high art, and literature all attest to the endurance of 'Cherry Ripe' in the mainstream for many years. Its initial success was nonetheless remarkable, and was appropriately enough itself immortalised in song on the Catnach satirical slip 'Medley of Melodists', which begins:

> We're all singing, sing, sing, singing,
> And we're all singing various songs and glees;
> And we're all singing like brisk humming bees, –
> Imitation of Street Singing;
> Cherry ripe, cherry ripe, still, still they sing,
> With cherry ripe now every place it does ring,
> For they're all singing, &c.
> The whole world for singing is now in a tune,
> And it will be overrun with ballad singers soon ...[131]

This song goes on to incorporate several further street hits, from the still-familiar tune of 'Buy a Broom', another of Vestris' hits, this time adapted from an old Viennese waltz, to a still more rarified Germanic import:

> In London you scarcely a street thro' can go,
> But the bailiffs hunting their prey with a view-hallo
> Hark follow, hark follow, hark follow, hark!
> Follow hark follow! –

This is a reference to the 'Huntsman's Chorus' from Carl Maria von Weber's Der Freischütz, the opera that took polite London by storm in the 1820s. Duly translated, this excerpt found its way onto the pages of Pitts and Catnach, for, notwithstanding its status as high culture and its original performance in five-part harmony by a full-scale professional operatic chorus (to say nothing of a thirteen-part orchestra), the chorus was based on a simple melody with a memorable refrain, suitable for both

[130] Charles Mackay, Memoirs of Extraordinary Popular Delusions, 3 vols. (1841), vol. 1, 336.
[131] Bod. Johnson Ballads 231.

solo and mass rendition: an idealised drinking song that could in fact function as such even in the dens of London.[132]

This was the key to the ballad-singer's mediation of the mainstream. Whatever a song's functional or physical origins, whether it was a seventeenth-century Irish jig for the fiddle like 'The Black Joke', an eighteenth-century stage ballad for soloist and small theatre ensemble, or an up-to-the-minute piece of bombast from the world of grand opera, the ballad-singer's function was, musically speaking, reductive. With ruthless efficiency, their task was to strip down any song to a bare skeleton, shorn of texture, harmony, and to some extent dynamics, with nothing left but a single vocal line. This should not be mistaken for a wholesale loss of musicality: rhythm, tone, tempo, and interpretation all remained. Rather, the performance of a song was reduced to an embodied, vocalised inter-action between singer and audience – which was in many ways a far more demanding test of its musical potential. With no arrangement, there was nowhere for a tune to 'hide'. This stripping down still remains to many the ultimate proof of a composition's quality, most notably in the realm of what is now considered to be 'popular music': perhaps the single most famous instance is Nirvana's acclaimed live album *MTV Unplugged in New York*, released in 1994.

As discussed in Chapter 3, a singer still had a host of musical and theatrical devices available to augment their performance: the key point is that, sonically, their repertoire – drawn from an incredibly broad range of musical sources – was reduced to an indiscriminately sparse palette. Their songs thereby achieved a powerful degree of *equivalence* and con-formity. Mainstream song culture therefore operated at the level of the lowest common denominator – that is, the level of the ballad-singer – which I do not mean pejoratively, but quite literally. It was this stripping away that enabled the existence of a shared, mainstream, musical culture, in a world lacking widespread access to the technologies that would enable the mobility of more complex forms of music. These technologies included not only recording and transmission devices, but also, more crucially, mass literacy and musical literacy. Via the minimalist operation of the ballad-singer, culture could be shared between court, stage, home, street, and public house; between town and country; between rich and poor. It only required that its cultural objects, the songs, be reduced to their most portable, which is to say simplest, incarnations. The result was a mainstream that was simultaneously impoverished and enriched.

The ballad-singer was not without parallel in this regard. Barrel organs, the coming force, provided access to music that could be performed

---

[132] http://ballads.bodleian.ox.ac.uk/search/roud/V7486.

without the slightest musical facility, and though organs could not communicate lyrics, they could substitute a degree of harmony. Nor is a mainstream willingness to sacrifice musical complexity for the sake of convenient access a phenomenon restricted to the nineteenth century: a similar thing occurred with the advent of mobile phone ringtones and, as high-fidelity purists would argue, the digital compression of songs by streaming services. Yet, for all the ballad-singer's skill, it cannot be maintained that their mediation of the mainstream represented an ideal state of affairs: by the nineteenth century, a widespread desire for musical variety and complexity was placing untenable pressure upon the status quo. By virtue of their very success in communicating a version of the latest music to the masses, ballad-singers became complicit in their own imminent demise.

### 'Words and Music Published': The Writing on the Wall

At some point after the middle of the century, probably in the 1860s, the Preston ballad printer John Harkness began to do something extraordinary to some of the ballad sheets he sent down to London.[133] It was not to the format: these were classic two-song broadsides, arranged in the usual way with a column per song, and headed by a large title or woodcut. Nor was it the fact that at least four of these broadsides included a song with an attributed author or singer, for these were stars of the music hall such as Harry Clifton and George Leybourne, and in borrowing their glamour Harkness was echoing earlier times when the name of Vestris or Braham would be used to help sell a pirated broadside. Harkness' great innovation was not an alteration but an addition: beneath the title, a strapline now informed the reader of where they could purchase the song's sheet music. These directions recommended two firms with whom Harkness must have had a close business relationship: the legend might read 'Words and Music published by Hopwood and Crew, 42, New Bond-st., London', or by 'C. Sheard, 192, High Holborn, London'. The earliest known sheet of this kind, SEC 896, read simply 'Music at Hopwood & Crew's London'.[134] This referred to the song in the left-hand column: 'Who's Coming Out for a Midnight Ramble. Written and Composed by Thomas Dodsworth. Sung with Great Applause by Geo Leybourne.'

Harkness' experiment was not absolutely without precedent. In 1829, Catnach produced *The Keepsake*, an outsized single-sheet compilation of

---

[133] http://ballads.bodleian.ox.ac.uk/search/?query=harkness&f_Printers=Harkness,%20J.&f_Locations=London.

[134] Bod. Harding B 11(4174).

sixteen songs (including 'The Wolf'), which remarkably featured five lines of notated melody for 'Will Watch, the Bold Smuggler', a song made popular some years earlier by Incledon, this inclusion of a melody line representing something rarely seen since the seventeenth century.[135] This sheet, however, was far from a conventional broadside, instead presaging the slightly later development that saw still larger sheets printed, crammed with dozens of songs. Mayhew links these formatting innovations to changes in distribution: London's ballad-singers became supplemented by 'patterers', 'long-song-sellers', and 'pinners-up', none of whom sang the songs they vended.[136] This appears to have been partly attributable to a total lack of musical facility, but more significantly to a reasonable response on the part of these sellers to the format of their products: with so many songs on offer at once, it made little sense to dedicate one's pitch to the performance of any one song. As one long-song-seller apparently stated:

I sometimes began ... with singing, or trying to sing, for I'm no vocalist, the first few words of any song, and them quite loud. I'd begin

'The Pope he leads a happy life,
He knows no care' –

'Buffalo gals, come out to-night;' 'Death of Nelson;' 'The gay cavalier;' 'Jim along Josey;' 'There's a good time coming;' 'Drink to me only;' 'Kate Kearney;' 'Chuckaroo-choo, choo-choo-choot-lah;' 'Chockala-roony-ninkaping-nang;' 'Pagadaway-dusty-kanty-key;' 'Hottypie-gunnypo-china-coo' (that's a Chinese song, sir); 'I dreamed that I dwelt in marble halls;' 'The standard bearer;' 'Just like love;' 'Whistle o'er the lave o't;' 'Widow Mackree;' 'I've been roaming;' 'Oh! that kiss;' 'The old English gentleman,' &c. &c. &c.[137]

This list returns us to our first descriptions of repertoire: it is generically mixed to the point of absurdity, including pieces of all ages and origins, and reduced in performance to a dizzying medley of snippets. It also makes more explicable the inclusion of a notated melody to an unfamiliar new tune, if the vendor was no longer expected to transmit it orally. In this light, Harkness' outsourcing to sellers of sheet music represented a further stage of development, giving access to an extended melody and keyboard accompaniment for which even the longest of ballad sheets could find neither space nor financial justification. Indeed, at one late point in his career Catnach apparently experimented with branching out into sheet music himself, advertising on one broadside: 'Just Published – a Variety of the most popular Songs of the day, set to MUSIC, for the

[135] Bod. Johnson Ballads fol. 12.   [136] Mayhew, *London Labour*, vol. 1, 3, 213, 221–3.
[137] Ibid., 271.

Voice, Violin, and German Flute, – the Cheapest Publications ever offered to the Public' – yet these publications, though consisting of the melody line alone, seem to have been sold so cheaply that the margin of profit was too slight to sustain the venture.[138]

There are significant musical differences between Catnach's one-off presentation of the melody of 'Will Watch, the Bold Smuggler', and Harkness' proxy delivery of 'Who's Coming Out for a Midnight Ramble?', differences attributable in large part to the half century that elapsed between their composition – and differences with ultimately fatal consequences for the repertoire of ballad-singers. This change was entangled with developments in literacy, education, economics, and class relations, yet it might be expressed most succinctly in the comparison of these two pieces of music. 'Will Watch, the Bold Smuggler' was composed by John Davy, a violinist and theatre hack come up to town from Devonshire, where he had been a protégé of William Jackson, an organist famous for his traditional, even reactionary views on songwriting and melody.[139] The result in this case is a perhaps self-consciously 'classic' nautical ballad, as that term would have been understood in 1811: written in 3/4, it adheres throughout to the key of B flat, and while its tenor range mostly spans only a ninth, from F to G, the melody's climax calls for a high B – very clearly a falsetto note for Incledon, its first singer.[140] The song's character is wholly conveyed by its melody line: in the separately published piano reduction, the left hand merely plays octaves in unison with the voice, occasionally shifting to a third below. That score, sold for 1s 6d, has appended to it a further reduction 'For the German Flute', which was of course just the vocal line, transposed – and it is this reduction that Catnach replicated (and probably pirated) on *The Keepsake*. In short, this was a highly generic tune of the type contemporaries called 'robust'; a simple melody that stood up on its own, the sort of thing ballad-singers had been performing for centuries – for, while their songs were entirely mixed in origin and genre, they tended to share these qualities of solo singability, allowing them to be picked up and repeated with relative ease, without losing much by reduction to this bare bones aesthetic. There was, in fact, no need for Catnach to reproduce the score, and this extraordinary move on his part probably had more to do with a desire to market this sheet as a one-off, collectable, prestigious commodity, a 'keepsake' in fact, with the use of musical notation intended primarily to enhance the sheet's cultural capital rather than

[138] Bod. Johnson Ballads 231.
[139] John Warrack, 'Davy, John (1763–1824)', *ODNB*, oxforddnb.com/view/article/7316. See also William Jackson, *Observations on the Present State of Music, in London* (Dublin, 1791).
[140] BL Mus H.1653.n (47).

serve an elucidatory purpose – especially when the song in question had been in circulation for eighteen years.

'Who's Coming Out for a Midnight Ramble?' is quite another matter. It is by no means a *difficult* song; indeed its span of a ninth, pitched comfortably in the middle range of a Victorian tenor, is less demanding than 'Will Watch'.[141] Its composer and lyricist Thomas Dodsworth, responsible for at least a dozen music-hall hits of the 1870–80s, is an otherwise wholly obscure figure, which if nothing else recommends him to the world of ballad singing. The arranger, W. G. Eaton, is every bit as untraceable. The song is in 2/4, the simplest of time signatures, which characterises mid-century blackface minstrelsy and music hall alike. And yet this is music of another order entirely to 'Will Watch'. The critical difference is less that the tune modulates from F to C, and back to F for the chorus – though the G# involved in that key change could easily confuse an untrained singer – but rather the consistent use of accidentals: a recurrent B natural and C# when in F, and G# when in C, that lend the tune its veering, off-kilter character, in keeping with its careering lyric of sprees and japes. The piano accompaniment, though no more complex than that of 'Will Watch', is far less dispensable: its dissonant chords and propulsive offbeat rhythm are more intrinsic to the song's identity – and the tune's logic – than would ever have been the case a generation earlier. This is still simple, highly generic music. But it was written at and for a piano, with the harmonic tricks and 'knees-up' rhythms enabled by that instrument very much at the forefront of the composition. When Harkness directed his purchasers to Hopwood's for the music, it was an admission of that music's necessity for any coherent performance.

This Hopwood and Crew score retailed at 3*s*, bringing into question our conception of the mainstream as a shared phenomenon: how could any music be a part of general culture when sold at such an exorbitant price? The sum is indeed out of all proportion to the score on offer, which might more reasonably retail at a shilling or less; the cost seems largely due to the lavish, coloured, full-page illustration of the singer George Leybourne ('Champagne Charlie') on its front cover. Yet the same publication's back cover may provide an explanation: this is taken up with reductions of no fewer than fourteen songs, all crammed on to a single page. It is conceivable that Hopwood and Crew sold just this page, or even excerpts therefrom, at a vastly reduced rate, as a by-product of their standard printing process, so that less affluent purchasers of the broadside could still obtain the music, albeit a little abbreviated, at an accessible price, while those better off bought the full score – the availability of these

---

[141] BL Mus H.1778.K (49).

snippets also explaining why anyone who bought the music might also need the broadside in order to obtain all the lyrics, as only the first verse is given in the shorter sheet music form.

The financial question thus disposed of, one just as fundamental remains: that of musical literacy and access to keyboards. If we are to accept the Harkness development as symptomatic of something happening to song culture more generally, then we must posit an effective revolution in the musical comprehension of the populace. It is this revolution that forms the subject of this book's final pages. It represents a new current in the mainstream, one that proved too strong for the ballad-singer's inherent limitations: an addition of harmony, texture, and self-sufficiency on the part of a newly aware and equipped audience, in the face of which our balladeers were left to sink or swim. The ballad-singer was ultimately undone, not by the actions of police or evangelists, not by rising noise levels or a dearth of topical material, but by changes in mainstream repertoire and the public's means of access thereto. This coming flood was apparent to some ballad-singers decades before 'Who's Coming Out for a Midnight Ramble?'. We might end by returning to the 1843 Westminster Court of Requests case of Morten versus Sadgrove. For Sadgrove, the ballad-singer, the writing was already on the wall:

Defendant: ... The profession was a good profession some years ago, but this new-fangled *singing for the million* has ruined it, and people learn to sing for themselves now, and their ears get so nice there is no pleasing them.— Commissioner (to plaintiff): Well, you must not be hard with him. Suppose he pays you 2s. a month?—This suggestion was immediately agreed to, and the song-writer and song-singer retired in amity to a neighbouring public-house, to discuss the present depressed state of their respective professions.[142]

---

[142] 'Court of Requests'. 'Singing for the Million' is a specific reference to the textbook and public classes of the German reformer Joseph Mainzer, who came to London in 1841. See Joseph Mainzer, *Singing for the Million: A Practical Course of Musical Instruction* (1841). As the Conclusion will make clear, I do not attribute any unique importance to Mainzer's role, rather seeing this as part of a wider trend towards the middle of the nineteenth century.

# Interlude IV
## 'Old Dog Tray'

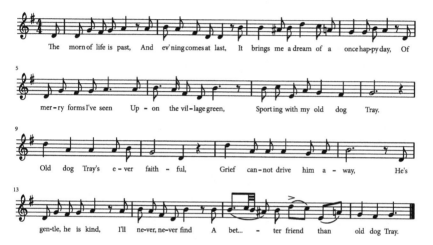

The morn of life is past, And ev'ning comes at last, It brings me a dream of a once hap-py day, Of

mer-ry forms I've seen Up - on the vil-lage green, Sporting with my old dog Tray.

Old dog Tray's e - ver faith - ful, Grief can-not drive him a - way, He's

gen-tle, he is kind, I'll ne-ver, ne-ver find A bet... - ter friend than old dog Tray.

Example IV.1  Stephen Collins Foster, 'Old Dog Tray', vocal reduction (1853)[1]

The forms I call'd my own
Have vanished one by one,
The lov'd ones, the dear ones have all pass'd away,
Their happy smiles are flown,
Their gentle voices gone;
I've nothing left but old dog Tray.
   Old dog Tray's, &c.

When thoughts recall the past,
His eyes are on me cast;
I know that he feels what my breaking heart would say.
Although he cannot speak,
I'll vainly, vainly seek
A better friend than old dog Tray.
   Old dog Tray's, &c.

[1] (1855; composed 1853) BL Mus H.2345/700–800 (745).

229

'Old Dog Tray' is a curious beast. It might justifiably be called the last great hit of the ballad-singer's repertoire, an embodiment of everything that characterised the mainstream described in the previous chapter. Yet it also represents much of what brought the ballad-singer down. In short, it has a good claim to be considered the street singer's swansong, and is as fit a place as any to begin the story of the end.

Considered in the form given here, it possesses most of the features of the mobile mainstream. It features just sixteen bars of highly memorable melody, comfortably contained within an octave and conforming to a generic AABA structure. Lyrically it is sentimental, even maudlin, by any standards, set in three verses with a simple chorus featuring a high degree of redundancy. Its author Stephen Foster, the most famous American songwriter of the nineteenth century, is never credited on broadsides, facilitating Londoners' ownership of a foreign production, and thereby enriching the mainstream. It may even have benefited from the precedent of Thomas Campbell's 'Poor Dog Tray', a quite different poem also sold as a broadside.[2] So far, so perfect for the ballad-singer's art. It was certainly a huge hit. All the later London printers – Disley, Fortey, Ryle, Such – carried it, and it even spawned an irreverent, satirical broadside 'Answer to Old Dog Tray', a metatextual phenomenon familiar to ballad culture of the eighteenth and even the seventeenth centuries.[3] In Sala's 1861 *Twice Round the Clock*, we encounter a typically disparaging mention at 5am – 'Never mind the noise of dogs barking … [and] of boys yelling the insufferable "Old Dog Tray,"' – a notice that suggests the song became fully established on the street.[4]

Sala mentions the song a second time in his chapter for 11am, set in a residential area near St Martin-in-the-Fields, central London – a location presumably chosen in homage to Hogarth's *Enraged Musician* of 1741, which depicts the spire of that church in the image's background. The passage is a classic list of the horrors of street music – 'First[,] Italian organ-grinder, hirsute, sunburnt, and saucy, who grinds airs from the "Trovatore" six times over, follows with a selection from the "Traviata," repeated half a dozen times, finishes up with the "Old Hundredth," and the

[2] http://ballads.bodleian.ox.ac.uk/search/roud/2668.
[3] http://ballads.bodleian.ox.ac.uk/search/roud/2667/?query=&f_Locations=London; Bod Harding B 11(2429).
[4] Sala, *Twice Round the Clock*, 25.

"Postmans' Knock,"' – and featuring in succession, three 'Hindostanee' singers with a tom-tom; a sham Highland dancer accompanied by bagpipes; acrobats with 'drum, clarionet, and all'; an 'eloquent beggar' and family; before, around the middle of the list, 'a lamentable woman with a baby begins to whimper "Old Dog Tray."' She is immediately drowned out by six Italian pipers, but not before we have recognised the stock figure of the pitiful ballad-singer, given a song to match her pathetic appearance.[5] In this context, 'Old Dog Tray' and its imagined singer are subject to the drawbacks of their lowest-common-denominator mode of performance: the stripped-down song, performed by a single voice, is no match for the riot of music and dance with which she competes, and even her conspicuous baby, considered as a prop, is no match for the percussion, harmony, and proliferation of musical timbre with which she must contend.

The perfect fit of singer and song brings us up against the old issue of representation: Sala evidently wishes to figure his 'whimpering' singer as abject, and so gives her a song to match – one that, though current, recognisable to his readership, and clearly associated with street performance, was also pitiful and concerned with loss. The conflation of song and singer suggests that the balladeer as a phenomenon, not merely her character within the song, has been left behind by the world. There are shades here of Wordsworth's more famous ballad-singer from *The Prelude*, as discussed in Chapter 1, 'single and alone' amidst a street similarly filled with foreign troupes of musicians.

Yet 'Old Dog Tray', for all its lyrical preoccupation with loss and nostalgia, was nonetheless a very modern sort of song. It is situational rather than narrative, reflecting the wider shift from the long-form strophic ballad, bordering on epic, to the more concise adoption of persona and position associated with many songs of the second half of the century.[6] More fundamentally still, its melody was clearly built upon – indeed, is only conceivable in relation to – the chord patterns associated with the piano. While singers necessarily shed that harmonic substructure in performance, as an essential part of the musical reductionism so vital to the operation of mainstream culture, those chords – sophisticated chords, presupposing a key signature and including distinctive sevenths and accidentals – are nonetheless heavily implied; ghosts still present beneath the bare melody. Indeed, when I discussed (and performed) this song in the self-consciously traditional and 'folk'-inflected surroundings of Cecil Sharp House,

[5] Ibid., 107–8.
[6] For this shift, see Bailey, *Popular Culture*, 134, where he writes: 'The more leisurely storyline of the ballad gives way to an episodic emphasis which exploits some social predicament in a quick succession of scenes or actions whose common import is punched home in a tag-line or chorus.' But note also Gammon, 'Not Appreciated in Worthing?', esp. 10.

auditors were keen to stress their dislike of its mannered, 'composed' style. Musically speaking, 'Old Dog Tray' may be slow and expressive rather than fast and precise, but it is closer kin to 'Who's Coming Out for a Midnight Ramble?' (Chapter 4) than to any ballad sung in the streets before the middle of the nineteenth century.

Tellingly, the earliest London scores of 'Old Dog Tray' arranged the chorus as a four-part harmony for a group of singers, emphasising the B-section, and provided a jaunty piano accompaniment straight out of the nascent music hall.[7] For a lone ballad-singer, this chorus was always something of an anomaly, taking up fully half of the song, and so hardly playing to the strengths of a solo performer. Yet conceived of as an ensemble piece, that chorus suddenly affords dynamic, harmonic, and indeed participatory social interest: it is easy to imagine large numbers joining in, whether at home or in a place of entertainment. Performed in a modern harmonic manner, rather than by a ballad-singer, it could have stood up well against Sala's six Italian pipers.

Then again, it did not even have to be *sung* to be enjoyed by listeners. One broadside song of around 1864, called 'Organ Grinder', features as its villain the eponymous grinder, who woos the narrator's sweetheart, a kitchen maid called Fan, as she cleans her employer's step.[8] He makes his appearance in verse four, 'A grinding, "Old Dog Tray."' Here is the memorable tune replicated with no musical effort or ability, but enhanced by simple harmony, cutting out the ballad-singer narrator. The song's narrative replicates the wider sonic contest: the grinder wins Fan's heart with his music, and they elope, the singer's only solace being the following wry reflection on the possibilities of the Street Music Act campaigned for by Charles Babbage and others:

> So I'll think no more of Fan and her organ man,
> But hope they'll get six months.
> *Spoken.* – With hard labour for disturbing Mr. Babbage in his
>   skyentific pursuits and mental miscalcuations.

Clearly the narrator-singer himself has no such fears of incarceration – and not without some justice. Perhaps the most remarkable thing about the immense discourse generated by the Street Music Act of 1864, an episode discussed at length by a number of recent works, is the conspicuous absence of the ballad-singer from that discourse.[9] Invariably, complaints

---

[7] BL Mus H.2345/700–800 (745); BL Mus H.1753 (13).
[8] Bod. Harding B 11(2867). The tune is unknown.
[9] The topic is treated extensively in works including James Winter, *London's Teeming Streets, 1830–1914* (1993); Bailey, *Popular Culture and Performance*; Assael, 'Music in the Air';

against Street Music were directed at, and defences mounted in favour of, Italian organ-grinders, German bands, and blackface minstrel troupes, with various other instrumentalists occasionally thrown in. The ballad-singer was almost never mentioned. This is a far cry from the start of the century, when irate writers were equally exercised whether 'an organ-grinder, or ballad-singer of the basest degree, [was] exhausting their whole stock of dissonance within two or three yards of your ill-starr'd ears'.[10] For this reason, I have set 1864 as the notional end of my chronology: if the ballad-singer was no longer to be considered a public menace, then her day must have been well and truly over.

'Old Dog Tray' may thus be seen as symptomatic of the ballad-singer's downfall: a fine, characteristic song, susceptible to parody – yet a song that, by the 1860s, could be enjoyed by other and more convenient means than listening to and purchasing from a street singer.[11] This applied to its print incarnations as well as its performances: the following Conclusion will discuss *The Old Dog Tray Songster*, dating from the 1860s, in which not only the titular song, but forty-two others, could be had for a single penny – that is, merely double the traditional cost of a single-song slip. While the singer in the street may have remained the most convenient, because most accessible, point of sale, any customer desiring a copy of the lyrics – perhaps after hearing the tune alone upon a barrel-organ, or after witnessing the song performed on the stage of a minor music hall – would receive vastly better value for money by taking her business to a shop, and buying a cheap songster. Although 'Old Dog Tray' was still available on numerous broadsides, its entry to the mainstream was therefore no longer dependent upon the ballad-singer: for this reason I would like to think of it as a swansong, and take its 'whimpered' performance in the midst of Sala's list of street musicians as a starting point for the end.

---

John Picker, *Victorian Soundscapes* (Oxford, 2003); and Gavin Williams, 'Engine Noise and Artificial Intelligence: Babbage's London', in James Q. Davies and Ellen Lockhart (eds.), *Sound Knowledge: Music and Science in London, 1789–1851* (Chicago, 2017), 203–26.
[10] John Beresford, *The Miseries of Human Life; or the Groans of Samuel Sensitive, and Timothy Testy*, 2 vols. (1807), vol. 1, 73.
[11] See http://vwml.org.uk/roudnumber/2667 for different print records of 'Old Dog Tray', and its appearance in as many disparate songsters, that is, book-form collections of lyrics, as on broadsides.

# Conclusion

> Misery [number 27] . . . On a sultry day, in London – being compelled by
> the heat to sit with the windows of a ground-room wide open, while an
> organ-grinder, or ballad-singer of the basest degree, are exhausting their
> whole stock of dissonance within two or three yards of your ill-starr'd
> ears[.][1]

This 'misery' came from a list of humorous observations about the
drawbacks of London life compiled in 1807. This early mention of
the organ-grinder, given equivalence to the more customary 'nuisance' of the ballad-singer, is highly unusual. By 1864, when the
debate over Bass' Street Music Act resulted in a vast amount of
printed discussion, the organ-grinder had become predominant,
even totemic, in discourse – whereas the ballad-singer was remarkable only for her near-total absence. People who complained about
street noise and music were no longer complaining about ballad-
singers. Clearly, the mainstream had changed for good. In this conclusion, I will explore precisely how and why this change occurred,
why it resulted in the end of the ballad-singer – and why, taking
a broader historical perspective, we might view the passing of the
singer with not only equanimity, but even a degree of optimism.

The bulk of contemporary comment upon the ballad-singer's mid-
century demise prompts us by contrast to focus upon the mentalities of
the learned and the propertied: of the 'brain-workers' who signed up to
Babbage's petition – those Victorians, in truth, who most resembled the
writer and imagined readers of this book. For such writers, discussing the
ballad-singer's end was primarily undertaken in a nostalgic mode, and
used as a means of dealing with larger issues of modernity.[2] Thus we find

---

[1] One of many topical 'miseries' listed as a form of observational comedy in Beresford, *The
Miseries of Human Life*, vol. 1, 73.

[2] Jerrold, 'The Ballad Singer' is the archetypal example, and contains practically all the
arguments listed in the following paragraph. As William Henderson observed in 1937,
citing Jerrold as the first great exponent, 'whenever anyone wrote about the street singers

234

held responsible for the phenomenon, everything from the New Police,[3] to decades of uninspiring peace since the great days of Nelson and Wellington,[4] to a passion for blackface minstrelsy,[5] with a vast number of words expended in attack upon immigrant communities:[6] foreign musicians who were better organised and equipped, louder, pushier, and more numerous than the singer – not only street musicians such as Parmesan organ-grinders[7] and German bands, but also the latest Italian and German composers, whose compositions were held responsible for degrading English ears.[8]

All these discourses might be collected under the general heading of 'crisis of modernity', which should not be taken as a form of dismissal: whole books could be and have been written on this precise issue, and it is only that I do not wish this to have been one of them. That the ballad-singer – no longer the noisy, intrusive, corrupting influence, but instead a victim of such influences – was so easily represented thus, is of interest. That the singer could so readily be made to stand for a particular conception of the early modern English past, a quieter, slower place, more localised and knowable, is significant, a testament to her essentially early modern social function in shaping and sustaining forms of community that seem to have been unrecognisable (at least to elite observers) in the new urban environment.[9] Nor was this argument wholly without merit. As demonstrated in Chapter 2, part of the ballad-singer's strength was her place in articulating the identity or grievance of a local community of neighbourhood, a model of spatial organisation resistant to both the absolute separation of public and private – or outdoor and indoor – and to the capitalist conception of the street as a conduit for the linear flow of goods and people, rather than itself constituting a site of petty commerce and exchange of all kinds. This final argument was not, however, one made by contemporaries. Indeed, the sum total of the discourse was not

of his own day he declared them to be on the point of extinction'. Henderson, *Victorian Street Ballads*, 9.
[3] Francis Place, 'Specimens of Songs Sung about the Streets of London', in Place, *Manners, Morals.*, f.144.
[4] Smith, *Little World of London*, 255.
[5] 'The English Serenader', *Theatrical Journal* 8, no. 388 (22 May 1847): 161–2.     [6] Ibid.
[7] The view, succinctly expressed in one newspaper, that 'The British ballad-singer has been destroyed—literally ground out of his livelihood—by the Italian organ-boy' was particularly widespread. See 'The Barbers and the Bakers', *Lloyd's Weekly Newspaper* 571 (30 October 1853).
[8] Harvey, 'Street Music of London', 343.
[9] See works as far apart in time as Strutt, *Glig Gamena Angel-Deod*, 142, 215; and Baring-Gould, *Strange Survivals*, 182–90. Compare with, from 1864 itself, William Allingham (ed.), *The Ballad Book: A Selection of the Choicest British Ballads* (1864), xii–xiv.

universally negative. Though predicated on loss, the argument of social reformers such as Francis Place was that the silencing of street song (because bawdy) was a good thing, indicative of working-class self-improvement and the efficacy of mass education; part of a wider legitimating move in order to lobby for an extension of the franchise.[10] By this reading, the displacement of the old by the modern was something to celebrate rather than mourn.

Place, however, was writing in perhaps disingenuous anticipation of the event, a generation before the 1860s and before even the influx of refugees from the Continent, precipitated by the upheavals of 1848, that some have pinpointed as the crucial moment of mainstream change.[11] One French travel narrative of the later period, for instance, reasoned that: 'As London serves as the gathering place for all the peoples and races of the earth, the street music reflects that cosmopolitan character.'[12] Still, we might do worse than take Place's proposition seriously: that for the many, the end of the ballad-singer was part of a narrative of opportunity, not of loss; that the inaudibility of 'Old Dog Tray' among the buskers was really about appetite and access: that we no longer hear the singer, not because she is silent, but because we – we, the people – are not. This proposition was put rather forcefully by one of the correspondents in the 1864 debate, James Parry of 4 Adelphi Terrace, a fashionable area just off the Strand, in a letter submitted to Michael Thomas Bass, who introduced the bill in Parliament:

It may be admitted that wandering street-players might have been needed formerly; but the whole thing is entirely changed now. Music is to be heard everywhere, by all classes, in their hours of recreation, at proper places and at all prices, from the Italian Opera House to the threepenny gallery at the East-end theatres. There is excellent music, both vocal and instrumental, at such places as the Canterbury Hall, the Oxford, &c. Then take all the choirs in full practice. Look at the monster amateur concerts at the Crystal Palace. It was but the other day advertised that a three-part song for female voices would be done by one thousand voices to each part. Until lately, a very nice little orchestra could be heard by taking a penny ice in Hungerford Market. Think of the thousands of charity children who learn to sing. Look at their annual gatherings in St. Paul's, and on one occasion in the Crystal Palace, heard by the Queen. Before closing this note, I will send you a list of all the

[10] Place, 'Specimens', ff. 143–67. See also Thale, *The Autobiography of Francis Place*, esp. xxv–xxvi.
[11] Winter, *London's Teeming Streets*, 71.
[12] Alphonse Esquiros, *The English at Home*, trans. Lascelles Wraxall, 2 vols. (1861), vol. 1, 288–9.

vocal societies now in operation. In short, music is going on everywhere, and at times when people want it and seek it.[13]

Parry's argument is highly partial, motivated by a desire for silence when and where he wished it, rather than a personal thirst for music. Yet it is eloquent, and even sensitive to personal economy: note the ingenious line about the penny ice as a means of accessing music (and, not incidentally, ice cream, also recently made available to the masses via the enterprise of Carlo Gatti). The same French account mentioned earlier is in accord, noting of London's 'open air' music that 'it is accessible to all, and costs nothing – it is the opera, the concert of the poor man.'[14]

Significantly, Parry's letter details opportunities not only to hear music but to learn and to make it. A growth in the number of cheap, accessible auditoriums is only one element in the narrative, though by no means a negligible one. Babbage himself defended his campaign by stressing that: 'The multitude of music-halls now established in all parts of London is such that those who enjoy street music may have a much larger quantity of it, and of a better kind, at a cheaper rate than that which in their own street disturbs all their neighbours.'[15] Two decades later, the antiquarian John Ashton endorsed this view, commenting that 'a new generation has arisen, who will not stop in the streets to listen to these ballads being sung, but prefer to have their music served up to them "piping hot," with the accompaniment of warmth, light, beer, and tobacco (for which they duly have to pay) at the Music Halls'.[16] Jacky Bratton's study of the 'Victorian Popular Ballad' expands upon these attractions, not only to audiences, but to writers:

The competition of the halls undermined the broadside ballads indirectly as well as by offering more for the customers' pennies. It also offered greater rewards and a better audience to the writers of songs; and the broadside presses, which had never paid more than a shilling or two for their material, found that the few shillings more a man might earn by selling to a music-hall singer, and the enormously greater reward he might reap by setting up to perform his own material, robbed them of all the versifying talent of the working classes.[17]

Pursuing this line of enquiry, Bratton concludes that the makers of and the market for topical songs moved to the halls, leaving the broadside 'impoverished' – a view that neglects the continued rampant piracy of

---

[13] James Parry to Michael Thomas Bass, 30 April 1864, cited in Michael Thomas Bass, *Street Music in the Metropolis. Correspondence and Observations on the Existing Law, and Proposed Amendments* (1864), 30.
[14] Esquiros, *The English*, vol. 1, 287.
[15] Charles Babbage, *A Chapter on Street Nuisances* (1864), 27.
[16] John Ashton, *Modern Street Ballads* (1888), v.
[17] Bratton, *The Victorian Popular Ballad*, 24–5.

music hall song by street sellers, just as theatrical song had always been pirated.[18] It is certainly true that the new songs composed for the street in this later period betray a state of creative exhaustion: many 'new' ballads were simply medleys of old titles, their verses comprising lists of other well-known songs, an enervated case of pop eating itself.[19] Yet it need not follow that the emergence of one new venue should necessarily eradicate what was, after all, more a mode of distribution than of pure entertainment – and distribution, in large part, of songs purloined from more buoyant tributaries of the mainstream. Taken in isolation, the music hall has insufficient explanatory power to be held wholly responsible for the death of the ballad-singer.

Evidently, song did not simply shift from the street to interior locations but, like a gas, expanded to populate the total available space. This did not mean vacating the street: as the 1864 debate makes plain, music did not abandon the outdoors, but proliferated and changed in character, and by no means involved the wholesale displacement of song by purely instrumental music. To a degree, some songs – particularly operatic arias – were experienced *as* instrumental music in the street. Blanchard Jerrold, son of Douglas, coined the phrase: 'The barrel organ is the opera of the street-folk.'[20] James Winter writes more expansively that:

The American writer James Fenimore Cooper visiting London at the beginning of Victoria's reign, enthused about the street music he heard: 'positively the best in the world,' better even, he claimed, than that of Venice or Naples. Instrumentalists who would in most large cities, he thought, be engaged by orchestras[,] walked the London streets and played Mozart, Beethoven, Meyerbeer, and Weber beneath one's window. Just the other evening, on his way to dinner, he had encountered a kind of wheelbarrow containing a 'grand piano on which someone was playing an overture of Rossini, accompanied by a flageolet.' A story went the rounds in the 1860s that Bellini once said to Rossini, 'My songs are sung in the streets of Paris and London.' 'Ah,' Rossini was supposed to have retorted, 'but mine *grind*!'[21]

This last anecdote suggests the mingling of vocalised and mechanised song, a plausible augmentation of the mainstream that mirrored the ongoing promiscuity of high and low song culture circulating at the level of the street. Winter continues:

---

[18] Ibid., 25, and see also 23–6.
[19] For three examples, see 'Chanting Benny, or the Batch of Ballads'; 'The Chaunt Seller, Or, A New Batch of Ballads'; and 'The Comic Song of Songs', Bod. Harding B 11(568), (583), and (761).
[20] Blanchard Jerrold, *London: A Pilgrimage. Illustrated by Gustave Doré with an Introduction by Peter Ackroyd* (1872, New edn 2006), 205.
[21] Winter, *London's Teeming Streets*, 77.

[S]elections from Italian opera were not the only musical fare served up by grid-dlers (glee singers), street-corner violinists, brass bands, or barrel-organs. Nevertheless, it was not just in concerts or choir rehearsals that the working class came in contact with 'high culture'; for every working man or woman who sang the *Messiah* at a local concert hall, there were many more who heard music from the classical tradition on the street.[22]

As early as 1859, *Household Words* was in agreement, suggesting that the elite vocal music most in demand on the street was performed instrumentally:

The harp, fiddle, and cornet which ply their trade at my window . . . are dissemin-ating among the populace, the politest strains of the Opera. Whenever they commence, we know who inspired their open-air music – whether it be Donizetti, Verdi, Mercandanti, or Bellini. Nothing is too high for them . . . They convey fashionable melodies to the ears of the cook as she ends her gossip with the grocer's man at the area steps; Mario and the glorious Royal Italian Opera band float the same notes more thrillingly and exquisitely, it is true, under the bandeaux of the beauties in the grand tier: but they are the same.[23]

Nor did this musical emancipation leave street vocalists unchanged. In *London Labour and the London Poor*, Mayhew's taxonomy of street per-formers classes the glee-singers mentioned by Winter, not with ballad-singers, who come under the category of 'street literature', but with instrumental musicians – a telling detail. Though the glee-singing reper-toire cited by Mayhew – 'Cherry Ripe', 'Home, Sweet Home' – is the same as the ballad-singer's, the performative mode is quite different: multiple 'trained' and harmonised voices, singing solely to entertain rather than to sell, and apparently 'only at night'. The stated remuner-ation for the pair of singers Mayhew gives us, varying from above three pounds a night 'on extraordinary occasions' to twenty-five shillings a week by the mid-century, is well above that which even two separate ballad-singers could expect to make, and is achieved partly by being invited off the street into private parties, suggestive of a performative style more in keeping with middling expectations of vocal music, or by periodic employment 'at the cheap concerts held at the public-houses'.[24] The glee, of course, was a far older form of English song, but the phe-nomenon of its performance on the street was new, indicative of a cultural shift that allowed for what we would now call 'busking'. This term in its modern sense was first recorded by Mayhew in 1851[25] – it is significant that there was no need for it before – and by 1881 had become common

---

[22] Ibid., 77–8.
[23] William Henry Wills and Eliza Lynn Linton, 'Street Minstrelsy', *Household Words* 478 (21 May 1859): 577–80, 577.
[24] Mayhew, *London Labour*, vol. 3, 194, 195–6.    [25] www.oed.com/view/Entry/25243.

enough for Hindley to offer the following curious statement in one of his antiquarian works: 'Our own taverns still supply us with ballad-singers – "*Buskers*" – who will sing of "*Jenkin and Julian*" – Ben Block or the Ratcatcher's Daughter "*for their meed* [sic].'"[26] Let us be plain: these singers were not ballad-singers; they performed for drink, rather than to sell songs – a paradigmatic shift achieved in the space of a generation. People continued to sing for gain, in the street and the public house, but they had ceased to be ballad-singers in the traditional sense. This suggests nothing less than a fundamental change in the way that Londoners conceived of and related to song.

In 1855, the journalist and statistician George Dodd contributed an article to Dickens' periodical *Household Words* that pondered the question of 'Music in poor neighbourhoods – how to get it, and of what kind?' Far from perceiving a *Land ohne Musik*, Dodd wrote that:

[Music] grows up even among the most lowly – and if it can be kindly led into a rational direction, so much the better for the workman and his wife and children ... The penny concert, the penny panoramas, the harmonic meetings, the banjo-player in a taproom, the sentimental singer up-stairs, the theatricals in a saloon – all indicate a want, a tendency, a natural yearning, which may lead to good, if properly managed.[27]

Clearly Dodd wished to distinguish between an ideal music – directed, dignified – and that which he saw as existing – disreputable, tawdry – and so his reformist, even evangelical tone was of a piece with a broader drive to encourage coordinated singing classes among the poor, of which Mainzer's 'Singing for the Million', mentioned in Chapter 4, was of early significance. Subsequent entrepreneurs, most notably the Hullah and Curwen families, were staggeringly successful, and played a major role in equipping much of the urban populace, of both sexes, with basic musical comprehension, principally of Tonic Sol-Fa systems of notation, and with the ability to sing in tune and in harmony.[28] This was clearly transformative in enabling new means of mass access to song; as early as 1840, the movement was seen by Jerrold as culpable in the decline of the ballad-singer, 'who, innocent of the superfluous theory of *do re mi*, warbled in his old wild naturalness'.[29] Yet as Dodd makes clear, this was not

---

[26] Hindley, *History of the Cries of London*, 8.
[27] George Dodd, 'Household Words', *Household Words* 12, no. 285 (8 September 1855): 137–41, 140–1.
[28] The best recent treatment of this major topic is Erin Johnson-Williams, 'Re-Examining the Academy: Music Institutions and Empire in Nineteenth-Century London', PhD thesis (Yale University, 2015).
[29] Jerrold, 'The Ballad Singer', 293.

simply a story of control and education achieved by paternalist (and capitalist) great men. In recognising 'a want, a tendency, a natural yearning', Dodd was acknowledging the degree to which this shift in musical engagement was instigated from below.

It would be disingenuous to pretend to the fiction of total historical detachment here: this is a nineteenth-century narrative that from the first has admitted of widely different historiographical interpretations. Take the music hall alone: if the ballad-singer was, in the twenty-first-century idiom, a dinosaur, then were the halls a catastrophic meteor, or an evolutionary phenomenon that saw the better singers turn into birds and take to the stage? Similar shades of valence inflect a less material shift around the middle of the century that lay at the centre of what Dodd, Jerrold, and others were observing. Jerrold puts it quite plainly: 'The public ear has become dainty, fastidious, hypercritical: hence, the Ballad-Singer languishes and dies ... in these chromatic days'.[30] Musical composition was undergoing a seismic development at all levels in this period, a change rooted in new approaches to harmony, which had profound implications for the ballad-singer's solo performance. This was the 'revolution' highlighted at the end of Chapter 4, exemplified by the differences between 'Will Watch' and 'Who's Coming Out for a Midnight Ramble?', and just as much in evidence in the difference between, say, J. S. Bach and Giuseppe Verdi, or between Thomas Arne and Arthur Sullivan. At its crudest, this is what musicology used to call the Classical versus the Romantic, and while the terms themselves are problematic, the tendencies are plain at the level of the mainstream. Bennett characterises this as a move from 'purely melodic, modal thinking, towards a reliance on harmonically conceived structures', while Scott writes:

> The appropriation of bourgeois song had its effects on working-class song ... most noticeably in the increasing fondness shown for the major key rather than the old modes. Furthermore, there was a growing assumption of accompanying harmony to tunes, and a tendency for them to imply the characteristic chord progressions of bourgeois songs.[31]

Contrary to Scott's first suggestion, it was not the practice of appropriation itself that was new, but rather the 'assumption of harmony' and dependence upon certain chord progressions and indeed modulations between major keys. Occurring across the mainstream, this change was manifest in opera and organ grinding, German and native brass bands, in blackface minstrelsy, on the deregulated theatrical stage, and in the hymns now permitted in Anglican as in Dissenting services. It can be

[30] Ibid., 289–91.    [31] Bennett, 'Music in the Halls', 3; Scott, *Singing Bourgeois*, 187.

heard in 'Old Dog Tray', a melody haunted by implicit underlying arpeggios. For song, this was the age of the piano – or at the very least, of the banjo or guitar.

Popular music scholarship has not always characterised this shift as benign. Vic and Sheila Gammon, writing of 'the musical revolution of the mid-nineteenth century', have argued that: 'Between about 1830 and 1860 a great deal of what was distinctive about the music making of artisans and the labouring poor was destroyed or went underground.'[32] The villain of their story is western notation, which, once learnt, is intolerant of other and earlier modes – something readily apparent in Chappell's song collections of this period, in which he takes great pains to fit modern bass harmonies to wayward early melodies.[33] I would like to propose that this change was less a top-down obliteration than a growing, bottom-up mainstream interest in the musical, or more specifically the compositional, properties of song. To draw upon both Chris Small and Edward Cone: the highly generic, strophic nature of many older ballads was itself a function of their primary purpose – to convey a narrative text – meaning that the music itself was less an object of aesthetic or embodied pleasure than a means of verbal articulation, whereas, by the mid-nineteenth century, a greater number of listeners invested more importance in the musical dimension of song, and correspondingly the lyrics of the biggest hits tended to be situational rather than narrative: lyrics in the service of music, rather than the reverse.[34] Of course, this was not an absolute binary, and old songs continued to be enjoyed, just as some new songs told narratives. Yet it was a clearly discernible trend that, combined with the increased importance of an accompanying instrument that could play chords, or of vocal harmony, was obviously incompatible with the craft of the ballad-singer. In fact, I think what I am arguing for is no less than the vernacular instantiation of the great shift in western musical thinking posited by Tomlinson: from a mentality that conceived of 'music' as fundamentally 'a sub-category of song', to a peculiarly European reorientation in which 'song is a kind of music'. This had already occurred at an elite level: now the masses, too, were hearing

---

[32] Gammon and Gammon, 'The Musical Revolution', 125. In response, see Russell, 'The "Social History" of Popular Music', esp. 144.
[33] Chappell addresses this in *A Collection of National Airs*, v, and in *Popular Music of the Olden Time*, vol. 1, xii, writes: 'In my former work, some [airs] had too much harmony, and others even too little, or such as was not in accordance with the spirit of the words. The musician will best understand the amount of thought required to find characteristic harmonics to melodies of irregular construction, and how much a simple air will sometimes gain by being well fitted.'
[34] Small, *Musicking*, 124–5; Cone, *The Composer's Voice*, 49.

songs as musical, rather than thinking of 'music-making [as] a songish thing'.[35]

There is another reason why I wish to concentrate on what was gained, rather than what was lost, and that is the intersection of this primarily musical development with corresponding changes in print culture. Discussion of the latter change has naturally focused on the implications for broadside ballads, rather than their singers, but the conclusion is the same: the informational content of the ballad sheet (whether read or heard) was supplanted by the newspaper, while a proliferation of cheap songbooks provided a new means of access to the cultural mainstream.[36] Even the special preserve of the street ballad, the dying speech and confession, was threatened, with Hindley positing a drop in sales of ninety per cent between their heyday and 1864.[37] Increasingly, those who might once have sung ballads on the street could be found instead peddling 'children's books and song-books': songs continued to be sold on the street, but in purely printed compilations, not as individual sung objects.[38]

This was in the first instance a metropolitan phenomenon. Writing in 1861, Hindley claimed that:

[E]ven in these degenerate days, when a ballad makes a real hit, from 20,000 to 30,000 copies of it will go off in a very short time. Then it finds its way into a book for town consumption. The chief circulation of the broad-sheet is in the country, where the conservative instinct is strong in this as in all other matters. The penny song-books, which have to a great extent superseded the broad-sheet in London, are not valued in the shires. 'They hold too much,' we have been told; 'the country people consider them too big, sir, and that it can't be all correct that's in them. So they like the sheet better, that they've been used to.'[39]

This may have been true in the south: one irony of the claim to London's forwardness in this regard is that in the north of England, particularly Northumbria, songs had more usually been sold in garlands and chap-books, rather than on broadsides, since the eighteenth century: only with

---

[35] Tomlinson, 'Vico's Songs', 198. See the Introduction for further discussion of this idea.
[36] Eric Mackerness, *A Social History of English Music* (1864), 133–4; Henderson, *Victorian Street Ballads*, 12 ('The cheap song-book and, above all, the cheap newspaper could no longer be withstood'); Lee, *Music of the People*, 85; Bennett, 'Broadsides on the Trial of Queen Caroline', 71 (speaking of the mid-century); Victor E. Neuburg, 'The Literature of the Streets', in H. J. Dyos and Michael Wolff (eds.), *The Victorian City: Images and Realities*, 2 vols. (1999), vol. 1, 191–209, 207. Contemporary writers concurred: see Hindley, 'Street Ballads', 416.
[37] Hindley, *Curiosities*, 159.
[38] Persons such as Nicholas Merry, cross-examined in POB t18390513-1573.
[39] Hindley, 'Street Ballads', 400.

heavy urban- and industrialisation did the great broadside printers of Birmingham, Manchester, Preston, and elsewhere begin to flourish.[40] The economic rationale of the broadside was peculiarly suited to the exploitation of the destitute and the labouring poor, who would only have small change available for leisure activities such as singing. A halfpenny for one to two songs, on highly perishable paper, had never represented good value when set against the economy of scale afforded by sixpenny and shilling songbooks, long since enjoyed by a middling market, who could afford the outlay of that much capital at once, and thereby receive, proportionally, far more songs per penny, in a higher-quality publication. The material developments that enabled the sale of penny songbooks in London may therefore be seen as liberating, giving the metropolitan poor a far better return on their expenditure: far from sentimentalising the broadside, we might see it as a particularly invidious form of consumer exploitation. This was the stance taken by the investigative journalist James Greenwood in 1867, writing apropos an expedition to the late Catnach's premises:

The singing public has kept pace with the reading public; and two songs, or two and a half, even though they be of the most pathetic character, printed on seven inches by five of dirty white tissue-paper, could hardly hope to realise a halfpenny while five-and-twenty square feet of politics and police news can be had, hot from the press, for a penny. No! The singing public has burst the chains that bound it to the flimsy halfpenny ballad, and will be pacified with nothing less for a penny than a 'Giant Warbler,' or a 'Doodah Songster,' or a 'Concert Companion,' sixteen pages at least, and with a coloured illustration.[41]

Greenwood conflates the dual innovations of the penny newspaper and the penny songbook as, in combination, vastly improving upon the broadside. While the use of newspapers by the working classes, who as early as the start of the century might club together to buy a communal paper or read one in a coffee house, was nothing new in itself, the access of the poor to papers was greatly enhanced by the repeal, in August 1855, of the onerous Newspaper and Stamp Duties Act, a levy increased as part of the infamous 'Six Acts' of 1819, and though reduced in 1836, still acting as a punitive restriction on the viability of a truly cheap press until its final abolition as the result of a long national campaign against what was perceived as a 'tax on knowledge'.[42] Taken together, a celebration of these hard-won reforms and technological innovations, themselves

[40] See Cox Jensen, *Napoleon*, 26.
[41] James Greenwood, *Unsentimental Journeys: or, Byways of the Modern Babylon* (1867), 130.
[42] The definitive account is Martin Hewitt, *The Dawn of the Cheap Press in Victorian Britain: The End of the 'Taxes on Knowledge', 1849–1869* (2014).

catalysed by a widespread increase in literacy effected by schools and
Sunday schools, and a corresponding increase in musical literacy thanks
to mass singing movements, might be seen as indulging in Whig History.
Yet it seems significant that the consequent decline of the broadside and
the ballad-singer was principally lamented by a handful of monied antiquarians. If the masses could learn a tune themselves at a cheap concert,
or even from some form of score, then why would they not obtain the
lyrics in a form that made economic and material sense, while continuing
to enjoy street performances by a wide range of musicians from Britain,
Europe, and the wider world?

Figure 5.1 is number eleven in a series of satirical illustrations published by William Spooner in the early 1840s, under the series title
'Eccentricities'.[43] The scorn with which it attacks the musical pretensions
of the working class is a sure sign that bourgeois sensibilities were
offended by the broadening of the mainstream. On the rear wall of the
barber's shop, we see the past: below a shelf of outmoded wigs are pasted
several individual song slips, representing the traditional means of access
of music for those in the foreground. Yet this poor young man is receiving
his music, not from a ballad-singer, but as ancillary entertainment while
being shaved, from the barber's daughter seated at a square piano. This
instrument is itself of a design that had been superseded by the 1840s,
a satirical detail that hints at actual practice: a second-hand keyboard
market would undoubtedly offer access to such instruments at well below
the going rate for an up-to-date pianoforte. In the dialogue below the
image, the pianist's suggestion of Cherubini's *Lodoïska*, first performed in
London in 1794, was presumably selected simply for the pun on 'whis-
kers' – yet the far weaker pun of 'Mus-hard', connoting 'moustache', is
infinitely more topical. Philippe Musard's London concerts, advertised as
*à la Musard*, were highly innovative promenade affairs, priced so as to
attract an audience of artisans, and featuring arrangements and interpretations that would come to be known as 'light classical'.[44] This middle-
class caricature thus contains predictable jibes indicating that the lower
orders, in patronising such music, were getting above their station: from
the caricatured faces, to the cockneyfied dialogue, to the visual joke that
the pianist, absurdly perched on a stool that leaves her short legs dangling,
is aspiring to an art form that is quite literally beyond her reach.

Perhaps, as a publisher, Spooner felt threatened or insulted by the
increasingly low prices at which illustrated songbooks were being retailed.

[43] I am extremely grateful to Sheila O'Connell for drawing my attention to this image.
[44] Scott, *Sounds of the Metropolis*, 41; Adam Carse, *The Life of Jullien* (Cambridge, 1951), 6,
40, 44.

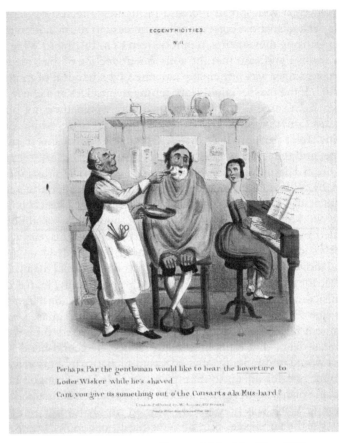

Figure 5.1  William Spooner, 'Eccentricities No. II', c.1840.
Lithograph (hand-coloured). © The Trustees of the British Museum

To return to the subject of the previous interlude: one of the penny
songbooks that Greenwood described, in this case published by
Thomas Goode of Clerkenwell, was entitled *The Old Dog Tray Songster*,
with Foster's sentimental lyric constituting the first of fully forty-three
songs.[45] This was a folded pamphlet arranged as sixteen pages; its frontispiece boasted a half-page illustrative woodcut of a sporting scene,
crudely water-coloured in five basic colours either by vendor or purchaser, and its aesthetic idiom was scarcely distinguishable from that of
a broadside. Yet its pages contained what might amount to or surpass

---

[45] *The Old Dog Tray Songster* (c.1860).

a singer's full repertoire: nearly fifty songs representing the breadth of the mainstream, from an English translation of the 'Marseillaise', to operatic excerpts, to 'Bold Robin Hood', to parodies of parlour standards, to Christy's Minstrel songs, to topical satire on national strikes. Three of the songs advertise where the sheet music might be obtained, while others give their most famous singers. 'Dearest, Then, I'll Love Thee More', for instance, directs the reader to 'Music—at Duff & Co's'. The score in question cost fully two shillings when published in 1849, but may subsequently have been sold at discount: it offers six pages of music including an ornate and harmonically involved piano accompaniment that would nonetheless have been comparatively easy to play, as the left and right hand always share a rhythm – nor does the arrangement alter across the three verses.[46] Nor did *The Old Dog Tray Songster* merely recommend music publishers. Many of its songs acknowledge their author, suggesting a more transparent and even legal appropriation of material into the mainstream than was the case in the broadside press. Printers of the latter – Ryle, Such, Fortey, Disley – also sold 'Old Dog Tray' as a broadside. But why consume the song in this form, when the vastly superior songster was available at about the same price?

In such thoroughly pragmatic decisions, the ballad-singer's fate was sealed. We need not mourn, for her custody of the mainstream had been a long one; she had endured unaltered for three centuries; that is, as long as the court composer, and considerably longer than the music hall star, the LP, or the iPod. For much of that time, ballad-singers fulfilled a vital and significant historical role: in mediating the musical mainstream, in disseminating news and opinion, in the construction of communities both local and national. Their ultimate displacement was a sign, not of the increasing quietness or impoverishment of mainstream culture, but of the opposite: of sonic and musical vibrancy, of increased literacy and access to newspapers, of the transnational influences of large-scale immigration to a newly global metropolis. Where some scholars would undoubtedly emphasise a sense of loss – and with good reason – within a narrative of unsolicited musical improvement and regulation perpetrated by Liberal reformers, I would rather stress the positives of an ever-more multicultural, dynamic working-class musical culture.[47] And after all, this buoyant state of affairs was in no small part thanks to the ballad-singer's abilities in affording mass access to modern, aestheticised melodies since at least the early eighteenth century. In short, I no longer think that their swift demise

---

[46] BL Mus H.1253 (7).

[47] For the counterargument, see especially Gammon and Gammon, 'The Musical Revolution'.

after such a long duration is something to be lamented, for, if ballad-singers were in chronological terms an especially tough sort of pit-canary, then they died of a surfeit of oxygen, not of toxins. I will end with an East End incident that, taken in isolation, is undoubtedly tragicomic, a case of one ballad-singer taking her personal revenge upon the Italian organ-grinders, and being thwarted by the New Police.[48] Yet, considering the case dispassionately, I think we might perhaps find some sympathy with the verdict, in favour of the injured Italian.

*Ellen Jones*, a ballad singer, was charged under the following circumstances: –

H. Fitzgerald, policeman 536, said—I was on duty last night in the Minories, and found the prisoner struggling with an organ-grinder. She would insist upon playing a tune on the organ, and struggled violently to get at the handle. Presently she made a regular rush at the Italian, and over he went, organ and all *(laughter)*.

THE LORD MAYOR. —Has any damage been done to the organ?
POLICEMAN. —Yes, my lord, to the amount of 5*s*.
THE LORD MAYOR. —Prisoner, what have you to say in answer to the charge?
PRISONER. —I was lushy, my lord. I was singing in a public-house, and he came and played in front of the house, which took away the halfpence that I ought to have had. I took hold of the organ-player's wrist and requested him civilly to go away, but he used bad language, and told me he would not. I did not like such low language as that, and therefore I own I did give him a gentle push, and down he went, and so did I *(laughter)*.
THE LORD MAYOR. —You had no business to touch him. What made you get drunk?
PRISONER. —I was very cold, and took a little gin and cloves. There was a good deal of drinking yesterday, my lord, in the Minories, because it was Guy Fawkes' Day.

The prisoner was ordered to pay 5*s*., the amount of the damage done to the organ.

---

[48] 'Police', *Standard* 10368 (7 November 1857).

# Bibliography

Unless specified, place of publication in all references is assumed to be London.

## Archival Material

British Library, Add. MS 27825: Francis Place, 'Collections relating to Manners and Morals'.
British Library, Add. MS 42952: 'Plays from the Lord Chamberlain's Office. Vol. LXXXVIII. June–August 1839'.
Cambridge University Library, Madden Collection.

## Newspapers and Periodicals

*Aberdeen Journal and General Advertiser for the North of Scotland* (1797–1876).
*Bell's Life in London, and Sporting Chronicle* (1822–86).
*Bell's Life in Sydney, and Sporting Reviewer* (1845–60).
*Britannic Magazine; or Entertaining Repository of Heroic Adventures* (1793–1807).
*British Stage and Literary Cabinet* (1817–22).
*Bury and Norwich Post* (1786–1931).
*Caledonian Mercury* (1720–1859).
*Chambers's Information for the People* (1842).
*Child's Companion; or Sunday Scholar's Reward* (1824–44).
*Daily News* (1846–1912).
*Director; a Weekly Literary Journal* (1807).
*Edinburgh Annual Register* (1808–26).
*Empire* (Sydney, 1850–75).
*English Gentleman* (1845).
*Era* (1838–1939).
*European Magazine and London Review* (1782–1825).
*Evening Standard* (1859–1905).
*Examiner; a Sunday Paper* (1808–36).
*Fraser's Magazine* (1870–82).
*Gentleman's Magazine* (1731–1922).
*Household Words: A Weekly Journal* (1850–9).
*Howitt's Journal* (1847–8).
*Hull Packet* (1793–1807).
*John Bull* (1820–92).

*Juvenile Companion and Sunday School Hive* (1854–71).
*La Belle Assemblée; or, Bell's Court and Fashionable Magazine* (1806–32).
*Ladies' Cabinet of Fashion, Music, and Romance* (1832–52).
*Lady's Monthly Museum; or, Polite Repository of Amusement and Instruction* (1798–1832).
*Lady's Newspaper* (1847–63).
*Lancaster Gazette and General Advertiser* (1803–94).
*Leigh Hunt's London Journal* (1834–5).
*Liverpool Mercury* (1811–1904).
*Lloyd's Weekly London Newspaper* (1843–1931).
*The London: A First-Class Magazine* (1867–8).
*London Magazine* (1820–9).
*Macmillan's Magazine* (1859–1907).
*The Mirror of Literature, Amusement, and Instruction* (1823–41).
*Monthly Magazine; or, British Register* (1796–1843).
*Monthly Review; or, Literary Journal Enlarged* (1749–1844).
*Morning Chronicle and London Advertiser* (1769–1865).
*Morning Post* (1772–1937).
*Musical Times and Singing Class Circular* (1844–1903).
*Musical World: A Weekly Record of Musical Science, Literature, and Intelligence* (1836–90).
*National Magazine* (Dublin, 1830–1).
*National Review* (1855–64).
*Notes and Queries* (1849–).
*Patriot: A Periodical Publication, Intended to Arrest the Progress of Seditious and Blasphemous Opinions, Too Prevalent In the Year 1819* (Manchester, 1819–20).
*Penny Satirist* (1840–6).
*Punch* (1841–1992).
*Satirist, Or, Monthly Meteor* (1808–14).
*Scots Magazine* (1739–1803).
*Scourge, or Literary, Theatrical, and Miscellaneous Magazine* (1811–16).
*Standard* (1827–1920).
*Theatre, or, Dramatic and Literary Mirror* (1819).
*Theatrical Journal* (1839–71).
*The Times* (1788–).
*Westminster Review* (1841–6).
*York Herald and General Advertiser* (1813–54).

### Electronic Databases

19th Century British Library Newspapers: http://find.galegroup.com/bncn/start.do?prodId=BNCN.
Bodleian Library, Broadside Ballads Online (Bod.): http://ballads.bodleian.ox.ac.uk.
British Museum Collection Database Online: http://britishmuseum.org/research/search_the_collection_database.aspx.
British Periodicals: http://ezproxy.ouls.ox.ac.uk:2303/home.do.

Eighteenth Century Collections Online: http://find.galegroup.com/ecco.
Folk Music of England, Scotland, Ireland, Wales and America: http://contempla
tor.com/folk.
House of Commons Parliamentary Papers: http://parlipapers.chadwyck.co.uk/h
ome.do.
The John Johnson Collection: http://johnjohnson.chadwyck.co.uk/home.do.
The Making of the Modern World: http://find.galegroup.com/mome/.
The Proceedings of the Old Bailey, 1674–1913 (POB): http://oldbaileyonline
.org.
Oxford Dictionary of National Biography (ODNB): http://oxforddnb.com/.
The Times Digital Archive: http://infotrac.galegroup.com/itw/infomark/0/1/1/
purl=rc6_TTDA?.

## Collections of, and Single, Songs

Aikin, John, *Essays on Song-Writing; With a Collection of Such English Songs as are Most Eminent for Poetical Merit* (1810).
Arnold, Samuel J., *Little Bess the Ballad Singer, As Sung with the Greatest Applause by Mrs. Crouch, Miss Leak, and Miss Poole* (n.d.).
Ashton, John, *Modern Street Ballads* (1888).
*The Ballad Singer, A New Song* (c.1800).
Bronson, Bertrand H. (ed.), *The Traditional Tunes of the Child Ballads*, 4 vols. (Princeton, 1959–72).
Chappell, William (ed.), *A Collection of National English Airs, Consisting of Ancient Song, Ballad, & Dance Tunes*, 2 vols. (1840).
Chappell, William (ed.), *Popular Music of the Olden Time; A Collection of Ancient Songs, Ballads, and Dance Tunes, Illustrative of the National Music of England*, 2 vols. (1855–9).
Dibdin, Charles I. M., *Mirth and Metre* (1807).
Dixon, James H. (ed.), *Scottish Traditional Versions of Ancient Ballads* (1845).
Dixon, James H. (ed.), *Ancient Poems, Ballads, and Songs of the Peasantry of England* (1846).
Dixon, James H. (ed.), *The Garland of Good-Will, by Thomas Deloney* (1851).
Motherwell, William, *Minstrelsy; Ancient and Modern, with an Historical Introduction and Notes* (Glasgow, 1827).
*The Old Dog Tray Songster* (c.1860)
Plumptre, James, *A Collection of Songs Moral, Sentimental, Instructive, and Amusing* (1805, 1806).
Speaight, George (ed.), *Bawdy Songs of the Early Music Hall* (1975).
Spedding, Patrick and Watts, Paul (general eds.), *Bawdy Songbooks of the Romantic Period*, 4 vols. (2011).
Spofforth, Reginald, *The Twelfth Cake, a Juvenile Amusement Consisting of Little Ballads* (1807).
*The Universal Songster, or, Museum of Mirth*, 3 vols. (1825–6).
Ware, William H., *London Now is Out of Town* (1811).
*Will Whimsical's Miscellany* (Chichester, 1799).
Wilson, Charles, *The Myrtle and Vine; Or, Complete Vocal Library*, 4 vols. (1800).

## Correspondence and Life-Writing

Anderson, Robert, *The Poetical Works of Robert Anderson*, 2 vols. (Carlisle, 1820).

Basset, Josiah, *The Life of a Vagrant, or the Testimony of an Outcast to the Value and Truth of the Gospel* (3rd edn, 1850).

Bewick, Thomas, *A Memoir of Thomas Bewick* (Newcastle, 1862).

Brown, William, *A Narrative of the Life and Adventures of William Brown* (York, 1829).

Burnett, John (ed.), *Useful Toil: Autobiographies of Working People from the 1820s to the 1920s* (Harmondsworth, 1984).

Burstow, Henry, *Reminiscences of Horsham* (Horsham, 1911).

Chatterton, Georgiana (ed.), *Memorials, Personal and History of Admiral Lord Gambier, G.C.B.*, 2 vols. (1861).

[Cochrane, Charles], *Journal of a Tour Made by ... J. de V., the Spanish Minstrel of 1828–9, through Great Britain and Ireland, a Character Assumed by an English Gentleman* (1847).

Dibdin, Charles, *The Professional Life of Mr. Dibdin, Written by Himself*, 4 vols. (1803).

Dodd, William, *A Narrative of the Experience and Sufferings of William Dodd, a Factory Cripple. Written by Himself* (2nd edn, 1841).

Gardiner, William, *Music and Friends: or, Pleasant Recollections of a Dilettante*, 2 vols. (1838).

Heaton, William, *The Old Soldier; The Wandering Lover; and other Poems; together with a Sketch of the Author's Life* (1857).

Hindley, Charles (ed.), *The Life and Adventures of a Cheap Jack. By One of the Fraternity* (1876).

Holcroft, Thomas, *Memoirs of the Late Thomas Holcroft*, 3 vols. (1816).

Kingsley, Charles, *Alton Locke, Tailor and Poet: An Autobiography*, 2 vols. (1850).

Knight, Charles, *Passages of a Working Life During Half a Century*, 3 vols. (1864).

Leatherland, J. A., *Essays and Poems, with a brief Autobiographical Memoir* (1862).

Lewis, Matthew G., *Journal of a Residence Among the Negroes in the West Indies* (1845, repr Stroud, 2005).

*The Life of Old Jemmy Catnach, Printer* (New edn, Penzance, 1965).

Love, David, *David Love's Journey to London, and his Return to Nottingham* (Nottingham, *c*.1814).

Love, David, *The Life, Adventures, and Experience, of David Love. Written by Himself* (3rd edn, Nottingham, 1823).

Magee, John, *Some Account of the Travels of John Magee, Pedlar and Flying Stationer, in North & South Britain, in the Years 1806 and 1808* (Paisley, 1826).

Maguire, Robert (ed.), *Scenes from My Life, by a Working Man* (1858).

Senelick, Laurence (ed.), *Tavern Singing in Early Victorian London: The Diaries of Charles Rice for 1840 and 1850* (1997).

Silliman, Benjamin, *A Journal of Travels in England, Holland, and Scotland, and of Two Passages Over the Atlantic, in the Years 1805 and 1806*, 2 vols. (2nd edn, Boston, 1812).

Smith, Charles M., *The Working Man's Way in the World* (3rd edn, 1857).

Somerville, Alexander, *The Autobiography of a Working Man, by 'One who has Whistled at the Plough'* (1848).

Speaight, George (ed.), *Professional & Literary Memoirs of Charles Dibdin the Younger* (1956).

Stott, Benjamin, *Songs for the Millions and Other Poems* (Middleton, 1843).

Taylor, Jane, *Memoirs, Correspondence, and Poetical Remains, of Jane Taylor* (4th edn, 1841).

Teasdale, Harvey, *The Life and Adventures of Harvey Teasdale* (7th edn, Sheffield, 1870).

Thale, Mary (ed.), *The Autobiography of Francis Place (1771–1854)* (Cambridge, 1972).

Thomson, Christopher, *The Autobiography of an Artisan* (1847).

Vincent, David (ed.), *Testaments of Radicalism: Memoirs of Working Class Politicians 1790–1885* (1977).

West, William, *Fifty Years' Recollections of an Old Bookseller* (Cork, 1835).

## Fiction and Poetry

Badcock, John, *Real Life in London; or, the Rambles and Adventures of Bob Tallyho, Esq. and his cousin, the Hon. Tom Dashall, through the Metropolis*, 2 vols. (1821).

Burrowes, John [John Freckleton], *Life in St. George's Fields, or, the Rambles and Adventures of Disconsolate William, Esq.* (1821).

Dickens, Charles, *Our Mutual Friend* (1864–5, New edn, Harmondsworth, 1971).

Edgeworth, Maria, *The Ballad Singer; or, Memoirs of the Bristol Family: A Most Interesting Novel in Four Volumes*, 4 vols. (1814).

Egan, Pierce, *Life in London, or, The Day and Night Scenes of Jerry Hawthorn, Esq.* (2nd edn, c.1870).

Goldsmith, Oliver, *The Vicar of Wakefield* (1800).

Johnstone, Charles, *Chrysal: or, The Adventures of a Guinea.*, 3 vols. (1760, New edn, c.1797).

Kelly, Isabella, *Joscelina: or, the Rewards of Benevolence. A Novel*, 2 vols. (2nd edn, 1798).

Lamb, Charles, *The Poetical Works of Charles Lamb. A New Edition* (1836).

Martineau, Harriet, *Illustrations of Political Economy: no. III, Brooke and Brooke Farm: A Tale* (3rd edn, 1833).

More, Hannah, *The Two Shoemakers. In Six Parts* (n.d.).

*The Surprising History of a Ballad Singer* (Falkirk, 1818).

Wordsworth, William, *The Prelude* (New York, 1850).

## Plays

Hoare, Prince, *No Song No Supper; A Musical Entertainment, In Two Acts* (1830).

Jerrold, Douglas, *Black-Ey'd Susan: A Drama, in Three Acts* (1829).

Jerrold, Douglas, *Sally in Our Alley. A Drama, in Two Acts* (1829).

Mayhew, Henry, *The Wandering Minstrel. A Farce, in One Act* (1834, New edn, New York, n.d.).

Moncrieff, William T., *Tom and Jerry; or, Life in London: An Operatic Extravaganza, in Three Acts* (2nd edn, 1828).

Moncrieff, William T., *Sam Weller or, The Pickwickians: A Drama in Three Acts* (1837).
Moncrieff, William T., *The Ballad Singer, in Three Acts* (1839), in British Library, Add. MS. 42952, ff. 248–327.

## Miscellaneous Primary Material

*An Act for Further Improving the Police in and near the Metropolis: (17th August 1839)* (1839).
*Advice to the Labourer, the Mechanic, and the Parent* (*c*.1800).
'Aleph' [William Harvey], *London Scenes and London People* (1863).
Allingham, William, 'Irish Ballad Singers and Irish Street Ballads', *Household Words* 94 (1852), repr. *Ceol* 3 (1967): 2–16.
Allingham, William (ed.), *The Ballad Book: A Selection of the Choicest British Ballads* (1864).
*An Address to the Public, From the Society for the Suppression of Vice* (1804).
Babbage, Charles, *A Chapter on Street Nuisances* (1864).
Baring-Gould, Sabine, *Strange Survivals: Some Chapters in the History of Man* (2nd edn, 1894).
Bartell, Edmund, *Hints for Picturesque Improvements in Ornamented Cottages, and Their Scenery* (1804).
Bass, Michael T., *Street Music in the Metropolis. Correspondence and Observations on the Existing Law, and Proposed Amendments* (1864).
Bee, John [John Badcock], *A Living Picture of London, for 1828* (1828).
Beresford, James, *The Miseries of Human Life; or the Groans of Samuel Sensitive, and Timothy Testy*, 2 vols. (6th edn, 1807).
Bigland, John, *An Historical Display of the Effects of Physical and Moral Causes on the Character and Circumstances of Nations* (1816).
Busby, Thomas L., *Costume of the Lower Orders of London. Painted and Engraved from Nature* (1820).
Carey, George Saville, *The Balnea* (1799).
Caulfield, James, *Blackguardiana: or, A Dictionary of Rogues* (*c*.1793).
*The Colonial Policy of Great Britain, Considered with Relation to Her North American Provinces and West India Possessions* (1819).
Colquhoun, Patrick, *A Treatise on the Police of the Metropolis* (6th edn, 1800).
Colquhoun, Patrick, *A Treatise on the Functions and Duties of a Constable* (1803).
Colquhoun, Patrick, *A Treatise on Indigence* (1806).
*The Dens of London Exposed* (1835).
*The Encyclopaedia of Anecdote* (Dublin, *c*.1800).
Esquiros, Alphonse, *The English at Home*, trans. Lascelles Wraxall 2 vols. (1861).
*The First Report of the Society Established in London for the Suppression of Mendicity* (1819).
Fletcher, Andrew, *The Political Works of Andrew Fletcher, Esq.* (1737).
'Folio, F.', *The Hawkers and Street Dealers of Manchester and the North of England Manufacturing Districts Generally... Being Some Account of their Dealings, Dodgings, & Doings* (Manchester, 1858).
Fox, William J., *Lectures Addressed Chiefly to the Working Classes*, 4 vols. (1846).
Gardiner, William, *The Music of Nature* (1832, New edn, Boston, 1841).

Greenwood, James, *Unsentimental Journeys: or, Byways of the Modern Babylon* (1867).

Gregory, George, *A Dictionary of Arts and Sciences*, 2 vols. (1806–7).

Hazlitt, William, *The Plain Speaker: Opinions on Books, Men, and Things. A New Edition* (1870).

*Heads of the People: Being Portraits of the English*, 2 vols. (1840).

Hindley, Charles, *Curiosities of Street Literature* (1871).

Hindley, Charles, *The Life and Times of James Catnach (Late of Seven Dials), Ballad Monger* (1878).

Hindley, Charles, *A History of the Cries of London, Ancient and Modern* (1881).

Hindley, Charles, *The History of the Catnach Press* (1887).

Hindley, Charles, *The True History of Tom and Jerry* (1888).

*History of the Westminster and Middlesex Elections; in the Month of November, 1806* (1807).

Hone, William, *The Reformists' Register and Weekly Commentary* (1817).

Hone, William, *The Every-Day Book; or, the Guide to the Year* (1825).

Horne, George, *Sixteen Sermons on Various Subjects and Occasions* (2nd edn, Oxford, 1795).

Howell, Thomas B. (ed.), *Cobbett's Complete Collection of State Trials*, 21 vols. (1809–26).

Jackson, William, *Observations on the Present State of Music, in London* (Dublin, 1791).

Jerrold, Blanchard, *London: A Pilgrimage. Illustrated by Gustave Doré with an Introduction by Peter Ackroyd* (2006).

Jerrold, Douglas, *The Essays of Douglas Jerrold. Edited by his Grandson Walter Jerrold with Illustrations by H.M. Brock* (1903).

Knight, Charles (ed.), *London*, 6 vols. (1851).

Leighton, John, *London Cries & Public Edifices. By Luke Limner Esq.* (1847).

Lhotsky, John, *Hunger and Revolution. By the Author of 'Daily Bread.'* (1843).

Mackay, Charles, *Memoirs of Extraordinary Popular Delusions*, 3 vols. (1841).

Malcolm, James P., *Anecdotes of the Manners and Customs of London during the Eighteenth Century*, 2 vols. (1810).

*Metropolitan Grievances; or, a Serio-Comic Glance at Minor Mischiefs in London and its Vicinity* (1812).

Millar, James, *The Friendly Society Guide: or, A Series of Letters, Conferences, and Essays on the Formation and Improvement of Benefit or Friendly Societies* (Dundee, 1825).

Molleson, Alexander, *Miscellanies in Prose and Verse* (Glasgow, 1806).

Morley, Henry, *Memoirs of Bartholomew Fair* (1859, repr. 1973).

*The Moving Market: Or, Cries of London. For the Amusement of Good Children.* (Glasgow, 1815).

*New Police Report for 1817. The Second Report of the Select Committee* (1817).

*The Observant Pedestrian; Or, Traits of the Heart: In a Solitary Tour from Cærnarvon to London: In Two Volumes, by the Author of The Mystic Cottager*, 2 vols. (1795).

Parker, George, *Life's Painter of Variegated Characters in Public and Private Life* (1789).

Parker, George, *A View of Society and Manners in High and Low Life*, 2 vols. (1791).

Plumptre, James, *Letters to John Aikin, M.D. on his volume of Vocal Poetry* (Cambridge, 1811).

'Rag, Jack' (ed.), *Streetology of London; or, the Metropolitan Papers of the Itinerant Club* (1837).

Rede, Lehman T., *The Road to the Stage; or, The Performer's Preceptor* (1827).

*Religious Tracts, Dispersed by the Society for Promoting Christian Knowledge*, 12 vols. (1800).

*Report from Committee on the State of Mendicity in the Metropolis, Ordered by the House of Commons to be Printed, 11 July 1815* (1815).

Reynolds, George W. M., *The Mysteries of London* (1850–6, New edn, Keele, 1996).

Rowlandson, Thomas, *Characteristic Sketches of the Lower Orders* (c.1820).

Sala, George Augustus, *Twice Round the Clock; or the Hours of the Day and Night in London* (1861).

Sala, George Augustus, *Gaslight and Daylight* (New edn, 1872).

Schlesinger, Max, *Saunterings in and about London. The English Edition by Otto Wenckstern* (1853).

Scholes, Percy A., *The Mirror of Music, 1844–1944: A Century of Musical Life in Britain as reflected in the pages of the Music Times*, 2 vols. (Oxford, 1947).

Shenstone, William, *Essays on Men and Manners* (Ludlow, 1800).

Slater, Michael (ed.), *Dickens' Journalism: Sketches by Boz and other Early Papers, 1833–39* (1996).

Smith, Albert R. (ed.), *Gavarni in London, Sketches of Life and Character: With Illustrative Essays by Popular Writers* (1849).

Smith, Charles M., *Curiosities of London Life: or, Phases, Physiological and Social, of the Great Metropolis* (1853).

Smith, Charles M., *The Little World of London; or, Pictures in Little of London Life* (1857).

Smith, John T., *Etchings of Remarkable Beggars, Itinerant Traders, and other Persons of Notoriety in London and its Environs* (1815).

Smith, John T., *Vagabondiana; or, Anecdotes of Mendicant Wanderers through the Streets of London; with Portraits of the Most Remarkable Drawn from the Life* (1817).

Smith, John T., *The Cries of London: exhibiting several of the Itinerant Traders of Antient and Modern Times* (1839).

Smith, John T., *A Book for a Rainy Day: or, Recollections of the Events of the Last Sixty-Six Years* (1845).

[Stanhope, Philip D.], *Chesterfield Travestie: Or, School for Modern Manners* (1808).

*The Statutes of the Realm*, 11 vols. (1810–28).

Strutt, Joseph, *Glig Gamena Angel-Deod, or, The Sports and Pastimes of the People of England* (1801).

*The Swell's Night Guide: or, a Peep through the Great Metropolis* (New edn, 1846).

Taylor, Edward, *Three Inaugural Lectures* (1838).

Taylor, Jane, *City Scenes; or, A Peep into London, for Good Children* (1809).

Thelwall, John, *The Poetical Recreations of The Champion, and his Literary Correspondents; with a Selection of Essays, Literary & Critical which have appeared in The Champion Newspaper* (1822).
Timbs, John, *Curiosities of London* (New edn, 1867).
Tuer, Alfred W., *Old London Street Cries* (1885).
'Unus populi', *A Letter to Mr. Scarlett on the Poor Laws* (1822).
Weston, Charles, *Remarks on the Poor Laws* (Brentford, 1802).

## Secondary Material

Abbate, Carolyn, *Unsung Voices: Opera and Musical Narrative in the Nineteenth Century* (Princeton, 1991).
Abbate, Carolyn, 'Music—Drastic or Gnostic?', *Critical Inquiry* 30 (2004): 505–36.
Anderson, Hugh, *Farewell to Judges & Juries: The Broadside Ballad & Convict Transportation to Australia, 1788–1868* (Victoria, 2000).
Andrews, Gavin, Kingsbury, Paul, and Kearns, Robin (eds.), *Soundscapes of Wellbeing in Popular Music* (Farnham, 2014).
Arata, Stephen, 'Rhyme, Rhythm, and the Materiality of Poetry: Response', *Victorian Studies* 53 (2011): 518–26.
Astbury, Raymond, *Black Entertainers in Victorian Dublin* (Milton Keynes, 2014).
Atkinson, David, *The English Traditional Ballad: Theory, Method and Practice* (Aldershot, 2002).
Atkinson, David, 'Folk Songs in Print: Text and Tradition', *Folk Music Journal* 8 (2004): 456–83.
Atkinson, David, *The Anglo-Scottish Ballad and its Imaginary Contexts* (Cambridge, 2014).
Atkinson, David and Roud, Steve (eds.), *Street Ballads in Nineteenth-Century Britain, Ireland, and North America: The Interface between Print and Oral Traditions* (Farnham, 2014).
Atkinson, David and Roud, Steve (eds.), *Street Literature of the Long Nineteenth Century: Producers, Sellers, Consumers* (Newcastle, 2017).
Atlas, Allan W., 'Belasco and Puccini: "Old Dog Tray" and the Zuni Indians', *Musical Quarterly* 75 (1991): 362–98.
Attali, Jacques, *Noise: The Political Economy of Music* (Manchester, 1985).
Baer, Marc, *The Rise and Fall of Radical Westminster, 1780–1890* (Basingstoke, 2012).
Bailey, Peter, *Popular Culture and Performance in the Victorian City* (Cambridge, 1998).
Banfield, Stephen, *Sondheim's Broadway Musicals* (Ann Arbor, 1993).
Banfield, Stephen, 'Review: *The American Popular Ballad of the Golden Era: 1924–1950*', *Journal of Music Theory* 44 (2000): 236–49.
Banfield, Stephen, 'Once Again: Scholarship and the Musical', *Journal of the Royal Musical Association* 138 (2013): 431–41.
Bann, Stephen, *Distinguished Images: Prints in the Visual Economy of Nineteenth-Century France* (New Haven, 2013).
Barclay, Katie, 'Composing the Self: Gender, Subjectivity and Scottish Balladry', *Cultural and Social History* 7 (2010): 337–53.

Barclay, Katie, 'Singing, Performance, and Lower-Class Masculinity in the Dublin Magistrates' Court, 1820–1850', *Journal of Social History* 47 (2014): 746–68.

Barclay, Katie, 'Sounds of Sedition: Music and Emotion in Ireland, 1780–1845', *Cultural History* 3 (2014): 54–80.

Barker, Hannah, and Vincent, David (eds.), *Language, Print and Electoral Politics, 1790–1832: Newcastle-Under-Lyme Broadsides* (Woodbridge, 2001).

Barricelli, Jean-Pierre and Gibaldi, Joseph (eds.), *Interrelations of Literature* (New York, 1982).

Barringer, Tim, Forrester, Gillian, and Martinez-Ruiz, Barbaro (eds.), *Art and Emancipation in Jamaica: Isaac Mendes Belisario and His Worlds* (New Haven, 2007).

Bartlett, Georgina, 'From the Stage to the Street: Theatre Music and the Broadside Ballad in London, 1797–1844' (Oxford University D.Phil. thesis, 2020).

Beaumont, Matthew, *Nightwalking: A Nocturnal History of London* (2015).

Beedell, Ann V., *The Decline of the English Musician, 1788–1888: A Family of English Musicians in Ireland, England, Mauritius and Australia* (Oxford, 1992).

Bell, Karl, *The Magical Imagination: Magic and Modernity in Urban England, 1780–1914* (Cambridge, 2012).

Ben-Amos, Dan, 'The Situation Structure of the Non-Humorous English Ballad', *Midwest Folklore* 13 (1963): 163–76.

Bender, Daniel, Corpis, Duane J., and Walkowitz, Daniel J., 'Sound Politics: Critically Listening to the Past', *Radical History Review* 121 (2015): 1–7.

Bennett, Anthony, 'Broadsides on the Trial of Queen Caroline: A Glimpse at Popular Song in 1820', *Proceedings of the Royal Musical Association* 107 (1980–1): 71–85.

Bennett, Anthony, 'Sources of Popular Song in Early Nineteenth-Century Britain: Problems and Methods of Research', *Popular Music* 2, Theory and Method (1982): 69–89.

Bennett, Anthony, 'Rivals Unravelled: A Broadside Song and Dance', *Folk Music Journal* 6 (1993): 420–45.

Bennett, Tony and Joyce, Patrick (eds.), *Material Powers: Cultural Studies, History and the Material Turn* (Abingdon, 2010).

Bergson, Henri, *Laughter: An Essay on the Meaning of the Comic*, trans. Cloudesley Brereton (1911).

Bernhart, Walter, Scher, Steven P., and Wolf, Werner (eds.), *Word and Music Studies: Defining the Field* (1999).

Bicknell, Jeanette and Fisher, John A. (eds.), *Song, Songs, and Singing* (Chichester, 2013).

Blackmur, Richard P., *Language as Gesture: Essays in Poetry* (1954).

Boase-Beier, Jean and Weninger, Robert (eds.), *Listening to Sing: Writing and Music* (Edinburgh, 2008).

Bohlman, Philip V., 'Herder's Nineteenth Century', *Nineteenth-Century Music Review* 7 (2010): 3–21.

Booth, Mark W., *The Experience of Songs* (New Haven, 1981).

Born, Georgina, 'Listening, Mediation, Event: Anthropological and Sociological Perspectives', *Journal of the Royal Musical Association* 135 (2010): 79–89.

Born, Georgina, 'For a Relational Musicology: Music and Interdisciplinarity, Beyond the Practice Turn', *Journal of the Royal Musical Association* 135 (2010): 205–43.

Born, Georgina (ed.), *Music, Sound and Space: Transformations of Public and Private Experience* (Cambridge, 2013).

Boswell, George, 'Reciprocal Controls Exerted by Ballad Texts and Tunes', *Journal of American Folklore* 80 (1967): 169–74.

Bourdieu, Pierre, *Distinction: A Social Critique of the Judgement of Taste*, trans. Richard Nice (1984).

Bowan, Kate and Pickering, Paul A., '"Songs for the Millions": Chartist Music and Popular Aural Tradition', *Labour History Review* 74 (2009): 44–63.

Bowan, Kate and Pickering, Paul A., *Sounds of Liberty: Music, Radicalism and Reform in the Anglophone World, 1790–1914* (Manchester, 2017).

Boykan, Martin, 'Reflections on Words and Music', *Musical Quarterly* 84 (2000): 123–36.

Braddick, Michael J. and Walter, John (eds.), *Negotiating Power in Early Modern Society: Order, Hierarchy and Subordination in Britain and Ireland* (Cambridge, 2001).

Brant, Clare and Whyman, Susan E. (eds.), *Walking the Streets of Eighteenth-Century London: John Gay's* Trivia *(1716)* (Oxford, 2007).

Bratton, Jacky S., *The Victorian Popular Ballad* (1975).

Bratton, Jacky S. (ed.), *Music Hall: Performance and Style* (Milton Keynes, 1986).

Briggs, Jo, 'Ballads and Balloon Ascents: Reconnecting the Popular and the Didactic in 1851', *Victorian Studies* 55 (2013): 253–66.

Bronson, Bertrand H., *The Ballad as Song* (Berkeley and Los Angeles, 1969).

Brown, Marshall, *The Tooth that Nibbles at the Soul: Essays on Music and Poetry* (Seattle, 2010).

Bucciarelli, Melania and Joncus, Berta (eds.), *Music as Social and Cultural Practice: Essays in Honour of Reinhard Strohm* (Woodbridge, 2007).

Buckley, Jenifer, *Gender, Pregnancy and Power in Eighteenth-Century Literature: The Maternal Imagination* (Basingstoke, 2017).

Burke, Helen M., 'The Revolutionary Prelude: The Dublin Stage in the Late 1770s and Early 1780s', *Eighteenth-Century Life* 22, no. 3 (1998): 7–18.

Burke, Peter, *Popular Culture in Early Modern Europe* (3rd edn, Abingdon, 2009, 1st edn, New York, 1978).

Burke, Peter, 'Postscript', *Italian Studies* 71 (2016): 259–63.

Butt, John, 'Do Musical Works Contain an Implied Listener? Towards a Theory of Musical Listening', *Journal of the Royal Musical Association* 135 (2010): 5–18.

Butterfield, Ardis, 'Repetition and Variation in the Thirteenth-Century Refrain', *Journal of the Royal Musical Association* 116 (1991): 1–23.

Bywater, Michael, 'Performing Spaces: Street Music and Public Territory', *Twentieth-Century Music* 3 (2007): 97–120.

Calhoun, Craig and Sennett, Richard (eds.), *Practicing Culture* (Abingdon, 2007).

Cannadine, David (ed.), *Trafalgar in History: A Battle and its Afterlife* (Basingstoke, 2006).

Carnell, Peter W., *Ballads in the Charles Harding Firth Collection of the University of Sheffield: A Descriptive Catalogue with Indexes* (Sheffield, 1979).

Carnelos, Laura, 'Street Voices. The Role of Blind Performers in Early Modern Italy', *Italian Studies* 71 (2016): 184–96.

Carse, Adam, *The Life of Jullien* (Cambridge, 1951).

Champion, Matthew S. and Stanyon, Miranda, 'Musicalising History', *Transactions of the Royal Historical Society* 29 (2019): 79–104.

Chandler, James and Gilmartin, Kevin (eds.), *Romantic Metropolis: The Urban Scene of British Culture, 1780–1840* (Cambridge, 2005).

Chantler, Ashley, Davies, Michael, and Shaw, Philip (eds.), *Literature and Authenticity, 1780–1900: Essays in Honour of Vincent Newey* (Farnham, 2011).

Chapin, Keith and Kramer, Lawrence (eds.), *Musical Meaning and Human Values* (New York, 2009).

Charosh, Paul, 'Studying Nineteenth-Century Popular Song', *American Music* 15 (1997): 459–92.

Chrisman-Campbell, Kimberley, *Fashion Victims: Dress at the Court of Louis XVI and Marie-Antoinette* (New Haven, 2015).

Chua, Daniel, *Absolute Music and the Construction of Meaning* (Cambridge, 1999).

Clark, Anna, *The Struggle for the Breeches: Gender and the Making of the British Working Class* (1995).

Clarke, Candace, *Misery and Company: Sympathy in Everyday Life* (Chicago, 1997).

Clayton, Tim, *The English Print, 1688–1802* (New Haven, 1997).

Clemit, Pamela (ed.), *The Cambridge Companion to British Literature of the French Revolution in the 1790s* (Cambridge, 2011).

Cockayne, Emily, *Hubbub: Filth, Noise & Stench in England, 1600–1770* (New Haven, 2007).

Cole, Michael, *The Pianoforte in the Classical Era* (Oxford, 1998).

Collison, Robert, *The Story of Street Literature: Forerunner of the Popular Press* (1973).

Cone, Edward T., *The Composer's Voice* (Berkeley and Los Angeles, 1974).

Connell, Philip and Leask, Nigel (eds.), *Romanticism and Popular Culture in Britain and Ireland* (Cambridge, 2009).

Cook, Nicholas, *Analysing Musical Multimedia* (Oxford, 2000).

Cook, Nicholas, *Music, Imagination, and Culture* (Oxford, 2002).

Cook, Nicholas, *Music, Performance, Meaning: Selected Essays* (Aldershot, 2007).

Cook, Nicholas and Everist, Mark (eds.), *Rethinking Music* (Oxford, 1999).

Corfield, Penelope J., 'Walking the City Streets: "The Urban Odyssey in Eighteenth-Century England"', *Journal of Urban History* 16 (1990): 132–74.

Costa, Marco et al., 'Interval Distributions, Mode, and Tonal Strength of Melodies as Predictors of Perceived Emotion', *Music Perception* 22 (2004): 1–14.

Cox Jensen, Oskar, 'The *Travels* of John Magee: Tracing the Geographies of Britain's Itinerant Print-Sellers, 1789–1815', *Cultural and Social History* 11 (2014): 195–216.

Cox Jensen, Oskar, *Napoleon and British Song, 1797–1822* (Basingstoke, 2015).

Cox Jensen, Oskar, Kennerley, David, and Newman, Ian (eds.), *Charles Dibdin and Late Georgian Culture* (Oxford, 2018).

Crawford, Thomas, *Society and the Lyric: A Study of the Song Culture of Eighteenth-Century Scotland* (Edinburgh, 1979).

Crick, Julia and Walsham, Alexandra (eds.), *The Uses of Script and Print, 1300–1700* (Cambridge, 2004).

Crosbie, Barbara, 'Half-Penny Ballads and the Soundscape of Eighteenth-Century Electioneering', *Publishing History* 70 (2011): 9–32.

Culler, Jonathan, *Theory of the Lyric* (Harvard, 2015).

Cunningham, Hugh, *Leisure in the Industrial Revolution, c.1780–c.1880* (1980).

Cunningham, Hugh and Innes, Joanna (eds.), *Charity, Philanthropy and Reform: From the 1690s to 1850* (Basingstoke, 1998).

Cunningham Woods, Francis, 'A Consideration of the Various Types of Songs Popular in England during the Eighteenth Century', *Proceedings of the Musical Association*, 23rd session (1896–7): 37–55.

Davey, James, 'Singing for the Nation: Balladry, Naval Recruitment and the Language of Patriotism in Eighteenth-Century Britain', *The Mariner's Mirror* 103 (2017): 43–66.

Davies, James Q. and Lockhart, Ellen (eds.), *Sound Knowledge: Music and Science in London, 1789–1851* (Chicago, 2017).

Davies, L. I., 'Orality, Literacy, Popular Culture: An Eighteenth-Century Case Study', *Oral Tradition* 25 (2010): 305–23.

Davies, Stephen, *Musical Meaning and Expression* (Ithaca, N.Y., 1994).

Davis, Jim, *Comic Acting and Portraiture in Late-Georgian and Regency England* (Cambridge, 2015).

Davis, Jim and Emeljanow, Victor, *Reflecting the Audience: London Theatregoing, 1840–1880* (Hatfield, 2001).

Davis, Michael T., '"An Evening of Pleasure Rather than Business": Songs, Subversion and Radical Sub-Culture in the 1790s', *Journal for the Study of British Cultures* 12, no. 2 (2005): 115–26.

Dawes, Kwame, 'Negotiating the Ship on the Head: Black British Fiction', *Wasafiri* 14, no. 29 (1999): 18–24.

Degl'Innocenti, Luca and Rospocher, Massimo, 'Street Singers: An Interdisciplinary Perspective', *Italian Studies* 71 (2016): 149–53.

Degl'Innocenti, Luca and Rospocher, Massimo, '*Street Singers in Renaissance Europe*', Special Issue of *Renaissance Studies* 33, no. 1 (2019): 1–158.

Dennant, Paul, 'The "barbarous old English jig": The "Black Joke" in the Eighteenth and Nineteenth Centuries', *Folk Music Journal* 10 (2013): 298–318.

DeNora, Tia, *Music in Everyday Life* (Cambridge, 2000).

Dentith, Simon, *Parody* (2000).

Dickie, Simon, *Cruelty and Laughter: Forgotten Comic Literature and the Unsentimental Eighteenth Century* (Chicago, 2011).

Dickinson, Harry T., *Caricatures and the Constitution, 1760–1832* (Cambridge, 1986).

Dillon, Elizabeth Maddock, *New World Drama: The Performative Commons in the Atlantic World, 1649–1849* (Durham and London, 2014).

Dugaw, Dianne, *Warrior Women and Popular Balladry, 1650–1850* (Chicago, 1996).

Dyos, H. J. and Wolff, Michael (eds.), *The Victorian City: Images and Realities*, 2 vols. (1999).

Eccles, Audrey, *Vagrancy in Law and Practice under the Old Poor Law* (Farnham, 2012).

Egri, Péter, *Literature, Painting and Music: An Interdisciplinary Approach to Comparative Literature* (Budapest, 1988).

Ehrenreich, Barbara, *Dancing in the Streets: A History of Collective Joy* (2007).

Elbourne, Roger, 'A Mirror of Man? Traditional Music as a Reflection of Society', *Journal of American Folklore* 89 (1976): 463–8.

Epp, Maureen and Power, Brian E. (eds.), *The Sounds and Sights of Performance in Early Music* (Farnham, 2009).

Epstein, James, *In Practice: Studies in the Language and Culture of Popular Politics in Modern Britain* (Stanford, 2003).

Epstein Nord, Deborah, *Walking the Victorian Streets: Women, Representation, and the City* (New York, 1995).

Etherington, Ben, 'Sound Gazes?', *Journal of the Royal Musical Association* 135 (2010): 39–43.

Eva, Phil, 'Home Sweet Home? The "Culture of Exile" in Mid-Victorian Popular Song', *Popular Music* 16 (1997): 131–50.

Everett, Walter, 'Deep-Level Portrayals of Directed and Misdirected Motions in Nineteenth-Century Lyric Song', *Journal of Music Theory* 48 (2004): 25–68.

Fahrner, Robert, *The Theatre Career of Charles Dibdin the Elder (1745–1814)* (New York, 1989).

Fairclough, Mary, *The Romantic Crowd: Sympathy, Controversy and Print Culture* (Cambridge, 2013).

Fitzgerald, Kelly, 'Singers as Songmakers: Individual Creativity and Expression Within the Making of Songs', *Béaloideas* 77 (2009): 80–102.

Fitzgerald, William, 'Listening, Ancient and Modern', *Journal of the Royal Musical Association* 135 (2010): 25–37.

Fitzpatrick, Martin et al. (eds.), *The Enlightenment World* (2004).

Foley, John M., *How to Read an Oral Poem* (Urbana and Chicago, 2002).

Foucault, Michel, *Discipline and Punish*, trans. Alan Sheridan (2nd edn, New York, 1995).

Fox, Adam, *Oral and Literate Culture in England, 1500–1700* (Oxford, 2000).

Friedman, Albert B., *The Ballad Revival: Studies in the Influence of Popular on Sophisticated Poetry* (Chicago, 1961).

Friedman, Albert B., 'The Formulaic Improvisation Theory of Ballad Tradition: A Counterstatement', *Journal of American Folklore* 74 (1961): 113–15.

Frith, Simon, *Performing Rites: On the Value of Popular Music* (Oxford, 1996).

Fulcher, Jane F. (ed.), *The Oxford Handbook of the New Cultural History of Music* (Oxford, 2011).

Fulford, Tim, 'Fallen Ladies and Cruel Mothers: Ballad Singers and Ballad Heroines in the Eighteenth Century', *The Eighteenth Century: Theory and Interpretation* 47 (2006): 309–30.

Fumerton, Patricia, *Unsettled: The Culture of Mobility and the Working Poor in Early Modern England* (Chicago, 2006).

Fumerton, Patricia (ed.), *Living English Broadside Ballads, 1550–1750: Song, Art, Dance, Culture, Special Issue of Huntington Library Quarterly* 79, no. 2 (2016): 163–342.

Fumerton, Patricia and Guerrini, Anita (eds.), *Ballads and Broadsides in Britain, 1500–1800* (Farnham, 2010).

Gammon, Vic, '"Not Appreciated in Worthing?" Class Expression and Popular Song Texts in Mid-Nineteenth-Century Britain', *Popular Music* 4, Performers and Audiences (1984): 5–24.

Gammon, Vic, 'The Grand Conversation: Napoleon and British Popular Balladry', *RSA Journal* 137 (1989): 665–74.

Gammon, Vic, *Desire, Drink and Death in English Folk and Vernacular Song, 1600–1900* (Aldershot, 2008).

Gammon, Vic and Gammon, Sheila, 'The Musical Revolution of the Mid-Nineteenth Century: From "Repeat and Twiddle" to "Precision and Snap"', in Trevor Herbert (ed.), *The British Brass Band: A Musical and Social History* (Oxford, 2000), 122–54.

Ganev, Robin, *Songs of Protest, Songs of Love: Popular Ballads in Eighteenth-Century Britain* (Manchester, 2009).

Gatrell, Vic A. C., *The Hanging Tree: Execution and the English People, 1770–1868* (Oxford, 1994).

Gatrell, Vic A. C., *City of Laughter: Sex and Satire in Eighteenth-Century London* (2007).

Gaunt, Richard A., 'Cheering the Member: Gladstone Election Songs at Newark', *Transactions of the Thoroton Society of Nottinghamshire* 114 (2010): 159–66.

Ghosh, Anindita, 'Singing in a New World: Street Songs and Urban Experience in Colonial Calcutta', *History Workshop Journal* 76 (2013): 111–36.

Gikandi, Simon, *Slavery and the Culture of Taste* (Princeton, 2011).

Golby, John M. and Purdue, A. William, *The Civilisation of the Crowd: Popular Culture in England, 1750–1900* (1984).

Gouk, Penelope and Hills, Helen (eds.), *Representing Emotions: New Connections in the Histories of Art, Music and Medicine* (Aldershot, 2005).

Gowing, Laura, *Domestic Dangers: Women, Words and Sex in Early Modern London* (Oxford, 1996).

Green, Bryan S., 'Learning from Henry Mayhew: The Role of the Impartial Spectator in Mayhew's *London Labour and the London Poor*', *Journal of Contemporary Ethnography* 31, no. 2 (2002): 99–134.

Gregory, E. David, *Victorian Songhunters: The Recovery and Editing of English Vernacular Ballads and Folk Lyrics, 1820–1883* (Lanham, 2006).

Griffin, Emma, 'Popular Culture in Industrialising England', *Historical Journal* 45 (2002): 619–35.

Groom, Nick, *The Making of Percy's* Reliques (Oxford, 1999).

Guillorel, Éva, Hopkin, David, and Pooley, William G. (eds.), *Rhythms of Revolt: European Traditions and Memories of Social Conflict in Oral Culture* (Abingdon, 2018).

Gustar, Andrew, 'The Life and Times of Black-Ey'd Susan: The Story of an English Ballad', *Folk Music Journal* 10 (2014): 432–48.

Hackman, Rowan, *Ships of the East India Company* (Gravesend, 2001).

Hadfield, Andrew, Dimmock, Matthew, and Shinn, Abigail (eds.), *The Ashgate Research Companion to Popular Culture in Early Modern England* (Farnham, 2014).

Hahn, Henry G., *The Ocean Bards: British Poetry and the War at Sea, 1793–1815* (Frankfurt am Main, 2008).

Hailwood, Mark, *Alehouses and Good Fellowship in Early Modern England* (Woodbridge, 2014).

Hall, Jason D. (ed.), *Meter Matters: Verse Cultures of the Long Nineteenth Century* (Athens, Ohio, 2011).

Halpern, Andrea R. et al., 'Perception of Mode, Rhythm, and Contour in Unfamiliar Melodies: Effects of Age and Experience', *Music Perception* 15 (1998): 335–55.

Hambridge, Katherine and Hicks, Jonathan (eds.), *The Melodramatic Moment: Music and Theatrical Culture, 1790–1820* (Chicago, 2018).

Harding, James M. and Rosenthal, Cindy (eds.), *The Rise of Performance Studies: Rethinking Richard Schechner's Broad Spectrum* (Basingstoke, 2011).

Harker, Dave, *Fakesong: The Manufacture of British 'Folksong', 1700 to the Present Day* (Milton Keynes, 1985).

Harms, Roeland et al., *Not Dead Things: The Dissemination of Popular Print in England and Wales, Italy, and the Low Countries, 1500–1820* (Leiden, 2013).

Harriman-Smith, James, 'Representing the Poor: Charles Lamb and the *Vagabondiana*', *Studies in Romanticism* 54 (2015): 551–68.

Harris, Bob and McKean, Charles, *The Scottish Town in the Age of the Enlightenment, 1740–1820* (Edinburgh, 2014).

Harris, Tim (ed.), *The Politics of the Excluded, c.1500–1850* (Basingstoke, 2001).

Hawley, Judith, 'Grub Street in Albion: or, Scriblerian Satire in the Romantic Metropolis', *Romanticism* 14, no. 2 (2008): 81–93.

Hayward, Sally, '"Those Who Cannot Work"', *Prose Studies: History, Theory, Criticism* 27 (2005): 53–71.

Heller, Benjamin, 'Leisure and Pleasure in London Society, 1760–1820: An Agent-Centred Approach' (Oxford University D.Phil. thesis, 2009).

Heller, Benjamin, 'The "Mene Peuple" and the Polite Spectator: The Individual in the Crowd at Eighteenth-Century London Fairs', *Past & Present* 208 (2010): 131–57.

Helsinger, Elizabeth, 'Listening: Dante Gabriel Rossetti and the Persistence of Song', *Victorian Studies* 53 (2009): 409–21.

Henderson, William (ed.), *Victorian Street Ballads: A Selection of Popular Ballads sold in the Street in the Nineteenth Century* (1937).

Hendy, David, *Noise: A Human History of Sound and Listening* (2013).

Henke, Robert, 'Meeting at the Sign of the Queen: The Commedia dell'Arte, Cheap Print, and Piazza Performance', *Italian Studies* 71 (2016): 171–83.

Hepburn, James, *A Book of Scattered Leaves: Poetry of Poverty in Broadside Ballads of Nineteenth-Century England*, 2 vols. (Cranbury, 2000–1).

Heppa, Christopher, 'Harry Cox and His Friends: Song Transmission in an East Norfolk Singing Community, *c*.1896–1960', *Folk Music Journal* 8 (2005): 569–93.

Herbert, Trevor (ed.), *Bands: The Brass Band Movement in the 19th and 20th Centuries* (Buckingham, 1991).

Hesmondhalgh, David and Negus, Keith (eds.), *Popular Music Studies* (2002).

Hewitt, Martin, *The Dawn of the Cheap Press in Victorian Britain: The End of the 'Taxes on Knowledge', 1849–1869* (2014).

Hewitt, Martin (ed.), *The Victorian World* (Abingdon, 2012).

Hewitt, Martin and Cowgill, Rachel (eds.), *Victorian Soundscapes Revisited* (Leeds, 2007).

Highfill, Philip H., Burnim, Kalman A., and Langhans, Edward A., *A Biographical Dictionary of Actors, Actresses, Musicians, Dancers, Managers, and other Stage Personnel in London, 1660–1800*, 16 vols. (Carbondale, 1973–93).

Hitchcock, David, *Vagrancy in English Society and Culture, 1650–1750* (2016).

Hitchcock, Tim, *Down and Out in Eighteenth-Century London* (2004).

Hitchcock, Tim, 'Begging on the Streets of Eighteenth-Century London', *Journal of British Studies* 44 (2005): 478–98.

Hitchcock, Tim et al. (eds.), *Chronicling Poverty: The Voices and Strategies of the English Poor, 1640–1840* (Basingstoke, 1997).

Hitchcock, Tim and Shore, Heather (eds.), *The Streets of London: From the Great Fire to the Great Stink* (2003).

Hofer-Robinson, Joanna, *Dickens and Demolition: Literary Afterlives and Mid-Nineteenth-Century Urban Development* (Edinburgh, 2018).

Holger Petersen, Nils et al. (eds.), *The Appearances of Medieval Rituals: The Play of Construction and Modification* (Turnhout, 2004).

Horgan, Kate, *The Politics of Songs in Eighteenth-Century Britain, 1723–1795* (2014).

Horn, David and Tagg, Philip (eds.), *Popular Music Perspectives: Papers from The First International Conference On Popular Music Research, Amsterdam, June 1981* (Göteborg and Exeter, 1982).

Howkins, Alun, 'The Voice of the People: The Social Meaning and Context of Country Song', *Oral History* 3 (1975): 50–75.

Humpherys, Ann, *Travels into the Poor Man's Country: The Work of Henry Mayhew* (Athens, Georgia, 1977).

Hunt, Arnold, *The Art of Hearing: English Preachers and Their Audience, 1590–1640* (Cambridge, 2010).

Hunter, David, 'Music Copyright in Britain to 1800', *Music and Letters* 67 (1986): 269–82.

Hutchins, Sean et al., 'The Vocal Generosity Effect: How Bad Can Your Singing Be?', *Music Perception* 30 (2012): 147–59.

Innes, Joanna, *Inferior Politics: Social Problems and Social Policies in Eighteenth-Century Britain* (Oxford, 2009).

Irving, David R. M., '"For whom the *bell* tolls": Listening and its Implications', *Journal of the Royal Musical Association* 135 (2010): 19–24.

Jackson, Jeffrey H. and Pelkey, Stanley C. (eds.), *Music and History: Bridging the Disciplines* (Mississippi, 2005).

Jackson-Houlston, Caroline M., *Ballads, Songs and Snatches: The Appropriation of Folk Song and Popular Culture in British Nineteenth-century Realist Prose* (Aldershot, 1999).

James, Louis, 'Taking Melodrama Seriously: Theatre, and Nineteenth-Century Studies', *History Workshop* 3 (1977): 151–8.

Johnson, James H., *Listening in Paris: A Cultural History* (Berkeley and Los Angeles, 1995).

Jones, Colin, *The Smile Revolution in Eighteenth Century Paris* (Oxford, 2014).

Jones, Peter T. A., 'Redressing Reform Narratives: Victorian London's Street Markets and the Informal Supply Lines of Urban Modernity', *London Journal* 41 (2016): 60–81.

Joyce, Patrick, *Visions of the People: Industrial England and the Question of Class, 1848–1914* (Cambridge, 1991).

Joyce, Patrick, *Democratic Subjects: The Self and the Social in Nineteenth-Century England* (Cambridge, 1994).

Joyce, Patrick, 'What is the Social in Social History?', *Past & Present* 205 (2009): 175–210.

Kaiser, Matthew, *The World in Play: Portraits of a Victorian Concept* (Stanford, 2012).

Karlin, Daniel, *The Figure of the Singer* (Oxford, 2013).

Kassler, Michael (ed.), *The Music Trade in Georgian England* (Farnham, 2011).

Kelley, Robin D. G., 'Notes on Deconstructing "The Folk"', *American Historical Review* 97 (1992): 1400–8.

Kennaway, James, *Bad Vibrations: The History of the Idea of Music as a Cause of Disease* (Farnham, 2012).

Kennaway, James (ed.), *Music and the Nerves, 1700–1900* (Basingstoke, 2014).

Kennerley, David, 'Debating Female Musical Professionalism and Artistry in the British Press, c.1820–1850', *Historical Journal* 58 (2015): 987–1008.

Kennerley, David, *Sounding Feminine: Women's Voices in British Musical Culture, 1780–1850* (New York and Oxford, 2020).

Kirk, John, Noble, Andrew, and Brown, Michael (eds.), *United Islands? The Languages of Resistance* (2012).

Kirk, John, Noble, Andrew, and Brown, Michael (eds.), *Cultures of Radicalism in Britain and Ireland* (2013).

Korczynski, Marek, Pickering, Michael, and Robertson, Emma, *Rhythms of Labour: Music at Work in Britain* (Cambridge, 2013).

Koven, Seth, *Slumming: Sexual and Social Politics in Victorian London* (Princeton, 2006).

Kramer, Lawrence, *Music as Cultural Practice, 1800–1900* (Berkeley and Los Angeles, 1990).

Kramer, Lawrence, *Critical Musicology and the Responsibility of Response: Selected Essays* (Aldershot, 2006).

Kramer, Lawrence, *Interpreting Music* (Berkeley and Los Angeles, 2011).

Laitinen, Riitta and Cohen, Thomas V. (eds.), *Cultural History of Early Modern European Streets* (Leiden, 2009).

Lamb, Jonathan, *The Evolution of Sympathy in the Long Eighteenth Century* (2009).

Lavery, Brian, *The Ship of the Line*, 2 vols. (2003).

Lee, Edward, *Music of the People: A Study of Popular Music in Great Britain* (1970).

Leppert, Richard, *The Sight of Sound: Music, Representation, and the History of the Body* (Berkeley and Los Angeles, 1993).

Leppert, Richard and McClary, Susan (eds.), *Music and Society: The Politics of Composition, Performance and Reception* (Cambridge, 1987).

Lightwood, James T., *Charles Dickens and Music* (1912).

List, George, 'An Ideal Marriage of Ballad Text and Tune', *Midwest Folklore* 7 (1957): 95–112.

Lloyd, Albert L., *Folk Song in England* (1969).

Lomax, Alan, 'Folk Song Style: Notes on a Systematic Approach to the Study of Folk Song', *Journal of the International Folk Music Council* 8 (1956): 48–50.

Lomax, Alan, 'Song Structure and Social Structure', *Ethnology* 1 (1962): 425–51.

Lomax, Alan, 'The Good and the Beautiful in Folksong', *Journal of American Folklore* 80 (1967): 213–35.

Lomax, Alan, *Folk Song Style and Culture* (Washington, 1968).

Lomax, Alan et al., 'A Stylistic Analysis of Speaking', *Language in Society* 6 (1977): 15–47.

Long, Eleanor R., 'Ballad Singers, Ballad Makers, and Ballad Etiology', *Western Folklore* 32 (1973): 225–36.

Longmore, Paul K., *Telethons: Spectacle, Disability, and the Business of Charity* (Oxford, 2016).

Mackerness, Eric D., *A Social History of English Music* (1964).

Maidment, Brian, *Dusty Bob: A Cultural History of Dustmen, 1780–1870* (Manchester, 2007).

Maidment, Brian, *Comedy, Caricature and The Social Order, 1820–50* (Manchester, 2013).

Makdisi, Saree, *Making England Western: Occidentalism, Race, and Imperial Culture* (Chicago, 2014).

Malcolmson, Robert W., *Popular Recreations in English Society, 1700–1850* (Cambridge, 1973).

Margulis, Elizabeth H., 'A Model of Melodic Expectation', *Music Perception* 22 (2005): 663–714.

Margulis, Elizabeth H., *On Repeat: How Music Plays the Mind* (Oxford, 2014).

Marsh, Christopher, *Music and Society in Early Modern England* (Cambridge, 2010).

Marsh, Christopher, '"The Blazing Torch": New Light on English Balladry as a Multi-Media Matrix', *The Seventeenth Century* 30 (2015): 95–116.

Marsh, Christopher, 'Best-Selling Ballads and their Pictures in Seventeenth-Century England', *Past & Present* 233 (2016): 53–99.

Marshall, Nancy R., *City of Gold and Mud: Painting Victorian London* (New Haven, 2012).

Mason, Laura, *Singing the French Revolution: Popular Culture and Politics, 1787–1799* (New York, 1996).

McCalman, Ian, *Radical Underworld: Prophets, Revolutionaries and Pornographers in London, 1795–1840* (Cambridge, 1988).

McClary, Susan, *Feminine Endings: Music, Gender, and Sexuality* (Minneapolis, 2002).

McClary, Susan, *Reading Music: Selected Essays* (Aldershot, 2007).

McColley, Diane K., *Poetry and Music in Seventeenth-Century England* (Cambridge, 1997).

McConachie, Bruce, *Engaging Audiences: A Cognitive Approach to Spectating in the Theatre* (Basingstoke, 2008).

McDowell, Paula, '"The Manufacture and Lingua-facture of Ballad-Making": Broadside Ballads in Long Eighteenth-Century Ballad Discourse', *The Eighteenth Century: Theory and Interpretation* 47, nos. 2–3 (2006): 151–78.

McGill, Josephine, 'Old Ballad Burthens', *Musical Quarterly* 4 (1918): 293–306.

McGill, Meredith L., 'What Is a Ballad? Reading for Genre, Format, and Medium', *Nineteenth-Century Literature* 71 (2016): 156–75.

McKean, Thomas A. (ed.), *The Flowering Thorn: International Ballad Studies* (Logan, Utah, 2003).

McLane, Maureen N., *Balladeering, Minstrelsy, and the Making of British Romantic Poetry* (Cambridge, 2008).

McShane, Angela, 'Drink, Song and Politics in Early Modern England', *Popular Music* 35 (2016): 166–90.

Mellers, Wilfrid, *Harmonious Meeting: A Study of the Relationship between English Music, Poetry and Theatre, c.1600–1900* (1965, repr. 2008).

Menzer, Paul, *Anecdotal Shakespeare: A New Performance History* (2015).

Merkin, Ros (ed.), *Popular Theatres? Papers from the Popular Theatre Conference* (Liverpool, 1994).

Merriam, Alan P., *The Anthropology of Music* (Evanston, Ill., 1964).

Meyer, Leonard B., *Emotion and Meaning in Music* (Chicago, 1956).

Middleton, Richard, *Voicing the Popular: On the Subjects of Popular Music* (New York, 2006).

Millar, Branford P., 'Eighteenth-Century Views of the Ballad', *Western Folklore* 9 (1950): 124–35.

Moore, Allan F. (ed.), *Analysing Popular Music* (Cambridge, 2003).

Morgentaler, Goldie, 'Dickens and the Scattered Identity of Silas Wegg', *Dickens Quarterly* 22, no. 2 (2005): 92–100.

Motherway, Susan H., *The Globalisation of Irish Traditional Song Performance* (Aldershot, 2013).

Mullen, John, *The Show Must Go On! Popular Song in Britain During the First World War* (Farnham, 2015).

Myers, Robin and Harris, Michael (eds.), *Spreading the Word: The Distribution Networks of Print, 1550–1850* (Winchester, 1990).

Navickas, Katrina, *Protest and the Politics of Space and Place, 1789–1848* (Manchester, 2017).

Nead, Lynda, *Victorian Babylon: People, Streets and Images in Nineteenth-Century London* (New Haven, 2000).

Neilands, Colin, 'Irish Broadside Ballads: Performers and Performances', *Folk Music Journal* 6 (1991): 209–22.

Negus, Keith, *Popular Music in Theory: An Introduction* (Cambridge, 1996).

Negus, Keith, 'Narrative, Interpretation, and the Popular Song', *Musical Quarterly* 95 (2012): 368–95.

'New Lights upon Old Tunes. "The Arethusa"', *Musical Times and Singing Class Circular* 35 (1894): 666–8.

Newman, Ian, 'Edmund Burke in the Tavern', *European Romantic Review* 24 (2013): 125–48.

Newman, Ian, 'Moderation in the Lyrical Ballads: Wordsworth and the Ballad Debates of the 1790s', *Studies in Romanticism* 55 (2016): 185–210.

Newman, Ian, *The Romantic Tavern: Literature and Conviviality in the Age of Revolution* (Cambridge, 2019).

Newman, Ian and Russell, Gillian, 'Metropolitan Songs and Songsters: Ephemerality in the World City', *Studies in Romanticism* 58 (2019): 429–49.

Newman, Steve, *Ballad Collection, Lyric, and the Canon: The Call of the Popular from the Restoration to the New Criticism* (Philadelphia, 2007).

Nicholls, David, 'Narrative Theory as an Analytical Tool in the Study of Popular Music Texts', *Music and Letters* 88 (2007): 297–315.

Nicholson, Eirwen E. C., 'English Political Prints and Pictorial Argument *c.*1640–*c.*1832: A Study in Historiography and Methodology' (University of Edinburgh PhD thesis, 1994).

Nicholson, Eirwen E. C., 'Consumers and Spectators: The Public of the Political Print in Eighteenth-Century England', *History* 81 (1996): 5–21.

Ó Madagáin, Breandán, 'Functions of Irish Song in the Nineteenth Century', *Béaloideas* 53 (1985): 130–216.

O'Byrne, Alison, 'The Art of Walking in London: Representing Pedestrianism in the Early Nineteenth Century', *Romanticism* 14, no. 2 (2008): 94–107.

O'Connell, Sheila, *The Popular Print in England, 1550–1850* (1999).

O'Gorman, Frank, 'Coventry Election Broadsides, 1780', *Yale University Library Gazette* 67 (1993): 161–9.

Obelkevich, James, 'In Search of the Listener', *Journal of the Royal Music Association* 114 (1989): 102–8.

Ogborn, Miles, *Spaces of Modernity: London's Geographies, 1680–1780* (New York, 1998).

Palmer, Roy, *A Touch on the Times: Songs of Social Change, 1770–1914* (Harmondsworth, 1974).

Palmer, Roy, *The Sound of History: Songs and Social Comment* (Oxford, 1988).

Palmer, Roy, '"Veritable Dunghills": Professor Child and the Broadside', *Folk Music Journal* 7 (1996): 155–66.

Parker, Roger and Rutherford, Susan (eds.), *London Voices 1820–1840: Vocal Performers, Practices, Histories* (Chicago, 2019).

Pawley, Alisun and Müllensiefen, Daniel, 'The Science of Singing Along: A Quantitative Field Study on Sing-Along Behaviour in the North of England', *Music Perception* 30 (2012): 129–46.

Pearce, Marcus T. and Wiggins, Geraint A., 'Expectations in Melody: The Influence of Context and Learning', *Music Perception* 23 (2006): 377–405.

Pearsall, Ronald, *Victorian Popular Music* (Newton Abbot, 1973).

Peddie, Ian (ed.), *The Resisting Muse: Popular Music and Social Protest* (Aldershot, 2006).

Pedersen, Susan, 'Hannah More Meets Simple Simon: Tracts, Chapbooks, and Popular Culture in Late Eighteenth-Century England', *Journal of British Studies* 25 (1986): 84–113.

Phelan, Peggy, *Unmarked: The Politics of Performance* (1993).

Philp, Mark (ed.), *Resisting Napoleon: The British Response to the Threat of Invasion, 1797–1815* (Aldershot, 2006).

Picker, John M., 'The Soundproof Study: Victorian Professionals, Work Space, and Urban Noise', *Victorian Studies* 42 (2000): 427–53.

Picker, John M., *Victorian Soundscapes* (Oxford, 2003).

Pickering, Mike, 'The Study of Vernacular Song in England', *Jahrbuch für Volksliedforschung* 33 (1988): 95–104.

Pickering, Mike, 'John Bull in Blackface', *Popular Music* 16 (1997): 181–201.

Pickering, Mike and Green, Tony (eds.), *Everyday Culture: Popular Song and the Vernacular Milieu* (Milton Keynes, 1987).

Pike, Lionel, *Pills to Purge Melancholy: The Evolution of the English Ballett* (Aldershot, 2004).

Platz, Friedrich and Kopiez, Reinhard, 'When the Eye Listens: A Meta-Analysis of How Audio-Visual Presentation Enhances the Appreciation of Music Performance', *Music Perception* 30 (2012): 71–83.

Porter, Gerald, *The English Occupational Song* (Umeå, 1992).

Porter, Gerald, 'Cobblers All: Occupation as Identity and Cultural Message', *Folk Music Journal* 7 (1995): 43–61.

Porter, Gerald, 'The English Ballad Singer and Hidden History', *Studia Musicologica* 49 (2008): 127–42.

Potter, Caroline (ed.), *Erik Satie: Music, Art and Literature* (Farnham, 2013).

Potter, John (ed.), *The Cambridge Companion to Singing* (Cambridge, 2000).

Potter, Tiffany (ed.), *Women, Popular Culture, and the Eighteenth Century* (Toronto, 2012).

Poulopoulos, Panagiotis, 'The Guittar in the British Isles, 1750–1810' (University of Edinburgh PhD thesis, 2011).

Preston, Cathy L. and Preston, Michael J. (eds.), *The Other Print Tradition: Essays on Chapbooks, Broadsides, and Related Ephemera* (New York, 1995).

Prineppi, Georgina, 'Sailors in British Broadside Ballads, 1800–1850' (University of Miama MMus thesis, 2015).

Rainey, David W. and Larsen, Janet D., 'The Effect of Familiar Melodies on Initial Learning and Long-term Memory for Unconnected Text', *Music Perception* 20 (2002): 173–86.

Reed, Peter P., '"There Was No Resisting John Canoe": Circum-Atlantic Transracial Performance', *Theatre History Studies* 27 (2007): 65–85.

Reed, Peter P., *Rogue Performances: Staging the Underclasses in Early American Theatre Culture* (New York, 2009).

Refini, Eugenio, 'Reappraising the Charlatan in Early Modern Italy: The Case of Iacopo Coppa', *Italian Studies* 71 (2016): 197–211.

Renwick, Roger deVeer and Rieuwerts, Sigrid (eds.), *Ballad Mediations: Folksongs Recovered, Represented, and Reimagined* (Trier, 2006).

Roach, Joseph, *Cities of the Dead: Circum-Atlantic Performance* (New York, 1996).

Rohr, Deborah, *The Careers of British Musicians, 1750–1850: A Profession of Artisans* (Cambridge, 2001).

Rolison, Jonathan J. and Edworthy, Judy, 'The Role of Formal Structure in Liking for Popular Music', *Music Perception* 29 (2012): 269–84.

Rothenberg, Molly A., 'Articulating Social Agency in *Our Mutual Friend*: Problems with Performances, Practices, and Political Efficacy', *ELH* 71 (2004): 719–50.

Rouse, Andrew C., 'The Forgotten Professional Popular Singer in England', *Studia Musicologica Academiae Scientiarum Hungaricae* 40 (1999): 145–58.

Rouse, Andrew C., *The Remunerated Vernacular Singer: From Medieval England to the Post-War Revival* (Frankfurt am Main, 2005).

Rudy, Seth, 'Stage Presence: Performance and Theatricality in Dickens's *Our Mutual Friend*', *Dickens Studies Annual: Essays on Victorian Fiction* 37 (2006): 65–80.

Russell, Dave, 'The "Social History" of Popular Music: A Label without a Cause?', *Popular Music* 12 (1993): 139–54.

Ryan, Marie-Laure (ed.), *Narrative across Media: The Languages of Storytelling* (2004).

Sack, Jessica S., 'Street Music and Musicians: The Physical and Aural Nature of Performance' (Oxford University M.Phil. thesis, 1998).

Salman, Jeroen, *Pedlars and the Popular Press: Itinerant Distribution Networks in England and the Netherlands, 1600–1850* (Leiden, 2014).

Salzberg, Rosa, *Ephemeral City: Cheap Print and Urban Culture in Renaissance Venice* (Manchester, 2014).

Salzberg, Rosa, '"Poverty Makes Me Invisible": Street Singers and Hard Times in Italian Renaissance Cities', *Italian Studies* 71 (2016): 212–24.

Sanders, Mike, '"God is Our Guide! Our Cause is Just!" The *National Chartist Hymn Book* and Victorian Hymnody', *Victorian Studies* 54 (2012): 679–705.

Schechner, Richard, *Performance Studies: An Introduction* (2002).

Schmuckler, Mark A., 'Melodic Contour Similarity Using Folk Melodies', *Music Perception* 28 (2010): 169–94.

Schulkind, Matthew D. et al., 'Musical Features that Facilitate Melody Identification: How do you know it's "your" song when they finally play it?', *Music Perception* 21 (2003): 217–49.

Scott, Derek B., *The Singing Bourgeois: Songs of the Victorian Drawing Room and Parlour* (2nd edn, Aldershot, 2001).

Scott, Derek B., *Sounds of the Metropolis: The Nineteenth-Century Popular Music Revolution in London, New York, Paris, and Vienna* (Oxford, 2008).

Seed, David, 'Touring the Metropolis: The Shifting Subjects of Dickens' London Sketches', *The Yearbook of English Studies* 34, Nineteenth-Century Travel Writing (2004): 155–70.

Sennett, Richard, *Flesh and Stone: The Body and the City in Western Civilisation* (New York, 1994).

Sennett, Richard, *Together: The Rituals, Pleasures and Politics of Cooperation* (New Haven, 2012).

Shannon, Mary L., *Dickens, Reynolds, and Mayhew on Wellington Street* (Farnham, 2015).

Shannon, Mary L., 'The Multiple Lives of Billy Waters: Dangerous Theatricality and Networked Illustrations in Nineteenth-Century Popular Culture', *Nineteenth Century Theatre and Film* 46 (2019): 161–89.

Shapiro, Anne D. (ed.), *Music and Context: Essays for John M. Ward* (Harvard, 1985).

Shepard, Leslie, *The Broadside Ballad: A Study in Origin and Meaning* (1962).

Shepard, Leslie, *John Pitts, Ballad Printer of Seven Dials, London, 1765–1844* (1969).

Shepard, Leslie, *The History of Street Literature* (Newton Abbot, 1973).

Shepherd, Janet, 'The Relationship Between Music, Text and Performance in English Popular Theatre, 1790–1840' (University of London PhD thesis, 1991).

Shepherd, John, *Music as Social Text* (Cambridge, 1991).

Shesgreen, Sean, *Images of the Outcast: The Urban Poor in the Cries of London* (Manchester, 2002).

Shields, Hugh, *Oliver Goldsmith and Popular Song* (Dublin, 1985).

Shoemaker, Robert, *The London Mob: Violence and Disorder in Eighteenth-Century England* (2004).

Simpson, Harold, *A Century of Ballads, 1810–1910, Their Composers and Singers* (1910).

Simpson, Paul, 'Street Performance and the City: Public Space, Sociality, and Intervening in the Everyday', *Space and Culture* 14 (2011): 415–30.

Simpson, Paul, 'Apprehending Everyday Rhythms: Rhythmanalysis, Time-Lapse Photography, and the Space-Times of Street Performance', *Cultural Geographies* 19 (2012): 423–45.

Simpson, Paul, 'Sonic Affects and the Production of Space: "Music by handle" and the Politics of Street Music in Victorian London', *Cultural Geographies* 24 (2017): 89–109.

Small, Christopher, *Musicking: The Meanings of Performance and Listening* (Hanover, N.H., 1998).

Smith, Bruce R., *The Acoustic World of Early Modern England* (Chicago, 1999).

Smith, Simon, *Musical Response in the Early Modern Playhouse, 1603–1625* (Cambridge, 2017).

Snowman, Daniel, *The Gilded Stage: A Social History of Opera* (2009).

Sorce Keller, Marcello, 'Why is Music So Ideological, and Why Do Totalitarian States Take It So Seriously? A Personal View from History and the Social Sciences', *Journal of Musicological Research* 26, nos. 2–3 (2007): 91–122.

Southern, Eileen, *The Music of Black Americans: A History* (3rd edn, New York, 1997).

Speaight, George, *Juvenile Drama: The History of the English Toy Theatre* (1946).

Spiers, Edward M., *Radical General: Sir George de Lacy Evans, 1787–1870* (Manchester, 1983).

St Clair, William, *The Reading Nation in the Romantic Period* (Cambridge, 2004).

Stedman Jones, Gareth, *Languages of Class: Studies in English Working Class History, 1832–1982* (Cambridge, 1983).

Stedman Jones, Gareth, *Outcast London: A Study in the Relationship between Classes in Victorian Society* (2nd edn, Harmondsworth, 1984).

Steedman, Carolyn, 'Cries Unheard, Sights Unseen: Writing the Eighteenth-Century Metropolis', *Representations* 118 (2012): 28–71.

Steedman, Carolyn, 'Mayhew: On Reading, About Writing', *Journal of Victorian Culture* 19 (2014): 550–61.

Stein, Mark, *Black British Literature: Novels of Transformation* (Columbus, Ohio, 2004).

Steinberg, Michael P., *Listening to Reason: Culture, Subjectivity, and Nineteenth-Century Music* (Princeton, 2004).

Stoddard Holmes, Martha, *Fictions of Affliction: Physical Disability in Victorian Culture* (Ann Arbor, 2004).

Storch, Robert D. (ed.), *Popular Culture and Custom in Nineteenth-Century England* (1982).

Storey, John, *Cultural Theory and Popular Culture: An Introduction* (5th edn, Harlow, 2009).

Street, John, *Rebel Rock: The Politics of Popular Music* (Oxford, 1986).

Taithe, Bertrand, *The Essential Mayhew: Representing and Communicating the Poor* (1996).

Taruskin, Richard, *The Danger of Music and Other Anti-Utopian Essays* (Berkeley and Los Angeles, 2009).

Thompson, E. P., *Customs in Common* (1991).

Tilly, Charles, *Contentious Performances* (Cambridge, 2008).

Tomlinson, Gary, *Metaphysical Song: An Essay on Opera* (Princeton, 1999).

Tomlinson, Gary, *Music and Historical Critique: Selected Essays* (Aldershot, 2007).

Trittschuh, Travis, 'The Ballad-Seller and His Kind', *Journal of American Folklore* 73 (1960): 54–56.

Valladares, Susan, 'Afro-Creole Revelry and Rebellion on the British Stage: Jonkanoo in Obi; or, Three-Fingered Jack (1800)', *Review of English Studies*, New Series (2018): 1–21.

van der Poel, Dieuwke, Grijp, Louis Peter, and van Anrooij, Wim (eds.), *Identity, Intertextuality, and Performance in Early Modern Song Culture* (Leiden, 2016).

van Dijck, José, 'Record and Hold: Popular Music between Personal and Collective Memory', *Critical Studies in Media Communication* 23 (2006): 357–74.

Veeser, Harold A. (ed.), *The New Historicism* (New York, 1989).

Vernon, David, *Politics and the People: A Study in English Political Culture c. 1815–1867* (Cambridge, 1993).

Vicinus, Martha, *The Industrial Muse: A Study of Nineteenth Century British Working-Class Literature* (1974).

Vicinus, Martha, *Broadsides of the Industrial North* (Newcastle, 1975).

Vincent, David, *Bread, Knowledge and Freedom: A Study of Nineteenth-Century Working Class Autobiography* (1981).

Ward, John M., 'Apropos "The British Broadside Ballad and Its Music"', *Journal of the American Musicological Society* 20 (1967): 28–86.

Watson, Ian, *Song and Democratic Culture in Britain: An Approach to Popular Culture in Social Movements* (Beckenham, 1983).

Watt, Paul, Scott, Derek B., and Spedding, Patrick (eds.), *Cheap Print and Popular Song in the Nineteenth Century: A Cultural History of the Songster* (Cambridge, 2017).

Weber, William, *Music and the Middle Class: The Social Structure of Concert Life in London, Paris and Vienna between 1830 and 1848* (2nd edn, Aldershot, 2004).

Weber, William, *The Great Transformation of Musical Taste: Concert Programming from Haydn to Brahms* (Cambridge, 2008).

Weliver, Phyllis (ed.), *The Figure of Music in Nineteenth-Century British Poetry* (Aldershot, 2005).

Welu, James A. and Biesboer, Pieter (eds.), *Judith Leyster: A Dutch Master and Her World* (Yale, 1993).

Weygand, Zina, *The Blind in French Society from the Middle Ages to the Century of Louis Braille* (Stanford, 2009).

Whipday, Emma, *Shakespeare's Domestic Tragedies: Violence in the Early Modern Home* (Cambridge, 2019).

Williams, Abigail, *The Social Life of Books: Reading Together in the Eighteenth-Century Home* (Yale, 2017).

Wilson, Blake, 'The Cantastorie/Canterino/Cantimbanco as Musician', *Italian Studies* 71 (2016): 154–70.

Wilson, James C. and Lewiecki-Wilson, Cynthia (eds.), *Embodied Rhetorics: Disability in Language and Culture* (Carbondale and Edwardsville, 2001).

Wilson, Kathleen, *The Island Race: Englishness, Empire and Gender in the Eighteenth Century* (2003).

Wilson, Kathleen (ed.), *A New Imperial History: Culture, Identity, and Modernity in Britain and the Empire, 1660–1840* (Cambridge, 2004).

Winfield, Rif, *British Warships in the Age of Sail 1793–1817* (Barnsley, 2008).

Winn, James A., *Unsuspected Eloquence: A History of the Relations between Poetry and Music* (New Haven and London, 1981).

Winter, James, *London's Teeming Streets, 1830–1914* (1993).

Wood, Gillen D'Arcy, *Romanticism and Music Culture in Britain, 1770–1840* (Cambridge, 2010).

Yeo, Eileen and Yeo, Stephen (eds.), *Popular Culture and Class Conflict, 1590–1914: Explorations in the History of Labour and Leisure* (Brighton, 1981).

Zucchi, John E., *The Little Slaves of the Harp: Italian Child Street Musicians in Nineteenth-Century Paris, London, and New York* (Quebec, 1992).

Zuckerkandl, Victor, *Man the Musician* (Princeton, 1976).

# Index

Printed by Printforce, United Kingdom